**Lone Wolf Terror
and the Rise
of Leaderless Resistance**

Lone Wolf Terror and the Rise of Leaderless Resistance

George Michael

Vanderbilt University Press ■ Nashville

This book is printed on acid-free paper.
Manufactured in the United States of America

Library of Congress Cataloging-in-Publication Data on file

LC control number 2011046021
LC classification HV6431.M483 2012
Dewey class number 363.325—dc23

ISBN 978-0-8265-1855-2 (cloth)
ISBN 978-0-8265-1857-6 (e-book)

For Wolfgang Vladimir

Contents

Acknowledgments

Several people assisted me in this study. I would like to thank all those who granted me interviews for this book, including Thomas P. M. Barnett, Harold Covington, Alan Dershowitz, Francis Fukuyama, Daveed Gartenstein-Ross, Rohan Gunaratna, Michael V. Hayden, Christopher Hewitt, the late Frederick Iklé, Anthony Joes, Edward Luttwak, Darren Mulloy, the late William L. Pierce, Paul Pillar, Daniel Pipes, John Robb, Martin van Creveld, and Laird Wilcox. Christopher Hewitt and Darren Mulloy offered suggestions on the manuscript that were very helpful.

I would also like to thank the staff at Vanderbilt University Press. I extend my special thanks to Eli Bortz for having confidence in this project. I greatly appreciate the editorial efforts of Ed Huddleston. Finally, I thank the University of Virginia's College at Wise and the Air Force Counterproliferation Center for allowing me time to complete this book.

Introduction

The face of terrorism is undergoing considerable change. There is a noticeable trend indicating the increasing frequency of lone wolf attacks by individuals and small cells with little or no connections to formal organizations. In the past few years, numerous lone wolf incidents carried out by assorted radicals have gained headlines. For instance, in April 2009, Richard A. Poplawski, a man who expressed racist views on extremist websites, fired on police in Pittsburgh, Pennsylvania, killing three officers.[1] Just a few weeks after that, an antiabortion activist, Scott Roeder, murdered a physician who performed late-term abortions.[2] In June of that year, a little-known but long-standing right-wing extremist, James von Brunn, opened fire at the United States Holocaust Memorial Museum in Washington, D.C., killing a guard.[3] In November, Major Nidal Malik Hasan, a Virginia-born Muslim psychiatrist in the US Army, allegedly went on a shooting rampage at Fort Hood, Texas, that killed thirteen people and left thirty-eight wounded.[4]

More incidents followed in 2010. On February 18, Joseph Stack, a fifty-three-year-old software engineer and tax protester, slammed his private plane into a building in Austin, Texas, that housed offices of the IRS, triggering a massive fireball that set the edifice ablaze and killed Stack and an IRS manager.[5] And on May 1, Faisal Shahzad, a seemingly upright and assimilated computer technician, a US citizen who lived in Connecticut but was born in Pakistan, attempted to detonate three bombs in an SUV parked in the heart of Times Square in New York City. Although he reportedly made contact with the Pakistani Taliban during a trip to Pakistan in 2008, after his arrest Shahzad insisted that he had acted entirely alone while in the United States.[6]

Lone wolf terrorism is not confined to the United States, as was tragically displayed on July 22, 2011, when a bomb placed in a Volkswagen exploded in Oslo, Norway, near the offices of the prime minister and other government buildings. The blast killed eight people and seriously injured eleven others. Less than two hours later, a lone gunman disguised as a police officer struck a summer camp operated by the youth organization of the liberal Norwegian Labour Party on the island of Utøya in Tyrifjorden. The second attack left sixty-eight people dead, many of them teenagers. The admitted perpetrator of both attacks, Anders Behring Breivik, had previously expressed anti-Muslim and anti-immigration sentiments on a website. In an online manifesto, Breivik counseled fellow travelers to emulate his terrorism by acting alone on their own initiative.[7] Ominously, his style of lone wolf terrorism suggests a high degree of planning and calculation, which could portend greater lethality of such attacks in the future. Breivik maintained no affiliations with hard-core extremists, though he was once briefly affiliated with a youth organization associated with the Far Right group Norwegian Progress, and he was not on the authorities' radar screen. Having no criminal record other than minor offenses, he was able to procure firearms and fertilizer for making his bomb without raising red flags. His attacks came out of nowhere.[8]

The increased frequency of these lone wolf attacks indicates a shift from terrorism by organized groups to terrorism by unaffiliated individuals.[9] To meet the challenge of seemingly random attacks such as these, in the summer of 2009 US authorities announced an effort to detect lone wolves who might be contemplating politically charged violence. Dubbed the "Lone Wolf Initiative," it began shortly after the inauguration of President Barack Obama and was launched in part because of a perceived rise in hate speech and increasing gun sales.[10] As reported, the Lone Wolf Initiative is one aspect of a broader strategy to combat domestic terrorism dubbed "Operation Vigilant Eagle."[11] As early as 1998, the FBI publicly announced that fringe groups could be planning attacks on their own initiative, as in the case of Eric Robert Rudolph, who supposedly drifted in and out of white supremacist groups before embarking on his one-man campaign of violence, which included bombing abortion clinics, a gay bar, and the Centennial Park at the 1996 Summer Olympic Games in Atlanta.

For obvious reasons, since the terrorist attacks of September 11, 2001 (9/11), the US government has been focused mainly on well-established terrorist groups, such as al Qaeda. However, recent lone wolf attacks suggest that leaderless resistance is becoming the most common form of terrorism in the United States and elsewhere in the West. In essence, leaderless resistance involves a kind of lone wolf operation in which an individual or a very small, cohesive group engages in terrorism independent of any official movement, leader, or support network.[12] To be effective, leaderless resistance assumes that many individuals and groups hold a common ideology and are willing to act on shared views in a violent or confrontational manner.

Despite these episodes of sporadic violence, some observers dismiss leaderless resistance as primarily a nuisance that poses no substantial or existential threat to the nation, something that could be consigned to the field of abnormal psychology. Others, however, believe there is a leaderless resistance trend that should be taken seriously, if for no other reason than the harm lone wolves can inflict. A case in point is the Beltway snipers. As a result of their violent escapades in the fall of 2002, John Allen Muhammad and Lee Boyd Malvo were charged with, or suspected in, twenty-one shootings in Alabama, the District of Columbia, Georgia, Louisiana, Maryland, Virginia, and Washington State. All totaled, they were believed to have killed ten persons and wounded three others in the Washington, D.C., metropolitan area alone. Although their campaign does not appear to have been ideologically driven, it could nevertheless serve as a model for an individual or group with a political agenda.[13]

In the current climate of fear in the United States, leaderless resistance has the potential to seriously disrupt the normal functioning of daily life. Jihadists operating in the United States would not have to resort to spectacular attacks in the style of 9/11 to be effective. Rather, any kind of seemingly random assassinations and bombings could be psychologically devastating to the public.[14] Furthermore, the most notorious lone wolves in the United States—Timothy McVeigh, Ted Kaczynski, and Bruce Ivins (the alleged sender of anthrax-laced letters)—wreaked havoc cheaply.[15] Inasmuch as lone wolves operate alone, they are likely more difficult to monitor because they lack ties to organizations that could already be under surveillance. As the case of Ted Kaczynski—the Unabomber—demonstrated, a highly intelligent and motivated person working alone can carry on a campaign of violence over the course of many years.

Increasingly, individuals and small groups are responsible for some of the most lethal acts of terrorism. Well-established organizations, such as Hezbollah, Hamas, the Revolutionary Armed Forces of Colombia (FARC), and al Qaeda, continue to mount operations. But individuals and much smaller cells, sometimes inspired by the same ideologies as more established groups, can autonomously act without central direction. In the contemporary world, the likelihood of major armed conflicts between nations has greatly diminished. Moreover, with the collapse of the Soviet Union, the world has entered a "unipolar" era in which a sole superpower, the United States, dominates. Sometimes referred to as the "new world order," this development has drastically changed the security environment within which terrorists operate. Fewer parts of the world than before are conducive to harboring large, clandestine groups, since many foreign governments are coordinating their counterterrorism efforts with the United States, as they seek to dismantle terrorist organizations and deny them funding and resources. This trend accelerated after 9/11.[16] Furthermore, with the collapse of the Soviet system, state sponsorship of terrorism has drastically declined.[17] Finally, new surveillance technology has enabled governments to better monitor dissident groups and potential terrorists. Large groups cannot operate as effectively as in the past because this monitoring makes them more vulnerable to infiltration and disruption.

On the other hand, the emergence of new technology has the potential to serve as a force multiplier for leaderless oppositional movements. In his book *Smart Mobs: The Next Social Revolution*, Howard Rheingold explained how ordinary people could harness new technologies to attain political and social goals. For example, "smart mobs" in Manila in 2001 overthrew President Joseph Ejercito Estrada in organized demonstrations coordinated by using cell phones to forward text messages. Similarly, cell phones, along with Internet-based platforms that permit the unregulated flow of information, were used to confront repressive governments during the Arab Spring revolts in 2011.[18] As far back as November 1999, antiglobalization activists have used mobile phones, websites, laptops, and handheld computers as part of their "swarming" tactics to halt meetings of the World Trade Organization.[19] Ominously, in recent years "flash mobs," organized through social media and telecommunications, have emerged in scattered US urban areas and have often turned violent.[20]

The Internet allows like-minded activists to operate on their own initiative without the direction of a formal organization, hence the emergence of leaderless resistance as a new operational strategy and the miniaturization of terrorist and insurgent movements around the world. As the political scientist and journalist Fareed Zakaria observed, the new face of terror consists of local groups across the world connected by a global ideology. Today we are witnessing the age of the "super-empowered individual" who, if adequately armed with a weapon of mass destruction (WMD), could effectively declare war on the world.[21] These developments mark a major departure from previous paradigms of warfare and conflict.

As John Robb presaged in his book *Brave New War: The Next Stage of Terrorism and the End of Globalization*, the rise of small-scale, "do-it-yourself" terrorism could become more worrisome than the centrally planned attacks about which the United States has been most concerned.[22] The US Department of State has observed a trend whereby more dispersed, localized, and smaller-scale groups are increasingly active in terrorism, often with great lethal effect.[23] This trend concerns authorities since all that connects the various individuals and cells is a common ideology, making them difficult to detect and deter. Supposedly, lone wolves are far less likely to leave paper trails and do not have superiors or contacts who can be monitored. A shared narrative and doctrine enable networks of such individuals to maintain a sense of cohesion and purpose without physical interaction.[24]

Could leaderless resistance presage a new paradigm of warfare? Chapter 1 surveys the evolution of contemporary conflict and strategy. In 1989 William Lind and others identified four generations of warfare.[25] First-generation warfare, which reached its zenith in the Napoleonic Wars in the early nineteenth century, was characterized by conflicts in which adversaries sought to amass huge armies that confronted each other on the battlefield in the hope of winning a single decisive victory. Second-generation warfare, which brought new technology and firepower to bear—for example, the machine gun and heavy artillery—nullified the power of mass formation of troops and resulted in stalemates and trench warfare. Such tactics exemplified combat in World War I. Third-generation warfare came to fruition during World War II, when improvements in armor, airpower, and communications allowed for highly maneuverable combat operations on an unprecedented scale. Firepower from both air and land forces could thus be synchronized against an enemy. This allowed a numerically inferior army to prevail over a larger army with greater resources, as evidenced by the Wehrmacht's stunning defeat of the French army in the blitzkrieg of May 1940. Virtually all forms of asymmetrical warfare are outgrowths of insurgent or guerrilla warfare. So-called fourth-generation warfare is a euphemism for the guerrilla movements that emerged in the twentieth century to challenge the European colonial powers, the United States, and the Soviet Union. Mao Zedong's peasant-based guerrilla strategy is widely considered to be a paradigm of fourth-generation warfare. Mao's main innovation was to add an ideological component to the guerrilla war framework, in which a single-party doctrine instilled a sense of revolutionary fervor in insurgents who were led by a unified command structure. Once the insurgency mobilized the peasant population and established a critical mass, it could launch large-scale attacks and ultimately overthrow the government. The emergence of new technology and more fluid forms of affiliation could usher in a fifth generation of warfare.

The Far Right subculture in the United States has led the way in theorizing on the concept of leaderless resistance, which is the topic of Chapter 2. In 1983 Louis Beam, a long-standing activist, first published the seminal essay "Leaderless Resistance," in which he proposed that the traditional hierarchical organizational structure was untenable under contemporary conditions. This work was disseminated through computer networks, which Beam was a pioneer in exploiting during the 1980s. Within the Far Right movement, there is an ongoing debate over the appropriateness of terrorism. Some activists believe in the efficacy of leaderless resistance, while others believe such an approach is doomed to failure. Although essentially a tactic of desperation, leaderless resistance has occasionally proved to be highly destructive, as evidenced by the Oklahoma City bombing in 1995.

Among the most adept at implementing the leaderless resistance approach have been the radical environmentalist and animal liberation movements, and they are the focus of Chapter 3. These so-called ecoterrorists have been responsible for a considerable amount of property damage, though not many fatalities. There are indications, however, that some representatives of the movement have adopted a more apocalyptic and misanthropic worldview and could thus be more inclined to wage lethal attacks in the future. Similarly, some radical activists in the animal liberation movement have targeted personnel affiliated with animal testing laboratories and could escalate their campaign of harassment to include deadly attacks.

After the Soviet Union collapsed, the world entered what Charles Krauthammer first characterized as the unipolar era. The emergence of the new world order has drastically changed the security environment, resulting in a less hospitable atmosphere for large terrorist groups. The greater coordination of counterterrorism efforts among nations is discussed in Chapter 4.

With the emergence of new technology, most notably the Internet, activists can operate on their own initiative. The Internet is at the center of the ongoing revolution in communications and networking, and the medium enables new forms of organization and greater dissemination of information. Like-minded people with dissident beliefs, who previously would have had a difficult time finding one another, can now network across national borders. At the 1999 World Trade Organization conference in Seattle, a disparate coalition of antiglobalization activists, labor union members, and assorted left-wing protesters demonstrated how "swarming" tactics could be employed without central leadership. Enhanced communication capabilities allow for new, more flexible models of organization and mass collaboration. Elements of globalization serve both to hinder and to facilitate insurgent and counterinsurgent efforts. Chapter 5 explores these trends.

One of the most worrisome aspects of the so-called new terrorism is the prospect of small groups, operating without constraints, getting their hands on WMD. New technology and access to WMD could create "super-empowered individuals" capable of unleashing a significant amount of violence on their own. Chapter 6 explores this danger, as well as the various types of WMD to which terrorists in the future could gain access and the hurdles they would need to surmount to carry out such attacks.

In the aftermath of 9/11, numerous jihadist lone wolves and small cells have attacked targets in the name of al Qaeda, though they often have had little or no formal connection to the organization. Chapter 7 chronicles the development of the contemporary Islamist resistance movement and discusses some of the theaters in which it has been active, including Afghanistan, Iraq, Europe, and the United States. Much of the discussion focuses on Abu Musab al-Suri, whose book *The Global Islamic Resistance Call* has emerged as the definitive treatise on leaderless jihad among scattered Islamist militants around the world today.

Some observers believe that a fifth generation of warfare is on the horizon, ushered in by the Internet, the pervasiveness of the media, porous borders, and the increasing proliferation and availability of WMD, all of which could enable individuals to cause tremendous damage.[26] Conceivably this fifth-generation warfare could take the form of leaderless resistance in which individuals and small cells commit acts of terrorism on their own initiative with no traditional command-and-control hierarchy. The Conclusion discusses pressing contemporary issues, such as globalization, immigration, multiculturalism, and the fragility of states, and how these affect insurgencies. In particular, two contemporaneous but contradictory trends in global politics—integration and fragmentation—are shaping contemporary forms of warfare, conflict, and terrorism. The increasing frequency of the lone wolf tactic suggests that it will feature prominently in conflict in the coming years.

As with variants of conflict and warfare that preceded it, the salience of leaderless resistance comes from a confluence of several political, social, and technological trends. Various factors unique to our age are leading to the miniaturization of terrorism, warfare, and conflict around the world. Though this development may seem insignificant, with the diminishing size of terrorist and insurgent groups suggesting weakness, the potential for destruction and disruption is perhaps greater than ever. New Internet platforms allow faster, more efficient communication for all—including terrorists. Greater interconnectedness also makes infrastructure more vulnerable to disruption as a perturbation could cascade throughout the system. The availability of more-lethal weapons and dual-use technology could lead to deadlier attacks. Finally, the historical process of globalization, although improving life opportunities for many people, can be highly disruptive as it upends relations among citizens, cultures, economies, societies, and governments. An overview of the evolution of warfare, conflict, and strategy will illustrate how the leaderless resistance trend began.

CHAPTER 1

The Evolution of Warfare, Conflict, and Strategy

To place leaderless resistance in context, a discussion of previous generations of warfare and conflict is instructive. To be effective, strategy must evolve to reflect the current operational environment. Throughout history, modes of warfare have been influenced by a number of social, political, economic, and technological factors. Earlier observers of warfare, such as Marquis de Vauban (1633–1707), understood the importance of science and technology and their implications for warfare.[1] Likewise, in his *Art of War*, Niccolò Machiavelli (1469–1527) observed the links between changes in military organization and developments in the social and political spheres. Such trends transformed warfare.[2]

In a seminal 1989 *Marine Corps Gazette* article, "The Changing Face of War: Into the Fourth Generation," William S. Lind and others identified four generations of warfare.[3] The advance from one generation of warfare to the next requires changes in various aspects of society, including politics, economics, and technology.[4] The starting point for Lind's schema was the era of the Napoleonic Wars in the early nineteenth century, during which first-generation warfare came into being.

First-Generation Warfare

Several developments allowed first-generation warfare to develop. The wealth of nations increased, which meant more resources for war were available. Improvements in agriculture freed up more farmworkers to be used as soldiers. The emergence of nationalism led to the mobilization of entire countries, and patriotism became a potent force that instilled greater enthusiasm in national armies. The increasing power of the state enabled the administration of such an ambitious undertaking. An innovation in communications introduced in 1794—the optical telegraph, or the semaphore—meant that messages could more quickly cross great distances, which let Napoleon keep in touch with Paris when he was in the battlefield.[5]

The Napoleonic Wars were characterized by a near-total mobilization of the resources of France. In 1793 the Committee of Public Safety, led by Robespierre, issued a decree—the *levée en masse*—which conscripted all human and material resources. In the face of the collapse of the Old Royal Army, the French Assembly made the bold decision to permanently requisition all citizens for national service.[6] This monumental action transformed the nature of war by involving an entire nation. With the entire economic and human resources of France behind him, Napoleon was able to wage a new style of warfare: total war. Previously war had often been considered the "sport of kings," and usually aroused little interest in the majority of the population.[7]

The son of a minor Corsican noble family, Napoleon Bonaparte rose to high command while still in his twenties, because of the French Revolution. As a citizen army replaced the professional army, the morale of the French soldier added a new element that Napoleon fully understood and cultivated. To inspire his army, he effectively united his men around a cause, the principles of the French Revolution, and later the glory of France as a growing empire.[8]

One of Napoleon's major innovations was the separation of field troops into self-contained divisions.[9] Napoleon divided his army into corps, which were further subdivided into divisions, brigades, regiments, and battalions that operated as autonomous units, but moved and fought together as a single entity.[10] He combined military leadership with political leadership, thus eliminating friction at the top and attaining a unity of command. An absence of checks and balances in this one-man rule, however, resulted in critical errors that ultimately brought down Napoleon's empire.[11]

Tactically, in first-generation war, adversaries sought to amass huge armies that confronted each other on the battlefield, each attempting to win a decisive victory.[12] In battle Napoleon always favored the offensive, with the central objective of annihilating an enemy's field forces. Everything else was secondary. To that end, he emphasized firepower. France's industrial and scientific infrastructure allowed the creation of heavy artillery, and Napoleon once opined that "God is on the side with the best artillery."[13] Having little respect for the sensibilities of European royal dynasties, he was not loath to annihilate opposing forces, fully understanding that the currency of politics is power.

Eventually Napoleon's adversaries adapted to his strategy by avoiding the decisive battles he so eagerly sought. Although his armies operated on a huge scale with unprecedented speed, his desire for hegemony in Europe led him to a strategic overreach that finally brought about his downfall.[14] The British navy's victory over the French fleet at Trafalgar in 1805 sank Napoleon's plans for an invasion of England. He imposed a European economic blockade of British goods, but England was able to surmount this challenge.[15] Next, in the Peninsular War, Spanish and Portuguese irregulars harassed the French army, forcing Napoleon to deploy a huge French force that was desperately needed elsewhere. Like the British, the Russians refused to meet Napoleon on his terms and even ceded the capital city of Moscow, thus using the strategic depth of Russian geography to wear his army down, which resulted in the disastrous Russian campaign of 1812. Finally, at Waterloo in 1815, the Duke of Wellington defeated Napoleon. Although Napoleon did not leave a written compilation of his thoughts on warfare, an adversary, a Prussian officer named Carl von Clausewitz, formulated his own strategy in a volume that became a classic text on the art of war.

Carl von Clausewitz

Carl Philipp Gottlieb von Clausewitz was born at Burg, near Magdeburg, in 1780. Having entered the army in 1792 as a *Fahnenjunker* (ensign) when he was only twelve, he had his baptism of fire the next year as part of a coalition of forces in a campaign that drove the French out of the Rhineland. Clausewitz attended the Prussian Military Academy (Kriegsakademie) in Berlin from 1801 to 1804, graduated at the top of his class, and captured the attention of General Gerhard Johann David von Scharnhorst (1755–1813). An astute officer, Clausewitz went on to serve as aide-de-camp to Prince Augustus of Prussia in the Jena campaign of 1806, during which he was wounded and taken prisoner. Sent to France, he stayed there for the remainder of the war, observing conditions in France that allowed him to see Prussia from a different intellectual and emotional perspective.[16] Upon his return home, he was placed on General Scharnhorst's staff and worked on reorganizing the Prussian army, which clearly needed reform, having been swiftly defeated by Napoleon's forces. Clausewitz attributed the army's 1806 defeat to Prussia's adherence to outmoded methods of warfare. Its opponent had been emancipated from such limitations.[17]

Appalled in 1812 by King Frederick William III's decision to join Napoleon in the fight against Russia, Clausewitz, along with several other Prussian officers, joined the so-called German Legion, a unit that fought alongside the Russian army. In 1815 he reentered the Prussian army, and in 1817 he assumed the directorship of the Kriegsakademie.[18] During his tenure there, Clausewitz attained the rank of general and produced his most important work, *On War*.[19] In 1831 he was appointed chief of staff to the Prussian army, deployed to observe the Polish rebellion against Russia, and he died after contracting cholera that same year.[20]

Edited by his widow, *On War* was published posthumously in 1832.[21] In it Clausewitz defines war as an act of violence "intended to compel our opponent to fulfill our will" and asserts that war is "not merely a political act, but also a real political instrument, a continuation of political commerce, a carrying out of the same by other means."[22] He viewed war as a legitimate instrument of national policy when waged for rational reasons. For Clausewitz, war was a serious means to a serious end and should thus be always subject to political design and oversight by the state.[23]

Seeing war as an instrument of policy, Clausewitz believed its ultimate prosecution should be carried out by political leaders, not the military.[24] The effective statesman, he believed, encompassed the gamut of power relations, political and military.[25] He also thought that soldiers should be allowed, even encouraged, to participate substantially in planning and conducting operations.[26] To be clear, Clausewitz made an important distinction between tactics—the art of winning battles—and strategy—the use of battles to obtain the objectives of a campaign.[27]

Military institutions, Clausewitz posited, depend on the economic, social, and political institutions of their respective states.[28] The Clausewitzian trinity, as it came to be known, consisted of interlinked citizens, army, and government. An important lesson he learned from observing Napoleon's campaign was that an entire nation should be mobilized in the service of a military objective. Prior to Napoleon, European monarchs feared that an armed citizenry could be destabilizing. Although Clausewitz was essentially conservative in outlook and aware of the potential danger of a mass army, he still favored this arrangement because he saw a strong, monolithic military and total mobilization of its power as necessary to exert the national will. Believing that the revolutionary fervor of the French armies had accounted for many of their victories, Clausewitz embodied this and other principles in a theory of warfare.[29]

Like Napoleon, Clausewitz emphasized the significance of the decisive battle. Rather than focusing on territory, he believed it was more important to destroy an opponent's military power. Thus an effective strategy concentrated forces at a decisive position. The "culminating point" was the moment when the chief objective of the campaign was accomplished.[30]

Clausewitz's model accounted for many intangible factors as well. He believed that a theory of war must consider the human element, including leadership, morale, perseverance, faith, zeal, courage, and boldness. And discipline was essential: he cited obedience as the most important factor in war.[31] To Clausewitz, when "genius" was combined properly with the emotional component of intuition, a commander in chief could attain preeminence on the battlefield.[32]

Clausewitz recognized that war had a high degree of uncertainty, or "friction." Like the great Chinese war strategist Sun Tzu, Clausewitz knew the importance of surprise. As he explained, the stratagem implied a concealed intention.[33] Although he conceded that troop deployment, surprise, and other tactics could affect the course of battles, he counseled that trying to achieve victory by such means was fanciful, especially the higher the level at which a war was waged, as between large armies, and the greater the number of people involved.[34] Experience, Clausewitz counseled, was one factor that could help an army overcome friction.[35]

Clausewitz effectively built on the fundamental concepts of eighteenth-century warfare and constructed much of the conceptual edifice that dominated the nineteenth century.[36] The Prussian army's victories of 1866 and 1870–1871 ensured that his thought would have a great influence on German foreign policy for years to come.[37] In his paradigm, the statesman appears as a supergeneral who possesses the final authority over his generals in the same way that the generals possess authority over lower-ranking officers and enlisted men.[38] This concept came into great force during World War II, when Germany's chancellor, Adolf Hitler, assumed control over all the country's military decisions. In American military academies, Clausewitz has attained preeminent status and *On War* is treated as a quasi-sacred text.[39] But his twentieth-century influence, according to some of his detractors, contributed to the calamity of World War I, during which second-generation warfare came to fruition.[40]

Second-Generation Warfare

Several innovations made second-generation warfare possible. The increasing wealth generated by industrialization, concomitant with the sheer volume of industrial output, provided the wherewithal to raise, support, and transport huge armies. After the Napoleonic Wars, the power of the state continued to increase in Europe. Better systems of public administration enabled governments to improve tax collection and raise the money for ambitious undertakings. New technology was brought to bear too. Steam power revolutionized transportation and logistics, making it much more efficient to transport personnel and materiel: armies and supplies could be moved by steamship and railroad. The telegraph, developed by Samuel Morse, allowed for rapid communications and made possible the greater coordination of forces. The new system allowed the micromanagement of wars from capitals, heralding centralized command and control. With enhanced communications, commanders could now organize huge troop movements at critical points on the battlefield, and the operational, or theater, level of war was born.[41] As nations became more interconnected by technological developments, they became ripe for world wars.[42]

Much had changed at the doctrinal level as well. The Napoleonic Wars served as a catalyst for Prussian military reforms, and other European armies were quick to follow. Perhaps the most important innovation was the creation of the German general staff, which became the brain of the army.[43] The chief of staff was expected not only to implement his commander's orders, but also to serve as a full partner in command decisions.[44] Furthermore, a new war academy, the Preußische Kriegsakademie, was created to train officers. After the reforms, the new Prussian army was much more flexible and responsive than its predecessor.[45]

An important innovation was the doctrine of *Auftragstaktic* (mission-oriented command), a new German philosophy of warfare emphasizing speed and the need to take the offensive. Officers were encouraged to respond to circumstances of the moment and take advantage of them. The key was an overall mind-set that allowed a unit to be built around a particular goal.[46] General Helmuth von Moltke (1800–1891) expanded on Napoleon's decentralized command structure, in which senior commanders were given considerable authority, but followed the general direction of his military doctrine. Moltke's version encompassed every element of war from mobilization to battle, enhanced by meticulous central planning by the general staff.

So decentralization of execution was combined with a centralized direction of purpose.[47] With these reforms, the German army was a flexible, cohesive war machine that was the envy of the world.[48]

Prior to World War I, war had consisted primarily of the employment of force against force. However, this epic conflict—the so-called Great War—turned into a vast exercise in the coordination of national resources, including factories, labor, and raw materials.[49] French military planners believed that heavy artillery and a large standing army would assure victory.[50] But the tactic of amassing huge columns of soldiers on the battlefield, standard during the Napoleonic Wars, proved unfeasible during World War I. Troops had formerly congregated for protection, but increased firepower and greater accuracy demanded that armies disperse.[51] As a consequence, stalemate ensued and resulted in trench warfare. Thus second-generation warfare favored defense over offense, and machine guns, magazine-fed rifles, rapid-fire artillery, and barbed wire were developed or put to use.

Patriotism became increasingly important and brought together millions of men under arms whose enthusiasm was sustained despite the horrific battlefield casualties in World War I.[52] Militarism suffused the zeitgeist, as writers such as Friedrich Nietzsche, Georges Sorel, Charles Péguy, and Gabriele D'Annunzio extolled elementary, even nonpolitical, bloodshed as a way to cleanse the world, which they saw as drowning in materialism and feminism.[53] Arguably, politics played little part in World War I. As war hysteria swept over Europe, people entered into the conflagration largely for the sake of fighting. Political restraints were overwhelmed, and politicians who resisted the tide were execrated.[54]

Between the two sides, over sixty-five million men were fielded—42,188,800 by the Allies and 22,850,000 by the Central Powers. Fifteen million people lost their lives in the war: more than 8.5 million soldiers and approximately 6.5 million civilians.[55] Air warfare notwithstanding, World War I did not involve much in the way of new military techniques. Rather it demonstrated the war-making value of massive industrial output. Ultimately Germany was defeated in a war of attrition because of the superior manpower and resources of its adversaries. Despite its desperate situation, Germany persisted and incurred a staggering loss: more than two million of its citizens dead (nearly 3 percent of its population). This high cost left an abiding sense of grievance on which Hitler was able to capitalize.[56]

Third-Generation Warfare

According to some interwar critics, World War I discredited the Clausewitzian—and by extension German—model of warfare. Chief among them was Basil Liddell Hart (1895–1970). At the start of World War I in August 1914, Liddell Hart joined the British army. After receiving a commission as a second lieutenant, he served with distinction in combat tours in France, during which he was wounded in a gas attack at the Battle of the Somme in July 1916. After leaving the army, he established a reputation as Britain's foremost military journalist, and later as a prominent military historian. The principal lesson he learned from the Great War was that it was folly to send mass formations of armed men in frontal assaults to face machine-gun garrisons. He reasoned that such tactics nullified Clausewitz's dictum of concentrating forces in a decisive point of attack. Direct attacks against an enemy's front should be avoided, Liddell Hart thought, believing that such an outdated practice would necessarily end in failure.[57] Such tactics, he argued, had led to the trench warfare in World War I in which so many soldiers had been killed. To prevent such a quagmire in subsequent wars, Liddell Hart advocated a form of maneuver warfare that would be based on the deployment of tanks, mobile infantry units, artillery, and aircraft against an adversary's headquarters and communications system. Rather than amassing forces in concentrated form, they should be deployed in an intelligent, strategic way to maximize their effectiveness.[58]

As was the case with second-generation warfare, the German general staff was in the forefront in the development of third-generation warfare. Diplomatically isolated after its defeat in World War I, and situated in a precarious geopolitical position, Germany faced the prospect of another multifront war. In the event of such a war, it was imperative for Germany that it win quickly. Surrounded on all sides by potential enemies, it could not afford to get bogged down in an attritional war in which adversaries collectively had greater manpower and resources. To counter this predicament, the German army developed maneuvering tactics that placed much responsibility on, and granted autonomy to, local commanders who sought to exploit opportunities as they arose.[59] During World War II, the Wehrmacht generated remarkably little paperwork, and orders from headquarters tended to be clear and brief. Officers and enlisted men were given incentives and rewarded for fighting prowess and risk-taking.[60] With this freedom of action, the blitzkrieg method was highly effective on the battlefield. The German military based its operation on the assumption that warfare was basically chaotic, and so its leaders built a high degree of flexibility into their command-and-control structure. Subordinate officers were encouraged to exploit fleeting opportunities presented by disorder as long as their actions conformed to their commanders' overall intent.[61] Maneuver warfare had been applied before World War II, albeit in more primitive form, but now improvements in armor and airpower permitted its application on an unprecedented scale and potentially enabled a numerically inferior army to prevail over a larger one with greater resources. Attacks could be better coordinated using aircraft and ground personnel.[62]

An early concept of third-generation warfare had been developed by the time of the German offensive in the spring of 1918, but third-generation warfare truly emerged in force with the blitzkrieg unleashed on May 10, 1940, with the German invasion of France.[63] Contrary to the accepted wisdom, the German campaign in Poland in September 1939 did not go smoothly. The vast majority of the Wehrmacht marched on foot and was supplied by horse-drawn transport. Nevertheless, the German general staff learned from the experience and implemented changes that led to the successful use of the blitzkrieg. What made the German Panzer Corps so effective during this offensive was that the tanks were equipped with radios, which transformed them "from stand-alone pieces of military hardware into a kind of coordinated group weapon," as Clay Shirky puts it. In effect, the blitzkrieg was a strategy based on using a smaller, more nimble force against a well-provisioned adversary.[64] Heinz Guderian, whose combined-arms tactics the Panzer attacks used, also employed other motorized vehicles for the breakthrough in France that had been so elusive in World War I. Whereas the French assumed a defensive posture behind the Maginot Line, Germany had learned from the previous war that trench warfare led to stalemate.

Hitler's experiences in the trenches during World War I led to some of his bad strategic decisions in World War II. The vast expanses of the Soviet Union made the blitzkrieg unfeasible there. Hitler realized the problem of "friction" in war, but believed it could be overcome by assertions of will. Even in 1940, after his victory over France, Hitler realized that the old core of Europe was too small and vulnerable to sustain a global conflict.[65] In the end, superior tactics were not enough for Germany to prevail over adversaries with far greater resources.

As the Israeli military historian Martin van Creveld has noted, the single most important factor driving twentieth-century warfare was technological progress.[66] The first two generations of warfare had emphasized scale and firepower. Third-generation warfare added emphasis on maneuverability. Technological developments drove the evolution from first- through third-generation warfare, and contributed greatly to increasing lethality, culminating in the atomic attacks on Hiroshima and Nagasaki in 1945. But factors other than technology, especially changes in politics, contributed to fourth-generation warfare, which often employs a sophisticated political-psychological element even though it may be fought with primitive tactics.

Fourth-Generation Warfare

Clausewitz's *On War* is a philosophical treatise that is considered to be the paradigm for first-, second-, and third-generation wars. These models basically involved direct confrontation between adversaries. In contrast, guerrilla warfare is designed to avoid direct confrontations with large forces. The term "guerrilla warfare" first gained currency in the early nineteenth century in Spain during the French occupation.[67] There the Peninsular War was a tremendous strain on Napoleon's army. Near the end of his life, Clausewitz presaged the growing importance of guerrilla warfare, which he referred to as "People's War," but he died before he could finish his drafts.[68] During the French occupation of Spain, he had studied the insurrection of armed civilians and regarded it as a model for his country.[69]

Although localized resistance movements emerged in Europe against the occupying French army during the Napoleonic period, they did not develop into national revolutionary ideologies. Rather, they remained parochial and xenophobic.[70] The major innovation of contemporary guerrilla war is the addition of revolutionary politics.[71] Since the 1930s, guerrilla wars have become less parochial and more national in character, and have often been inspired by revolutionary ideologies connected to international movements, thus giving them greater cohesion than in the past.[72] During the first few decades after World War II, most insurgents were animated by Marxist-Leninist ideology that gave voice to their anticolonial aspirations. More recently, a disparate array of Islamic fighters scattered around the world find inspiration in al Qaeda's extreme Salafist interpretation of Islam.

Since World War II the great majority of wars have been low-intensity conflicts. The extreme lethality of nuclear weapons has made direct conflict between military superpowers too dangerous.[73] But this has not stopped so-called proxy wars in which states support insurgencies. As a result, guerrilla war became the dominant form of warfare from the early 1950s to the end of the Cold War.

Thomas X. Hammes, a retired US Marine Corps colonel, expounded on the nature of contemporary insurgency in his study *The Sling and the Stone: On War in the 21st Century*. Building on Lind's framework, he described fourth-generation warfare as an evolved form of insurgency that endeavors to use all available networks—political, social, and military—to convince the enemy's decision makers that their strategic goals are unattainable or not worth the cost.[74] Unlike earlier forms of warfare, it does not aim to defeat the enemy's military forces. Rather, it directly targets the minds of the enemy's decision makers to destroy their political will to carry out the struggle. Since all forms of asymmetrical warfare are outgrowths of insurgent warfare, an examination of them is in order to better understand the dynamics of contemporary armed conflict and terrorism.[75]

Tactics and Strategies

Guerrilla warfare is essentially the strategy of using one's supposed weakness against an enemy's strength and cleverly using terrain to conceal rebel forces from the enemy. Typically guerrilla fighters implement a Fabian strategy, named after the campaign of Fabius Maximus against Hannibal of Carthage in the third century BC, in which Fabius evaded battle in order to gain time and thus erode the morale of his enemy.[76] The Roman general nibbled away at the Carthaginians' rear guard and avoided a decisive battle, thus exhausting Hannibal and his forces.[77] Guerrilla fighters usually do not have a technical advantage over regular armies, nor do they have a tactical advantage. Nevertheless, they often have an operational advantage since they fight elusively without trying to defend territory against a determined attack, and they choose when and where to fight.[78]

Establishing a secure base is crucial for an insurgency. Under the best circumstances the base will be near an international border, rough in terrain, and away from easy transportation.[79] Mountainous areas are considered to be conducive to insurgencies because they offer cover and are more difficult for conventional forces to traverse. It is also preferable to have guerrilla strongholds in close proximity, in order to facilitate planning, command, control, and communications.[80] Still, an axiom of guerrilla warfare is that insurgents should not attempt to hold a particular piece of territory in the face of a determined attack.[81]

Gaining the support of the people, noncombatants, is essential for an insurgency. Without a critical mass of support, an insurgency will not get far. As David Galula wrote in his classic study *Counterinsurgency Warfare: Theory and Practice*, during its embryonic phase any resistance movement is "as vulnerable as a new-born baby."[82] At minimum, a prerequisite for an insurgency is a cause that appeals to both active and passive supporters. Initially in an insurgency, the population can be divided into three segments: those who support the insurgents; those who want to see the insurgents defeated; and, usually the largest group, those who are neutral, or uncommitted. Thus, in order to prevail, the insurgency must offer a political cause that can mobilize the uncommitted majority.[83] Insurgents must demonstrate that they have momentum and will ultimately succeed. By maintaining the military initiative, they can leave the impression that they are gaining the upper hand.[84]

In order to be successful, leaders have to marshal the resources to mount a viable insurgency. The defense analyst Jeffrey Record once argued that the single most important factor that determines the likelihood of an insurgency's success is external support. The greatest impetus for this support during the Cold War was the continuous rivalry between the major communist powers and the West.[85] But external support can take many forms.[86] Record found few examples of colonial or postcolonial insurgencies that prevailed without foreign assistance. Superior will is important, but to be viable it must be backed with the force of arms.[87] To make his case, he cites numerous examples, including the American Revolutionary War, in which the rebels received vital support from France. In the Peninsular War, Spanish and Portuguese rebels benefited from the presence of British troops on the peninsula. Likewise, in the Vietnam War, the Vietnamese communists received assistance from both the Soviet Union and China. Even in China, Mao's forces received large quantities of captured Japanese weapons that the Soviets had taken from the surrendered Kwangtung Army. During the Soviet-Afghan War, the mujahideen received substantial covert support from the CIA through the Pakistani Inter-Services Intelligence (ISI).[88]

By contrast, the track record for insurgents is less impressive in conflicts in which they did not receive outside support. Although the FLN (Front de Libération Nationale) eventually prevailed in Algeria, the rebels owed their victory primarily to the international community and French elite opinion regarding the open and widespread use of torture against the insurgents.[89] In the so-called Malayan Emergency, the insurgency was restricted almost entirely to the minority ethnic Chinese segment of the population and thus never attained broad-based support.[90] Likewise, plans for guerrilla warfare conducted by Germans foundered after the end of World War II. Allied intelligence officers foresaw an unprecedented terrorist campaign in the wake of the German defeat. The Werewolf operation led by Hitler's commando extraordinaire, Otto Skorzeny, was organized to fight Allied occupation forces, and operatives were trained, but the guerrilla force was crushed by the massive Allied advance. Moreover, occupied Germany was surrounded by adversaries or other countries under occupation, thus rendering outside support untenable.[91]

During the twentieth century, guerrilla warfare was most successfully implemented in Asia, where many centuries earlier a Chinese scholar contributed greatly to contemporary guerrilla war theory.

Sun Tzu

Around the year 500 BC, the philosopher Sun Tzu produced a treatise—*The Art of War*—that in some ways anticipates contemporary asymmetrical warfare. According to Sun Tzu, war is governed by constant factors.[92] All warfare, he averred, is based on deception. He believed that war should be waged swiftly, counseling that in no instance had a country ever benefited from a protracted war, and thought that war should be avoided if possible. Like Clausewitz, Sun Tzu knew that the decision to wage war was a serious one, that war should not be entered into for base reasons or no reason at all. If war were necessary, then the goal should be to win with minimal bloodshed. There was also an important psychological component to his strategy: "If you know the enemy and know yourself, you need not fear the result of a hundred battles. If you know yourself but not the enemy, for every victory gained you will also suffer a defeat. If you know neither the enemy nor yourself, you will succumb in every battle."[93]

Sun Tzu saw war and peace as two sides of the same coin. An effective military leader, he proposed, could win without a battle being fought: the true mark of military genius was the ability to discourage one's adversary from fighting in the first place. This was consistent with Sun Tzu's view that minimizing damage inflicted on an enemy's land, people, and infrastructure would make it easier to convert the vanquished into citizens, rather than having them resist or rebel.

Timing was crucial for Sun Tzu. When a commander had an enemy where he wanted it, he should strike like a thunderbolt.[94] He recommended that a general always keep the opponent off balance by mixing tactics—both direct and indirect—in an endless series of maneuvers. Rather than seeking to surround an enemy army, Sun Tzu counseled that an outlet should always be left open so that a desperate foe would not be pressed too hard to fight. He also emphasized the primacy of morale in the effectiveness of an army. It was imperative, he believed, for a commander to first become attached to his men. Once he gained their trust, they should be kept under control by iron discipline. He also stressed the importance of intelligence and espionage, arguing that the best information is obtained from spies.

Modern insurgency is often based on Sun Tzu's concept of turning weakness to strength. If the enemy is strong, he counsels, evade it. In modern military parlance this is asymmetry, in which competing forces are out of balance. Through asymmetrical warfare a weaker power could attain a political objective against a more powerful adversary.[95] Presumably Sun Tzu had a significant influence on Mao Zedong.

Mao and the Chinese Communist Revolution

Mao Zedong, who led the communist revolution in China, is considered the chief theoretician of fourth-generation warfare. Not unlike Sun Tzu, Mao saw the principal target in warfare not as enemy soldiers but the collective mind and will of their political leaders. He believed that independent guerrilla operations were but one step in a broader total war, and one aspect of revolutionary struggle.[96]

The son of an industrious farmer, Mao was born in the Hunan Province in central China in 1893. Although raised in austerity, he received a thorough secondary education and was most interested in history and political science. A keen observer of his times, Mao noticed that the Chinese government was unable to meet the needs of the peasants with whom he grew up. His experience as a private soldier in a corrupt and inefficient army further increased his political awareness.[97] From an early age he sought to think of ways to free China from colonialism and help it develop into a strong country. To that end, he joined the Chinese Communist Party (CCP) in 1921, the year it was founded.[98]

Early in his political career Mao denounced the concept of "pure guerrilla warfare," preferring that the Red Army establish and consolidate revolutionary bases. However, as time went on, he became convinced that an urban revolutionary focus was unfeasible in China.[99] Since its population was overwhelmingly rural, Mao reasoned that only China's peasantry could make up his forces and provide it with food and an extensive intelligence network.[100]

The classic Maoist insurgency model is based on his notion of a people's war. According to Mao in his treatise *On Guerrilla Warfare*, successful guerrilla warfare progresses through three phases. In the first phase—the strategic defensive—insurgents seek to mobilize and organize the people and achieve ideological unification and coherence. Like Clausewitz, Mao understood that war was inherently a political undertaking.[101] Mao considered roughly 15–25 percent of the population to constitute a "significant segment" necessary for a revolutionary movement to take hold.[102] In order for guerrillas to prevail, Mao theorized, they must establish control over an area of the countryside. From a secure base, rebels could endure even a prolonged struggle against government. This position of security leads to the second, longest phase—the strategic stalemate—in which insurgents seek to establish their organization through small-scale attacks and acts of terrorism against government targets. During this phase, neither side can mount major offensives. Finally, in the third phase—the strategic offensive—insurgents escalate their activities to include larger-scale attacks. Once they reach a critical mass, the guerrilla forces are transformed into regular forces that seek to control select territories.

According to conventional wisdom, popular support is critical for the insurgency as it passes through each stage. Without it, the rebels would lose momentum, at which point the counterinsurgency forces could gain the advantage.[103] Although the model assumes an orderly, sequential progression from one stage to the next, victory can come at any point if a government suddenly loses its will to continue the struggle.[104] It is crucial that the guerrilla campaign appear purposeful and not chaotic, otherwise it will fail to generate the great popular expectations necessary for its eventual success through each stage of its development.[105]

Mao realized that the most formidable hurdle in a revolution is to get people to join, fight, and possibly die for his cause.[106] He intuitively understood the efficacy of decentralized networks and organized his communist forces accordingly into a number of independent cells that could not be defeated en masse.[107] As he appraised his own strategic situation, he saw decentralization forced on guerrillas because they lacked a well-developed communications system.[108] His tactical approach prefigured the rise of leaderless resistance decades later.

Mao's peasant-based approach had an enduring influence, as it would come to dominate guerrilla strategy in the twentieth century. His revolutionary model resonated with insurgent movements around the world. Soon anticolonialist movements would challenge the old order. The first wave of modern guerrilla warfare appeared in Africa and Asia after 1945. For roughly twenty years there were rebellions against Western colonial powers in struggles for national independence. Often anticolonial movements contained a strong socialist component in the agendas of the rebel groups. By the late 1950s, the Soviet Union and China championed wars of "liberation," while the United States saw itself as the guardian of "world order." The communist ideology was attractive to many national liberation movements because it allowed rebels to view their sacrifices not as transient acts of rebellion but as contributions to an historical process whose outcome was certain. Furthermore, even a superficial sympathy for communist ideas was enough to attract support from the Soviet Union and its allies, which was often indispensable in military terms.[109] One of the lengthiest insurgencies of the last century—the Vietcong's efforts in Southeast Asia—received support from both the Soviet Union and China and humbled the United States in what became one of the major US foreign policy setbacks of the Cold War.

Vietnam

One of the most drawn out and successful guerrilla conflicts in history took place in Vietnam. For more than three decades Vietnamese communists persisted, and they finally succeeded in taking control of the entire country in 1975. The origins of the conflict can be traced back to 1941, when Ho Chi Minh formed the Vietminh, an umbrella organization that included all the nationalist resistance movements. Its principal military leader and chief strategist was General Võ Nguyên Giáp, who created an army out of a ragtag collection of peasants infused with a deep sense of purpose. During the Second World War, Ho's guerrillas had been active in the anti-Japanese resistance. By war's end, hardly any Japanese or French units were stationed in Vietnam. As a result, the partisans rapidly asserted control over the country, and by June 1945 six mountain provinces were largely under their sway. When the communists entered Hanoi, they took over with hardly a shot fired.[110] By defeating the Japanese, the Vietminh attained the stature of a national liberation army. On September 2, 1945, the Democratic Republic of Vietnam was proclaimed, based in Hanoi and led by Ho.

The strength of Ho Chi Minh's appeal was his call for Vietnamese independence, a point on which the French could not compete.[111] On December 19, 1945, full-scale war returned when Vietminh units attacked French garrisons. During the war with France, which lasted from 1946 to 1954, the Vietnamese had a numerical superiority almost from the start.[112] Ensconced in the garrison at Hoa Binh, the French sought to draw the Vietminh into a decisive battle.[113] Despite his Maoist orientation, Giáp too sought a decisive engagement in the style of Clausewitz. In May 1954 at Dien Bien Phu he committed roughly half his forces to defeat the French army, and he succeeded—resulting in the French decision to leave Vietnam.[114]

In 1960 Ho organized the National Liberation Front (NLF)—dubbed the Vietcong by its opponents—to conduct guerrilla warfare in the south. According to T. X. Hammes's analysis, the Vietcong were able to prevail for a variety of reasons. First, they possessed abiding determination and a belief that they would eventually be victorious. Second, they exhibited remarkable ingenuity in overcoming problems. They often employed tactics that were beyond the training and experience of the US forces. Although the Vietcong consistently lost on the battlefield, they won the war. As Hammes points out, strategically they shifted the force from the battlefield to the political arena, as evidenced by the Tet Offensive of 1968.[115]

By the spring of 1967, Vietcong losses had reached horrendous levels. Facing an increasingly desperate situation, its leaders decided to mount a spectacular operation that would reverse their decline. The original objective of the Tet Offensive was to instigate a general uprising among the people in South Vietnam. This was the major Vietnamese innovation to Mao's concept of guerrilla warfare. During the operation, virtually every major town and city, as well as the most important US bases, came under attack. Although the combined communist forces of the North and South wreaked considerable havoc, the Vietcong were destroyed as an effective military organization. In fact, the main reason they were able to launch the surprise attack, despite the US intelligence that something big was in the offing, was because General William Westmoreland believed such an operation would be suicidal.[116] Approximately fourteen thousand South Vietnamese and four thousand US troops were killed in the offensive, but casualties were far higher for their adversaries, who lost somewhere between forty-five thousand and eighty-four thousand fighters.[117] At least militarily, the Tet Offensive "was the greatest defeat sustained by the Communists in [the] entire conflict."[118]

The Tet Offensive illustrated the primacy of politics in guerrilla warfare. The Vietcong were effectively destroyed but won a huge political victory. Although the US military was winning all the battles, from that point on it was losing the war. The assault represented a tipping point by raising doubts in the minds of moderate Americans, not just the antiwar segment of the population, about the feasibility of winning the war. Not long after, the venerable television news anchor Walter Cronkite essentially proclaimed that the war could not be won, and President Lyndon B. Johnson subsequently announced he would not seek reelection.[119] At that point, the US defeat was all but certain.[120] The last US ground forces withdrew from South Vietnam in August 1972, and Saigon fell in April 1975 after the North Vietnamese Army launched the largest conventional invasion on the Asian continent since the Chinese intervention in the Korean War, taking South Vietnam, which had been abandoned by the United States.[121] During the evacuation, Harry Summers, a US Army infantry colonel, told a North Vietnamese colonel that the NVA had never defeated US forces on the battlefield, to which the NVA colonel responded, "That may be so, but it is also irrelevant."[122] The Vietnam War had a catalyzing effect on Marxist-Leninist-inspired revolutionary movements around the world, including those in Latin America. Several Latin American theorists would modify Mao's strategy.

Latin America

Fidel Castro launched his first attempt to overthrow the dictatorship of Fulgencio Batista in 1953, when he and his army of two hundred men stormed an army barracks outside Santiago, Cuba, in the hope of sparking a popular uprising. Most of the attackers were killed, and Castro was captured and sentenced to fifteen years in prison, but he was released under a general amnesty after serving just eleven months. Exiled to Mexico, he returned to launch another invasion in December 1956, when he, along with eighty-one followers, arrived on the shores of Oriente, the easternmost province of Cuba.[123] Batista's government was fragile, as even middle-class support had dwindled. Batista had alienated practically all key strata of Cuban society, including the Catholic Church and business elites. His army command was corrupt and lacked combat experience.[124] Diplomatically isolated, Batista earned the open disdain of the Eisenhower administration, which even imposed an arms trade embargo on Cuba.[125] According to some estimates, Castro never commanded more than fifteen hundred armed men during the revolution. Nevertheless, he was able to prevail in an island country whose population was close to seven million.[126] Castro effectively skipped the first phase of Mao's revolutionary model, in that his small guerrilla band never attempted a broad-based mobilization of the national community and instead picked up support as it moved toward Havana. Because Batista was broadly unpopular, this approach was feasible.[127] The Cuban Revolution electrified revolutionaries in many parts of the world, who often cited it as the prototype of how to conduct a guerrilla war. Chief among them was Castro's colleague Ernesto "Che" Guevara.

While in Mexico City in 1956, Guevara met Fidel Castro and joined his rebel army. His medical skills made him invaluable. After the triumph of the Cuban Revolution in 1959, Guevara assumed a series of positions in the new government led by Castro, but in 1965 he left the country to spread the revolutionary struggle. An internationalist who believed that revolution should transcend national borders, Guevara first traveled to Congo and then returned to Latin America with the goal of inciting a hemisphere-wide revolution. He went to Bolivia, but his band of revolutionaries failed to win the support of the peasants there. On October 8, 1967, he and his remaining guerrillas were captured by the Bolivian army, and he was executed the next day. In death he attained the status of a martyr. Arguably, his chief contribution was symbolic rather than tactical or strategic. He even became an icon of the counterculture in the United States.[128]

According to Guevara, the Cuban Revolution offered three principal lessons. First, popular forces could prevail over a state army. Second, it was not necessary to wait until all conditions were perfect before mounting an insurrection. The rebellion could precipitate these conditions. Strategically parting company with traditional Marxists, Guevara believed that human consciousness was more important in creating a revolutionary climate than material conditions. To bring about revolution, a vanguard needed to politically educate the masses, not wait for the capitalist economy to collapse. Third, as in the case of Mao, the countryside should be the focus of fighting.[129]

Tactics are widely discussed in Guevara's opus *Guerrilla Warfare*. Consistently Guevara argued that guerrillas have to be seen as the vanguard of the people, without whose support they cannot prevail. Guerrillas must have adequate knowledge of the countryside in which they fight, and should use hit-and-run tactics to keep the enemy off balance. They should engage the enemy only when they believe they can win, and always by surprise. After the initial phases of the guerrilla struggle have passed and revolutionaries attain wide popular support, then they can increasingly take on the features of a regular army, deliver a death blow to the enemy, and attain power. Until victory, the essential task of a guerrilla is to survive to fight another day. Guerrilla bands must remain mobile and travel lightly, preferably in bands of no more than fifteen. Guevara's handbook contained much practical advice, explaining how guerrillas could attack enemy convoys, establish a good supply system and medical services, plan acts of sabotage, and set up a war industry in liberated zones.[130]

The French socialist Régis Debray followed up on Guevara's ideas in a book titled *Revolution in the Revolution?* Tactically Debray advanced Guevara's *"foco* theory" of guerrilla war in which a *foquismo*—a small guerrilla band or foco (center)—would inspire the people by demonstrating that resistance was possible.[131] Guevara had posited that by using violence, a revolutionary movement could mobilize popular support quickly, avoiding the necessity of prior political mobilization. Violence could transform a political situation and create an environment conducive to revolution. However, when Guevara applied this approach in Bolivia, he and his guerrillas were crushed. As Mao and Giáp both realized, in most situations, this approach was not effective because it exposed the rebel movement at its weakest moment.[132]

Robert Taber, a CBS investigative journalist who traveled to Cuba in the late 1950s to cover the burgeoning revolutionary movement, wrote an important treatise on guerrilla warfare titled *The War of the Flea*. Although somewhat romanticizing guerrillas, the book expressed interesting insights on the nature of insurgency, and it has been widely cited. According to Taber, there was something unique about the 1960s zeitgeist that fostered the spread of insurrection. He describes a "will to resist" that became nearly universal. According to Taber, once a critical mass is reached, a guerrilla movement possesses several advantages over its adversary. First and foremost, the guerrillas determine when and where to strike, forcing the government into a reactive, defensive posture. With the people behind them, the guerrillas can wage a protracted war, and all they really need to do is survive. The government, on the other hand, must expend more and more resources as the conflict drags on, losing political capital along the way. Likening guerrillas to fleas that irritate a dog, Taber observed that their campaigns can also inflict economic damage, as it may discourage foreign investment. By repeatedly striking the enemy, a guerrilla campaign serves as an educational tool and propaganda weapon. Despite widespread poverty and disaffection, the peasants of Latin America demonstrated limited revolutionary potential. This occasioned a shift in strategic thinking toward cities as loci of insurgencies.

The Urban Guerrilla

For years the rural model of insurgency was preferred by revolutionaries, but as countries became more urban, some theorists sought to formulate a guerrilla strategy that could be applied in cities. Guevara had seen urban terrorism as a supplemental tactic, part of a broader insurgency based in the countryside. At worst it was a dangerous aberration, as Castro and Guevara came to be firmly convinced that the city was the graveyard of the revolutionary freedom fighter. But with the defeat of rural guerrillas in Latin America by the middle of the 1960s, urban terrorism gained popularity in Europe, North America, and Japan.[133]

The urban guerrilla strategy to shift insurgent activity from the countryside was deemed necessary because of urbanization taking place throughout the world. In 1900 roughly 5 percent of the world's population resided in cities of one hundred thousand inhabitants or more. A century later that figure had reached 45 percent. In an increasingly urban world, it is more likely that soldiers will find themselves fighting in cities.[134]

One early theoretician of urban guerrilla warfare, Abraham Guillén (1913–1993), had fought to defend the Spanish Republic against the forces of Francisco Franco. In his *Strategy of the Urban Guerrilla*, published in 1966, he observed that Latin America had the fastest-growing rate of urbanization in the world at that time, so it was not conducive to rural-based guerrilla warfare in the style of China or Cuba. Instead he advocated a strategy of progressive harassment in which insurgents would mount small operations to wear down a government.[135] In some urban guerrilla models, the objective is to first capture the capital city and then proceed to conquer the countryside—effectively the Maoist model in reverse.[136]

Some Latin American revolutionaries believed that terrorism could be used to galvanize the masses and infuse them with the spirit of revolt. More than any other figure, the Brazilian revolutionary Carlos Marighella theorized on the concept of the urban guerrilla. Best known for his tract *Mini-manual of the Urban Guerrilla*, he propounded a strategy to move revolutionary violence from the countryside to the city. Marighella believed revolutionary violence could be based in urban areas and directed by a small group of urban guerrillas. In his framework, urban operations laid the groundwork for guerrilla outbreaks in the countryside, which was supposed to be the decisive theater.[137] According to Marighella, urban terrorism would begin with two distinct phases: the first designed to bring about actual violence, the second to give meaning to the violence. Targets were supposed to have symbolic significance. Like some contemporary proponents of leaderless resistance, Marighella argued that violence did not have to be structured or coordinated in order to provoke a crisis that would create a climate conducive to revolution.

In Uruguay a group called the Tupamaros, founded in 1963 by Raúl Sendic, implemented a strategy of urban revolution, concentrated in Montevideo, the capital.[138] With the proper constellation of political, social, and economic factors, the Tupamaros believed they could obtain power. Initially the government had a difficult time dealing with the situation, but it eventually responded harshly. Marighella and the Tupamaros believed that people would flock to the revolutionaries if government repression was employed but the opposite was true. The general population in Uruguay was fearful of the revolutionary violence and supported the government's severe counterterrorism measures. Consequently, the left-leaning administration was defeated in the election of 1971 and a right-wing, authoritarian government came to power. Soon after, martial law was declared and a brutal counterterrorist campaign ensued. Indirectly the Tupamaros had accomplished the opposite of what they had intended.

The Tupamaros modified the revolutionary tradition in Latin America, believing that urban guerrillas could blend in with the masses of the city, not unlike rural guerrillas in the jungle of the countryside. After the failure of their campaign, the consensus among revolutionary theoreticians was that urban guerrilla warfare was not viable.[139] Despite their failure, the Tupamaros became a model of urban terrorism for many left-wing terrorist groups in the late 1960s and 1970s, including the Red Army Faction in Germany, Direct Action in France, the Red Brigades in Italy, and the Weather Underground in the United States. For decades, the vast majority of guerrilla movements were animated by left-wing ideologies, and as a consequence often received substantial support from the Communist bloc. The 1979 Soviet invasion of Afghanistan, however, proved to be a watershed and ultimately set in motion developments that led to the dissolution of the Soviet Union.

The Soviet-Afghan War

The central government in Afghanistan has always been weak, exercising only limited control over the countryside. In December 1979 the besieged, Moscow-supported People's Democratic Party administration asked the Soviet Union to send a contingent of troops to ward off the incipient mujahideen and foreign mercenaries.[140] The Soviets complied, invading Afghanistan with an army trained to fight a high-intensity conventional war on the plains of Europe and ill suited to conducting counterinsurgency operations.[141]

The Soviet army never deployed enough forces to conduct a successful counterinsurgency campaign in Afghanistan. Throughout the war, Soviet troop strength was between 80,000 and 115,000, with about 35 percent of those forces dedicated to securing lines of communications and bases. Nor did the Soviets seriously attempt to win the hearts and minds of Afghans. Chronically underdeployed, the Soviets sought to depopulate areas from which the mujahideen received support. Such operations engendered a massive humanitarian and refugee crisis in which roughly one-third of Afghan's prewar population of sixteen million fled across the border, in what one observer called "migratory genocide."[142] The scorched-earth policy alienated the Afghan people and made them more sympathetic to the mujahideen. Over time, Islamic jihad animated the mujahideen, thus complementing the domestic dimensions of the struggle with a fervent religious element as well.

The fourteen-hundred-mile-long Afghanistan-Pakistan border served as a lifeline to the resistance. Without the support of the Pakistani and US governments, it is far from certain that the resistance would have prevailed.[143] Prince Turki bin Faisal, the head of Saudi intelligence, coordinated the training and support of the mujahideen with the CIA and Pakistan's ISI.[144] It is estimated that the US government gave approximately $3.1 billion to foreign volunteers in Afghanistan. Saudi Arabia is reported to have matched that amount.[145] To counter military advances that the Soviet army had made in the war during the mid-1980s, the US government made the critical decision to provide Stinger anti-aircraft missiles to the mujahideen. By doing so, the United States crossed the threshold and significantly increased its stake in the war. These weapons were quite successful in neutralizing the Soviet fleet of heavily armored MI-24D helicopters, which had been inflicting heavy casualties on the Afghan rebels.[146] As a consequence, the Soviets sharply cut back their air operations, and their hold on Afghanistan became increasingly untenable.[147]

The war took a tremendous toll on the Soviet Union. Diplomatically, it strained relations with the Islamic world, for obvious reasons. China interpreted the invasion as an effort by the Soviet Union to encircle it, and declared that the withdrawal of Soviet forces was a precondition for improved relations between the two countries. Large majorities in the United Nations annually voted that all troops should leave Afghanistan. India—a Soviet ally—was the only country in the region to recognize the government in Kabul and extend aid to it. In eight years of fighting, Soviet forces suffered between 48,000 and 52,000 casualties, including at least 13,000 to 15,000 deaths.[148] Although these were relatively low figures when compared to "the Great Patriotic War," as the Soviets called World War II, there were numerous hidden costs. Strain was placed not only on the country's fragile economy but on people's faith in government. The Soviet Union tumbled a few years later.[149]

Why Do Insurgencies Arise?

According to the military historian Martin van Creveld, "attempts by post-1945 armed forces to suppress guerrillas and terrorists have constituted a long, almost unbroken record of failure—a record that, as events in contemporary Iraq and Afghanistan testify, continue to the present day."[150] If guerrillas have been so successful since World War II, a question arises: how do insurgencies develop and attain critical mass?

Weak governance provides fertile ground for insurgencies. Usually a government can respond to unlawfulness swiftly and effectively, but when a state is substantially weakened and cannot provide adequate protection to its population, insurgents can assert alternative authority. Through terrorism, insurgents demonstrate that the government does not have a monopoly on force, intimidating part of the population into passivity. Ideological indoctrination will win over some segments of the population, but the rest are kept in line through force and are motivated by self-preservation.[151]

A disparity in motivations can also affect the outcome of a conflict. Insurgents tend to take a long view of history, while counterinsurgents tend to take a short view; thus the former can often outlast the latter.[152] And superior strength of commitment can compensate for military inferiority.[153]

The democratic framework of contemporary Western governments has been implicated as a cause of failure in guerrilla war. In his study *How Democracies Lose Small Wars*, Gil Merom argues that the domestic structure of democracies makes it difficult for such governments to prosecute small wars. On the home front, a variety of factors—including sensitivity to casualties, a repugnance for brutal military behavior, and a commitment to democratic life—militate against prosecuting small wars for a long time. Significant changes in Western societies have brought an aversion to prolonged small wars that do not seem to serve a compelling national interest, thus increasing the chance of success for insurgents. In particular, the increasingly educated liberal middle class exerts significant influence in the marketplace of ideas, and all of society becomes more aware of the implications of war. Ongoing casualties instill war weariness, particularly in wars that are considered nonessential, thus threatening to undercut public support. To compensate, state leaders are tempted to use greater firepower and higher levels of brutality. As revulsion to the conduct of the war grows, the antiwar sentiment intensifies. Merom's central argument is that democracies do not do well in small wars because they find it difficult to continually escalate violence and brutality to secure victory. Although they may have formidable military resources, they are restricted by their domestic structure and by their most articulate citizens, who voice opposition to war as the conflict persists. Thus there is a complex interplay between the structure of democratic societies, their militaries, and the strategy of insurgents.[154]

Warfare and strategy are not static, but evolve to reflect the social, political, economic, and technological trends of their eras. In recent years, sporadic attacks by small groups and individuals acting on their own initiative without the direction of a parent organization have raised the prospect that a fifth generation of warfare may be just over the horizon.

Some observers have noted a similar historical "wave" process with regard to terrorism. David C. Rapoport, emeritus professor of political science at the University of California, Los Angeles (UCLA), examines broad cycles in the history of terrorism over the past 125 years. As he sees it, a certain zeitgeist defines each major wave of modern terrorism. According to Rapoport, each wave has a life cycle of about one generation, and terrorists use tactics unique to that wave to reach their goals and employ language artfully to express their ideologies and justify their actions. The first wave commenced in Russia during the late 1880s and later appeared in western Europe and the Balkans. This "anarchist wave" was the first real global terrorist experience. The second wave appeared in the 1920s and was informed by anticolonialism. The Treaty of Versailles after World War I raised the aspirations for self-determination among people living under the yoke of colonialism. World War II accelerated this trend, as more and more erstwhile colonial subjects attained their independence or approached it. The third wave was spearheaded by the "New Left," which criticized "the establishment" in the West for not living up to its democratic ideals. Radicals in the West such as the Weather Underground, the Red Army Faction, and the Red Brigades drew inspiration from, and sought to make common cause with, liberation movements in the third world, including the Vietcong and the Palestine Liberation Organization (PLO). Rapoport marks 1979 as the year the fourth wave was born. That year three important events occurred: the Iranian Revolution, the start of a new Islamic century, and the Soviet invasion of Afghanistan. The first three waves were all inspired by secular ideologies that generally called for greater democracy, self-determination, and social justice. By contrast, the fourth wave, informed by militant Islam, marks a departure from this. In a sense the fourth wave is antidemocratic in that it rejects secularism and explicitly calls for elements of a theocracy, including the establishment of *sharia*, or Islamic law. The tactic of suicide terrorism is the major innovation of the fourth wave. Rapoport cautions that the Islamic terrorism wave may outlast the previous waves since it is inspired by religion, which has proven to be far more durable than secular ideologies.[155]

Expanding on this framework, Jeffrey Kaplan, a professor at the University of Wisconsin–Oshkosh, writes that a fifth wave of terrorism has emerged that is characterized by tribalism and a desire to create a utopian society to be realized in this lifetime. Movements in this category—including the Khmer Rouge in Cambodia and the Lord's Resistance Army in Uganda—became disillusioned with the terrorist worldviews that gave birth to them and developed inward-looking, local orientations. Though they may still maintain regional and international contacts and patterns of alliance, they do not identify with the wave whose ideologies once may have animated them.[156] Reminiscent of the dictum of the late speaker of the house Tip O'Neill that "all politics is local," this analysis suggests that local conditions continue to catalyze terrorists and insurgent groups, notwithstanding the influence of globalization and transnational movements.

Although conflicts between states are declining in number, a great deal of conflict persists within states. Moreover, population growth, although subsiding, makes for a crowded world in which grievances and instability can flourish. Concomitant with these trends are the historical process of globalization, greater availability of weapons of mass destruction, and greater connectivity occasioned by the Internet and other new communications technology. These could give rise to a fifth generation of warfare characterized by unaffiliated individuals and small groups united by a common ideal, a topic that will be discussed in the Conclusion. First a review of some case studies and an examination of forces shaping the contemporary landscape of conflict are in order. Even the United States faces internal challenges, as the next chapter explains.

CHAPTER 2

Leaderless Resistance and the Extreme Right

Political extremism has long been a feature of US history. Some historians cite the Anti-Masonic Party of the early nineteenth century as the first reactionary movement in US politics.[1] A few decades later, the Know-Nothing movement arose as a backlash amid an influx of largely Irish Catholic and southern German Catholic immigration. Shortly after the Civil War, the fraternal vigilante group known as the Ku Klux Klan emerged in Pulaski, Tennessee, and along with it came the first large-scale right-wing violence in the country. In 1915 the release of D. W. Griffith's critically acclaimed feature film *The Birth of a Nation*—which lionized the Reconstruction-era Ku Klux Klan—was the catalyst for the creation of the second-generation Klan, whose estimated membership reached three to six million in the 1920s. In the next decade, the dynamism of fascism in continental Europe inspired similar movements in the United States, including Gerald Winrod's Defenders of the Christian Faith, William Dudley Pelley's Silvershirts, Fritz Kuhn's German American Bund, the Italian American Fascist League of North America, and Father Charles Coughlin's Christian Front. The specter of communism in the 1950s provided an opportunity for the Far Right to return and regain respectability under the banner of McCarthyism. Moreover, the Supreme Court's *Brown v. Topeka Board of Education* decision in 1954 galvanized the racialist Right, and the third-generation Ku Klux Klan emerged along with overtly fascist groups such as the National Renaissance Party, the National States Rights Party, and the American Nazi Party.

During the 1990s, the extreme Right appeared to gain ground as a social movement. What is more, trends in technology, such as the Internet, enabled the movement to reach a larger audience than it had in the past. Horrific acts of political violence—most notably the 1995 bombing of the Alfred P. Murrah Federal Building in Oklahoma City—and high-profile confrontations with law enforcement authorities seared right-wing terrorism into public consciousness. In the aftermath of 9/11, as a result of greater vigilance by government, the extreme Right experienced a number of setbacks, as many of its representatives were arrested and prosecuted. The year 2008, though, witnessed the beginning of a polarization in the United States that could revive the extreme Right. The financial meltdown and ensuing economic crisis created conditions for greater grievance as the ranks of the unemployed grew. The election of the country's first African American president, Barack Obama, seems to have had a catalyzing effect, not only on the extreme Right but on the more respectable conservative movement as well. The Tea Party movement gained momentum in 2009 and was instrumental in Republican Party successes in the 2010 congressional elections. Although the extreme Right remains a marginalized movement, it persists and has demonstrated a remarkable capacity to continually reinvent itself.

As the noted scholar of political violence Ted Robert Gurr observed, the principal reason right-wing terrorism has been unsuccessful and short-lived in the United States and western Europe is because extremist groups have generated little public support. In this they differ from community-based terrorist groups such as the Irish Republican Army (IRA), the PLO, and ETA (the Basque nationalist organization).[2] Likewise, as the Israeli prime minister, Benjamin Netanyahu, once pointed out, virtually no support exists in the United States for a lengthy terrorist campaign because the "potential sympathizers willing to listen to the cynical theories of terrorist ideologists and collaborate with them in their grisly deeds do not constitute a 'sea' but a collection of puddles at most."[3] As a consequence, some representatives of the extreme Right argue that a strategy that focuses on attaining broad-based support is unfeasible in the United States today. What's more, changing demographics—it is projected that over half the country's population will be nonwhite by midcentury—makes a racially exclusionary party untenable at the national level. For these and other reasons, some elements of the extreme Right have decided that a strategy of revolution and terrorism based on leaderless resistance is the only viable alternative to reach their political and social goals.

The Response to the Extreme Right

As a highly stigmatized and marginalized movement, the extreme Right faces significant repression, despite the long tradition of civil liberties in the United States. Among Western democracies, the US response to political extremism is unique. In the Federal Republic of Germany there is an agency called the Verfassungsschutz (Office of the Protection of the Constitution), which can recommend to judiciary the dissolution of extremist groups it deems a threat to Germany's constitutional democracy.[4] Likewise the British government has occasionally invoked the 1965 Race Relations Act to justify the raids of homes and offices of such groups as the National Front and the British National Party. Even in Israel, where the Far Right enjoys significant grassroots support, the government outlawed the late Meir Kahane's Kach movement because of its extremist platform.[5] Other democracies appear to have much more legal latitude than the United States in responding to political extremism and violence.

While it is axiomatic that terrorism is carried out by extremists, the vast majority of extremists are not terrorists. This presents a conundrum to authorities. Because of First Amendment protections, the government does not officially have the authority to disband groups just because they espouse unpopular ideas. From a comparative legal perspective, the US government appears to be more constrained than other governments in responding to political extremism. What is often ignored, though, is that private nongovernmental organizations (NGOs) have inserted themselves into this area of public policy and have done much to fill the void. In essence, the response to right-wing extremism in the United States is a joint effort by the government and private watchdog groups.

The origins of the close working relationship between the federal government and NGOs in this area can be traced to the 1930s. By 1936, President Franklin D. Roosevelt was concerned that hostile fascist and communist governments might have a subversive influence on some Americans. With the defeat of fascism in Europe in the next decade, the US extreme Right was discredited, demoralized, and in retreat. Events in the 1950s, however, allowed it to rebound, and the Klan emerged again in the aftermath of the *Brown v. Topeka Board of Education* decision. In 1956 the FBI commenced a campaign of surveillance and disruption of left-wing groups, COINTELPRO (Counter Intelligence Program), and in 1964 this effort was expanded to include the Klan and various "white hate groups."[6] Cumulatively COINTELPRO measures had a devastating effect on the morale of dissident groups, creating so much suspicion among members that they were reluctant to initiate violence of any kind. From the perspective of government officials, these efforts were generally successful as the program effectively neutralized targeted groups.

When details of COINTELPRO came to light, however, both a legislative and public backlash ensued. In addition to the extreme Right, numerous antiwar and civil rights activists had been targeted by the program. The negative publicity surrounding COINTELPRO pressured the Justice Department to make changes to the law enforcement and investigative policies of the FBI. Hence, the "Levi Guidelines" were adopted on April 5, 1976, in an attempt to depoliticize the bureau. When determining whether to investigate a dissident group, the FBI had to consider the likelihood that terrorism will occur, the magnitude of the threat, the immediacy of the threat, and the danger to privacy and free expression posed by an investigation.[7] The guidelines marked a significant departure from traditional policy, moving federal law enforcement away from preventive functions. Furthermore, these changes came on the heels of the Privacy Act of 1974, aimed at stopping the FBI from spying on people because of their political beliefs. As a result, the FBI devoted less attention to terrorism and focused on traditional law enforcement.[8] The number of domestic intelligence cases initiated dropped from 1,454 in 1975 to 95 in 1977.[9] Significantly, however, nothing in the guidelines precluded the FBI from opening an investigation based on information received from private groups.

The number of so-called watchdog groups, NGOs that monitor the activities of the extreme Right, has grown considerably over the past few decades; the most prominent are the Anti-Defamation League (ADL), the Southern Poverty Law Center (SPLC), and the Simon Wiesenthal Center (SWC).[10] By far the most important is the well-financed ADL, which maintains thirty-three regional offices in US cities, as well as offices in countries including Austria, Canada, and Israel.

Through its nationwide intelligence apparatus, the ADL has been able to closely monitor developments on the extreme right. Arguably second in influence and stature is the Southern Poverty Law Center (SPLC), headquartered in Montgomery, Alabama, and founded by the mediagenic Morris Dees. The SPLC's major innovation is the use of civil suits to hold extremist groups responsible for the actions of their individual members. Thus the SPLC is among the NGOs most feared by the extreme Right.

These NGOs take a multifaceted approach to countering terrorism and extremism. For example, when the contemporary militia movement surfaced in 1994, both the ADL and the SPLC crafted legislation that proscribed paramilitary training by unauthorized groups. The thrust of the legislation was to make it illegal to operate paramilitary camps.[11] The ADL has taken the lead in sponsoring hate crime laws that are occasionally used to prosecute perpetrators of right-wing violence insofar as extremists choose targets they perceive as "outsiders" for no other reason than some ascriptive characteristic such as race or ethnicity. By 2009 the ADL's model hate crime statute or a facsimile thereof had been adopted in all but five states.[12] That year Congress passed, and President Barack Obama ratified, new legislation that enhances the federal government's ability to address hate crimes. The ADL had long lobbied for the law.[13] Although perpetrators of hate crimes are usually juveniles or young adults without much wealth, the SPLC has on occasion used civil suits to hold extreme Right organizations responsible for the actions of their law-breaking members. Using this novel and controversial tactic, the SCLC has won judgments against Louis Beam's Knights of the Ku Klux Klan, Robert Shelton's United Klans of America, Tom Metzger's White Aryan Resistance (WAR), and more recently Richard Butler's Aryan Nations. The SPLC contends that the principal aim of its suits is to bankrupt the organizations and individuals responsible for crimes, effectively putting them out of business.[14]

By far the most effective mechanism for countering the extreme Right, though, has been in the area of intelligence sharing. Again the ADL has taken the lead. FBI documents obtained under the Freedom of Information Act (FOIA) indicate that the ADL has made considerable efforts to cultivate a close working relationship with the FBI.[15] The SPLC has moved into this area as well and, as Morris Dees has said, the organization "has long shared intelligence with law enforcement agencies."[16] In 2010 the Department of Homeland Security announced the creation of a "countering Violent Extremism Working Group" whose members included Richard Cohen, the president and CEO of the SPLC.[17] The cumulative efforts of these NGOs have done much to neutralize the extreme Right in the United States.

As a testament to the effectiveness of the monitoring groups, some right-wing terrorists have planned attacks against them. On several occasions Morris Dees has been marked for assassination.[18] In 1983 the SPLC's facilities were subjected to an arson attack.[19] In 1986 members of a right-wing group allegedly conspired to blow up the SPLC headquarters with a military rocket.[20] In 1996 Willie Ray Lampley, a militiaman from Oklahoma, was convicted of conspiracy for planning a bombing campaign that would have included gay bars, an abortion clinic, and offices of the SPLC and the ADL.[21] And Buford O'Neal Furrow, the gunman who attacked a Los Angeles Jewish day-care center on August 10, 1999, and shot to death a Filipino American postal carrier later that day, had originally planned to attack the Simon Wiesenthal Center headquarters but changed his mind after observing the tight security there.[22]

After 9/11, the federal government returned to a more proactive approach to countering right-wing extremism. Some representatives of the movement expressed consternation that the government's war on terror could spill over into a witch hunt against domestic extremists and dissidents. Several arrests in the months following 9/11 gave credence to such concerns.[23] The FBI stepped up monitoring of several extremist organizations, including the National Alliance, the Aryan Nations, the World Church of the Creator, branches of the Ku Klux Klan, and the Christian Identity movement, as well as individual activists including the Holocaust denier Ernst Zündel and the white nationalist and former Ku Klux Klan grand wizard David Duke. Several arrests suggested a high degree of political motivation by the government.[24] In the aftermath of 9/11, law enforcement authorities increasingly prosecuted any illegal activity by extremists, while at the same time infiltrating groups seen as most dangerous, to try to prevent terrorist attacks.[25] Facing both monitoring groups and government repression, the extreme Right has moved toward a leaderless resistance approach. A review of some notable cases of right-wing terrorism illustrates this trend.

Episodes of Right-Wing Violence

As the terrorism researcher Christopher Hewitt observed, one distinguishing characteristic of contemporary political violence in the United States is that a significant and growing number of terrorist acts are committed by unaffiliated individuals, people who are not members of terrorist organizations. Moreover, heavy surveillance and infiltration by law enforcement agencies and monitoring groups make any coordinated terrorist action by a large organization unfeasible if not impossible. Extreme Right terrorism will most likely continue to consist of isolated actions by lone wolves.[26] Significant episodes of violence punctuated the current wave of right-wing terrorism, which commenced in the 1980s and eventually influenced the strategic and tactical development of leaderless resistance.

Gordon Kahl and the Posse Comitatus

The farm crisis of the 1980s provided a seedbed for right-wing extremism in the US heartland. One of the most prominent organizations in the Midwest was the Posse Comitatus, which espoused a radical decentralization and antistatism—as exemplified by its name, which translates as "power of the county," suggesting there is no legitimate form of government above the county level. Despite its sometimes bombastic rhetoric, the Posse posed only a minor irritant to authorities. That changed, however, on February 13, 1983, when the Posse affiliate and tax resister Gordon Kahl became embroiled in a confrontation with federal officials in Medina, North Dakota. A group of US marshals sought to serve Kahl a warrant for tax violations. Extremely distrustful of authorities, he refused to be served and a shootout ensued in which two marshals were killed and four other people were wounded, including Kahl's son, Yorie. Remarkably, Kahl, a sixty-three-year-old farmer and World War II veteran, single-handedly forced the authorities to retreat.[27]

Kahl evaded law officers for almost four months, but on June 3, 1983, they finally caught up with him in Lawrence County, Arkansas. Still defiant, he managed to mortally wound a local sheriff, who also happened to fire a shot that struck Kahl in the head and killed him. Not realizing that Kahl was dead, the officers attempted to force him outside his bunker dwelling by pouring fuel down its chimney. The structure went up in flames, sparking rumors that the FBI had summarily executed Kahl, then incinerated his corpse and murdered the sheriff to cover up the truth.[28] As a result, Kahl entered the extreme Right's pantheon of martyrs and his death inspired the creation of an underground terrorist group, the Order.

The Order

Shortly after Gordon Kahl's death, the annual Aryan Nations Congress met at the group's compound in Hayden Lake, Idaho, in the summer of 1983. At that meeting, a young, charismatic member of the National Alliance (a prominent Nazi-style organization), Robert Jay Mathews, hatched the idea of creating an underground group to avenge Kahl's death. Mathews used his considerable powers of persuasion to draw nearly fifty members into his clandestine terrorist group, "the Order."[29] During 1983 and 1984, the group went on a crime spree that included armored car heists, robberies, bombings, and at least five homicides.[30]

Although the Order was racist and anti-Semitic, it gave its highest priority to targeting the state and prominent institutions. Mathews instructed Order members to avoid petty conflicts with racial minorities as that would distract the group from its primary mission. A list of enemies marked for assassination was compiled, including Morris Dees, former secretary of state Henry Kissinger, the banker David Rockefeller, the television producer Norman Lear, and the international financier Baron Elie de Rothschild.[31] Despite such lofty intentions, the Order settled for a Denver-based Jewish radio personality, Alan Berg, as its first target. An acerbic talk show host, Berg occasionally berated Far Right callers on air. On the night of June 18, 1984, a team of Order assassins followed Berg to his townhouse. The gunman, Bruce Pierce, shot Berg twelve times with a MAC-10 firearm. Berg died almost instantly from his wounds.[32]

As expected, the Order caught the attention of authorities, and the FBI identified the group as the most serious domestic terrorist threat.[33] Ultimately a counterfeiting operation led to the group's demise. A recruit who was not an official member, Tom Martinez, agreed to become an informant for the FBI after his arrest for passing counterfeit money the Order had printed. He set up two of his colleagues, including Mathews, in a sting operation at a hotel, and a shootout ensued. Mathews managed to escape after wounding an officer. Undaunted, he issued a "declaration of war" against the United States government, which was sent to several newspapers. Finally the FBI caught up with him at Whidbey Island in Washington State. With Mathews refusing to be taken alive, a two-day standoff followed during which he engaged in several shootouts with SWAT teams. Eventually the law enforcement agents lost their patience, and on December 8, 1984, dropped white phosphorous illumination flares onto the roof of the house in which Mathews was barricaded. This sparked a fire that engulfed the structure, and Mathews perished. A concerted effort by federal, state, and local law enforcement agencies eventually crushed the Order, and many of its members are now serving long prison sentences.

The Order's campaign caught many in the radical Right by surprise. Some criticized their exploits as ineffectual and quixotic, while others lionized incarcerated members as exemplary "Aryan warriors" and "POWs."[34] Although the Order tactically did not really achieve much, symbolically it marked a significant change in the orientation of the extreme Right. The US government was now seen as the enemy and the extreme Right began to take on a more revolutionary posture, as it no longer wanted to preserve the status quo. Now it sought the overthrow of the government, which it believed was controlled by Jews—some Order members spoke of "ZOG" (Zionist Occupation Government). On a more instrumental level, the Order distributed much of its funds to aboveground organizations around the country. It was hoped that the money—much of it from robbing banks and armored cars—could be used to cement the fragmented elements of the racialist Right.[35] For example, Mathews gave $200,000 to Glenn Miller for his White Patriot Party, which was active in North Carolina during the 1980s, and he allegedly donated $250,000 to Tom Metzger and WAR.[36] It is also strongly suspected that Mathews gave a substantial amount of money to William L. Pierce. If true, the Order significantly contributed to the success of one of the most important organizations on the revolutionary racialist Right. Possibly with money from Mathews, Pierce established his National Alliance on a solid footing and relocated its headquarters to West Virginia.[37]

William L. Pierce and *The Turner Diaries*

Robert Jay Mathews drew inspiration for his organization from the novel *The Turner Diaries*, written by his ideological mentor William Pierce, the founder and chairman of the National Alliance, under the pseudonym Andrew Macdonald. So intrigued by the book, Mathews made it required reading for all members of the

Order. Since it has also been connected to several significant episodes of right-wing terrorism, a brief examination is in order.[38]

The late William Pierce (1933–2002) was arguably the most influential revolutionary theoretician that the American extreme Right has produced. In that fractious milieu in the late twentieth century, Pierce was seen as the movement's elder statesman. He earned a PhD in physics from the University of Colorado and went on to become a tenured professor at the University of Oregon. Soon tired of the academy, he went to work in 1966 as the editor of *National Socialist World*—a journal published by the late George Lincoln Rockwell's American Nazi Party. By 1970 Pierce had broken with that organization to run the National Youth Alliance under the tutelage of Willis Carto. The group soon collapsed, but out of its remnants Pierce in 1974 created the National Alliance, an organization he would continue to lead until his death in 2002. He is best known for writing *The Turner Diaries*, the story of an apocalyptic race war that convulses America. Published in 1978, the novel gained him considerable notoriety and was thought to have inspired right-wing violence. Pierce was largely responsible for the creation of a genre of literature in which a story is told interspersed with ideological digressions and, as some charge, ideas for carrying out terrorist attacks. Perhaps the most widely read book in the subterranean world of the extreme Right, the novel had sold between 350,000 and 500,000 copies by 2000—an astounding figure for an underground book.[39]

Cleverly written as fiction, *The Turner Diaries* tells the story of a cellular white-supremacist revolutionary group that conducts a terrorist campaign against the US government, which it regards as merely a front for a Jewish cabal working behind the scenes. The rest of the novel recounts a race war that besets the world at the close of the twentieth century. In the story, the protagonist, Earl Turner, is an important yet relatively low-level member of a resistance movement known as the Organization, which has waged a war against "the System." For his exemplary service as a revolutionary, Turner was selected to be a member of a quasi-monastic inner circle of the Organization, known as "the Order." The Organization's exploits include armed robberies to procure funds to carry out its struggle. Government buildings and other important institutions are targeted. The objective is to weaken "the System" and to polarize the population. A struggle of apocalyptic proportions follows, as American society implodes under the weight of racial strife. The book contains some graphic descriptions of violence. A veritable race war leads to ethnic cleansing writ large and degenerates into the most bestial behavior, including cannibalism. In a grisly orgy of retribution, the Organization punishes "race-traitors" in a spectacle called "the Day of the Rope," in which tens of thousands are strung up on lampposts, power poles, and trees throughout Southern California. Eventually the Organization acquires nuclear weapons, and a global atomic war ensues, involving the United States, the Soviet Union, and Israel.

Turner's final mission is to fly a small crop duster equipped with a nuclear bomb on a kamikaze mission to destroy the Pentagon. Selflessly, he agrees and succeeds, delivering a fatal blow to the system. From that point on, the Organization gains the upper hand, and by 1999, "just 110 years after the birth of the great one [Adolf Hitler]," victory is clearly in sight. After the conquest of the United States, the revolution spreads throughout the world. The book closes with a millennial tone. Out of the ashes of devastation, the West experiences renewal of its civilization and is once again master of its own destiny.[40]

Much has been made of Pierce's novel—it has been referred to as a "blueprint for revolution" and the "bible of the racialist right."[41] At the cusp of the new millennium, *The Turner Diaries* was mentioned several times in an FBI document titled "Project Megiddo" that warned of the prospect of violence around the turn of the century by groups with apocalyptic worldviews.[42]

Subsequent underground groups inspired by the Order have attempted to model their organizational structure on the group and have even appropriated its name. Shortly after the demise of the Order, a new group emerged calling itself the Brüder Schweigen Strikeforce II or Order II, but it was quickly crushed by the FBI.[43] In 1998 the FBI arrested members of a group called the New Order, which drew inspiration from the original organization. Its members allegedly planned to attack the Southern Poverty Law Center and ADL offices.[44] Another organization to which the Order had a direct connection was the Covenant, the Sword, and the Arm of the Lord.

The Covenant, the Sword, and the Arm of the Lord

In the late 1970s, a Christian Identity minister, Jim Ellison, founded a community in Arkansas known as the Covenant, the Sword, and the Arm of the Lord (CSA). Over the years it took on a paramilitary orientation, as members believed that enemies would one day besiege their compound, which in a sense they did. Ellison stockpiled many weapons and taught members how to use them in a mock village called "Silhouette City."[45] The CSA compound came to be seen as a safe haven for those in the extreme Right underground who sought to evade law enforcement officials.

The CSA was linked to several episodes of terrorism. For example, Ellison and another member, Richard Wayne Snell, firebombed a Jewish community center in Bloomington, Indiana, and a gay church in Springfield, Missouri.[46] In another incident, Snell fatally shot a pawnbroker in Texarkana, Arkansas. Finally, during a routine traffic stop, Snell opened fire on an Arkansas state trooper and fatally wounded him. The CSA also planned several other serious terrorist attacks but failed to carry them out.[47]

By 1985 the violence and terrorism emanating from the CSA had captured the attention of federal authorities. In April that year, the FBI deployed for the first time its elite antiterrorist unit, the Hostage Rescue Team, which quickly surrounded the CSA compound. Although the CSA had demonstrated a proclivity for violence, Ellison surrendered without incident after negotiation. As Brent L. Smith observed, during the 1980s right-wing extremists were usually based in rural parts of the United States and stayed in fixed bunker–style camps that allowed authorities to identify them—and arrest them—with ease. Thus they were apprehended and prosecuted in large numbers.[48] As a consequence, a new consensus began to emerge among these groups on strategy.

The Rise of Leaderless Resistance

After the demise of the CSA and the Order, the revolutionary Right went into a period of retrenchment and soul-searching. From this interlude emerged a change in their tactics. The terrorism analyst Bruce Hoffman asserts that terrorist groups learn from past mistakes and adjust accordingly.[49] The extreme Right had learned that an organization that grew to the size of the Order would eventually fall prey to infiltration and then soon be crushed. The CSA demonstrated that it was not feasible for terrorist groups to congregate in a compound that could easily be identified and surrounded.[50]

Having learned from the errors of the Order and the CSA, the violence-prone extreme Right now employs leaderless resistance. With the movement organizationally fragmented, leaderless resistance makes a virtue out of necessity. Moreover it dovetails with the Internet and new communications technology. Although advocates of the leaderless approach have theorized extensively on the concept, it remains largely a construct of academic scholars and journalists who use it to attribute the often unorganized and sporadic nature of right-wing violence to a larger operational plan. There is anecdotal evidence that several perpetrators using this approach were psychopaths with little if any ideological sophistication. That said, leaderless resistance should not be dismissed as merely a topic for abnormal psychology, for as the terrorism analyst Christopher Hewitt noted, political violence often occurs within a context reflecting the political zeitgeist. Terrorism is almost always linked to a wider social movement. Klan terrorism in the South was part of a broader pattern of white resistance to the civil rights struggle. Black terrorism, including killings by the Black Panther Party and assorted Black Muslim cults, was associated with the rise of the Black Power movement. Leftist terrorism emerged in the context of widespread student opposition to the Vietnam War. Therefore, in order to understand the current upsurge in terrorism, it must be located within its political and social context.[51]

Leaderless resistance arises in large measure because of the failure of organized right-wing terrorism. Despite its audacious, seemingly desperate nature, some of the most lethal incidents of right-wing violence in the United States fall under this category, and it should not be taken lightly.[52] According to government prosecutors, the most lethal act of domestic terrorism—the Oklahoma City bombing—appears to fit the leaderless resistance category.

The Oklahoma City Bombing

On April 19, 1995, exactly two years after the culmination of the Waco siege of the Branch Davidians, the Murrah Federal Building in Oklahoma City was bombed, killing at least 168 and wounding many others. Until 9/11, this attack had been the most lethal act of domestic terrorism carried out in the United States. Subsequent investigation implicated Timothy McVeigh as the chief culprit for the attack. He had some accomplices, including Terry Nichols and Michael Fortier, but the scope of their involvement is still uncertain.[53] McVeigh and Nichols are reported to have attended meetings of the Michigan Militia, but the group did not welcome them. To the contrary, members of the group thought they were loose cannons and should not be granted membership.[54] In the FBI's own description, "one of its most extensive investigations" failed to turn up a significant militia connection to the bombing.

Although McVeigh may not have had any formal affiliation with extremist groups, there is evidence suggesting he was a denizen of the Far Right subculture. Although he did not evince obvious racism, he actively explored the propaganda of the racialist Right. For instance, he obtained a trial membership in a Ku Klux Klan organization based in North Carolina but declined to renew because he felt the Klan was "manipulative to young people." Moreover, he felt the government was his real enemy, not racial minorities.[55]

Nevertheless, McVeigh was enamored of *The Turner Diaries*, distributed it among his army buddies, and even went so far as to sell the book at a loss at gun shows.[56] The anti–gun control theme, not racism, is what seems to have most resonated with McVeigh. This is somewhat surprising since the Second Amendment theme is really incidental to the novel—racism is its leitmotif. Still, the gun laws are presented in the book as links in a chain, which ultimately lead to the loss of individual rights, and McVeigh seems to have identified with the protagonist, Earl Turner. When he was arrested, police found photocopied pages of the book in an envelope in his car, pages on which the following sentences were highlighted: "The real value of our attacks today lies in the psychological impact, not in the immediate casualties. More important, though, is what we taught the politicians and the bureaucrats. They learned this afternoon that not one of them is beyond our reach."[57]

During McVeigh's trial, prosecutors argued that the book served as his blueprint for the Oklahoma City bombing.[58] In one passage, Turner's unit is assigned to blow up the FBI headquarters in Washington, D.C. The objective is to destroy a computer center that could be used to monitor the aboveground members of the Organization, a complex located in a sub-basement. At 9:15 a.m. one day, a bomb explodes and destroys the building, presaging the detonation at the Arthur P. Murrah Federal Building at 9:02 a.m. on April 19. Earl Turner's fictional bomb was made out of ammonium nitrate—and so was Timothy McVeigh's. McVeigh was obviously aware of William Pierce's National Alliance. Records indicate that several times he called an Arizona chapter's recorded phone message line.[59]

After the Oklahoma City bombing, William Pierce downplayed the connection between McVeigh and *The Turner Diaries* and disavowed the attack, mostly for tactical reasons, maintaining that it served no real purpose during that particular period of "resistance."[60] Moreover, Pierce pointed out that McVeigh's methods and motives differed substantially from those of the characters depicted in *The Turner Diaries*. The only similarity he found was that of bombs delivered in a truck. Finally he maintained that the events described in his novel were "predictions" of trends that he extrapolated would lead to the unraveling of society, rather than specific exhortations for violence.[61] He claimed that he wrote the book merely to spread his ideology and attract more supporters.[62] Nevertheless, according to statements made by McVeigh not long before he was executed, *The Turner Diaries* did have a profound influence on him and was instrumental in his choice of target.[63]

Now dead, Timothy McVeigh remains an enigmatic figure. By some accounts he appeared the veritable paragon of the leaderless resistance concept, though some of his later letters from prison suggest that he favored a mass uprising, not lone wolf operations. He also displayed a strong sense of despair and desperation, attitudes that correspond with the leaderless resistance concept.[64] Some observers found coincidences in the Oklahoma City bombing that suggested a larger conspiracy at work than government prosecutors asserted. Some speculated that McVeigh had connections with remnants of the Covenant, the Sword, and the Arm of the Lord. Not long before the bombing, McVeigh placed a phone call to Elohim City, an encampment where some former members of the CSA lived. Its leader, Robert Millar, was the spiritual adviser to Richard Wayne Snell, the CSA member responsible for at least two homicides. Snell was executed the day of the Oklahoma City bombing. Hours before his execution, Snell saw news of the bombing on television and is reported to have remarked, "[Arkansas] Governor Tucker, look over your shoulder. I wouldn't trade places with any of you or any of your political cronies. Hell has victory. I'm at peace." To add further mystery, the CSA's former leader, James Ellison, testified in 1988 that in 1983 he and Snell had visited the Murrah Building and talked about blowing it up. A former leading CSA member who has since repudiated his extremist views, Kerry Noble, said he was convinced that McVeigh carried out the plot hatched by Snell and Ellison.[65]

According to statements he made shortly before he was executed, McVeigh claimed that he called Elohim City searching for a prospective hideout, not to enlist the help of others in the commission of his terrorist act. The person he was trying to reach was not there at the times the calls were made.[66] Thus McVeigh was not able to convey his request. He adamantly maintained that members of the community had no foreknowledge of the bombing.

In addition to conjecture linking the bombing to the CSA, there are theories purporting an Islamic connection to the incident. Stephen Jones, McVeigh's defense attorney, was one of the main purveyors of this theory.[67] McVeigh dismissed this theory as "nonsense" and a "red herring."[68]

It is telling to note how the radical Right responded to the Oklahoma City bombing. Although McVeigh was usually depicted as a fellow traveler of the militia movement, I know of not one instance of a militia leader publicly condoning the attack. The opposite was true, as often militia leaders blamed the attack on a government conspiracy. A view held by many in the militia movement was that the government deliberately orchestrated the attack and tried to implicate militias, thus creating a crisis in which new antiterrorist legislation could be enacted that would spark a witch hunt against the Far Right.[69] This sentiment was given a veneer of credibility after the release of an independent report by retired US Air Force brigadier general Benton Partin, who had been responsible for the testing and design of many non-nuclear weapons used by the air force. His report concluded that the single bomb supposedly used in Oklahoma City could not have caused so much destruction. He asserted that the destruction was caused mainly by several "demolition charges attached to supporting column bases, at locations not accessible from the street, to supplement the truck bomb damage."[70] Partin opined that a "classic cover-up" had followed the incident.[71]

In contrast, the racialist Right seemed much less likely to ascribe the attack to some larger conspiracy involving the government or unknown others. Like their militia counterparts, most leaders in the racialist Right did not condone the attack, but this was due to its lack of tactical efficacy rather than any moral revulsion. However, some of the more radical proponents of leaderless resistance did praise the attack, including Alex Curtis, who designated McVeigh the "lone wolf of the century," and Tom Metzger, who lauded McVeigh in an editorial in his newspaper, *WAR*.[72] Still another theory linked McVeigh to a broad conspiracy involving a small racist criminal gang.

The Aryan Republican Army

Around the time of the Oklahoma City bombing, a six-man group of bandits calling themselves the Aryan Republican Army was making headlines in the Midwest for a series of bank robberies that confounded authorities. Its members were Peter Langan, the putative ringleader, as well as Richard Lee Guthrie Jr., Scott Anthony Stedeford, Kevin William McCarthy, Michael William Bresica, and Mark Thomas. The Aryan Republican Army is reported to have been responsible for robbing twenty-two banks and netting some $250,000 in cash. Although the goals of these renegades are still murky, they are alleged to have consorted with some of the most notorious figures in the Far Right underground, including the residents of Elohim City, Dennis Mahon, who held leadership positions in a variety of white separatist groups, and possibly even Timothy McVeigh. The criminologist Mark Hamm writes that Langan made plans so that one member from each cell would be selected to have contact with other cells in order to safeguard operations. Hamm posits a theory that the Aryan Republican Army was part of a larger conspiracy and revolutionary division of labor in which the bandits would use their money to fund right-wing revolutionaries. He strongly suspects that members of the Aryan Republican Army were instrumental in the Oklahoma City bombing and provided funding for the attack.[73]

Authorities eventually closed in on the Aryan Republican Army and put an end to its campaign. Although its significance is disputable, it could presage a pattern in other countries of criminal enterprises funding terrorist and revolutionary movements. Events of the mid-1990s, most notably the Oklahoma City bombing, fueled an ongoing debate in the extreme Right on resistance and terrorism.

The Development of the Extreme Right's Theoretical Approach to Terrorism

Decades before leaderless resistance gained currency in the extreme Right, the concept was promoted by Richard Cotton, a radio broadcaster and subsequently a key figure in the National Youth Alliance (which would later evolve into the National Alliance). In 1965 his newsletter discussed creating phantom cells and implementing the leaderless resistance strategy. At a conference a year later sponsored by the Congress of Freedom, Cotton again discussed phantom cells as outlined by Colonel Ulius Louis Amoss (see below). Despite his advocacy, it would be years before the concept would take hold.[74]

Aware that they are part of a relatively small and marginalized movement, most in the extreme Right realize that the forces arrayed against it—government and the monitoring organizations—are collectively much more powerful. Consequently there has always been a conservative majority in the extreme Right who have believed it would be foolhardy to prematurely engage in revolutionary violence. Such an approach would almost certainly lead to organizational suicide. Thus the more conservative elements have advocated a strategy that would concentrate on using propaganda to build a revolutionary majority. This came to be known as the theory of mass action.[75]

A leading proponent of mass action was George Lincoln Rockwell, founder of the American Nazi Party, which was most active in the 1960s. Rockwell believed that events and trends such as racial integration, school busing, the Vietnam War, race riots, and rising crime would engender urban mayhem and create favorable conditions for his party. Extrapolating, he predicted that a full-blown race war would commence by the end of the decade.[76] In light of this projected crisis, Rockwell entertained the idea that his party could win national power by 1972, but in 1967 he fell to an assassin's bullet, and with his departure some elements of the extreme Right became disillusioned with the conservative approach. Foremost among them was Joseph Tomassi, a member of Rockwell's successor organization, the National Socialist White People's Party, who eventually departed and founded the National Socialist Liberation Front (NSLF), a neo-Nazi organization that patterned itself on the left-wing models of the Weathermen and the Symbionese Liberation Army. Correctly he saw that in the early 1970s the idea of a Nazi-style party winning popular support was futile. However, the NSLF campaign was reckless, its revolutionary arm was quickly crushed, and, like Rockwell, Tomassi was killed by a disgruntled member of his group. Although the organization never succeeded in striking a serious blow against "the system," according to Jeffrey Kaplan its "contribution to the leaderless resistance concept [was] incalculable."[77] Still, the approach had not yet been named, and the idea would languish until the early 1990s.

Another resistance approach occasionally used by the Far Right has been the cellular model.[78] The Far Right version of this approach can be traced back to an anonymous tract titled *The John Franklin Letters*, which was popularized by the John Birch Society in 1959. The Birch Society promoted the book as a call to resistance in the wake of a communist takeover, which the group believed was just around the corner. Although no author's name was listed, there was suspicion in the movement that the prominent Far Right intellectual Revilo P. Oliver had written it.[79] The story centered on a resistance group called "the Rangers" that mounts a campaign of sabotage against the government, which has been taken over by a nebulous communist conspiracy.[80] Although the Birch Society was organized on the cellular model, its members were loath to engage in any political violence.

The Minutemen, a Far Right group that gained notoriety during the 1960s, also adopted the cellular structure with a centralized command structure. Its leader, Robert DePugh, published a manual for activists—*Blueprint for Victory*—which gave advice on political, military, economic, and psychological warfare.[81] Though the Minutemen discouraged lone wolf operations, some of its members were implicated in violence, and the organization was effectively shut down by authorities.[82] Similarly, the Order endeavored to implement a cellular structure and carry out missions in small groups. There were even plans to split the organization into interlocking separate cells. Involved in some spectacular incidents, the Order was resoundingly quashed after a concerted effort by government authorities. The crushing defeat of the Order and the CSA ushered in a debate in the Far Right movement on the best strategy of "resistance" to employ. Thus the concept of leaderless resistance was reexamined and updated for current conditions.

Jeffrey Kaplan observed that the movement's discourse became increasingly shrill and millenarian by the late 1980s.[83] The mass action theories of previous generations were seen as unrealistic. The cellular model had been discredited with the demise of the Order. A period of despair and hopelessness seemed to settle over the movement. However, two events—the ambush of Randy Weaver's home in Ruby Ridge, Idaho, in 1992, and the siege of the Branch Davidians' compound at Waco in 1993—again galvanized a broad segment of the Far Right. Previously isolated voices calling for leaderless resistance now found a more receptive audience.

Leaderless resistance had several proponents during the 1980s. For example, in 1984 Jack Mohr of the Christian-Patriots Defense League wrote a letter to his supporters in which he described his "Citizens Emergency Defense System" as employing leaderless resistance.[84] But the concept really crystallized and gained new currency as a result of an October 1992 meeting in Estes Park, Colorado, called by a Christian Identity minister, Pete Peters. This event provided a forum for the articulation of a new leaderless resistance approach. Prior to the meeting the concept was vaguely recognized by some, but it was now given a name and disseminated to a much larger audience. This event, more than any other, popularized the notion in the Far Right subculture.[85]

One of the speakers at the conference was Louis Beam, a firebrand orator and long-standing activist. Peters included Beam's essay on leaderless resistance in a published report on the meeting.[86] In his essay, Beam identifies the late Colonel Ulius Louis Amoss as the source of inspiration for his theory. A former operative of the Office of Strategic Services (OSS), Amoss had written about mounting resistance in the event that the United States was taken over by communists during the Cold War. According to Beam, an organized approach was untenable under then-current conditions—the government was too powerful and would not allow the existence of any potentially threatening oppositional organizations. The leaderless resistance model proffered by Beam rejected the pyramid structure in which the leadership is located at the top and the mass of followers at the bottom. He reasoned that in a technologically advanced society such as the contemporary United States, the government, through means such as electronic surveillance, could easily penetrate a group's structure and uncover its chain of command. From there, the organization could be effectively neutralized from within by infiltrators and agents provocateurs.

Beam considered the communist cellular system, but determined that it was inappropriate for the Far Right because the movement did not have the resources that the communist cells had—central direction, outside support, and adequate funding. As a strategic alternative, Beam invoked the "phantom cell" model of organization as described by Amoss. This approach draws from the "Sons of Liberty" or the "Committees of Correspondence"—organizations of Revolutionary War patriots who opposed British colonial rule—as a basis of resistance. According to Beam's historical interpretation of this approach, it operated in small, independent cells with no central command or direction. Applying this model, Beam argued that it was the responsibility of individuals to acquire the necessary skills and information to carry out what needed to be done. Members ought to take action when and where they see fit. Organs of information, such as newspapers and leaflets (and now the Internet), enable each person to keep informed of events.

Leaderless resistance, Beam concedes, is a "child of necessity," but he argues that all other alternatives are either unworkable or impractical. Furthermore, he points out that this approach presents an intelligence nightmare for authorities since it is difficult to infiltrate "a thousand different small phantom cells opposing them."[87] The essay was disseminated through computer networks, which Beam was a pioneer in using during the 1980s.[88] Beam's revolutionary approach quickly caught on and ushered in a period of theorizing and debate on resistance and terrorism within the Far Right. The government and monitoring groups were quick to notice and saw this as evidence of the development of a loose, widespread, Far Right terrorist network.[89]

Perhaps unintentionally, William Pierce of the National Alliance contributed to the popularity of leaderless resistance with the publication of his novel *Hunter*, in some ways the sequel to *The Turner Diaries*, again under the pseudonym Andrew Macdonald. More so than *The Turner Diaries*, *Hunter* includes ideological digressions from the dialogue. *Hunter* tells the story of a lone wolf assassin, Oscar Yeager, a Vietnam veteran and contractor who does work for the Defense Department in the Washington, D.C., area. The book begins with Yeager as a racist, though not yet an anti-Semite. Initially he murders interracial couples, hoping to encourage others to replicate his acts.

As the story develops, Yeager meets Harry Keller, the local leader of the National League (read National Alliance), who informs him that despite surface appearances the most serious adversaries whites face are not blacks, but Jews. At first, Keller's anti-Semitism makes Yeager feel uncomfortable, but as time goes on he begins to identify with Keller's ideology and becomes a full-blown anti-Semite. Not surprisingly, Yeager's murder spree captures the attention of the FBI. An astute agent, William Ryan, determines that Yeager is the culprit, but rather than arrest him, he offers Yeager freedom with the proviso that he work for Ryan to carry out rogue operations. At his behest, Yeager wages a one-man terror campaign against politicians and liberal activists, among others. Ryan seeks to become the head of a new agency called the Committee for Public Safety, a KGB-style organization. From there, he plans to clean up the nation's problems. Like Keller, Ryan also educates Yeager on "the Jewish issue," but whereas Keller is more idealistic, in the sense that he believes white non-Jews can organize and regain control of their destiny, Ryan is more cynical and believes that things are too far gone, and that therefore they must reconcile themselves to current realities. Another character, Saul Rogers, enters the story. A former high school teacher and current member of the National League, he becomes a popular televangelist who introduces subtle racialist themes in his sermons. For this, he incurs the wrath of Jewish defense groups that seek to censor his program, after which Rogers drops the semblance of philo-Semitism and instead selectively emphasizes the anti-Jewish themes of the New Testament. The story climaxes when Agent Ryan orders Yeager to kill Rogers because his program is stirring up people and could disrupt the order he seeks to establish. However, Yeager balks at the idea, which leads to a heated argument between the two over the best means for accomplishing the ends they seek. Yeager closes the debate by shooting Ryan to death.[90]

Although *Hunter* has been characterized as advocating leaderless resistance, William Pierce rejected such a strategy as unviable. As with *The Turner Diaries*, he claimed that ideological propagandizing and not a call for terrorism was his intention with the novel.[91] Despite the stridency of his rhetoric, Pierce did not endorse leaderless resistance, which he once characterized in his National Alliance bulletin as "simply an excuse for losers, cowards, and shirkers to do nothing except talk to each other."[92] Regardless of his intentions, *Hunter* fit well into the Far Right's 1990s zeitgeist when the leaderless resistance approach was popular.[93] Since the extreme Right is closely monitored by the government and private watchdog groups, leaderless resistance is arguably its most feasible approach to violent revolutionary activity. To that end, these novels present a high degree of plausible deniability for their authors.[94]

Another contribution to the theory of leaderless resistance came from the late David Lane, the most celebrated of the imprisoned members of the Order. Lane exhorted "Aryan warriors" to adopt a mentality devoid of any compunction about destroying the system. In his essay "Wotan," he distinguished between two arms of the resistance movement. The aboveground, political arm, concerns itself mostly with the dissemination of propaganda. The underground, or "Wotan," is recruited from the ranks of the political arm.[95] Activists deciding to enter the underground realm are advised to sever all ties with the political arm, lest they compromise it to prosecution and persecution by authorities. Wotan members are encouraged to develop a "totally revolutionary mentality" and not concern themselves with ethical implications of terrorism: "those who do not share his cause are expendable and those who oppose his cause are targets." Lane's essay shows an increasing preoccupation with anonymity and the idea that the number of terrorists who make up a cell should be drastically reduced: "Wotan are small autonomous cells, one-man cells if possible. No one, not wife, brother, parent or friend, knows the identity or actions of Wotan."[96] Some proponents of leaderless resistance advise that only lone wolf operations are proper for current conditions in the United States.

For a time the most vociferous advocate of the lone wolf approach to leaderless resistance was Alex Curtis, who operated the *Nationalist Observer* website while living in San Diego. Like Louis Beam, Curtis reasoned that dissident groups could now be too easily infiltrated, making it impossible to mount an effective campaign of resistance. Moreover, those organizations that suggest such actions, even in an abstract way, could be slapped with a civil suit for "vicarious liability," in which they are blamed for influencing the violent actions of others. Curtis instructed his readers to act entirely as individuals.

Like David Lane, Curtis envisaged a two-tiered resistance structure with an aboveground propaganda arm and a second tier of lone wolves. He advised against formal memberships and meetings, as they offered opportunities for authorities and monitoring groups to identify activists and gather information on them and their sympathizers. In 1998 he created a website that included an audio "update" that reviewed episodes of right-wing violence. He also sent out regular e-mail messages to an estimated eight hundred subscribers.[97] In these media, he pointed out mistakes and offered suggestions on how they could be avoided. He counseled lone wolves not to cooperate with authorities and to respond to them with only five words—"I have nothing to say." In addition, he produced a "security issue," which taught readers how to avoid detection by authorities and what to do if arrested. For Curtis, the end justified the means. He once contemplated the suitability of illegal drug sales as a way to further the racial revolution.[98] Moreover, he had no compunction about the most lethal methods of terrorism. One issue of his bimonthly *Nationalist Observer* contained an article that described biological toxins that could be used for weapons of mass destruction, including the Type A bubonic and typhoid toxins.[99]

Curtis saw leaderless resistance as a means by which to provoke a crisis atmosphere that would polarize the population along racial lines. He actually welcomed hate crime laws, believing their selective use against whites would engender hostility among them. According to Curtis, leaders in the movement should never condemn hate crimes perpetrated by whites.[100] Although random hate crimes appear to have little tactical value, he saw them as a means by which to foment a revolutionary atmosphere.[101]

Curtis's violent rhetoric caught the attention of authorities and monitoring organizations. In November 2000, the ADL issued a report titled "Alex Curtis: Lone Wolf of Hate Prowls the Internet." About a week later he was arrested with two others for various civil rights violations. The arrests were the culmination of an extensive two-year joint investigation by the FBI and the San Diego Police Department dubbed "Operation Lone Wolf." Apparently failing to follow his own advice, Curtis allegedly acted with others to harass several prominent figures in the San Diego area, including Congressman Bob Filner (D-CA), La Mesa mayor Art Madrid, regional ADL director Morris Casuto, and the director of the Heartland Human Relations and Fair Housing Association, Clara Harris.[102] Despite the amateurish characteristics of the alleged offenses, the authorities took Curtis and his accomplices seriously. Curtis was charged with three federal counts of conspiracy to violate civil rights. For each count, he faced ten years in prison and a $250,000 fine, but in March 2001 he pleaded guilty after an agreement with prosecutors that they would recommend that he serve no more than three years in prison. Curtis also agreed to apologize publicly and privately to his victims. In June 2001 he received a three-year prison sentence and agreed not to consort with activists in the white nationalist movement after his release.[103]

Over the past two decades, the leaderless approach has gained popularity on the Far Right. Even Liberty Lobby, an organization that appealed to an older and less radical segment of the movement, released a publication on the subject.[104] Yet the Far Right has not unanimously endorsed this approach. In light of some of the seemingly farcical examples of lone wolf activism, some critics find it futile and counterproductive because it brings negative publicity and unwanted attention from authorities. Instead, they call for a more gradualist approach to effect their revolutionary goals. Ironically some of those advocating this new approach are associated with the National Alliance, an organization connected to many incidents of right-wing violence.

Writing under the pseudonym Eric Hollyoak in 2000, Steven Barry wrote a scathing critique titled "The Fallacy of Leaderless Resistance" in *Resistance* magazine, the organ of the National Alliance's record label, Resistance Records.[105] A retired

US Army Special Forces sergeant, Barry claims to have had much experience in counterinsurgency warfare during his twenty-five-year military career.[106] He took issue with the amateurish approach of leaderless resistance, saying he could find no historical examples of its successful application. In his view, it amounts to little more than anarchy that degenerates into banditry, has no operational utility, and is fundamentally flawed. According to Barry, leaderless resistance appeals to the "lowest (or most psychotic) common denominator" within any given organization. Moreover, it plays into "the enemy's" hands, since connected organizations can be subject to vicarious liability lawsuits initiated by watchdog groups such as the Southern Poverty Law Center.

According to Barry, armed resistance is a subset of a larger strategy of political warfare, which also includes ideological warfare, organizational warfare, psychological warfare, intelligence warfare, and mass warfare. He sees the leaderless resistance approach as organized backwardly. Careful planning and organization, he counsels, must precede armed resistance. In order to plan successfully, a policy-making body is necessary, with a centralized chain of command through which it can issue orders. Furthermore, Barry points out that no underground resistance group is capable of sustaining itself without a support system and infrastructure—friends and accomplices who provide intelligence, safe houses, escape routes, and supplies—which the Far Right does not have. Barry's recommendations are reminiscent of the strategic approach used by the Shining Path in Peru, which spent ten years creating a clandestine organizational structure before embarking on a campaign of violence in the 1980s.[107] In conclusion, Barry was highly critical of armed right-wing violence, and saw lone wolf resistance as futile. Not even the Order escaped his caustic pen. He thought the Order's campaign was doomed to fail because it had no real support network.

Barry's article precipitated a hailstorm of controversy on the revolutionary Right. For many of its adherents, the exploits of the Order were beyond reproach. The most vociferous proponents of leaderless resistance, including Alex Curtis and Tom Metzger, harshly criticized Barry for what they saw as heresy. The imprisoned Order members Richard Scutari, Gary Lee Yarbrough, and Randy Duey also took issue with Barry and pointed out that William Pierce had no reservations about accepting largesse from the Order. Duey conceded that there was room for variety in revolutionary strategy, but his inclination was to do without leaders. Moreover, he argued that the Order sought to act as a catalyst spurring others: "If a thousand Eric Rudolphs or twenty-five Orders arose, the system would really be in danger."[108] Curtis and Metzger said that the leaderless resistance approach was not meant to be a permanent strategy, but was the most viable approach at present. According to their reasoning, society will eventually break down, at which time an organized resistance infrastructure will naturally develop.

Just where Pierce stood on the issue of resistance and terrorism has long been a topic of speculation. Pierce's opinion was often ambiguous. In some of his broadcasts, he gave veiled praise to Islamic terrorists who carried out spectacular attacks. Some saw Pierce as a cheerleader on the sidelines, one who "built bombers, not bombs" and instigated others to commit acts of terrorism. In examining his pronouncements closely, however, it is evident that he favored a more gradual approach to resistance and revolution. He criticized random acts of violence, such as the attacks by Buford O'Neal Furrow, not for moral reasons but because he believed such acts gave his opponents a reason to crack down on the extreme Right before it was in a position to mount effective resistance. He counseled that such "resistance" must be properly directed in a disciplined manner. He stressed the need to build a revolutionary infrastructure before the extreme Right could physically oppose "the system." Pierce elaborated on his position in an interview with me:

WP: My view of the matter is that we can't afford any kind of systematic illegal activity. By that I mean any scheme to raise money illegally or not pay our taxes, rob banks, or assassinate people. We can't do that, because certainly, if we did, we would get caught and lose. I don't have any experience with that sort of thing. I have other things to do. I just believe that eventually we would wreck the whole operation if we tried to operate illegally. So we have to work within the law at this stage. It just doesn't make sense for us to be illegal. What's to be gained by being illegal?

GM: Do you see yourself permanently playing the role of a propagandist or do you think that someday, if conditions allowed for it, that your organization could transform itself into a group that actually physically confronts the system, if you will?

WP: We do what seems to me makes sense to do at any given time. We cannot win ultimately unless we are able to communicate with the people much more effectively than we are now.

So all of our efforts have been aimed at building up a communications and multimedia infrastructure. If ten years from now the Jews are successful in outlawing the First and Second Amendments, we may have to do other things. We may be forced to be much more confrontational than we are now. I just hope that the timing is such that we are not forced into a position where we can't win. . . .

History has a habit of catching people by surprise. . . . And it happened over and over and over again that the established regime, which should have been able to maintain control, loses control because it was overwhelmed and events snowballed on them. They weren't able to keep up with what happened, what happened too fast and caught them by surprise.

I don't know what's going to happen. I really don't. I'm just doing what I have to do now because we can't win without being able to communicate with the people. So that's what I'm trying to do. When we can do that a lot more effectively than we're doing now, we'll think about what we're going to do next.[109]

Repeatedly Pierce maintained that conventional politics was futile for his move-ment and that armed struggle was inevitable. He had no illusions about the extent of his influence and power, and he warned that any premature resistance or terror-ism would only provoke the government into repressive measures that the extreme Right would be unable to counter. Thus, Pierce and his National Alliance concen-trated on building a multimedia propaganda network. To that end he produced a weekly Internet radio program, *American Dissident Voices*, in which he analyzed the predicament of the extreme Right. He ascribed great significance to the news and entertainment industry, which he averred was under the control of a tight Jewish cabal. On July 23, 2002, Pierce died of cancer. After his death, his organization experienced a number of setbacks, but it continues to this day under the leadership of Erich Gliebe. While he was alive, Pierce commanded great respect in the white nationalist movement. Although Pierce did not explicitly call for a campaign of violence, because he did not believe the extreme Right was prepared for such an undertaking, in the final years of his life he occasionally offered indirect praise for Islamic terrorists such as Osama bin Laden and spoke admirably of Palestinian suicide bombers who were "paying a terrible price" in attempts to liberate their land. A close reading of his pronouncements suggests that he thought violence would one day be necessary to achieve his organization's aims. Through his writings and broadcasts he formulated a doctrine of revolution, and, in doing so, created a poten-tially effective foundation for leaderless resistance. Such an approach requires ideo-logical cohesion and coherence so that members of a movement who act on their own initiative can work toward the same goals, however broadly defined. No other person, with the possible exception of David Duke, commanded such authority on the extreme Right. For his part, Duke consistently condemns violence, not only for tactical reasons but out of principle, at times making him come across as a kind of white nationalist Gandhi.

Leaderless resistance continues to have currency on the extreme Right, and a number of loose cannons ignored Pierce's admonitions for restraint. An undated essay posted on several extreme Right websites in the first decade of the twenty-first century, titled "Advice for Lone Wolves," counseled activists on the approach. The anonymous author asserts that for the past thirty years the movement has failed to produce any tangible results. Barring any major economic or social disruption, the author argues, the movement's only hope is for small groups or individuals to commit acts of resistance on their own. These lone wolves should keep illegality to a minimum and avoid petty crimes, the author writes. They should hold jobs that al-low them time to engage in revolutionary acts. When committing acts of terrorism, activists should not announce them to the media—such communication provides a link between perpetrator and act that police can use in their investigations. In order to blend in and avoid detection, lone wolves should eschew things like tattoos that would make them identifiable. They should adopt the mind-set that once they inflict significant damage, the enemy—the "Iron Heel"—will never stop hunting them. If captured, they should remain silent and never grovel, so as not to discredit the movement.[110]

In a libertarian vein, Jefferson Mack made a contribution to leaderless resistance theorizing in a book published by Paladin Press, *Invisible Resistance to Tyranny*. The book offers advice to so-called invisible resisters, who Mack counsels should choose their own course of action depending on opportunities available to them. By being "bad citizens," people can undermine the government. To prevent being identified as a troublemaker, resisters should avoid direct confrontation with law enforcement and other authorities. By appearing as good citizens, they can sabotage the system from within, especially if they work for the government and have access to confidential information. Mack advances a leaderless strategy implemented by like-minded individuals. Despite advocating small cells, he counsels that it is important to have a network of sympathizers who can provide support, intelligence, and safe houses should the need arise. Rather than advertising meetings or creating membership organizations, Mack recommends, resisters should meet local fellow travelers and gather informally so they do not raise suspicion. He argues that the most effective "freedom fighters" would be organized into squad-sized units of five to eight persons, all of whom would know each other well (and have known each other for a long time). To be effective, he points out, freedom fighters do not have to engage in violence. To mislead authorities they can claim to be members of an outlawed group, thus causing the police to chase a phantom organization. Similarly they could take credit for things they do not even do. For example, if a politician dies in an automobile accident, they could claim responsibility even when they had nothing to do with the incident. For targets, Mack identifies political leaders and their staffs, leaders of "anti-freedom special interest groups," military and police personnel involved in the "suppression of political dissidents," known collaborators, and foreign occupation troops (e.g., United Nations personnel), but counsels that resisters should avoid targeting ordinary citizens and police officers.[111]

Despite the popularity of leaderless resistance, some counsel that the approach is wrongheaded and will never seriously challenge the status quo. These people advance a traditional insurgent strategy that involves building a cadre of guerrillas.

Harold Covington and the Northwest Volunteer Army

Harold Covington has earned a controversial reputation in the extreme Right subculture. Highly literate and articulate, he has done a significant amount of writing and theorizing on strategy.[112] Yet he has also been involved in bitter internecine feuds that have led some activists to impugn his movement credentials. He attained notoriety for his connection to the so-called Greensboro Massacre that occurred on November 3, 1979, when members of a neo-Nazi organization, the National

Socialist Party of America (NSPA), and a local Ku Klux Klan chapter clashed with demonstrators led by members of the Communist Workers Party at a "Death to the Klan" rally in Greensboro, North Carolina. After a series of disputes between the two sides, a shootout ensued in which five members of the Communist Workers Party were killed.[113] At that time Covington was the leader of the NSPA and a principal organizer of counterdemonstrators, but he was conspicuously absent from the actual event. Rumors surfaced that he was an informant and agent provocateur for the FBI, Bureau of Alcohol, Tobacco, and Firearms, or CIA. Covington categorically denies these allegations.[114]

Beginning in 2003, Covington published a quartet of novels based on a white separatist insurgency in the Pacific Northwest.[115] In his scenario, the United States has long been in terminal decline. Outsourcing, the importation of cheap "coolie labor," and other baleful economic trends have decimated the white working class. Because of massive immigration from Latin America, unskilled labor jobs pay peon wages. Working-class white families blow their money at Indian-owned casinos. Government entitlements have been chipped away and replaced with "faith-based" initiatives that are far less substantial. Senior citizens without money and health insurance are often euthanized in order to save the government money.

In Covington's novels, white Americans are described as a degraded lot. Virtually everybody is dysfunctional. Feminism has taught women to hate men. Religion is spiritually shallow—fundamentalist Christianity continues but it amounts to little more than a "theological smokescreen for Zionism." As Covington describes, everyone is "wretchedly, bitterly, soul-destroyingly unhappy." Although there is incessant blather in the media that the United States is the land of liberty, ordinary white people are always afraid. To complain about this state of affairs would be to risk prosecution under the "Dees Act."[116] A restrictive firearms law—the Schumer Act—prevents most citizens from owning guns.[117] Those patriots who choose to pursue electoral politics are brutally repressed, arrested, and prosecuted on trumped-up charges. To make matters worse, the US military is overstretched, bogged down in a series of endless small wars in the Middle East, thus putting the federal government in a terrible fiscal predicament. These military excursions have taken their toll on the economy.

Set in the not-too-distant future, the novels extol the exploits of the Northwest Volunteer Army (NVA). The catalyst for the NVA's campaign was an incident in Coeur d'Alene, Idaho. Federal agents there sought to seize a child from the Singer family under provisions of "It Takes a Village"—a program that allows the government to seize children (invariably white) from recalcitrant families and sell them to wealthy families, in order to generate revenue. In this particular incident, a spontaneous uprising ensues and federal agents are ambushed by gunfire from other families who reside on the same street as the Singers, setting in motion the revolt for which the NVA had long planned. Although the federal authorities quash the rebellion by the end of the day, the symbolic significance is so great that it ignites a war of national independence .

Frequently in the novels Covington refers to contemporary conflicts in the Middle East as a source of inspiration. Although the odds may seem overwhelmingly stacked against them, Covington argues that the small, yet highly effective insurgency in Iraq proves that a small separatist movement can be successful. The NVA eventually opens up a second front in the Pacific Northwest, a region chosen for its large forested expanses that provide an ideal setting for guerrilla warfare. The basic unit of the NVA is the company, consisting of just a few fighters. Each company is supposed to be part of a brigade, which is the main operational combat unit. The largest units are called flying columns. Finally, general headquarters coordinates strategy on a national level, dealing with intelligence and propaganda. There are also supporters who keep the fighting units in the field. The highly mobile units use hit-and-run tactics to keep the enemy off balance. Communication is compartmentalized for security reasons.

The NVA's campaign is described as a classic colonial war. To those who criticize his revolutionary model, Covington retorts that the US government rests on a foundation of sand. He admits it would not be feasible to mount a nationwide guerrilla campaign. In the late 1980s he dallied with the idea of southern nationalism, or the creation of a separate white southern state. By the late 1990s, however, he had shifted his separatist strategy to the idea of establishing a white state in the Pacific Northwest. Likewise steering clear of grandiose schemes to foment a nationwide white revolution, the protagonists in Covington's novels instead seek to mount a separatist guerrilla campaign in a region of the country. Covington himself exhorts racially conscious whites to migrate to the area in order to obtain a critical mass. If a guerrilla war could be conducted in a defined territory, with insurgents making limited demands, theoretically the government could be persuaded to let a few states secede if it found the cost of continuing to put down such a rebellion excessive. A frequent refrain in Covington's novels: "In a colonial war, the generals never surrender! The *accountants* surrender!" Thus the insurgents seek to mount a war of attrition that will eventually persuade the US government to relinquish territory. Their strategy of economic warfare includes attacking several targets. The NVA succeeds in shutting down the region's legalized gambling industry, and paralyzes the legal system by assassinating judges. Internal Revenue Service offices and agents are attacked, as are white "collaborators." Establishments that employ nonwhites are burned to the ground. In order to instill a new sense of nationhood, residents and establishments are punished for flying the US flag, which is derided as the "Masonic dishrag." In its stead, a tricolor blue, white, and green flag has been chosen as the symbol of the new republic.

To meet the security challenge, the federal government creates a special Federal Anti-Terrorist Police Organization (FATPO) to combat the insurgents. Composed mostly of nonwhites, the agents brutally repress the local white population, thus further estranging them from the government. But the insurgents soldier on and eventually the war of attrition takes its toll on the US government. Preparing for another offensive in the Middle East in defense of Israel, the government is overstretched and its leaders decide to concentrate military efforts in the Middle East rather than continuing the counterinsurgency in the Pacific Northwest. Concomitant with this development, Mexican irredentists demand a separate "Aztlán" nation in the US Southwest, with the proviso that the government in Washington, D.C., provide tax money to the fledgling semiautonomous province of Mexico. With the enactment of NAFTA, a gradual affinity developed between Mexico and the US southwest. A coalition of Hispanic politicians now clamors for a new country of their own. Chelsea Clinton, president of the United States, announces on television that the federal government has agreed to hold an armistice conference in Longview, Washington. After stormy negotiations, the government finally cedes Idaho, Oregon, Washington, parts of Western Montana, and most of Wyoming to the rebels for the creation of the Northwest Republic, based on the precepts of white separatism and National Socialism.

Reaction to Covington's novels has been mixed in the white nationalist movement. Writing on the Vanguard News Network, an extreme Right website, Michael O'Meara described Covington's series as the most authoritative treatment of white separatism in the English language, finding it infinitely more readable and convincing than *The Turner Diaries*. According to O'Meara, the purpose of political fiction is to get to those who cannot be reached through rational discourse. Others, however, have criticized Covington's strategy for its lack of vision because its protagonists do not endeavor to take over the whole country. Moreover, some argue that if most of the racially conscious whites congregated in one region, they would be sitting ducks for "ZOG," the so-called Zionist Occupation Government. Even if successful, the new republic would be "surrounded by hostile muds [nonwhites] with nukes."[118]

Inasmuch as the extreme Right movement is so small in the United States, it is unreasonable for members to think seriously of attaining critical mass nationwide. Covington's books seem to take this into account, positing a migration of racialist whites to the Pacific Northwest so that they can attain a critical mass regionally. Although many white nationalists may agree with this strategy, there seem to be many obstacles. First and foremost would be the challenge of finding suitable employment. Members of the white nationalist movement appear to be chronically cash-strapped, and as a group do not have the wherewithal for such an undertaking. Covington discussed these hurdles in a conversation with me:

> Getting white Americans to change their patterns of behavior in any manner whatsoever, never mind in some radical and life-altering way, is extremely difficult. We definitely have our work cut out for us.
>
> White nationalists are almost all either working class or former members of the old middle class who have achieved downward mobility, so to speak, and, as such, you're right, we're all pretty much destitute. This is par for the course. For a variety of psychological reasons I am sure you're already familiar with, a small strata of Robespierre-like middle-class intellectuals invariably

end up leading revolutions, but in our case this almost never implies middle-class levels of affluence. In this our people are typical of American whites as a whole, who are drowning in a sea of debt and who have been experiencing falling living standards for several generations now. There is also a strong element of what the Marxists call lumpenproletariat among us. (You will note many of my characters in the novels are of this class, albeit very sanitized and idealized.) This again is par for the course; people with anything to lose or any stake in the existing system very seldom engage in revolutionary or radical political activity, except for that small cadre of middle-class intellectuals I mentioned, most of whom are motivated out of personal resentments of various kinds.

As to relocation to the homeland, yeah, this situation never fails to bemuse me. I am asking our people to do something that 150 years ago, hundreds of thousands of white Americans did willingly and eagerly—leave everything they have in the rest of the country behind, pack all their worldly goods into a wheeled vehicle, and light out westward into the unknown. A century and a half ago the Great Plains were crawling with wagon trains of white people doing this very thing, risking life and limb and braving the weather, starvation, Indian attacks, and disease to reach this beautiful land. Now I am lucky if I can persuade a dozen people per year to undertake the same journey in a matter of days, in air-conditioned comfort down smooth interstate highways, with soft Best Western and Holiday Inn beds to sleep in at night. Nowhere else have I seen a worse example of how the white man's character has degenerated, how we are no longer the men and women our ancestors were. I have little to offer in the way of a solid answer to this question except that somehow or other *it has to be done.*[119]

Obstacles to forming a guerrilla army notwithstanding, Covington remains critical of the leaderless resistance approach:

My personal respect for Louis Beam is immense. Louis's article "Leaderless Resistance" was brilliant and spot on in the context of the times in which it was written.

That said, Louis tripped over the same obstacle that I and everyone else who has ever tried to do anything with "the Blob" [white masses] have tripped over—the wretchedly poor character of the twenty-first century white American. Louis's concept of leaderless resistance was based on the assumption that actual acts of resistance would in fact take place, and that never happened.

I largely blame the Internet for that. Right after Louis published his groundbreaking thesis, along came the Internet, and the White man was given an easy out, a way to satisfy his hunger for feel-good factor without risk and without effort. The Internet is political empty calories. The Internet is sterile. It produces nothing but more Internet. But the fact is that the Internet satisfies that nagging little bit of shame and remorse and self-contempt that tells the White man that he really should be doing something about "all of this nigger and Jew shit." The White man can sit down in his basement rec room with a cold beer and a bowl of nachos, spend an evening pounding on his keyboard, and then get up and say, "Hey, I really got a lot done for the race tonight." But he didn't. All he did was let off steam into cyberspace where it will dissipate overnight, kind of like pissing into the ocean.

There would be a definite place for leaderless resistance in the movement, sure, if we could ever get anybody actually to do anything. But it basically turned into yet another excuse for the white man to do nothing. "Shhh, I can't help you, Harold. I have to keep a low profile, I'm practicing leaderless resistance."[120]

In 2006 a Northwest Front Party convention was held, during which a "Northwest American Republican Constitution" was drafted that called for a "whites only" republic. On his *Radio Free Northwest* program, Covington exhorts whites to relocate to the Pacific Northwest. To date he has attracted few volunteers, but he has produced a concrete plan for a guerrilla campaign in America.

The Extreme Right and American Politics

Despite Covington's lamentations, the ever-expanding medium of the Internet gives individuals and groups without access to the marketplace of ideas a chance to have their views heard. It might also facilitate leaderless resistance. The extreme Right's foray into cyberspace came in the mid-1980s, when three electronic bulletin boards were launched: Aryan Nations Liberty Net, White Aryan Resistance, and Liberty Bell.[121] For the most part, these bulletin boards were unsophisticated and did not reach many people. However, that changed on March 27, 1995, when Don Black, a close associate of David Duke, launched Stormfront.[122] Since then, Stormfront has come to host many right-wing websites and serves as an important entry point for people who seek them. As of early 2009, board membership exceeded 159,000, and over five and a half million posts had been submitted on the site in over 450,000 discussion threads.[123] The Internet has also facilitated the convergence of white nationalist movements around the world. As Jeffrey Kaplan and Leonard Weinberg observed in their study *The Emergence of a Euro-American Radical Right*, scattered elements of the extreme Right in the West, faced with declining white birth rates, sweeping third-world immigration, diminishing life opportunities for working-class youths, and perceived cultural decadence, have come to feel like strangers in their lands. Communicating through chat rooms and other Internet forums, they have found solace in the slogan "white power" and sought to develop a new pan-Aryan identity based on race and civilization, an identity that transcends national borders.[124]

Not surprisingly, the use of the Internet by right-wing extremists has caused much consternation among monitoring groups. To meet the challenge, in 1999 the ADL created HateFilter, a program that blocks access to Far Right websites.[125] Relatedly, pressure is occasionally exerted on Internet service providers to prohibit offensive discourse on bulletin boards and persuade dot-com merchants to restrict the sale of items with extremist themes.[126] Yet some observers believe that the pre-occupation with the construction of a "cyber Reich" distracts movement affiliates from more tangible and meaningful activism, such as public marches and demonstrations, thus diluting their attempts to influence the real world.[127]

Since the demise of the Order, there has not been any significant organized threat of terrorism and violence from the racialist Right. The modus operandi of right-wing terrorists has changed, and now virtually all act individually without any directive from the extremist groups with which they are sometimes affiliated. Plausible deniability adds to the effectiveness of the leaderless resistance strategy.[128] Individuals and groups that espouse revolution can avoid criminal liability by denying formal connections to lone wolves.[129] In that vein, from 2002 to 2007 the FBI reportedly employed an agent provocateur, Hal Turner, a New Jersey blogger, who published provocative information intended to cause other parties to act in a way that would lead to their arrest.[130] The primacy of leaderless resistance in the racialist Right presents a challenge for authorities since it makes it more difficult to identify the source of threats. It is much easier to infiltrate a large organization than a clique of a few individuals, and easier to know what its members are thinking than to read the mind of a lone wolf. Leaderless resistance is symptomatic of organizational and financial weakness, but lone wolves are still capable of grabbing attention with sporadic violence.

For example, on June 11, 2009, an eighty-eight-year-old man with a long history of involvement in extremism, James von Brunn, walked into the US Holocaust Memorial Museum in Washington, D.C., armed with a .22-caliber rifle and gunned down a security officer, after which he himself was shot and wounded. The guard he shot, Stephen T. Johns, died that same day. Von Brunn was later charged with murder. After the incident, police discovered in his car a notebook with a handwritten note that read: "You want my weapons—this is how you'll get them. The Holocaust is a lie. Obama was created by Jews." Previously von Brunn had been arrested in December 1981, after a bizarre incident in which he sought to arrest members of the Federal Reserve Board of Governors. Armed with several weapons, including a sawed-off shotgun, he ran past security guards as he entered the headquarters of the Federal Reserve building in Washington, D.C., where the board was meeting at the time. He was arrested before he could enter the room. Convicted of several offenses, including attempted kidnapping, second-degree burglary, and assault with a dangerous weapon, he served six and a half years in prison. Several months after his attack in 2009, he died in custody before he could be brought to trial for murdering Johns.[131]

Since the early 1980s, the US extreme Right has evolved from a movement characterized by ultrapatriotism to one increasingly characterized by a revolution-ary outlook. This can be explained in large part by some social trends that have significantly changed the texture of the United States. For those on the extreme Right, the United States is not the same country they once knew. What is more, many in the movement consider the "damage" done too great to be repaired by conventional methods. Only radical solutions, they believe, can save the nation and race. From their perspective, this increasingly desperate predicament demands that the old order be torn asunder and a new one built on the ruins. Out of destruction it is believed that the remnants of Western civilization will give rise to a new golden age characterized by creativity and (white) racial solidarity.[132] However, in order to arrive at this much-heralded new era, some trigger event or catalyst is seen as being necessary to usher in a revolutionary epoch, which would include great tribulation and sacrifice. On that note, the presidential candidacy of Barack Obama seemed to alarm some segments of the white nationalist movement. In October 2008, twenty-year-old Daniel Cowart of Bells, Tennessee, and eighteen-year-old Paul Schlessel-man of West Helena, Arkansas, were arrested for crimes connected with an alleged plot to rob a gun store, target students at a largely black high school, and then at-tempt to assassinate Obama.[133]

In October 2010, a *Time* magazine cover story attributed a resurgence of the radical Right to "the tectonic shifts in American politics that allowed a black man with a foreign-sounding name and a Muslim-born father to reach the White House."[134] The Obama presidency and the persistent economic recession appear to have emboldened the Far Right. For instance, in the spring of 2010, an organization calling itself the Guardian of the Republic issued letters to all fifty state governors urging them to resign within three days or face removal. Around the same time, the FBI arrested nine members of the Hutaree Christian militia group after they alleg-edly conspired to kill police officers in a plot to trigger a civil war and bring about the collapse of the federal government.[135] The militia movement, which had been in retreat since the Oklahoma City bombing in 1995, has experienced a resurgence. The Southern Poverty Law Center reported a sharp increase—almost a tripling—in the number of extremist groups in the months after Obama's electoral victory, to 932.[136] A Department of Homeland Security report released in April 2009 specu-lated that the prolonged economic downturn could create fertile recruiting ground for extremist groups. The report also warned that veterans returning from the wars in Iraq and Afghanistan could be recruited and radicalized by such groups. Such a prospect was feared because these veterans could use their skills and knowledge from military training and combat. The most serious threat, the report mused, came from lone wolves who embrace the tactics of leaderless resistance and carry out acts of violence.[137]

In Europe increasing concern over immigration and globalization appears to have bolstered the electoral fortunes of several Far Right parties, including the Movement for a Better Hungary and the Austrian Freedom Party.[138] In the United States, consternation over immigration has fueled the rise of self-styled vigilante groups such as the Minuteman Project, which Chris Simcox and James Gilchrist created in 2004 to patrol the US-Mexico border. According to the Southern Poverty Law Center, a considerable number of white nationalists have volunteered for the project.[139]

The principal weakness of the extreme Right in the United States has been its lack of ideological coherence and its failure to develop a platform to appeal to a sizable portion of the public. This has inhibited the movement from developing a sense of unity that would allow it to mobilize effectively and widely. By contrast, as a political activist in the 1920s and earlier 1930s, Adolf Hitler demanded that the various German nationalist parties merge with his Nazi Party—the NSDAP—and adopt its platform. As Hitler wrote in *Mein Kampf*, only with the power of a singular ideology could the nationalist Right prevail over its Marxist opponents. Similarly, the international communist movement of the early twentieth century, despite its various factions, developed an ideology around which activists could organize and seek political power. More recently, Osama bin Laden's vision of Islamism attracted radical Muslims around the world, despite the fact that his formal organization has been severely damaged by military action led by the United States. By contrast, the US Far Right's lack of ideological coherence has undercut any unified sense of mission among its followers and thus makes implementation of the leaderless resistance approach less feasible. The radical environmentalist and animal liberation movements have proven far more adept at using this tactical method.

CHAPTER 3

Ecoextremism and the Radical Animal Liberation Movement

For more than two decades, elements of the radical environmental and animal liberation movements have demonstrated skill in implementing the leaderless resistance approach. Although the two movements have separate origins, over the years they have converged. Today there is considerable overlap in membership and a high degree of cross-fertilization. An element of misanthropy often runs through both movements as well. And both have adopted a similar decentralized organizational model in which activists commit acts of vandalism, and sometimes terrorism, without direction from a central command-and-control apparatus.

Background

The origin of the contemporary environmental movement can be traced back to the 1960s and grew out of the burgeoning counterculture in many Western countries.[1] Antecedents of the movement can be found much earlier. According to the researcher Donald Liddick, the first intellectual effort to recognize the inherent value of the natural world was advanced by the transcendentalists, a New England dissident movement that arose in the 1830s and was highly critical of established churches. Inspired by eighteenth-century Romanticism and nineteenth-century writers such as Ralph Waldo Emerson and Henry David Thoreau, they exalted nature and introduced the notion of an "oversoul," or a divine moral force, that inhered in every living thing. They saw the earth as possessing a spirit of its own, with humans representing just one part of a diverse, natural world. An organized environmentalist movement did not emerge, though, until the late nineteenth century. In his 1864 book *Man and Nature*, George Perkins Marsh outlined the principles of conservation and argued that human dominion over the planet carried a responsibility to safeguard the environment.[2]

Although usually identified as being on the political Left, the environmentalist movement has a long pedigree on the Right as well. For example, the roots of the "religion of nature" that figures prominently in some fascist movements can be traced back to the nineteenth century. The Enlightenment ideas of positivism, rationalism, universalism, and democracy that swept over Europe eventually spawned a countermovement known as German Romanticism. Charles Darwin's *On the Origin of Species*, published in 1859, added a scientific veneer to this development. Darwin's theory of evolution was later applied to the social sciences and transformed into Social Darwinism, which became popular in the second half of the nineteenth century. In Britain, its chief proponent, Herbert Spencer, used the concept to buttress laissez-faire economic policies. In contrast, in Germany it tended to take the form of nature worship and racial mysticism. The German zoologist Ernst Haeckel, for example, saw in evolution a unifying force that explained the cosmos as an all-embracing whole. It was he who coined the term ecology.[3] In 1904 Haeckel founded a group called the German Monist League, which stressed the oneness and unity of reality. A "world soul" was conceptualized as a project in which all forms of life evolved upwardly. Nature was seen as a neutral force, not favoring any particular race or species. Spencer's "survival of the fittest" maxim, conceived after reading Darwin, applied to all creatures without favor. Out of this struggle, perfection would result. Inherent in the religion of nature was a strident critique of Christianity, which was attacked for turning people away from a reverence for nature. Instead of worshiping an anthropomorphic god, Monists emphasized pantheistic worship of nature. Monism gained popularity with the fledgling neopagan movement, as well as proto-Nazi groups, which shared a desire for the creation of a new Germanic faith as a substitute for traditional Christianity, whether Catholic or Protestant. The Nazi race theorists saw existence as an eternal struggle in which only those having the requisite will would survive. Integral to the Nazi mission was restoration of the "natural order," which would result in a "new man."[4] Despite this rightist pedigree, today there is very little overlap between the extreme Right and the radical environmentalist movement. The latter, with its leftist and egalitarian ethos, looks askance at the former's racism and anti-Semitism.[5]

In the United States, the early conservation movement was composed primarily of representatives of the upper middle class and included such prominent public figures as Theodore Roosevelt, the twenty-sixth president, and Gifford Pinchot, first chief of the Forest Service and later governor of Pennsylvania. Conservationists sought to promote human advancement by managing the use of natural resources, yet some people believed that the conservation movement did not go far enough and called for preservation. (In essence, conservationism calls for the proper use of the environment, while preservation seeks to keep nature in its original state.) To that end, in 1892 John Muir founded the Sierra Club with the intention of preserving the pristine beauty of California's Sierra Nevada range. Aldo Leopold, like Muir, was also critical of the conservation movement and cofounded the Wilderness Society in 1935, helping lay the foundation for modern environmental and animal rights debates.

During World War II and immediately after, the focus on economic growth detracted from concern for environmental causes, but events soon reenergized the movement. First, David Bower and the Sierra Club were able to halt construction of dams in Colorado's Dinosaur National Monument. Second, the construction of the Glen Canyon Dam in Utah in 1956, and the subsequent creation of Lake Powell, gave rise to an invigorated and politically sophisticated environmental lobby. Finally, in 1962, Rachel Carson published *Silent Spring*, which documented the detrimental effects of pesticides on the environment. The book is widely credited for helping launch the modern environmental movement.[6]

Awareness of environmental problems grew over the ensuing decades. Problems such as oil spills and toxic waste sites prompted the federal government to formulate policies aimed at protecting the environment. For example, the National Environmental Policy Act was enacted in 1969, creating national standards for assessing the potential impact of major federal projects on the environment. The Clean Air Act of 1963 stemmed from a perceived need for cleaner air in urban areas. Similarly, the Clean Water Act of 1972 sought to make water safe for swimming, protect fish and wildlife, and eliminate contamination from discharged pollutants. The first Earth Day was celebrated on April 22, 1970, with twenty million people at schools across the country participating in related events and 250,000 people marching in Washington, D.C.[7] Over the years, the environmental movement became increasingly complex and a split emerged. A mainstream segment preferred to effect change through democratic, legal, and nonviolent means. Another segment veered toward "direct action," which often included criminal tactics to further the environmental agenda.[8] The first truly proactive environmental group emerged in the late 1960s with the creation of Greenpeace. Initially the group protested the US government's underwater nuclear tests near Alaska's Aleutian Islands, but later it expanded its actions to include the disruption of whaling and seal-hunting operations.[9]

Although the environmental movement has a long pedigree, criminal and violent acts from its members did not emerge until the last decades of the twentieth century. As Liddick observed, the contemporary movement is far removed from the elite conservation and animal welfare movements of the nineteenth century and the more mainstream environmental and animal protection groups that emerged later. An eventual leading figure in the radicalization of the movement, Edward Abbey, began sawing down billboards in New Mexico in 1958. Others were active in the early 1970s with similar operations. For example, the Arizona Phantom sabotaged coal-mining operations in Black Mesa, Arizona, destroying railroad tracks and heavy equipment. The "Billboard Bandits" sawed down billboards across Michigan. A Tucson-based group called the "Eco-Raiders" cut down billboards, destroyed newly constructed houses, pulled up survey stakes, and dumped thousands of cans and bottles on the doorstep of the Kalil Bottling Company. Authorities apprehended five college students believed to have been responsible for the Eco-Raiders' campaign of vandalism. Their exploits may have been a model for the small gang of activists depicted in Abbey's influential novel *The Monkey Wrench Gang*, which can be read as a call to militant action. The book would serve as an operational model for subsequent groups, such as Earth First! and the Earth Liberation Front (ELF).[10]

First published by Lippincott in 1975, *The Monkey Wrench Gang* received good reviews and was sold in mainstream bookstores. The novel is believed to have inspired some environmentalists to radicalize their activism, and is also thought to have at least indirectly inspired the creation of Earth First! in 1980 (a group Abbey never joined, though he associated with its members and occasionally wrote for its organ). The tale involves four main characters who band together to mount a campaign against industrial firms and developers in the US Southwest. The leader of the group is A. K. "Doc" Sarvis, MD, a middle-aged widower who practices surgery in Albuquerque. His lover, Bonnie Abbzug, is a Jewish woman from the Bronx in her midtwenties, with a master's degree in French literature. They are joined by George Washington Hayduke, a twenty-five-year-old Special Forces veteran of the Vietnam War, who never settled back into society upon his return to the States. Finally, Joseph Fielding Smith, better known as "Seldom Seen," a so-called Jack Mormon with three wives, rounds out the group. After bewailing the degradation of the environment, they decide to engage in direct action—a campaign of sabotage against the culprits. Forswearing violence against people, they exclusively target bridges, tractors, bulldozers, billboards, power stations, and railroad cars. Through their exploits they attain notoriety, and eventually all but one are arrested. They plea-bargain and receive minor sentences, and in the end reunite with Hayduke, or "Rudolph the Red," who managed to evade capture and has assumed a new identity. Back together, they contemplate mounting a new campaign.[11] In the years since its initial publication, *The Monkey Wrench Gang* has exerted a strong influence on the radical environmentalist movement.[12] The extremist wing of the movement has shown itself to be among the most adept practitioners of leaderless resistance—a theoretical approach to terrorism that favors violence by individuals or small cohesive groups.[13] This was the modus operandi of the Monkey Wrench Gang.

By the 1980s, a backlash to the environmental movement had emerged, and both the Reagan and George H. W. Bush administrations tended to favor industry interests and property rights over environmental concerns. For the most part, the Clinton administration followed the same course. Frustrated by unsuccessful efforts to effect change through conventional methods, some in the environmental movement turned to direct action.

Earth First!

According to one story, in 1980, while on a weeklong hiking and camping trip in the Pinacate Desert in Mexico, five environmental activists—David Foreman, Ron Kezar, Bart Koehler, Michael Roselle, and Howie Wolke—discussed ways to further the goals of their movement.[14] Out of this meeting, Earth First! was formed. All the founding members had previously been affiliated with mainstream environmentalist groups, but they decided that direct action was necessary to avert a looming environmental catastrophe and save the planet. Previously Foreman had served as the chief Washington lobbyist for the Wilderness Society. Initially, in addition to environmentalists, the group attracted an assortment of anarchists, radical leftists, and pagans.[15]

The first Earth First! action took place in 1981, when approximately seventy-five people gathered to demonstrate near the Glen Canyon Dam. By 1984, a campaign of "monkey wrenching" had begun. David Foreman's 1985 book *Ecodefense: A Field Guide to Monkeywrenching* provided practical advice on what he called "ecotage." Members occasionally used a controversial tactic known as "tree spiking." In one incident in 1984, a twenty-three-year-old millworker was severely injured after his saw blade struck an eleven-inch spike that had been driven into a tree. Although Earth First! denied responsibility, it was obvious that the spike had been put there intentionally.[16]

According to the radical environmental worldview, the earth was being raped and exploited by humans, not unlike the pattern of oppression of women, minorities, and other marginalized groups. The philosophy of "deep ecology" was formulated by the Norwegian philosopher Arne Naess, who decried "anthropocentrism" and advanced the notion of "biocentrism" in its stead. Biocentrism posits that all life forms—from single-cell organisms to humans—are of equal value.[17] Rather than protecting the environment, deep ecologists call for an actual rollback of civilization and a re-creation of wilderness.[18] Deep ecology presupposes radical changes, in contrast with the "shallow ecology" of mainstream environmentalism. According to Liddick, deep ecologists believe that only by drastically reducing the human population can a "post-apocalyptic, millenarian, primitive, earth-centered utopia come into being."[19]

Taking this supposition seriously implies that some ecoextremists could have a predilection for real terrorism. A small group known as R.I.S.E., founded in November 1971 and based near Chicago, espoused a blend of radical environmentalism and millennialism. The core of R.I.S.E.—two teenagers, Allen Schwandner and Stephen Pera—was able to acquire and grow small quantities of several infectious diseases.[20] The group planned on unleashing a series of bioattacks that it hoped would wipe out most of the human race, but was thwarted before it could act. Chicago police found out about the plans and arrested the leaders in 1972. R.I.S.E. members believed that humans were destroying the environment, and so needed to be eliminated. Out of the ruins, they envisioned, a small select group would live in harmony in nature. The group's grandiose ambitions were not matched by the scientific and technical expertise to carry out its plot. Still, it raised the prospect of a group, motivated by an apocalyptic worldview, willing to carry out attacks producing mass casualties.[21] That possibility arose again in July 2000, when unknown animal rights activists and environmental extremists, protesting against a conference on genetic engineering, left three jars containing low concentrations of a cyanide compound at different locations in downtown Minneapolis.[22]

A few environmental activists have publicly gone so far as to assert that AIDS was a welcome development insofar as it could drastically reduce the human population. Some environmental cults, such as the Church of Euthanasia and the Voluntary Human Extinction Movement (VHEMT), call for the elimination of the human race to save the earth.[23] On a less sinister note, in a 1987 article Edward

Abbey suggested that the United States should close its borders to immigrants as a measure to curb the nation's population.[24] By doing so, he displeased some on the political Left, which tends to favor an open-borders immigration policy.

The worldview of Earth First! contained an element of traditional, left-wing anticapitalism, as it excoriated the US government and corporations for their greed and held them responsible for the destructive cycle of overconsumption and resource depletion. Moreover, they implicated hierarchy and bureaucratic authority as the chief culprits. From its inception, Earth First! rejected a rigid organizational structure in favor of a movement shaped by a shared culture manifested in symbols, stories, and songs. Despite claims of an absence of an organizational structure, formal membership, or leadership, Earth First! includes numerous incorporated organizations, such as Daily Planet Publishing, the Fund for Wild Nature, the Trees Foundation, and the Earth First! Direct Action Fund.[25]

Earth First! experienced two major setbacks in 1989 and 1990. First, five members were arrested in a major FBI sting in 1989. The "Arizona Five," as they came to be known, were implicated in operations carried out by a splinter group called EMETIC (the Evan Mecham Eco-Terrorist International Conspiracy). Formed in 1987, the group was responsible for a number of major sabotage attacks in the late 1980s. An FBI investigation—code named THERMCOM—revealed that EMETIC had conspired to simultaneously damage power transmission lines at three nuclear facilities in Arizona, California, and Colorado.[26] After their arrest, the Arizona Five became the first environmental terrorists officially designated as such by the FBI in the United States. Among those arrested was David Foreman, the most prominent cofounder of Earth First! He later pleaded guilty only to distributing his book *Ecodefense* to the conspirators and was released on probation.[27] The second Earth First! setback came about a month after power lines were toppled in an "Earth Night" 1990 action for which the organization took credit near Santa Cruz, California.[28] On May 24, two members—Judi Bari and Darryl Cherney— were injured when an explosive device detonated in Bari's Subaru. At the time, the two were coordinating a massive protest effort known as Redwood Summer. The FBI and the Oakland police suspected that Bari and Cherney had made the bomb and that it had accidentally detonated as they drove through Oakland.[29]

Disagreements over tactics opened a breach in the ranks of Earth First!, which had grown throughout the 1980s to a peak of about ten thousand members. New members from the West Coast brought with them interest in a variety of social justice issues, of which environmental concerns were just one. They favored civil disobedience over monkey-wrenching. This softer approach alienated some of the more "biocentric" activists in the movement, prompting Foreman to leave in 1990, complaining that leftists who favored humanism over biocentrism had infiltrated the movement.[30] As underground activists became marginalized and isolated from other members of their movement, a process of continued radicalization occurred, which produced more violent activists, including lone wolves, bent on carrying out acts of terrorism.[31] Over the years, the movement would become more prone to vandalism, leading to the creation of even more radical spinoff organizations.

Earth Liberation Front

Founded in Brighton, England, in 1992, the Earth Liberation Front (ELF) formed after Earth First! activists distanced themselves from illegal activities.[32] The ELF slogan—"the burning rage of a dying planet"—suggests its radical bent. The organization has been responsible for well over $100 million in property damages since 1997. In October 1996, a US branch of ELF announced its existence with an attack on a US Forest Service truck in Oregon's Willamette National Forest.[33] Essentially a leaderless movement, ELF has no official membership or central organization. Rather, ELF activists (sometimes referred to as "elves") and cells act independently and remain anonymous to the public, thus maximizing their fluidity of movement. Structurally, ELF activists work in small, autonomous cells of two to five persons. Members of one cell are not known to others, ensuring operational security. With no formal membership, ELF does have guidelines that exhort activists to cause economic damage to firms that despoil the environment, to educate the public on the harm being done to the environment, and to take all necessary precautions to avoid harming life. Basically, anyone who follows these guidelines is considered a member of ELF. Liddick writes that an element of anarchism informs ELF's ideology, as members see the destruction of the global capitalist economy as a prerequisite to saving life on earth.[34]

Some ecoextremists extol revolutionary strategies that sound similar to the leaderless resistance approach advocated by extreme Right revolutionaries. The researcher Paul Josse argues that by implementing leaderless resistance, ELF can avoid ideological cleavages within its movement. Various ideological orientations are subsumed in the movement, which remains focused on direct action. By concentrating on the narrow goal of halting the degradation of nature, ELF eliminates opportunities for ideological debates, thus enabling unanimity of purpose unlikely in an organization characterized by a hierarchical structure.[35] Typically the existence of ELF cells becomes known only after an illegal direct action is claimed. Cells are often formed when like-minded activists meet while participating in aboveground activities.[36]

The first recognized ELF actions in the United States occurred in 1996, when operatives struck McDonald's restaurants, gluing their locks and spray-painting the buildings with slogans. In 1997 ELF claimed responsibility for another attack in the United States, when operatives burned a Bureau of Land Management horse corral in Oregon.[37] A year later, ELF made headlines when a cell called "the Family" claimed responsibility for arson at a ski resort in Vail, Colorado, that caused $12 million in damages.[38] The most destructive incident, however, occurred on August

1, 2003, when arsonists set fire to a housing complex under construction and destroyed a hundred-foot crane in San Diego, causing losses estimated at $50 million.[39] For the radical environmentalist movement globally from 1956 to 2005 the vast majority of such actions took place in North America and Europe, with 47.5 percent occurring in the United States, followed by 9.8 percent in Great Britain.[40] Car dealerships and sports utility vehicles have been frequently targeted. Instructional manuals popular in the radical environmental movement, such as the *ALF Primer, ARSON—Around with Auntie ALF,* and *Setting Fires with Electrical Timers: An Earth Liberation Front Guide,* provide instructions on how to prepare and use incendiary devices.[41] The eponymous *Earth First!* journal once recommended burning trees to save them from loggers.[42] Although most acts of ecosabotage have not been lethal, they have been costly to victims. According to the FBI's head of domestic terrorism, ELF alone was linked to six hundred criminal acts committed between 1996 and 2002, totaling $43 million in damages.[43] Collectively in the United States, the radical environmental movement has committed hundreds of arsons and acts of vandalism, causing damages of more than $100 million.[44]

For years, radical environmentalists have held that human beings should not be harmed or endangered in acts of ecoresistance. Nevertheless, an ideological framework for justifying causalities has been forged. Proponents of deep ecology draw a moral equivalence between sentient and non-sentient beings, and thus mountains and protozoa are considered of equal worth to humans. Furthermore, they assume that the human population has grown far too large and must someday be drastically reduced if the planet is to remain viable. Human civilization must be eradicated, and in its place humans will live in harmony with other creatures. An element of misanthropy informs this worldview, as humans, deemed a threat to the survival of life on earth, are derogated. Thus a millenarian quality suffuses the movement, which could conceivably justify the use of WMD to bring about a more sustainable planet.[45]

Nevertheless, most radical environmentalists do not condone sabotage that risks human life. Since 1985 only four fatalities have been attributed to ecoterrorists.[46] According to the researcher Bron Taylor, several characteristics of the movement militate against the use of violence. First, the environmentalist movement is not as isolated from the mainstream as other dissident movements, such as neo-Nazis. As such, members usually do not sever their connections to those outside the movement. Furthermore, the egalitarian and antiauthoritarian ethos of the movement works against the emergence of a charismatic leader who can exert overarching control over other members. A commitment to free speech and debate in the movement allows for moderating opinions to be heard, thus tempering radicalism that might emerge. There is also the general belief in the movement that all life is sacred, and therefore people should not be harmed. Finally, environmentalist gatherings often contain a strong element of frivolity and revelry that would seem to decrease the likelihood of violence emanating from the movement.[47]

After the protests at the World Trade Organization meetings in Seattle in November 1999, ELF began to assume a more anticapitalist and antiglobalization orientation.[48] Many elements of the radical environmental movement champion causes usually associated with the political Left. For example, some ecoextremists have become increasingly strident in their opposition to the war on terror, and to the wars in Iraq and Afghanistan. A former spokesman for the Earth Liberation Front, Craig Rosebraugh, exhorted antiwar activists to escalate their opposition. Among his suggestions to foment revolution were to attack US financial centers, provoke large-scale urban rioting, attack media centers of power, spread the battle to the individuals responsible for war (i.e., leaders in government and US corporations), publicly announce that the antiwar movement does not support US troops; target US military establishments within the United States, and finally, when engaging in these actions, to strike hard and fast and then retreat in anonymity.[49] Not long after he released his manifesto, on March 28, 2003, five cars and a van at the navy recruiting headquarters in Montgomery, Alabama, were spray-painted with antiwar slogans and a truck was set on fire, for which ELF issued a communiqué claiming responsibility.[50]

Born in Portland, Oregon, on April 15, 1972, according to his memoirs, Rosebraugh had a happy and normal childhood. While in college, he developed a leftist worldview and became highly critical of capitalism, American society, and US foreign policy. Eventually he came to the conclusion that the political system in the United States could only be changed through a campaign that included an element of political violence. Explicitly rejecting the notion of reform, he embraced the revolutionary idea of tearing down the US power structure. In fact, he argues that a key reason why "justice" struggles have not gone further in the United States is their reformist, rather than revolutionary, orientation.[51]

To further his revolutionary cause, Rosebraugh wrote a manifesto titled *The Logic of Political Violence: Lessons in Reform and Revolution*. In it, he explained his odyssey from a position of nonviolence, introduced to him while he was attending a community college in Oregon in the early 1990s, to his belief in the efficacy of political violence. At first impressed by Mohandas Gandhi's nonviolent campaigns, he abandoned that approach after studying history and experiencing antiwar protests, and by the mid-1990s had come to believe that social and political change was highly regulated in United States, with only nonviolent methods and occasional use of civil disobedience approved for reaching political goals.[52] For his master's degree, obtained at Vermont's Goddard College, he wrote a thesis titled *Rethinking Nonviolence: Arguing for the Legitimacy of Armed Struggle*. Although he still espoused nonviolence in public, privately he began to question it.[53] More often than not, he discovered that force, or the threat of it, was successful in effecting meaningful social and political change.

To make his point, Rosebraugh includes several case studies from history in *The Logic of Political Violence*. First he cites the example of Jewish resistance in World War II, arguing that Hitler could not be deterred from his genocidal ambitions—only armed resistance could have succeeded. In the case of the US civil rights movement, Rosebraugh concedes that African Americans made gains, but he believes that the movement was reformist in orientation and thus achieved far less than it might have. He argues that Martin Luther King, with his strategy of nonviolent civil disobedience, was assisted in large part by the more radical exponents of the Black Power movement, who made whites and the US government more amenable to his approach. In the case of the Vietnam-era antiwar movement, he criticizes protestors for their minimal goals, ignoring wide-ranging social and political transformation for the price of merely ending the war. Further, he argues that the antiwar movement had less to do with ending the war than the effective guerrilla campaign of the Vietcong and its support by the North Vietnamese government. In the Algerian Civil War, Rosebraugh sees a paradigm for an effective revolutionary strategy. The Algerian rebels unabashedly implemented a campaign of terrorism that created the conditions for revolution, transforming the anger, resentment, and feeling of alienation among Algerians into revolutionary behavior and prevailing over the more powerful French army. Rosebraugh likewise praises the Cuban revolutionaries led by Fidel Castro, finding it instructive that a revolution could begin before revolutionaries knew what kind of regime they wanted to implement. Finally, he cites the case of the 1916 Easter Rebellion in Ireland, which, although initially a failure, granted legitimacy to the fledgling Irish Republican movement and set the stage for its victory in the next decade.[54]

Despite his belief in the strategic viability of political violence, Rosebraugh acknowledges that "as the military technology in countries such as the United States become increasingly advanced, the ability for a successful armed insurrection by the mass of people against such a force greatly decreases. Not that it is impossible, but it is increasingly difficult." He concedes that a revolutionary atmosphere does not currently exist in America. Nevertheless, he finds solace in the bromides of Castro and Guevara that insurrectionists can create their own conditions for revolution. In order for the nonviolent approach to work, Rosebraugh notes that it is necessary for opponents to have a conscience and possess the capability of seeing the evil in their ways so that they will voluntarily change. But he believes this sort of scenario is unlikely given the precedents of US history, and he argues that political violence is necessary, though he calls for an eclectic strategy that could include nonviolent tactics. More often than not, he avers, even when a nonviolent campaign has been successful, it has been because an opponent was coerced into changing and affected by outside pressures.[55]

On February 12, 2002, Rosebraugh was subpoenaed to testify before Congress in a special session called "The Emerging Threat of Eco-Terrorism."[56] In his testimony, he opined that the United States is "based upon murder, exploitation, and ultimate genocide." Further, he described the US government as "the most extreme terrorist organization in planetary history."[57] In early 2003, he and Leslie James Pikering founded a group called Arissa, whose aim is to spur more dramatic direct action.[58] Another organization with which Rosebraugh is affiliated is the Animal Liberation Front (ALF), which he joined after spending a night in jail with an ALF activist in 1997.[59]

The Radical Animal Liberation Movement

Like the environmental movement, the animal welfare movement has a long history. Organized efforts to protect animals began in England in the late eighteenth and early nineteenth centuries. The Royal Society for the Prevention of Cruelty to Animals and the National Anti-Vivisection Society sought to prevent the abuse of animals in the nascent biomedical research industry. Other organizations, such as the Society for the Suppression of Vice (which later became the League Against Cruel Sports), sought to abolish hunting and animal sports.[60] In the United States, Henry Bergh founded the American Society for the Prevention of Cruelty to Animals (ASPCA) in 1866.[61] For decades the movement was solidly mainstream, refraining from illegal acts. While the use of criminal means to further the goals of the animal rights movement began much later, a direct action approach can be traced back to 1960s England, when a group known as the Hunt Saboteurs Association disrupted fox hunts by using bull horns and spraying chemicals that masked the scent of foxes, thus confusing the dogs. In 1972, two hunt saboteurs—Ronnie Lee and Cliff Goodman—decided that more militant action was needed. Hence the Band of Mercy was formed and began using direct action to free animals.[62] Presumably, the group took its name from the original Band of Mercy, started in 1894 to thwart fox hunting. In November 1973 the new group launched its first attack on the animal research industry: operatives set fire to a half-completed facility for the Hoechst Pharmaceutical firm.[63]

In his influential 1975 book *Animal Liberation*, Peter Singer adopted utilitarian reasoning to argue that the benefits of eating animals and using them in biomedical research were minimal compared with their suffering. He advanced the notion of "speciesism" to imply that humans had discriminated against animals just as they had discriminated against women and certain minorities throughout history. He argued that it was unconscionable to use animals to serve human needs for any reason, whether for food, clothing, the production of medicine, or entertainment.[64] The fullest articulation of animal rights appeared in Tom Regan's 2001 book *Defending Animal Rights*. Most animal rights activists believe that mammals and other vertebrates should be accorded the most rights. The common benchmark is sentience, the ability to process sensory inputs. Animal rights activists occasionally compare factory farming and the use of animals for food and experiments to slavery and the Holocaust.[65] Thus those who engage in direct action outside the law justify their purpose as high-minded.

Although there had been sporadic earlier acts of criminality on behalf of animal rights, the first sustained campaign began in 1976, when Ronnie Lee created the Animal Liberation Front (ALF) with thirty others in England. Two years earlier, Lee had been caught attempting to firebomb a medical facility and sentenced to a year in prison. While incarcerated, he decided to adopt an organizational model based on small, decentralized, autonomous cells. Members of other groups, such as Greenpeace and the Sea Shepherd Conservation Society, were involved early on in ALF.[66] Within ten years ALF had grown to fifteen hundred activists and was believed responsible for causing roughly six million pounds sterling, or about $9.5 million, in damage annually to British businesses and research facilities.[67] Its exploits gained the organization international notoriety and inspired a movement worldwide. ALF's stated goal is to stop animal suffering through direct action, which includes illegal activities to rescue animals and inflict damage on businesses and facilities that use and abuse animals. There is no formal membership. Rather, activists are bound by an ideology and earn the right to regard themselves part of ALF after carrying out illegal actions consistent with the organization's guidelines.[68] The first documented ALF operation in the United States occurred in March 1979, when activists masquerading as lab workers "liberated" research animals from the New York University Medical Center.[69]

Although it is essentially an underground group, there are aboveground organizational structures that promote ALF's objectives, such as the North American Animal Liberation Press Office (NAALPO), which has sometimes defended criminal ALF operations.[70] There are also newsletters and journals that carry stories on ALF attacks. A spinoff group, the Animal Rights Militia (ARM), founded in England in 1982, advocates a more proactive approach for advancing animal rights, including abandoning ALF's admonition against taking all necessary precautions to avoid harming people. Another animal rights organization, the Justice Department, emerged in 1993 and conducted, according to the *Independent*, "the most sustained and sophisticated bombing campaign in mainland Britain since the IRA was at its height."[71] Ominously breaking from the philosophy of not jeopardizing human lives, the group claimed responsibility for sending envelopes with blades dipped in rat poison to roughly eighty researchers, hunting guides, and others in Canada and the United States.[72]

In the worldview of animal liberationists, the killing of sentient nonhuman animals is not unlike murder. Accordingly, violence could be justified to prevent such killing, not unlike the justification some antiabortion activists have used to support attacks on doctors and clinic personnel.[73] An ALF spokesman, "Screaming Wolf," once wrote a primer titled *A Declaration of War: Killing People to Save Animals and the Environment* in which he counseled activists to operate in a leaderless fashion and take action according to their own conscience to stop human oppression. On at least one occasion, an animal liberation activist was involved in a terrorist fatality. On May 6, 2002, Volkert van der Graaf assassinated the Dutch politician Pim Fortuyn in Hilversum. Motives for the assassination are not entirely clear, but Fortuyn had previously come out in favor of lifting a ban on the breeding of fur animals.[74]

Arguably the most potent and enduring campaign of radical animal rights activism was undertaken by a group called Stop Huntingdon Animal Cruelty (SHAC), whose members launched a concerted effort to shut down Huntingdon Life Sciences (HLS), one of the largest animal-testing companies in the world. Founded in 1999 by Greg Avery and Heather James, SHAC began its campaign in England after a video made by People for the Ethical Treatment of Animals (PETA) was broadcast on television, showing abuse of lab animals inside an HLS facility. As of 2006, SHAC operatives had bombed eleven privately owned vehicles and attacked numerous residences of HLS employees. They have also attacked companies that do business with HLS, including an insurance company (Marsh) and an investment bank (Stephens Inc.). As a consequence, these firms broke off their business contacts with HLS. Some employees of another HLS affiliate, Chiron, were subjected to repeated late-night visits by SHAC activists.[75]

There is a significant aboveground leadership within the radical animal rights movement, including mainstream organizations such as PETA, cofounded by Alex Pacheco and Ingrid Newkirk in 1980 and based in Norfolk, Virginia.[76] In recent years, the Humane Society Legislative Fund, an affiliate of the Humane Society of the United States (which has absorbed the Doris Day Animal League and the Fund for Animals), has emerged as an influential lobbying group in Washington, D.C., with a reported $120 million annual budget.[77] Activists and organizations are essential in providing inspiration and have been crucial to the movement's success. According to the research of Wesley Jamison, who uses a stratified pyramid to conceptualize the structure of the animal rights movement, the most influential members compose the top 1 percent. Active members account for roughly 4–5 percent. A third tier consists of "attentive members," making up about 10 percent. Finally, "general members" account for about 85 percent of the movement. A significant trend observed by Liddick is the takeover and radicalization of traditional animal rights organizations. He cites PETA, writing that it explicitly defends—and in effect sponsors—criminal activities by some of the more radical organizations. For example, PETA has taken out full-page ads condoning ALF criminality, and on some occasions PETA members have carried out ALF-like direct actions.[78] Likewise, Greenpeace has engaged in civil disobedience to protect whales and other wildlife. One activist, Paul Watson, a former member of the Canadian Coast Guard, left Greenpeace to form the Sea Shepherd Conservation Society (SSCS), which promotes marine environmental issues. SSCS operates by using aggressive vigilante tactics, such as ramming vessels, to disrupt whaling.[79] Not unlike Sinn Féin in its relationship to the Provisional Irish Republican Army, the Sea Shepherds are believed to have unofficially supported a group known as Orcaforce that has attacked and sunk several whaling ships.[80]

There is increasing overlap and cooperation between the ecodefense and animal liberation movements.[81] In a communiqué released in 1993, ELF declared solidarity with ALF.[82] The aforementioned arson of the ski resort in Vail was believed to have been a joint ALF-ELF operation. Likewise, in January 2003, activists who claimed to be fighting for both the environmental and animal liberation causes took responsibility for an action against the pharmaceutical company Novartis in Bern, Switzerland.[83] An important ALF activist, Rodney Coronado, gained notoriety for sinking two whaling ships and destroying a whale processing station in Iceland. More than any other person, Coronado represents the cross-fertilization between the two movements.[84] Convicted for his role in the firebombing of an animal research laboratory at Michigan State University, he served a three-and-a-half-year prison sentence.[85] According to official statistics, violent incidents arising from ALF occurred at a rate of eighty per month in the United Kingdom in 1995. A report from the US Department of Justice listed 313 such cases over several years, but Great Britain is the setting for the vast majority of illegal actions related to animal rights.[86] In 2006 ALF claimed responsibility after a firebomb was placed on the doorstep of a house owned by Lynn Fairbanks, a University of California researcher. According to some sources, the attack prompted Congress to pass the Animal Enterprise Terrorism Act.[87]

By 2008, ALF activists were increasingly taking protests to the homes of researchers, in what became known as "home demonstrations," involving noise-making and assorted vandalism. As a consequence, the US Department of Justice launched "Operation Backfire" to crack down on ALF and ELF direct action. At a press conference, the FBI announced that charges had been filed against nine American and two Canadian activists who called themselves "the Family," alleging that they had participated in ALF and ELF direct actions.[88] Some environmentalists have decried government repression against the movement, calling this a "Green Scare." Still, campaigns of harassment by the likes of ALF and ELF continue to demonstrate the havoc that lone wolves can wreak. To date, the most infamous lone wolf associated with the radical environmental cause is Ted Kaczynski.

The Unabomber

Some elements of the radical environmental movement have appropriated Ted Kaczynski as one of their own. For example, in the spring of 2002, *Green Anarchist* listed him as a "POW" and carried an article by Kaczynski in which he urged the movement to "eliminate the entire techno-industrial system."[89] A number of environmental activists have expressed sympathy for Kaczynski, but for his ideas more than his tactics.[90] His antitechnology worldview has endeared him to many in the radical environmental movement. In some ways his philosophy is reminiscent of the Luddites active in England from 1812 to 1817, who destroyed machines in factories for fear that they were obviating human labor. Since Kaczynski is an archetypical lone wolf, a brief sketch of his political odyssey is in order.

Kaczynski's early life appears relatively normal. Although he seems to have been socially awkward, quiet, shy, and unkempt, his biographer Alston Chase maintains that he was not the "filthy hermit he was made out to be." Although his childhood was unhappy, it was not markedly different from that of his peers. His adolescence was troubled but unremarkable. His social life in high school and college is described as average. He grew up in a Polish working-class neighborhood in Chicago, where his parents made conflicting demands on him. They encouraged him to develop his intellect and think for himself, but they also stressed conformity.

Kaczynski's highly developed intellect seems to have contributed to his loneliness insofar as he had few peers who could relate to him. In 1958 he began his undergraduate studies at Harvard at the age of sixteen.

According to Chase, it was as an undergraduate at Harvard that Kaczynski first encountered ideas that he would weave into an ideology of revolution and incorporate in his Unabomber critique of "technological society." Chase, also a Harvard grad, observed that the curriculum at that time fostered a "culture of despair," which reflected recent events. The Great Depression had underscored the fragility of the US economy. The carnage of the Second World War had demonstrated how technological knowledge, when not guided by moral purpose, could cause unprecedented destruction. By the early 1960s many of the faculty had lost faith in the idea that morality was rational, and this was reflected in the revised general education curriculum at the university. The final straw for Kaczynski—the experience that Chase believes set him on his future course of action—was a series of experiments in which he participated while at Harvard. Led by the esteemed psychologist Henry A. Murray, who headed the Department of Social Relations, the experiments subjected participants to a highly stressful form of interrogation intended to incite anger and ridicule their beliefs. Conducted during the Cold War, the research was intended to further knowledge on interrogation and brainwashing, which interested the US government at that time as part of psychological operations. Murray, regarded as the cofounder of humanistic psychology, had worked for the Office of Strategic Services (precursor to the CIA) during World War II.[91]

At age twenty, Kaczynski graduated from Harvard and entered graduate school at the University of Michigan, where he received a PhD in mathematics in 1967. That same year, he joined the Department of Mathematics at the University of California, Berkeley, as an instructor. He tired of the academy, however, and moved to Great Falls, Montana, in 1971. That summer he began building a small cabin near the town of Lincoln, eighty miles southwest of Great Falls on a lot that he and his brother, David, had purchased.[92]

A voracious reader, Kaczynski enjoyed literature and books on history and science. An expert on etymology, he was fluent in several languages, including Spanish and German, and had also studied Finnish, Russian, French, Egyptian, and Chinese. Chase asserts that Kaczynski may have become a cold-blooded killer not despite his intellect, but because of it. Two strains of his personality, one psychological, the other intellectual, converged to form the mind of a killer.[93]

On May 25, 1978, Kaczynski began a campaign of terrorism when he left a package in the parking lot of the Science and Engineering Building at the University of Illinois at Chicago Circle campus. The next day Terry Marker, a security guard, was slightly injured in the explosion that occurred when he opened the package. In the years to come, Kaczynski sent sixteen bombs to targets including universities and airlines, killing three persons and injuring twenty-three others. His campaign ended on April 24, 1995, when a package bomb he had mailed killed the president of the California Forestry Association, Gilbert Murray. Kaczynski was arrested on April 3, 1996, after one of the longest and costliest FBI investigations ever, dubbed UNABOM—"UN" standing for "university" and "A" for "airlines." At his trial, he justified his actions as an attempt to slow down the inexorable march of technology.[94]

In a journal entry, Kaczynski wrote that his violence was motivated mainly by a desire for personal revenge.[95] Nevertheless, Kaczynski also seemed motivated by ideology. In June 1995 he promised that he would desist from further bombings if either the *Washington Post*, the *New York Times*, or *Penthouse* magazine would publish his 35,000-word critique of technology titled "Industrial Society and Its Future," now more often referred to as the "Unabomber Manifesto." At first, the proposition set off a flurry of debate in the media over the ethics of publishing such a document—the work of a killer—under duress. Then-US Attorney General Janet Reno encouraged its publication in hopes that someone might recognize its authorship and provide a lead to solve the Unabomber case. Reluctantly, on September 19, 1995, both the *Post* and the *Times* published the essay in toto in a special supplement. In it, Kaczynski rails against technology for breaking down local, human-scale communities. His critique blends common narratives of both the Left and the Right. For example, he decries big government but also big business, arguing that both are inevitable consequences of industrialization. In order to appeal to a large audience, he offers a "veritable salad of ideas," emphasizing themes from ecology because he thought it would make his treatise more popular, Chase writes. Chase describes the diatribe as "a compendium of philosophical and environmental clichés that expresses concerns shared by millions of Americans."[96]

Kaczynski sought to use his trial to expound on his views. Adamantly opposed to a defense based on insanity, he was quite willing to accept the death penalty if the trial allowed him to showcase his antitechnology philosophy. When he discovered that his defense team would press for the insanity defense, he attempted to commit suicide in his cell by hanging himself with government-issued underpants. Eventually he agreed to a guilty plea that would spare him the death penalty, but that meant life in prison without possibility of parole. From his prison cell, he occasionally corresponds with journalists and academics to clarify his views.

Over time, as evidenced by some of his writings, Kaczynski seems to have developed a greater ideological affinity for the environmental movement.[97] His last two victims, both of whom died, could be perceived as antienvironment. According to prosecutors, Kaczynski had claimed in an anonymous letter to the *New York Times* that his penultimate victim Thomas Mosser, an executive at Burson-Marsteller, was responsible for helping to improve the image of the Exxon Corporation after the *Exxon Valdez* oil spill. The last victim, Gilbert Murray, was the president of the California Forestry Association, although the intended target was William Dennison, past president of the association (when it was known as the Timber Association of California). According to some sources, Kaczynski was influenced by Earth First! and chose at least one of his victims from the *Live Wild or Die!* magazine's "Eco-Fucker hit list."[98]

In a letter to Donald Liddick, however, Kaczynski disavowed all connections to radical environmentalists and even went so far as to state that groups like ELF should be resisted. Further, he added that he was "not particularly interested in animal rights." His overriding concern is with bringing about the collapse of technological civilization, a civilization he believes benefits groups that are often classified as left-wing, including gays and lesbians and other minorities. Leftists have nothing to gain from the collapse of the technological society, he writes, so their commitment to acting to bring about its collapse is suspect. The values of the Left are "essentially the soft values of modern society," he writes, and a movement dominated by such values will never take the severe measures necessary to bring down the techno-industrial system, nor would such a movement be prepared for the harsh consequences of the collapse of the system. Kaczynski counsels that people who sincerely want to destroy technological society must divorce themselves from a movement dominated by the political Left because the latter will impede the emergence of any genuine revolutionary movement.[99]

Kaczynski's philosophy is difficult to pigeonhole. Consistently rejecting traditional ideologies, he maintains that his critique of industrialization transcends the traditional political spectrum. Not unlike the libertarian Right and some social conservatives, he decries big institutions because they diminish individual liberty. As he sees it, the "system" cannot be reformed. Rather, it must be destroyed if humans are to survive in a meaningful way and be self-actualized. Otherwise, society's most important decisions will be made by computers, and humans will be fated to become slaves. Nevertheless, there is also a teleological element to his prognostications, not unlike the tenets of "scientific socialism," in the sense that Kaczynski also believes the system will eventually collapse on its own. Although he has been described as a misanthrope, he appears desperately concerned about the human condition. In formulating his worldview he liked to cherry-pick ideas he admired from other thinkers and discard the rest. He flirted with the radical environmental movement, perhaps because he believed it would be most amenable to his way of thinking, and for a while he corresponded with *Earth First!*—the eponymous journal published by the radical environmental group. Chase sums up his way of thinking as "a 'Fourth World' philosophy of cultural primitivism."[100]

Opposition and the Road Ahead

Although the radical environmental movement has attracted attention by causing substantial property damage and even loss of life, it has failed to alter public opinion significantly. It has, however, managed to make previously labeled "radical environmental" organizations, such as Greenpeace and the Sierra Club, appear more moderate. Despite all the damage that the radical environmental and animal liberation movements have wrought, Liddick believes that their future looks dim. As the number of their attacks has grown, the US government has taken notice.

Since the late 1990s, the FBI has identified violent ecoextremists and radical animal liberation activists as the most serious domestic terrorism threat in the country. The government has responded to their vandalism and harassment with new laws aimed at punishing more harshly activists who target animal-testing laboratories and their affiliates. Thirty-two states have followed suit and enacted laws to protect animal-testing enterprises. A rider attached to the Drug Act of 1983 makes tree spiking a felony. Furthermore, private industry has responded by pooling resources to discredit their opponents through education, advertising, and lobbying.[101] In May 2005, John Lewis, the deputy assistant director of the FBI, discussed the threat posed by animal rights extremists and ecoterrorists before a congressional committee. He pointed out that from January 1990 to June 2004 such groups had claimed credit for more than twelve hundred criminal incidents in the United States, resulting in millions of dollars in damage and loss. To meet this threat, he announced that the FBI had formed numerous joint terrorism task forces with law enforcement agencies around the country.[102]

Despite a lack of demonstrable achievement, the radical environmental movement persists, and some elements of the radical Left have mounted effective protests without central leadership, as demonstrated by the events in Seattle during the 1999 meetings of the World Trade Organization. As a consequence of the dissolution of the Soviet Union in the early 1990s, and the general decline in the fortunes of Marxism, many young people turned to environmentalism, which they sought to combine with left-wing ideology.[103] Previously some radical left-wing groups received support from the Soviet bloc, but after 1989 such state sponsorship has evaporated.

CHAPTER 4

The Strategic Implications of the New World Order

The collapse of the Soviet Union drastically changed the security environment within which terrorists operate. During the Cold War, several Eastern bloc states were covert supporters of terrorist groups. At the time, supporting terrorism was viewed as furthering the foreign policy objectives of the Soviet bloc.[1] In her classic study *The Terror Network*, Claire Sterling maintained that for much of the period from the late 1960s to the early 1980s, the Soviet Union was at the center of a global terrorist apparatus.[2] Soviet-supported terrorism was designed to advance the influence of the communist superpower. Near the end of the Cold War, however, Soviet leaders realized that collaboration with terrorists produced few tangible benefits and complicated relations with the United States and the West, with which they were seeking to improve relations.[3] Initially after the Cold War, terrorism went into steep decline, in large part because several leading terrorist groups lost material support from communist states in the East and from their client states, such as Cuba.[4] Left-wing terrorist groups lost credibility as the broader political Left became concerned more about social and identity issues than redistributive economic policies.

In an era of globalization dominated by the United States, states presumably would have more to gain by accommodation with the West than by confrontation. This development militates against the viability of large terrorist organizations, which are more vulnerable to state repression and disruption, since the governments of these countries are now coordinating their counterterrorist efforts with the United States. As a consequence, terrorism by small groups and lone wolves is becoming increasingly prevalent.

The Unipolar Era

The collapse of the Soviet Union ushered in a new era of global integration. Francis Fukuyama's 1989 article "The End of History?" presaged the coming zeitgeist. As he observed events around the world that year, governments were converging on a model of a free-market democracy. According to his analysis, all other ideologies had been effectively exhausted and discredited, and no credible alternatives remained. All that was left was mere fine-tuning.[5] Similarly, in 1990, on the cusp of the first Gulf War, Charles Krauthammer announced that the world had entered the "unipolar" era. Even before the collapse of the Soviet Union, he assumed that the Cold War was over and that the new era would be characterized by a period of US global hegemony. With this window of opportunity, he argued that the United States should establish a global order to its advantage. Krauthammer's article proved prescient when, the next year, President George H. W. Bush announced the emergence of a "new world order," suggesting a convergence of interests among the great powers of the world.[6] In the years afterward, the "new world order" came to imply unprecedented globalization, with the United States playing the leading role. Throughout the 1990s and beyond, the US military attained global preeminence, with the US defense budget roughly equivalent to the combined defense spending of the rest of the world. As the historian Paul Kennedy has observed, "There exists no equal in history to such a disproportionate share, even if we [go] back to the time of the Roman Empire."[7]

As the 1990s began, a new era of American triumphalism was foreseen, a period of unprecedented tranquillity and economic opportunity. With old-style Palestinian terrorism diminishing, in September 1993 a historic Middle East peace agreement was signed on the White House lawn. Even Middle Eastern countries that previously supported terrorism, such as Syria and Iran, retreated substantially from this tactic and no longer targeted the United States. Muammar Gaddafi, the most flamboyant Middle Eastern sponsor of terrorism during the 1980s, forswore his involvement in international terrorism and sought to cultivate the image of Libya as a reformed state ready to enter the community of nations.[8]

Still, conflict and terrorism did not disappear, and others began to express a less sanguine view of globalization, seeing disturbing trends antagonistic to democratization, namely the return of tribalism and violent religious fundamentalism. In 1993 US senator Patrick Moynihan saw the specter of violent ethnic conflict leading to "pandemonium" in various parts of the world.[9] That same year, the eminent Harvard professor Samuel Huntington introduced his "clash of civilizations" model of international relations, in which he asserted that conflict in the twenty-first century would be most pronounced along "civilizational fault lines." In his analysis, culture and cultural identities were "shaping the patterns of cohesion, disintegration, and conflict in the post–Cold War world." Especially worrisome to Huntington was the potential for violence emanating from the Islamic world. Huntington contended that Islam and the West had been engaged in a "quasi-war" for several years and were on a collision course.[10]

In the twenty-first century, in light of 9/11, some fear that history has returned and that the triumph of liberal democracy predicted by Fukuyama was merely an interlude between the Cold War and a new era characterized by civilizational and cultural conflict.[11] Some wonder if perhaps the West was not triumphant after all, but merely enjoying a respite before resuming its long-predicted decline. As the conservative commentator Patrick J. Buchanan pessimistically mused, "the end of history" may have been only a "temporary truce, a phony peace, an armistice, a time of transition from a day of Western dominance to a day when the West pays tribute."[12]

Fukuyama remained relatively optimistic about the future. As he noted, the influence of militant Islam is limited, with virtually no appeal to non-Muslims. Moreover, he sees no extant ideological alternatives to liberal democracy that could pose any serious challenge.[13] But Fareed Zakaria says that Fukuyama does not fully appreciate the threat that the United States and the new world order pose to militant Islam—a threat militant Muslims feel intensely. Zakaria posits that perhaps one side can restart history unilaterally.[14] In that vein, Norman Podhoretz, a prominent neoconservative theorist, characterized the 9/11 attacks as the opening salvo of World War IV.[15]

The Global War on Terror

The events of 9/11 put counterterrorism at the top of the national agenda. The government was strongly criticized in many quarters for its failure to anticipate and prepare for such a horrific eventuality, though the Clinton administration had actually given high priority to domestic terrorism. Throughout Clinton's tenure, a flurry of new antiterrorist laws were enacted, including the Anti-Terrorism and Effective Death Penalty Act of 1996, and related presidential directives were issued.[16] Funding for counterterrorism was substantially increased as well.[17] Much of the impetus for these efforts came from the perceived threat of domestic right-wing extremists and citizen militias. The 1995 bombing of the Murrah Federal Building in Oklahoma City was seen as a harbinger of further domestic terrorism. Although Clinton placed counterterrorism high on his agenda, the effort was mostly behind the scenes and he did not attempt any sustained public education on the issue. Consequently, when George W. Bush took office, there was little public or congressional pressure to respond to the threat posed by Osama bin Laden and al Qaeda.[18]

In the aftermath of 9/11, Congress called for more vigilant measures to root out potential terrorists at home and abroad.[19] To meet the challenge, President Bush issued several executive orders that, among other things, blocked terrorist financing, established an Office of Homeland Security, and allowed for the detention and trial of some noncitizens in military tribunals.[20] In 2003 the Department of Homeland Security was created, entailing the most thorough reorganization of the government bureaucracy since the creation of the Department of Defense in 1947. After the 9/11 attacks, Attorney General John Ashcroft and FBI Director Robert Mueller refocused the bureau's efforts on detecting terrorist plans and thwarting future attacks.[21] To that end, greater emphasis has been placed on intelligence collection and sharing.

Intelligence Sharing

Fundamental to new counterterrorist initiatives is improved intelligence gathering and analysis. The well-coordinated attacks of 9/11 showed a gaping hole in that area. The 9/11 Commission Report found that the government was structured to fight the Cold War, not to combat terrorism, and thus called for the creation of a national intelligence director to coordinate intelligence among all government agencies. Previously, a so-called firewall between the CIA and the FBI blocked most intelligence sharing, and there was a history of entrenched bureaucratic resentment and distrust between the two agencies.[22]

Some critics charge that the Clinton administration gave short shrift to intelligence.[23] Prior to 9/11, for example, the FBI was skittish about infiltrating mosques to collect intelligence on Islamic extremists lest the agency offend the sensibilities of Muslims.[24] Intelligence-gathering efforts in the United States were also constrained by the legacy of COINTELPRO, the FBI program to disrupt political dissident groups. Since 1976 the FBI has officially conducted surveillance of extremist and potentially violent groups under the attorney general's guidelines established after revelations of misconduct arising in COINTELPRO. Under these guidelines, the FBI could not investigate a suspected terrorist group without evidence of criminality. After 9/11, the Justice Department recalibrated this policy and relaxed its guidelines.[25] Augmenting these investigatory functions, government authorities increasingly prevail on private monitoring and intelligence-gathering organizations for information.[26]

The federal government increased intelligence sharing with foreign countries as well, seeking the cooperation of foreign governments to help track down suspected terrorists and their supporters. Shortly after 9/11, President Bush announced to the world, "Either you are with us or you are with the terrorists." The new nature of war has occasioned a shift in focus from traditional military invasions to the risk of infiltration of society by individuals.[27] Increasingly countries are more willing to share information from databases on suspected terrorists. Over the past several years, the United States has experienced many successes, as many al Qaeda operatives, including several senior-level leaders, have been captured in foreign countries. If the global war on terror is to succeed, international cooperation—most importantly with Pakistan—is crucial. The Pakistani military and the ISI have been implicated in supporting Islamist terrorism in the region and may have aided Osama bin Laden—a reasonable inference given his long residence at a safe house in Abbottabad, Pakistan, near prominent military installations. Nevertheless, there have been a number of arrests of high-profile terror suspects in Pakistan.[28]

Regarding greater interstate cooperation in the realm of intelligence since 9/11, General Michael V. Hayden, the former director of both the National Security Agency (NSA) and the CIA, was generally pleased the level of cooperation, as he explained to me:

It is an imperfect world and we are all part of the human condition, so nothing is perfect. But to a degree that I think would surprise many people, countries, even when the political discourse between them gets really chippy [belligerent], seem to continue deep intelligence cooperation. And I think there are reasons for that. One is that the people cooperating are professionals [and] are part of the permanent government. . . . Second, their states have great demands on them. . . . In many ways, the intelligence relationship between states has actually been the bedrock. It has remained stable, even when political relations have gone unstable.

So, by and large, there has been remarkable cooperation. [As] director of the CIA, in about thirty months, I visited about fifty countries. Certainly my deputy and I have visited about fifty countries and none of those were tourist stops. Those were all business trips. And by the way, a lot more than fifty [representatives of countries] came to visit us at Langley [Air Force Base]. So there was a lot of that kind of cooperation in a way that might surprise people.

One of the more challenging sets of relationships we had was with the Europeans. We simply viewed ourselves to be a nation at war. They viewed themselves not to be at war. In fact, they didn't agree with the concept that we were at war. And therefore there were limits sometimes on their cooperation. But by and large, there is an awful lot of work that goes on between intelligence services. They are friendly, and at least non-enemy.[29]

New technology has enhanced the government's ability to monitor potential terrorists and their supporters. Surveillance has become more pervasive and powerful on the ground and in orbit.[30] The Foreign Intelligence Surveillance Act of 1978 (FISA) permits intelligence gathering on US citizens within the country if they are suspected of engaging in, assisting, or agreeing to assist in international terrorism as agents of a foreign country.[31] Internet communications are frequently monitored. In 1999, the FBI began approaching Internet service providers and encouraging them to install a program called Carnivore, which can download all electronic transmissions flowing through servers, from e-mails, to website visits, chat room discussions, and more.[32] Reportedly, Carnivore's ability to track down Osama bin Laden's e-mail was critical in thwarting several of his planned strikes.[33] The pervasiveness of monitoring prompted Osama bin Laden to frequently change his location, thus inhibiting his operations. The global war on terror is treated as a military problem as well.

Military Action

The 9/11 terrorist attacks provoked a ferocious response from the US government. Initially there was broad-based sympathy for the United States, and many countries offered assistance, even if only symbolic, which provided tremendous legitimacy to US efforts to eradicate the Taliban and al Qaeda in Afghanistan. For the first time in its history, NATO invoked Article 5 of its charter, which stipulates that an attack on one member state should be considered an attack on all, and that all should assist a member state that has been attacked. Although Operation Enduring Freedom—the US government's name for the war in Afghanistan—has been mainly a US military effort, NATO countries have played a leading role in the stabilization and reconstruction phases of the mission. Moreover, for a few months after 9/11, AWACS (Airborne Warning and Control System) aircraft from NATO patrolled US skies.

Concerning the broader international community, the United States invoked Article 51 of the UN Charter, which states that member nations have the right to self-defense in response to an armed attack, but added that because an armed attack could also be launched by nonstate entities, a principle of state responsibility implied that a country was obligated to prevent terrorists from operating on its soil; otherwise it too could become a legitimate target. To bolster this claim, the Bush administration first demanded that the Taliban hand over Osama bin Laden and other parties responsible for the attacks on 9/11, and proceeded with military operations only after the Taliban refused. For the war effort, the United States entered into a number of bilateral agreements with individual countries, most critically Pakistan, whose cooperation was essential. Despite regional rivalries, Russia supported the US intervention by allowing the United States to use bases in the former Soviet republics in central Asia, over which it still exerted a strong influence. Middle Eastern governments helped out as well.[34] In sharp contrast to the Soviet invasion of Afghanistan in 1979, which was met with a call for jihad from the Muslim world, Operation Enduring Freedom was met with a "deafening silence," as the noted Middle East studies professor Fawaz Gerges put it.[35] No prominent Muslim clerics declared a defensive jihad.

In a speech delivered not long after 9/11, Bush reinforced the doctrine of self-defense to fit the contemporary world. He announced that the United States would make no distinction between countries that sponsored terrorism and those that harbored terrorists. By doing so, he implied that he would be willing to use military action against countries in which terrorists resided. This sea change in foreign policy prodded governments in the Middle East to cooperate with US authorities, and they began handing over terrorists and providing intelligence leads.[36]

Fresh from a successful first phase of Operation Enduring Freedom, by April 2002 President Bush began to publicly call for a policy of regime change in Iraq. By June 2002 he announced that he would launch preemptive strikes against those countries believed to pose a serious threat to the United States. Furthermore, he added that the United States would be willing to take unilateral action if support from the United Nations and traditional allies was not forthcoming. This approach, which would later be dubbed "the Bush Doctrine," caused considerable consternation from some in Bush's cabinet, most notably Secretary of State Colin Powell, who worried that a military operation against Iraq could destabilize the whole Middle East. However, the hawks in the administration carried the day.[37]

Ultimately President Bush became convinced that a strategy of preemption was necessary. Two factors featured prominently in this: first, the prospect of another massive surprise attack similar to 9/11; and second, the proliferation of weapons of mass destruction adding to the potential lethality of future terrorism. If these two factors converged in the hands of terrorists or a rogue state, the United States could be on the receiving end of terrorism of unprecedented magnitude.[38] Public opinion also helped the Bush administration in the days leading up to the Iraq War. A *Washington Post* poll found that approximately 70 percent of Americans surveyed believed that Saddam Hussein had a role in the 9/11 attacks.[39]

International support was less forthcoming for the US invasion of Iraq. The Bush policy of preemption was seen by many in the international community as an overreach of authority. At first the Bush administration pursued a unilateral approach, but then, encouraged by Colin Powell, it decided to internationalize the issue by taking it to the United Nations. Powell made his case there, but the United Nations failed to authorize military action. Instead, after long negotiations, it adopted Resolution 1441, which determined that Iraq was in material breach of the 1991 ceasefire terms and would face "serious consequences" if it failed to comply fully. Despite these efforts, the Bush administration failed to secure extensive international support. Although the international community was unable to restrain the United States, it nevertheless denied it legitimacy. All the same, the administration sought to create the impression of a large and diverse "coalition of the willing," which totaled forty-one countries, the majority of which offered little more than permission to put their names on the list.[40]

In March 2003 the Bush administration finally launched its military campaign against Saddam Hussein, dubbed Operation Iraqi Freedom. After just a few weeks of battle, US and coalition troops won a decisive victory despite pockets of fierce Iraqi resistance. Elation was short-lived, however, as a loose collection of former members of the ruling Baath Party, foreign fighters, elements of al Qaeda, and regular Iraqi citizens bent on revenge and restoring national honor coalesced to wage a guerrilla war of resistance. By the summer of 2003, Iraq appeared to have emerged as the pivotal theater in the war on terror.

Arguably, the war in Iraq diverted resources away from the fight against al Qaeda in Afghanistan and intensified the appeal of global jihad. Opposition to the Iraq War prevented numerous countries from shouldering the burden with the United States in the struggle against terrorism. Nevertheless, there was still a considerable collective effort to combat terrorism since many countries perceived al Qaeda as a serious threat to international order.[41]

Interstate Cooperation

Although terrorism was on the international agenda prior to 9/11, there was not a strong sense of urgency about it. Immediately afterward, there were several international measures taken to strengthen international counterterrorism efforts. The day after the 9/11 attacks, the UN Security Council passed Resolution 1368, which unequivocally condemned the attacks as a threat to international peace and security and expressed the readiness of the United Nations to combat all forms of terrorism. On September 28, 2001, the UN General Assembly adopted Resolution 1373, which condemned terrorism and called for increased cooperation to combat it. The United Nations also designed a "Global Programme against Terrorism" under its Office of Drugs and Crime. The thrust of the program was to criminalize terrorism and its financing, and to encourage interstate cooperation bilaterally, regionally, and internationally. To monitor and assist implementation, the Security Council established the Counterterrorism Committee (CTC), with one representative from each of the council's fifteen members. The World Bank and the International Monetary Fund assisted the CTC in these efforts as well. In addition, the International Treaty for the Suppression of Terrorism Financing, initially adopted by the UN General Assembly in December 1999, was strengthened. Not to be left out, Arab governments increased regulation of alternative remittance systems based on trust, such as the *hawala* system. Furthermore, charities came under greater regulation and scrutiny, some of them having been implicated in commingling funds with terrorist groups. This action was remarkable, considering the politically sensitive nature of the issue in the Islamic world.[42]

Other international bodies besides the United Nations condemned the 9/11 attacks and outlined recommendations to confront the newly perceived threat. Besides NATO invoking Article 5 of its charter for the first time, the Organization of American States (OAS) adopted a resolution on September 21, 2001, calling for members to take effective measures to prevent terrorist groups from operating within their territories. Moreover, the ministers of the OAS Permanent Council began drafting a hemispheric antiterrorism treaty and planned to convene a meeting of the Inter-American Committee against Terrorism (CICTE).[43]

Traditionally the thrust of US counterterrorism policy has been to work with allies to apply economic sanctions against state sponsors.[44] The Export Administration Act of 1979 has been important in this regard. Those countries that resist the United States run the risk of economic sanctions—a substantial threat. There is evidence suggesting that economic sanctions may cause more damage and pain that the use of violent force.[45] Because of their enormous political and economic influence, member nations of the G8 (Group of Eight) acting together can effectively punish countries believed to sponsor terrorism.[46]

One of the most worrisome aspects of contemporary terrorism is the prospect of a radical group obtaining a WMD. Osama bin Laden unequivocally stated his intention to acquire weapons of mass destruction to supplement his capabilities. Reportedly, al Qaeda attempted several times to acquire WMD, including nuclear weapons, albeit without success. Al Qaeda's previous large-scale acts of terrorism suggest that the group would have no compunction about using WMD. Prior to 9/11 there were a number of antiproliferation treaties, including the Chemical Warfare Convention, the Biological Weapons Convention, and the Nuclear Non-

Proliferation Treaty, all of which gained greater salience after the attacks. After seven years of negotiation, the United Nations established the International Convention for the Suppression of Acts of Nuclear Terrorism. Bilateral action was also taken. For example, the 1991 Soviet Nuclear Threat Reduction Act (later renamed the Cooperative Threat Reduction Program), which sought to secure loose weapons and stores of fissile materials from the former Soviet Union, was improved in the aftermath of 9/11 and led to the creation of the G8 Global Partnership against the Spread of Weapons and Materials of Mass Destruction.[47] And in May 2003 the Bush administration announced another multilateral agreement—the Proliferation Security Initiative—to combat the transportation of WMD.[48]

The war on terror created new opportunities in US foreign relations, including new possibilities for US dialogue and cooperation with China and Russia in security areas, since both have an interest in quelling Islamic radicalism.[49] For many years Russia has been involved with the jihadist struggle, first in Afghanistan in the 1980s, and then, since the early 1990s, fighting Muslim separatists in the breakaway republic of Chechnya. After the Beslan school massacre in September 2004, the Russian conflict with jihadism intensified. But there are still several factors that work against greater cooperation between Russia and the United States in the global war on terror, though both countries are targeted by jihadist forces and so share an interest in combating radical Islam.[50] Although Russia has had little success in political and economic unification with the Commonwealth of Independent States, it has succeeded in the realm of security cooperation with newer organizations with narrower membership and more closely defined goals. In 2001, for example, Russia and its most loyal allies in central Asia—Kyrgyzstan, Tajikistan, and Uzbekistan—joined the new Shanghai Cooperation Organization (SCO) with China, a country that confronts a potential jihadist challenge in the form of a separatist movement in its Uygur province of the Xinjiang region.[51] The SCO was originally conceived as a coordinating body to deal primarily with the problems of "terrorism, separatism, and political extremism" in central Asian, focusing primarily on the Taliban and, by extension, al Qaeda.[52] In the summer of 2007, Russian, Chinese, and central Asian forces took part in joint maneuvers against a notional terrorist enemy.[53]

Although initially reluctant to fully support the global war on terror led by the United States, countries such as Saudi Arabia, Indonesia, and Morocco finally joined the effort with enthusiasm after suffering from spectacular terrorist operations. At first leaders of these countries denied they had a problem with native-bred terrorism on their own soil, but they now are arresting and prosecuting home-grown mujahideen. The crackdown by Western and Saudi banking authorities and Arab states on private contributions further diminishes the resources of terrorists.[54]

In military interventions, cooperation has been mixed. While many countries offered assistance to the US military effort in Afghanistan, support was far less forthcoming for the 2003 invasion of Iraq. In order to sustain a global war on terror, the United States must forge a multilateral coalition to support military interventions. Although the US military is formidable in fighting conventional wars, it has difficulty winning peace once major combat operations are over. Furthermore, it is difficult to sustain the domestic political support necessary to keep US troops deployed in conflict zones for long.[55]

Contributions from allies—including military personnel—are necessary to sustain the global war on terror (sometimes dubbed "the long war"). In his book *Combating Jihadism: American Hegemony and Interstate Cooperation in the War on Terrorism*, Barak Mendelsohn argues that when faced with a threat to the international order, states come together to meet the challenge. A drive for self-preservation facilitates interstate cooperation, not unlike how threatened people bond within states. The role of the world hegemon is of vital importance in setting the international agenda and taking the lead in preserving order. Yet, as Mendelsohn points out, interstate cooperation is not automatic. Rather it requires a consensual understanding that societies are under attack worldwide, coupled with an articulation of strategies and policies consistent with recognized international principles. Internationally, nonhegemon states combined provide a normative framework that restricts the hegemon's actions. Although the hegemon may be tempted to act unilaterally, when it does so against the desires and norms of a large number of other states, cooperation tends to falter, as evidenced by the US experience in Iraq. Opposition to the Iraq War prevented numerous countries from shouldering the burden in Iraq with the United States.

Despite differences over Iraq, governments after 9/11 have increased coordination of their counterterrorist efforts. This development has made it more difficult for traditional terrorist networks to operate. Increasingly the United States is promoting an international agenda that seeks to create a less hospitable world for terrorism. For instance, suppliers of nuclear technology to terrorist-harboring states are hit with sanctions. Moreover, countries that support international terrorism face diplomatic isolation and economic and military sanctions. To this end, financial assets of terrorists and their supporters are sometimes frozen in the West. Greater intelligence sharing between the United States and its allies disrupts terrorists' ability to operate. More effective surveillance hinders terrorists and aids in the apprehension, arrest, and conviction of terrorism suspects. Finally, there is more shared training and cooperation between allied militaries and law enforcement officials, especially special forces, to counter the terrorist threat.[56]

The 9/11 attacks prompted an international effort to eradicate terrorism. As a consequence, large terrorist groups are on the defensive as governments coordinate efforts to dismantle them, and they are increasingly vulnerable to disruption. However, small groups and lone wolves are still able to mount terrorist operations. Despite the enormous progress in international cooperation, some aspects of the contemporary world redound to the favor of oppositional and terrorist groups, including the Internet, the new media, enhanced information technology, and new models of organization.

CHAPTER 5

The Wiki Revolution
and the New People Power

Recent technological developments have transformed organizational models and methods of collaboration. The Internet is at the center of the ongoing revolution in communications, enabling new forms of organization and greater dissemination of information. Prior to the Internet, physical proximity usually determined one's associates, but now people are linked across great distances and national borders.[1] Over two billion people worldwide now have Internet access, and when they organize, they tend to do so by affinity. The communities of affinity forged through the Internet build a sense of collective identity, resulting in "virtual communities" not unlike the "imagined communities" Benedict Anderson wrote about in his study on nationalism.[2] Like-minded dissidents, who previously had a difficult time finding one another, can now form groups more easily.[3] New communications technologies have greatly reduced transmission time and costs, while substantially increasing the complexity and scope of the information that can be shared.[4]

The origins of the Internet go back to 1964, when the US Defense Department began experimenting with a new computer network based on "digital packet messaging."[5] Over the years, the network it pioneered grew slowly but steadily. By 1971 there were twenty-three hosts, and ten years later eight hundred.[6] By 2010 the network included an estimated 769 million hosts.[7] In 2011, an estimated 2.1 billion people around the world used the Internet.[8] Accompanying this trend have been improvements in the technical qualities of computers, which have enhanced the Internet's capabilities.

The Internet offers several advantages for political activists, including decentralization and ease of access. It represents many communications breakthroughs in a single medium.[9] As a result, it empowers dissident movements in a number of ways. First, it allows greater interconnectivity, the power to communicate and network with far more people and more quickly than ever before. Second, it enables covert communication and anonymity. Third, Internet access is inexpensive, thus increasing its availability. Fourth, the Internet allows dissidents to circumvent restrictions on speech and avoid censorship.[10] The communications revolution has empowered individuals, making it possible to move money, products, information, and ideas across borders, previously done mostly by governments and big corporations.[11] Of course, the Internet can also be used by terrorists to disseminate propaganda, communicate, raise money, and plan and coordinate operations.

New Models of Organization

In his classic study *The Logic of Collective Action* (1965), Mancur Olson argued that group formation is difficult because potential members find little incentive to join. According to Olson, rational individuals weigh the costs and benefits of creating and joining associations. Initially, the costs of membership and participation usually exceed tangible benefits, making collective action problematic.[12] When benefits are widely diffused, a free-rider problem also sometimes inheres in the process of group formation: why should individuals join if they will receive collective benefits whether they join or not? Those who form groups must find ways to surmount these problems.

Since there are a plethora of interest groups, clearly there must be ways to overcome the challenges of forming them.[13] Traditionally, the powerful, affluent, and well-connected have had a decided advantage in group formation, but new communications technologies have lowered the cost of organizing and have made it possible for people to more easily pool resources.[14] It is also easier for people to cooperate and collaborate outside traditional institutions and organizations.[15] New networks and communications tools enable people to act together in ways not possible before.[16]

The Internet's significant reduction of transaction costs has facilitated interest group formation as well. Ronald H. Coase first expounded on the concept of transaction costs in a 1937 article, "The Nature of the Firm." He found that vertically integrated firms combined many tasks in their production process because it was cheaper to do them in-house. Information costs also discouraged managers from working more with other firms. With the new technology, however, it is often cheaper to get things done outside the organization.[17] What is more, new social tools make possible serious, complex work that can be done by "loosely structured groups, operating without managerial direction and outside the profit motive."[18]

But just how viable are online networks? One might intuit that with electronic interaction a real sense of togetherness is lacking compared with physical meetings, as well as the trust, solidarity, and sense of shared purpose necessary to sustain political and social movements. However, the psychologists John A. Bargh and Katelyn Y. A. McKenna found that the intensity of online relationships can rival those developed offline.[19] For example, reputational management, or social filtering systems, support new forms of broad-based cooperation, such as the online auction house eBay, whose users can rate transactions with other users.[20]

The communications revolution can be exploited by terrorists in making possible new forms of organizations. Throughout most of the twentieth century, terrorists embraced centralization and the leadership principle.[21] Ted Robert Gurr looked at the organizational structure of terrorist groups and found that in most instances large groups were successful in launching lengthy terrorist campaigns but small groups were usually unsuccessful. Historically, most terrorist groups have been small and ephemeral because they failed to generate broad support, and conventional wisdom was that in order to have a major effect, terrorist groups had to be large. According to Gurr, groups became large because they embraced popular issues and had mass appeal.[22]

Developing a viable terrorist group is no easy task. Its leaders have special organizational problems. First, they must communicate within an infrastructure of secrecy, which typically prevents good communication. Although decentralization allows autonomy, it makes coordination more difficult because the group must always be on guard for informants, which is the most important factor leading to the arrest of terrorists.[23] Further, terrorist groups must maintain internal discipline, or they risk fragmentation. Finally, terrorist groups must consider logistics and have active supporters.[24] As the terrorism scholar Jessica Stern pointed out, mobilizing terrorist recruits and supporters requires an effective organization with resources and logistical plans or procedures. The organization must have a mission with enough appeal to attract a sizable number of recruits and financial backers.[25] No matter how acute or widespread popular disaffections are, the masses do not rise spontaneously. They require mobilization.[26]

Chris Anderson, editor in chief of *Wired* magazine, developed the concept of the "long tail" to explain how new Internet platforms, such as Amazon, enable firms to employ a niche marketing strategy in which they can sell large volumes of unique items to a larger number of customers instead of selling only a lesser variety of popular items in large quantities. The major reason for this is because the Internet lets customers choose from a vast number of products.[27] The long-tail operation makes it easier for a highly specialized company to be viable and enter a market without having a locally concentrated customer base. The same principle can be applied to insurgency and terrorism. Because of new technology, a large popular following is no longer necessary for a terrorist group to survive over time. A small number of geographically dispersed people can share an extremist cause without broad popular appeal, thus making niche terrorism possible.[28]

By the 1990s, terrorism analysts began to talk of a new type of terrorism in which the actors were less organizationally structured and more fluid in their operations. Like-minded extremists formed ad hoc conspiracies, and lone wolves committed some of the most lethal acts of terrorism.[29] Without traditional leadership structures, amorphous, mission-driven organizations having no center of gravity are difficult to target. The ideologies that motivate such movements can be broadly conceived to appeal to potential followers who can act on their own volition.[30]

The Internet has enabled the creation of virtual organizations, allowing like-minded people to find information about particular ideologies. The organizational ties among these people are often tenuous, but people discovering information can be recruited by an actual group through connections made on the Internet. So-called all-channel networks are collaborative arrangements wherein individuals and small groups are all connected. Historically, the all-channel network has been difficult to sustain because it required dense communications. With the information revolution, however, this style of network has been gaining strength.[31] Often autonomous and self-sufficient, all-channel networks are too dispersed for authorities and opponents to destroy in one fell swoop. Moreover, because members come from a wide range of backgrounds, a movement can better recruit from different segments of the population. The multiplicity of varied groups allows for a division and specialization among them and a greater adaptation to circumstances. Because different groups apply a variety of approaches, the movement is able to learn from those that fail, thus enhancing the reliability of the movement's system.[32]

New research suggests that decentralized networks can be viable. In their book *The Starfish and the Spider: The Unstoppable Power of Leaderless Organizations*, Ori Brafman and Rod A. Beckstrom identify various decentralized networks that have prevailed despite efforts to destroy them, such as the Apache Indians, the al Qaeda network, the Animal Liberation Front, and music sharers on the Internet. By their very nature, decentralized networks are resilient when attacked.[33] Brafman and Beckstrom use the metaphor of the starfish, which when cut in half grows into two starfish. Since it has no brain—no "central command"—the starfish can continue to function and replicate. This contrasts with a spider, which can be rendered helpless if it loses one of its appendages. So-called spider organizations are characterized by hierarchy and have physical headquarters. "Starfish organizations," in contrast, have autonomous circles that work toward common goals. With the growing popularity of the Internet, the barriers to creating such circles have been dramatically lowered. Because these circles are virtual, they are amorphous and difficult to identify and target. What holds them together are shared norms that develop, as members spend more time interacting with one another and develop trust.[34] Knowledge and an egalitarian ethos suffuse these organizations.

Behind the most successful virtual circles, Brafman and Beckstrom observe, is a catalyst, a leader who has the vision to guide it, more through inspiration than by diktat. They identify Osama bin Laden as having been an exemplar in this regard and argue that he became powerful because he never took a traditional leadership role. Circles usually do not form on their own, so it is necessary for a leader to develop an idea, share it with others, and lead by emotion and example. Catalysts usually know many people and are skilled at making connections and bringing people together who would not otherwise meet. Essentially, they provide the drumbeat for organizations. They assume a peer relationship with their following and tend to lead by inspiration rather than coercion. Crucial in holding the decentralized circle together is a shared ideology.[35] Shared narrative and doctrine enable such networks to maintain their sense of cohesion and purpose.[36]

The egalitarian nature of the Internet allows people to have a greater voice and communicate directly with others around the globe. The longer people have used the Internet, the more likely they are to participate in social-capital-building activities.[37] Technology has leveraged persons within organizations, thus allowing them to make change easier than in the past.[38] These technological trends enable enhanced international collaboration.

Collaboration

The Internet has enabled mass collaboration globally. The online encyclopedia *Wikipedia*, for example, demonstrates how thousands of dispersed volunteers can create a fast, fluid, and innovative product that can outperform some of the largest and best-financed enterprises.[39] One of the reasons *Wikipedia* works is that everyone is free to start an article. And because it is easier to get someone to add to a project once it has been started, it is not necessary to have experts write the initial articles. The number of people who are willing to start a project is much smaller than the number of people who are willing to contribute once it has been created.[40]

Mass collaboration has its genesis in the open source movement in software. In 1986, Linus Torvalds envisaged an operating system that could be available to anyone. Users would be permitted to modify it, with the proviso that they not license it or restrict its use. That year, the Linux operating system was created by a collaborative effort of numerous independent programmers.[41] Effective peer production mixes elements of hierarchy with self-organization and relies on meritocratic principles of organization, in that the most skilled and experienced members of a community provide leadership and facilitate contributions from others in the community.[42] The community provides a context within which incentives exist, as members identify talent and evaluate their output. Behind the most successful "crowdsourcing" efforts is a collaborative effort between the crowd and highly motivated individuals who guide them.[43]

The desire to create and collaborate is not new, but new technology makes it much easier for people to connect and work on common endeavors. Crowdsourcing taps into a deep-seated desire of humans to interact. In previous epochs, the knowledge and talent dispersed around the world always outstripped the capacity of humans to harness those invaluable qualities. As a consequence, much talent "wither[ed] on the vine for want of an outlet." Crowdsourcing enables talent and knowledge to be matched with those who need it. An exponential rise in the level of education worldwide implies that there are now many more talented people than ever before.[44] A mechanism for distributing all that knowledge has emerged through the Internet. Many people feel that their talents are underused in their jobs. Collaboration is one way to alleviate this feeling.[45]

Why do members of a community contribute? Basically, because they enjoy it, feel passionate about a particular issue, and revel in the idea of creating something of value.[46] Moreover, there are also benefits in feelings of solidarity, as many people feel a deep commitment to their communities of affinity.[47]

Creativity is bolstered when it is the work of many hands.[48] In his popular book *The Wisdom of Crowds*, James Surowiecki identified the conditions under which collaborative minds could solve complex problems. First, participants must be drawn from a large pool to ensure a diverse array of approaches. Second, the participants must exercise independence and not have their opinions determined by the opinions of those around them. Third, there must be decentralization, meaning that the individuality, or "local knowledge," of participants must not be impaired. Finally, there must be some method of aggregating and processing each individual contribution.[49] Similarly, as Don Tapscott and Anthony D. Williams observed, "peering" works when tasks can be broken down into small pieces so that individuals can contribute increments independently of other producers. The costs of assembling those pieces into the finished product, including providing the quality-control mechanisms, must be low.[50]

New tools based on community, collaboration, and self-organization are changing the ways in which things are created and undermining hierarchical lines of authority. The growing accessibility of information and technology puts tools into the hands of people all over the world who are now capable of collaborating on a truly global scale. As Tapscott and Williams note in their book *Wikinomics: How Mass Collaboration Changes Everything*, we are entering an era in which productive capability will be more dispersed than ever before. As a consequence, creation will be fast, fluid, and persistently disruptive. In such a world, "only the connected will survive." As they see it, the new art and science of "wikinomics" is based on four ideas—openness, "peering," sharing, and acting globally.[51] Such trends presage a decline in hierarchies, though they will not altogether disappear.

An example of crowdsourcing is the so-called Anonymous group linked to numerous episodes of Internet "hacktivism." Anonymous, which is essentially leaderless, can be traced back to 2003 with the launch of the imageboard (a type of Internet forum devoted to the posting of images) known as "4chan," which became linked to various hacktivist subcultures. Members maintain online anonymity while performing acts of civil disobedience, with the primary goal of promoting Internet freedom. With increasing notoriety, the concept of Anonymous as a collective of unnamed individuals became an Internet meme.[52] In July 2011, twenty or more arrests of suspected Anonymous hackers were made in the United States, the United Kingdom, and the Netherlands following "Operation Avenge Assange." The group attacked PayPal, MasterCard, and Visa after they froze the accounts of WikiLeaks, a Website created by the embattled Australian journalist Julian Paul Assange that publishes secret information.[53]

Crowdsourcing can be applied to insurgency and terrorism as well. In his study *Brave New War: The Next Stage of Terrorism and the End of Globalization*, John Robb, a US counterterrorism operation planner and former air force officer, presages an open source style of warfare based on networks, not unlike those that predominate in the software industry.[54] In open source efforts, the collective weight of the volunteers exceeds that of contributions from any individual, company, or group of companies. Similarly, in the realm of insurgency, a seemingly simple operation such as an attack using an improvised explosive device (IED) often requires a division of labor consisting of a financier, a bomb maker, an "emplacer," and a "triggerman."[55] Robb expounded on his theory of "open-source" warfare:

An open source movement has a process structure. It has a unifying ideal. Plus there are lots of interactions, coordination, a lot of sharing of technique and capability. . . . To a certain extent, there is a leadership cadre, but they just offer broad strategic guidance. Al Qaeda is operated pretty much on an open source basis. You have the leadership group. They offer strategic advice, they give moral credibility. They set the objectives and the plausible promise of the group. And occasionally they move that plausible promise forward by making attacks. They mount their own, but they are relatively infrequent. Everything else is done at the periphery.

So, to an extent, it's not totally leaderless. It's just a different kind of organizational type. I've never really seen a truly leaderless organization. . . .

There's a whole methodology associated with how the tactics are developed [and] how they are shared. And it actually translates into the technology realm with "tinkering" networks. Tinkering is a kind of open source activity. . . .

IED manufacturing, the techniques, and everything else is done on a tinkering basis. People come up with new methodologies. And then people call each other to ask questions about how to do stuff. They post methodologies on the web, even video instruction. And while some of those methodologies are wrong, there is a kind of "wisdom of crowds" effect. The community points everyone to the right stuff. So tinkering is a kind of technology development parallel to the organizational structure.[56]

Related to Robb's open source warfare, new swarming tactics could become increasingly prevalent as an operational approach as well.

Swarming Tactics and the Antiglobalization Movement

In 1999 two Rand Corporation researchers, John Arquilla and David Ronfeldt, predicted that the old hierarchical structures of terrorist groups would give way to flatter organizations that would be more network based, enabled by new information technology. Relatedly, they referred to "swarming" as an operational innovation whereby dispersed nodes of a network of forces might converge on a target quickly from multiple directions to accomplish a task, then disperse immediately until the next "pulse" or operation.[57] Arquilla and Ronfeldt identified swarming as a form of "netwar," which they defined as "an emerging mode of conflict (and crime) at societal levels, short of traditional military warfare, in which the protagonists use network forms of organization and related doctrines, strategies, and technologies attuned to the information age."[58] What distinguishes netwar from previous forms of conflict is the networked organization of the belligerents. Many of the groups are leaderless, yet their members are able to combine in swarming attacks.[59] The emergence of so-called amateur terrorism is related to the spread of information technologies that give dispersed groups and individuals the ability to conspire and coordinate attacks across considerable distances.[60] The Zapatista movement in Mexico, for instance, has employed a form of netwar. Reaching out to a range of NGOs, it has impelled the Mexican government to call a halt to military operations on several occasions.[61] Swarming is most effective when it is designed around the deployment of small, dispersed, and networked maneuverable units.[62]

The Internet facilitates swarming in several ways. For example, in the fall of 1999, diverse elements of the antiglobalization movement converged in Seattle and disrupted important meetings of the World Trade Organization (WTO). Through the Internet, various groups and activists were able to coordinate their efforts and swarm, or come together. Much of the cohesion stemmed from improvised communications, including cell phones, radios, police scanners, and portable computers. Employing this hardware, activists were able to access continuously updated web pages and other sources that gave reports from the street. In part, the WTO protests succeeded because of a combination of strategic surprise and tactical openness. The "Battle of Seattle" was fought not only in the streets but also in the so-called infosphere.[63]

During the demonstrations, the "Black Bloc"—a loose coalition of anarchists, legitimate demonstrators, and opportunist criminals—was able to come together for short-term activism. The police were not prepared for this type of postmodern, networked conflict.[64] The main organizer of street activity was the Direct Action Network (DAN), whose members provided a nucleus of blockades around which crowd actions were directed. Another major actor was organized labor, mainly the AFL-CIO (American Federation of Labor and Congress of Industrial Organizations), an institution with a top-down leadership structure. Although its main body had no interest in joining with DAN, after a few days of protests there was spillover from union crowds into DAN's street action. Whereas the AFL-CIO had planned on holding a march in downtown Seattle to bring attention to its labor concerns, DAN and other like-minded activist groups sought to shut down the WTO meetings altogether by enclosing the conference site.[65]

The actions in Seattle demonstrated that the political Left had adopted swarming tactics and formulated its own version of leaderless resistance. Two leading proponents, the Italian Marxist Antonio Negri and the Duke University professor Michael Hardt, theorize that "autonomist Marxism" can serve as a model for overthrowing the global capitalist system.[66] Rather than the masses of workers acting in unison in revolt, as Lenin and Mao prophesied, Negri and Hardt argue that a patchwork of autonomous "multitudes" can effectively oppose the current capitalist version of globalization and replace it with an alternative globalization based on socialism.[67] Variegated protest groups—anarchists, environmentalists, and working-class laborers—can organize against a common foe. Although they may lack a single leader, organizational hierarchy, and common ideology, they are nonetheless held together by a shared opposition to the current process of globalization, as evidenced by the Seattle protests.[68]

As Negri and Hardt see it, for the first time in history democracy is possible on a global scale. The main threat they see to such a proposition is a perennial global state of war, which they argue is incompatible with democracy as it places severe demands on citizens and leads to curtailment of civil liberties and infringement of rights.[69] Although the United States is currently in a hegemonic position, Negri and Hardt argue that it cannot continue to operate unilaterally, hence the growing trend of multilateralism, albeit sometimes under US direction. The cost of unilateral wars is too much even for the United States to bear. As Negri and Hardt explain, the network they endeavor to develop is democratic and seeks to build a freer, more egalitarian global order, in contrast to other contemporary distributed networks, such as al Qaeda, that retain a strict hierarchical core and central command and control, and whose goals are to resuscitate old regional social and political bodies under a religious authority.[70]

Negri and Hardt maintain that the multitude, despite myriad differences, can find commonality, work together to attain democracy, and create an alternative globalization. Whereas previous revolutionary movements were led by vanguard parties with centralized leadership, they argue that a new networked "movement of movements" can successfully effect change. Negri and Hardt cite the 1999 protests in Seattle as the embryonic display of this model. A variety of movements, groups, and activists came together to oppose the "neoliberal" orientation of the global economic order sometimes referred to as the Washington Consensus.[71] Antiglobalization activists created their own Independent Media Centers (Indymedia) in cities where major protests occurred.[72] By exploiting new forms of communication, such Indymedia activists can break the information monopoly of the traditional corporate media and become actively involved in the production of information.[73] Increasingly, dissident and terrorist groups are also taking advantage of the new media.

The New Media

Previously in the unipolar era, the United States was thought to have a near monopoly on soft power, which Joseph Nye referred to as the ability to determine the framework of the debate in international affairs.[74] However, the popularity of the Internet has led to a diffusion of soft power around the world. As of 2011, the global penetration rate of the Internet was estimated to be 30.2 percent of the population.[75] Extremist and terrorist groups are now exploiting the new media and youth culture as powerful recruitment tools to communicate their views and incite violence. On web portals such as YouTube, people can bypass the mainstream media and post videos themselves, making them directly available to all.[76] The new participatory culture has pervaded the media, as consumers are increasingly interacting with each other to produce a greater "collective intelligence."[77]

The new media developed concomitant with Web 2.0, which arose after the dot-com bubble burst in 2000. Out of the rubble, a new crop of web-based companies and services emerged that offered interactivity and "user-generated content," ushering in a new era of communications that allowed much greater and broader participation from users, not only in commerce and social networking but in terrorism and insurgency as well.[78] Web servers are now often used to create platforms where people can co-create their own services, communities, and experiences.[79] Bloggers post news items from other sources, links of interests, and personal commentary on websites.[80] Although most blogs lack the quality and prominence of commercial media, they nevertheless point to the increasing ease with which individuals can create their own news and entertainment and bypass established sources.[81] There has been a transfer of these creative capabilities from professional classes to the general public.[82] In this sense, culture is returning to an earlier period, before the advent of the mass media, when it was primarily created at the grassroots level.[83]

The Internet is blurring the difference between news providers and news consumers. The new media allow far more amateur participants to contribute to the generation of news stories. Some new media platforms even rival those of the traditional media in size, and offer inspiration and research sources for journalists.[84] Activists, with little formal coordination, can have a big impact, as evidenced by the case in which bloggers brought attention to the errors of a *60 Minutes* program, broadcast during the 2004 presidential election campaign, involving President George W. Bush's service in the Texas Air National Guard.[85] No longer does a writer have to go through a gatekeeper to reach readers. Furthermore, the web has drastically reduced the cost of publishing globally. With costs of production and distribution now minimal, amateurs can and do operate as journalists. All these factors have led to a huge increase in broadcasting and narrowcasting capability. Arguably, not since the invention of the printing press by Johannes Gutenberg has there been such a revolution in the media.[86]

Increasingly there is cross-fertilization between the old media (e.g., major television networks and the press) and the new media (e.g., YouTube, MySpace, and Facebook). In his book *Convergence Culture: Where Old and New Media Collide*, Henry Jenkins argues that the new media will not supplant old media. Rather, a synthesis will emerge. Today there is a flow of content across multiple media platforms. In old media, control was largely centralized, and since the 1980s there has been greater consolidation and concentration, with fewer gatekeepers. But the digital revolution has led to a democratization of the media. We are now in an era of transition, with digitization providing the conditions of convergence.[87] A dialectic between the old and new media is under way, in which consumers increasingly participate, contributing and modifying content. Prior to the Internet, newspapers essentially spoke directly to their audience in monologue. In contrast, today many newspaper websites offer the opportunity for conversation among readers.[88] Just as radio did not destroy the print media, so television did not destroy radio.[89] Convergence implies a change in the way media are produced and consumed.

The expansion of media was an important factor in the rise of terrorism in the 1970s.[90] Contemporary terrorism gained prominence in the media age that allowed the more widespread dissemination of news around the world. Today media products created by major networks can be recycled and refashioned to fit the designs of dissident groups. For example, local affiliates supplement al Qaeda central and combine archival material with local content. Groups as varied as Hezbollah, Hamas, the Liberation Tigers of Tamil Eelam (LTTE), the Shining Path of Peru, and White Aryan Resistance have propaganda videos on YouTube. The increased availability of sophisticated, inexpensive video-making tools and interactive online network platforms has revolutionized terrorists' online communications.[91] The democratization of the media has empowered many people who previously would not have had a voice in the marketplace of ideas. Moreover, there are now flexible communications tools available that allow new ways of coordinating collective action outside traditional institutions and organizations.[92] But social networking platforms are not without perils for terrorist groups, as portals such as Facebook can provide a trove of information for monitoring agencies, though jurisdictional and constitutional limits on what can be retrieved are not legally clear. To date, most social networking sites have cooperated with federal officials requesting emergency access to information.[93]

In their study *War 2.0: Irregular Warfare in the Information Age*, Thomas Rid and Marc Hecker examine the intersection of technology and insurgency. Two contemporaneous trends—the growing popularity of the World Wide Web and the rise of insurgencies—are shaping the course of modern warfare. As they observed, military research once spurred new media technologies, such as radio, television, and the Internet, but that asymmetry has been reversed. Now the new media shape contemporary warfare. New technology has increased the options for irregular forces more so than for governments and their armies, but in counterintuitive ways. Rid and Hecker find a reversal of historic trends. First, regular armies engaged in counterinsurgency operations are refining the use of modern information technology for *external* purposes, to reach local populations in theaters of operations and win their hearts and minds. In contrast, insurgents are increasingly using the Internet for *internal* purposes, to communicate with fellow irregulars. Still, insurgents and their supporters have become increasingly sophisticated in getting out their side of the story. New podcasting capabilities enable amateurs to record and disseminate graphic battlefield images. In sum, recent innovations in information technology have leveled the playing field for irregular forces.[94]

Modern technology facilitates leaderless resistance in a number of ways. For instance, the Internet can serve as a conduit for information flow, which enhances recruiting. Moreover, increasingly secure communications, strengthened through such methods as encryption, free e-mail accounts, Internet Relay Chat, steganography, anonymous remailers, and web-based bulletin boards, make it potentially more difficult to link messages with an individual, thus enhancing operational security.[95] Through Internet gathering points such as chat rooms, dispersed individuals can share information and develop a common worldview that subsumes their local agendas in support of a common goal.[96] Some groups avoid membership lists and recruit on the Internet. Through this medium one can become a true believer in an ideology without any formal organizational connection.[97] Furthermore, websites can even instigate terrorism without any specific connection to perpetrators. For example, the Nuremberg Files, a website operated by an antiabortion activist in Oregon, listed the names and addresses of doctors who performed abortions. Operated by Neal Horsley, the site contained unsubtle suggestions that there should be some kind of retribution against them. In February 1999 the site was removed by its Internet service provider after a red line was drawn through the name of Dr. Barnett Slepian the same day he was killed by an antiabortion assassin.[98]

Trends in technology and networking are contributing to the miniaturization of terrorist groups. Although traditional hierarchies will not disappear, they are losing some of their advantages. Usually it is more difficult to coordinate a group as it increases in size, because as a group grows it becomes less likely that every member can interact directly with everyone else. Coordination, communication, and organization all become increasingly difficult as groups get larger.[99] Increased surveillance, government repression, and coordinated counterterrorism efforts have constrained large terrorist organizations in the aftermath of 9/11. But the new organizational structures described above are thought to be highly resilient and adaptable. As they are more network based than in the past, they have fewer characteristics of a formal organization. Rather, cells interact with one another when the need and opportunity arise. Moreover, the network can be supported by a nonviolent following that sympathizes with its ideology and can provide intentional—and perhaps also unwitting—support. For instance, people may donate money to charities that, in addition to humanitarian projects, also support terrorist groups. What holds the network together is a shared mission.[100] The reduction in costs and advances in communications and the increasing potential lethality of terrorist devices mean that terrorist groups can now operate effectively without state support.[101]

This new organizational paradigm presents numerous challenges to counterterrorism agencies since traditional hierarchies have a difficult time fighting networks. Furthermore, contemporary terrorists often operate in the "cracks and gray areas of society, striking where lines of authority crisscross," as Arquilla and Ronfeldt put it. As a result, it is not always clear which agencies should take responsibility in countering a particular terrorist threat. Finally, in a federal system such as the United States, terrorists can easily traverse jurisdictional boundaries, thus confusing the question of who has primary authority in handling such cases. To adapt to this situation, some observers argue, government should develop networks that share information and pool resource to counter the new networked terrorism—saying, in essence, that it takes a network to fight a network.[102] Such efforts become all the more critical now that it is possible for small cells, and even individuals, to cause considerable damage, because weapons of mass destruction are more widely available.

CHAPTER 6

Weapons of Mass Destruction and Leaderless Resistance

What makes leaderless resistance so potentially dangerous is the prospect of an individual or small cell obtaining a WMD or employing innovative tactics in a particularly lethal manner. Historically, technological advances enhanced the disruptive potential of terrorism. In fact, one reason for the rise of modern terrorism was the increasing availability of firepower to groups seeking to overthrow the government. For example, the introduction of dynamite in the late nineteenth century was a catalyst for the anarchist movement, which launched bombing campaigns in Europe and America.[1] The terrorist attacks of 9/11 brought together two threats that were much more ominous in combination than they were in isolation: radical Islam and the availability of WMD.[2]

Today there is much consternation over the increasing availability of WMD. In her study *The Ultimate Terrorists*, Jessica Stern of Harvard University argued that the likelihood of terrorists using WMD today is greater than in the past for several reasons. For one thing, such weapons are more readily available. A steady dissemination of dual-use equipment enables production of chemical and biological weapons, knowledge of their existence continues to increase, and motivations of terrorists are changing, with modern terrorists likely to be inspired by millenarian and extremist ideologies instead of the secular ideologies that animated earlier terrorists. With the breakup of the Soviet Union, new concerns arose about the security of nuclear weapons and the greater risk of a black market for WMD, components, and related expertise. The Soviet Union's collapse left eighteen thousand nuclear warheads in the hands of leaders of new countries, though there is no evidence that any of these weapons ever left government control.[3] And chemical and biological weapons are proliferating. Despite efforts to suppress proliferation, US intelligence agencies estimate that over twenty countries have or are developing nuclear, chemical, or biological weapons along with ballistic missile systems to deliver them.[4] Finally, advances in technology make it easier to carry out WMD attacks.[5] Although Stern concedes that the probability of WMD attacks is still low, they could be devastating.[6]

One could add that since US armed forces are so superior to other militaries, international adversaries have few alternatives to asymmetrical, unconventional attacks. Even Francis Fukuyama, a noted optimist on the future of international relations, agrees that leaderless resistance could be worrisome if conjoined with

WMD: "The only way [leaderless resistance] could really be serious is if they get hold of weapons of mass destruction. . . . I always have thought that's really the only way in which they could ever constitute anything considered a strategic threat to the United States."[7]

Nuclear Weapons

The most worrisome aspect of modern terrorism is the prospect of a radical group obtaining a nuclear weapon. On the eve of the Nuclear Security Summit in April 2010, President Barack Obama announced that the prospect of nuclear terrorism was "the single biggest threat to U.S. security . . . short-term, medium-term and long-term."[8] Likewise, former CIA director George Tenet once said he believed that the main threat of WMD was the nuclear threat, and that al Qaeda was making efforts in that direction.[9] During the Cold War, the nuclear balance of terror was thought to be logical, with the United States and the Soviet Union pursuing their foreign policy goals rationally and thus reluctant to initiate nuclear warfare. Some observers fear, however, that nuclear-armed extremist groups would not follow such logic because of their radical worldviews.[10]

What is more worrisome is that some terrorist organizations with the most violent histories, such as al Qaeda, have the financial wherewithal to purchase WMD.[11] Osama bin Laden explicitly stated more than once his ambition to acquire WMD.[12] Nuclear terrorism could be catastrophic. A study by the Rand Corporation of a hypothetical attack on the port of Long Beach, California, estimated that a ten-kiloton nuclear device would kill 60,000 persons instantly or soon thereafter, while exposing another 150,000 to harmful radioactive water and sediment. The total economic cost of such an attack would exceed $1 trillion.[13]

Although state officials would presumably be reluctant to convey a nuclear weapon to a terrorist group, rogue elements in a regime might be willing to do so. Reportedly some elements of the nuclear sector in Pakistan sympathize with al Qaeda and its jihadist goals. The prospect of Pakistani nuclear scientists selling their wares on the black market is unsettling—and not just hypothetical, as illustrated by the case of Dr. Abdul Qadeer Khan, who was implicated in covertly selling nuclear technology and expertise to countries around the world. Because of his activities, knowledge of how to build nuclear bombs has been disseminated widely. In 1998 Osama bin Laden's representatives approached the Khan network but were rebuffed.[14] However, bin Laden fared better with Khan's longtime rivals Sultan Bashiruddin Mahmood and Chaudhry Abdul Majeed, two retired senior engineers at the Pakistan Atomic Energy Commission. In August 2001 the two had long discussions with bin Laden, Ayman al-Zawahiri, and other al Qaeda officials about the prospect of building WMD. Not long after 9/11, Pakistani authorities placed Mahmood and Majeed under house arrest.[15] Mahmood's son told the Associated Press that his father had sympathized with the Taliban and met with Osama bin

Laden several times between 2000 and July 2001. During one encounter, bin Laden was supposed to have asked how to build a nuclear bomb.[16] Prior to this incident, for two years in the mid 1990s, Zawahiri and two of his top lieutenants traveled extensively to Russia, Yemen, Malaysia, and Singapore, during which they may have sought to procure WMD.[17] According to a 2001 article in *USA Today*, al Qaeda and the Taliban had contacted at least ten Pakistani nuclear scientists since 1999.[18]

Although both the US and Russian governments have substantially reduced their arsenals since the Cold War ended, many warheads remain. According to the Federation of American Scientists, as of 2010, the total US inventory of nuclear weapons was 9,600 warheads, of which 2,468 were operational. For Russia, those figures were 12,000 and 4,650, respectively. Worldwide there are approximately 22,600 nuclear warheads.[19] Thus there are still many that could fall into the wrong hands.

Nuclear terrorism could effectively nullify airpower or intercontinental missiles deployed to intercept a nuclear payload, because terrorists themselves would physically operate as the delivery system.[20] Conceivably, terrorists could smuggle a nuclear bomb into the country and then detonate it, making an SDI-style defense useless. Alternatively an attacker could ship a fully assembled nuclear weapon to a major port, with a time-delay, global-positioning, or tamper-detonating system, effectively making the port of entry the target.[21]

How plausible are these scenarios? Though their probability is quite low, their potential ramifications are so consequential that they need to be considered. Nevertheless, despite the alarming prospect of nuclear terrorism, the obstacles to obtaining such capabilities are formidable. Neither nuclear weapons nor nuclear technology have proliferated to the degree once feared. Although such weapons have been around for over sixty years, the so-called nuclear club stands at only nine members—the United States, Russia, China, the United Kingdom, France, India, Pakistan, North Korea, and Israel (whose government has never confirmed its arsenal). What is more, even if a terrorist group procured a nuclear warhead, sophisticated security measures would be difficult to surmount. For example, devices known as permissive action links are designed to prevent the unauthorized use of nuclear weapons.

Acquiring fissile material with which to build a bomb would also be challenging. The single greatest obstacle to producing a nuclear weapon is acquiring weapons-grade highly enriched uranium (HEU), the production of which requires large facilities, sophisticated equipment, and highly skilled expertise that in total would be beyond the capabilities of a clandestine terrorist group. Obtaining HEU on the black market might be possible, but there would still be tough challenges in constructing the actual nuclear device. If states seeking nuclear capability face such difficulties, it follows that it would be even more challenging for terrorist groups with far fewer resources and no secure geographic area in which to operate. Still, over the past several decades the number of nuclear reactors has steadily expanded. As of 2010, 442 commercial nuclear reactors operated worldwide. In the United

States there are 104 reactors at sixty-five plants sites in thirty-one states. Amid concern about global climate change, nuclear power is seen as an attractive alternative to burning fossil fuels to generate electrical power, and the number of nuclear reactors worldwide is projected to double by the end of the century. Nuclear reactors can produce plutonium, which might be used for the pit (core) of a nuclear weapon. With the number of reactors growing, some observers fear a concomitant increase in fissile material that could get into the hands of rogue states or terrorist groups and be used for a nuclear bomb. From the perspective of terrorists, though, plutonium would probably not be the preferred fissile material. Would-be nuclear terrorists would probably have to settle on the less sophisticated gun-type nuclear device as opposed to the more challenging implosion device.[22] This would rule out plutonium as usable material, since it can only be used effectively in the implosion design.[23] Terrorists would probably prefer smaller tactical nuclear weapons to so-called strategic nuclear weapons anyway, because of their greater portability and the less stringent security measures surrounding them, making them tempting targets for theft.[24]

Even if a rogue regime were to develop nuclear weapons, it would be reluctant to convey them to terrorist groups over which it did not exercise tight control. To be implicated in supplying nuclear weapons to terrorist groups would run the risk of serious retaliation from any targeted countries as well as the international community. Conceivably, though, nonstate actors would operate under a different matrix of constraints. With no official home base, they would be less likely to fear a retaliatory strike.[25] And though it is highly unlikely that a state would convey a nuclear weapon to a terrorist group, it is conceivable in the case where a regime felt particularly threatened. In such a scenario, a collapsing regime could transfer a nuclear weapon to a terrorist group in order to exact revenge on an adversary. Moreover, if a regime collapsed, state control over nuclear weapons could evaporate, thus allowing a terrorist or criminal group to obtain weapons from the nuclear arsenal.[26] Most pressing in this regard is the disposition of Pakistan's arsenal of nuclear weapons, the security of which is in question. What is more, the Pakistani military and the ISI have been implicated in supporting Islamist terrorism in the region and may have provided support to Osama bin Laden.

In several former Soviet republics during the early 1990s, the security at some nuclear sites was often less than adequate. Moreover, the Russian government was not even aware of the location and amount of much fissile material because of its poor accounting practices. Russia's HEU-fueled reactors constitute about one-third of the world's total and contain more than half of all civilian-owned HEU in the world.[27] Securing nuclear materials in Russia is imperative. As Joseph Cirincione, president of the Ploughshares Fund (a public foundation that supports nonproliferation), once pointed out, would-be nuclear terrorists will think like Willie Sutton, who once explained that he robbed banks because "that's where the money is." Caring little about a state's geopolitical orientation, terrorists will go where the nuclear material is.[28] Under the aegis of Project Sapphire, the US and Russian governments worked together to secure and transport fissile material from Kazakhstan to the United States.[29] The prospect of unaccounted fissile material needs to be taken seriously, as the International Atomic Energy Agency (IAEA) identified 1,562 confirmed incidents of nuclear smuggling as of 2010.[30]

It would not be easy to acquire a nuclear bomb on the black market. Despite concerns over "loose nukes," nuclear facilities are usually well protected. In 1997, a Russian general, Alexander Lebed, alleged that eighty-four "suitcase" bombs were missing from the Russian military arsenal.[31] Echoing Lebed's claim, a Russian defector, Stanislav Lunev, asserted that dozens of these weapons were covertly deployed in the United States during the Cold War.[32] Initially, the Pentagon acknowledged that the United States and the Soviet Union had built such devices.[33] Later Lebed recanted and returned to the official Russian line that no such weapons existed in the Russian arsenal.[34] US officials generally remain unconvinced by Lebed's initial story since they were never mentioned in any Soviet war plans.[35] Furthermore, nuclear weapons require considerable maintenance and cannot simply be mothballed, or their operability would expire over time. Finally, there is no evidence that the Chechen rebels or al Qaeda has acquired such weapons, despite stories to the contrary.[36]

Empirical evidence does not support the supposition that acquiring nuclear weapons is an easy task. In 1992 Osama bin Laden attempted to purchase highly enriched uranium in South Africa, to use in building a nuclear bomb.[37] He tried again in 1993, reportedly agreeing to purchase a complete nuclear missile or highly enriched uranium from the former Soviet arsenal.[38] And in September 1998 he reportedly paid $2 million to a man in Kazakhstan who promised to deliver a Soviet-made suitcase nuclear device.[39] In addition, bin Laden made remarks in which he claimed that his organization had acquired nuclear and chemical weapons, and threatened to use such weapons if the United States used them against his forces.[40]

Despite efforts by al Qaeda spanning more than a decade, there is no credible evidence that the organization has succeeded. The group has occasionally fallen victim to nuclear scams in which operatives have purchased useless material at high cost. Likewise, the Chechen rebels, who would seem to be the most advantageously situated to acquire nuclear weapons, because of their connections to organized crime and their experience in the Russian military, appear to have been unsuccessful as well.[41]

With the technological hurdles to obtaining nuclear weapons so high, terrorists could settle for less-sophisticated alternatives, such as nuclear sabotage. Research-based nuclear reactors on urban university campuses might be accessible. Roughly half the high-power operational research reactors in the United States are within ten miles of metropolitan areas in which five hundred thousand or more people reside.[42] If terrorists could corrupt an insider, they might be able to sabotage a site.[43] As the nuclear accident at Chernobyl in 1986 illustrated, the effects of an attack or sabotage could be devastating.[44]

For small groups or lone wolves intent on nuclear terrorism, employing a radioactive dispersal device, or "dirty bomb," is a more feasible option. A dirty bomb consists of radioactive material conjoined with conventional explosives, which when detonated would disperse harmful radiation, possibly rendering an area uninhabitable for a long time. According to one author, in the closing days of World War II, the Nazi regime contemplated such an attack, in conjunction with the Japanese, on the west coast of the United States.[45] Decades later, in 1995, a team of Chechen rebels planted a crude device in Ismailovsky Park in Moscow, but alerted authorities to its location. Although the device contained only a small amount of radioactive material, it raised the worrisome prospect of low-budget nuclear terrorism. A few years later, in 1998, a container emitting high levels of radiation was discovered on a Moscow rail line.[46] The container was defused, and the identity of the perpetrator was not revealed. In 2002, the prospect of a "dirty bomb" scenario made headlines in the United States with the arrest of Jose Padilla. A former Chicago gang member who had converted to Islam in prison, after his release Padilla traveled to Afghanistan and Pakistan, where he met senior al Qaeda leaders and allegedly sought to acquire materials with which to construct a dirty bomb.[47] More attempts followed. In 2006, a British citizen named Dhiren Barot was convicted of plotting a series of attacks in London using radiological dispersal devices.[48] More recently, the neo-Nazi sympathizer James Cummings procured radioactive and conventional explosive materials, which he planned to use for a dirty bomb to be detonated in Washington, D.C., in order to assassinate Barack Obama.[49]

Although not as deadly as a conventional nuclear device, a dirty bomb still threatens economic and societal disruption. Cleaning up radiation after an attack would entail ripping down contaminated structures and sending them to a special dump.[50] The prospect of a dirty bomb is worrisome because radioactive materials are so widely available in industrial economies that it might be impossible to prevent determined terrorists from gaining access to them. Increasingly, biotoxins are available as well, making them another potential terrorist threat.

Biological Weapons

Biological weapons could be even more lethal than nuclear bombs. Diseases killed millions of people in the last century. Smallpox caused the death of approximately 500 million people in the twentieth century, compared to the estimated 320 million who died as casualties of war (military and civilian), from influenza during the 1918 pandemic, and from AIDS, all combined.[51] The prospect of using smallpox as a biological weapon exists, as vaccinations for the disease long ago ceased.[52]

Adding to these fears is the difficulty of detecting biological weapons.[53] Moreover, the hurdles for acquiring and developing biological weapons are relatively lower than for other WMD, such as nuclear weapons. Producing effective biological weapons involves three essential steps. First, a seed stock or a pathogenic or toxin-producing organism, must be acquired. Second, the microorganism or toxin must be produced in bulk. Finally, the most significant technical hurdle, a system must be devised capable of dispersing the agent in an infectious or toxic concentration as a respirable aerosol.[54] Prior to 9/11, civilian laboratories were not well guarded and would rarely check whether those placing orders were acquiring them for legitimate use, despite several threats of biowarfare attacks in the United States.[55] And not just threats: in September 1984 an attack was engineered by followers of the Rajneesh sect in Oregon. Led by the Bhagwan Shree Rajneesh, the cult attracted thousands of adherents and accumulated substantial financial resources. Followers contaminated salad bars in restaurants in Oregon, using salmonella bacteria, in an attempt to influence a local election by incapacitating voters. No one died, but public officials identified 751 local persons who became sick during the subsequent outbreak.[56]

Representatives of the US Far Right have been implicated in cases involving biotoxins as well. In 1995 the FBI arrested members of the Patriots Council, a Minnesota-based tax protest group, for allegedly manufacturing and planning to use ricin, a highly toxic biological substance.[57] Although ricin is effective as a weapon for assassination, it is not suitable for inflicting mass casualties.[58] Two years later, in April 1997, the Washington, D.C., offices of the B'nai B'rith received a suspicious package that contained a leaky petri dish and a note indicating that the package might contain microbes of the plague or anthrax. The perpetrator was never identified, but the intended target suggests that the attack came from an anti-Semitic group or individual.[59]

To date, the most worrisome cases of bioterrorism have involved anthrax. Anthrax occurs naturally and is usually found in the blood of grazing animals, such as cows, goats, and sheep. The majority of victims are afflicted with cutaneous anthrax, an easily treatable and rarely fatal skin infection. When weaponized, though, spores can result in pulmonary anthrax, which produces lesions and hemorrhaging, and is fatal in ninety-nine cases out of a hundred within one week of onset.[60]

In 1998 the FBI arrested Larry Wayne Harris and William Job Leavitt for allegedly possessing anthrax, but dropped the charges after it was apparent that they had possessed only a harmless strain used in veterinary vaccines. Prior to that incident, in 1995, Harris had pleaded guilty to illegally obtaining bubonic plague bacteria through the mail from a microbiological firm, the American Type Culture Collection (ATCC).[61] Although a loophole in the law made the transaction legal, authorities arrested him for mail fraud because he misrepresented himself on the purchase order. Such transactions must comply with US export control laws, which have subsequently been tightened.[62] According to prosecutors, Harris had boasted to undercover informants several times of planning attacks involving biological agents. He claimed he had first become interested in biological warfare while stationed at a microbiology laboratory at Aberdeen Proving Ground while in the US Army. In the early 1970s, he attended Ohio State University, where he studied microbiology and later worked for biological firms. For a while Harris had been affiliated with the Aryan Nations, and he once admitted he was on the governing board of William Pierce's National Alliance. He also authored an underground press book, *Bacteriological Warfare: A Major Threat to North America*.[63]

A lone wolf could use anthrax for lethal effect, as the case of Dr. Bruce Ivins demonstrates. Shortly after 9/11, two waves of letters laced with anthrax were sent to various media representatives and US lawmakers. Letters in the first wave went to headquarters of ABC News, CBS News, NBC News, and the *New York Post*, all located in New York City, and to the *National Enquirer* at American Media Inc. (AMI) in Boca Raton, Florida. A second wave was sent to the Washington, D.C., offices of Senators Tom Daschle (D-SD) and Patrick Leahy (D-VT). The anthrax was weaponized, suggesting that it could only have been produced in a sophisticated military lab beyond the expertise of a nonstate terrorist group.[64] By early November 2001, five people had died from the contaminated letters and another seventeen were sickened.[65] Had the anthrax been employed more effectively, it could have done even greater damage and possibly shut down the nationwide postal system.[66]

Early in the investigation, the FBI identified Dr. Steven Hatfill as a suspect. Although Hatfill was never charged, the FBI investigated him thoroughly for five years. Eventually he was cleared and awarded $5.8 million for his claim that the Justice Department and FBI violated his privacy and ruined his career. In August 2008 another doctor, Bruce Ivins—a research scientist at the US Army Medical Research Institute of Infectious Diseases (USAMRID)—was identified by the FBI as the person responsible for the anthrax-laced letters. The sixty-two-year-old microbiologist lived in a modest home not far from where he worked at Fort Detrick, Maryland. Earlier Ivins had undergone treatment for mental illness, and he had spent a week in a psychiatric ward that year. On July 27, 2008, before he could be arrested, Ivins is said to have consumed a heavy dose of prescription Tylenol with codeine. He collapsed in his home and was taken to a hospital, where he died two days later.[67] Although the case against him was circumstantial, a seven-year FBI investigation—"Amerithrax"—concluded that Ivins was solely responsible for the attacks.

Some experts, though, were highly skeptical of the government's case, as Ivins seemed an unlikely suspect and believe that there is compelling exculpatory scientific evidence. An unprepossessing scientist, he was a churchgoing, piano-playing husband and father of two adopted children. The anthrax found in the letters sent to the offices of Senators Daschle and Leahy was highly sophisticated, causing some experts to believe that producing such a weaponized form of the toxin was beyond Ivins's capacity. Richard Spertzel, the former head of the biological weapons section of UNSCOM from 1994 to 1999,[68] averred that the anthrax used in the letters to Daschle and Leahy could not have been made at the laboratory where Ivins worked. Furthermore, the particles were coated with a material not previously used in that fashion. And according to an FBI leak, each particle was given an electric charge that caused the particles to repel each other at the molecular level, thus increasing the likelihood of retention of the spores in lungs. Spertzel concluded that the potential lethality of this anthrax exceeded that of any type of powdered product found in the now defunct US Biological Warfare Program. Although he believes Ivins was a brilliant scientist, Spertzel does not think he had the knowledge or access to technology necessary to produce the anthrax used in the attacks. Representative Rush Holt (D-NJ) introduced H.R. 1248—"The Anthrax Attacks Investigations Act of 2009"—which called for a national commission to study the matter further. Adding to suspicion are the strange deaths of several prominent microbiologists since the attacks. While these deaths have raised eyebrows in some quarters and have provided grist for Internet conspiracy mills, others counter that the number of scientists who have died is within statistical norms for the profession.[69]

If the government's case against Ivins is to be believed, then it illustrates the destructive potential of lone wolf terrorism using bioweapons. Still, there are difficult hurdles that would have to be surmounted to launch an effective bioattack. When an agent is released, it is very difficult to control the spread of the disease. Milling biological weapons into a small granular powder would require considerable expertise of the sort found in government laboratories, probably beyond the capabilities of a terrorist group.[70] The pathogen particles would need to be large enough to reach the intended victims and yet small enough to be inhaled into their lungs. If airborne, the pathogen would need to survive the ultraviolet rays of the sun, as well as drying and heating, until it was inhaled. Likewise, food-borne and waterborne pathogens would have to survive holding temperatures and pH levels of the food and water in which they were placed.[71]

Nevertheless, biological weapons offer several advantages to terrorists. First, they are cheaper and easier to acquire than other WMD. Second, pathogens could be released and transmitted throughout a targeted community with comparative ease. Third, the delay between infection and onset of disease would take days, weeks, or even months, thus compounding terror.[72] Finally, as John Robb points out, bioweapons dovetail well with the leaderless resistance approach to terrorism:

> The true type of leaderless resistance is when the technology enables an individual to declare war on the world by himself. And we're reaching that point, at least with biotech, pretty quickly. . . . The [likes of] computer viruses [will] crop up in the biotech field in the next decade. I'm more concerned about that than I am nuclear terrorism, because nuclear terrorism requires mastery of the nuclear cycle. If it [were] that easy to acquire nuclear weapons, Iran would have a massive arsenal right now. So, if it takes a state-level infrastructure to actually build them, maintain them, and use them effectively, then that's not the perfect tactic for small groups. Biotech, on the other hand, is all about decentralization. It is all about doing things on a small scale.[73]

Despite the advantages of biowarfare, terrorists may seek out less sophisticated methods.

Chemical Weapons

Although less lethal than bioweapons, chemical weapons have been employed by terrorists. Unlike nuclear devices, chemical weapons are well within the reach of individuals and small groups, much more available, and far easier to fabricate. The first terrorist group to mount major attacks with chemical weapons was the Japanese cult Aum Shinrikyo (Supreme Truth). Some observers believed the cult portended a new type of terrorist group that would indiscriminately employ weapons of mass destruction. Aum Shinrikyo was founded in 1987 by a charismatic former yoga instructor, Chizuo Matsumato, known within the cult as Shoko Asahara. Left almost completely sightless by infantile glaucoma, he attended schools for blind children. Virtually all the other students were completely blind, but Asahara, with limited eyesight, was able to do favors for classmates, and came to be accepted as their leader. Perhaps as a result of this experience, Asahara developed a messiah complex.[74]

Aum Shinrikyo, which operated from 1987 to 1995, was one of the most innovative terrorist organizations in recent history. Especially novel was the cult's apocalyptic ideology, which sought to usher in a global Armageddon from which the cult's members would emerge to build a new order based on the precepts advanced by Asahara, whose theology syncretized elements of Hinduism, Buddhism, Shinto, and anti-Semitic and anti–Free Masonry conspiracy theories. Enamored of high technology, Asahara sought to randomly inflict high casualties, believing in a distorted type of karma—*poa*—that would redeem his victims and provide them with favorable afterlives. To that end, the group pursued sophisticated weaponry, including nuclear, biological, and chemical weapons. The group's formidable resources—its coffers held an estimated $1 billion—enabled it to procure and develop WMD. Asahara managed to attract highly trained scientists, including chemists, electrical engineers, physicians, and biologists, providing expertise that allowed the group to pursue its nefarious schemes.[75]

Originally Aum Shinrikyo planned to release nerve gas in the United States in 1994, but for reasons unknown, it settled instead on the Japanese city of Matsumoto, where sarin gas released in 1994 killed seven people and injured more than 150.[76] On March 20, 1995, the cult released sarin gas in the Tokyo subway system, killing five persons and injuring roughly 5,500 more.[77] If the cult had acquired high-grade sarin and dispensed it as an aerosol, the Tokyo attack might have resulted in thousands of deaths.[78] The most effective way to spread chemical agents in the air is to release them in an enclosed area in the manner of the Tokyo subway attack.[79]

As the case of Aum Shinrikyo illustrates, chemical weapons suitable for mass-casualty attacks can be acquired by nonstate entities with moderate technical skills.

Furthermore, they could be manufactured in a kitchen or basement in sufficient quantities for mass-casualty attacks.[80] In 2007 a spate of bombings in Iraq used improvised explosive devices designed to disperse chlorine gas. And in 2005, an individual linked to al Qaeda—Kamel Bourgass—was arrested and convicted after conspiring to attack London with ricin.[81]

Representatives of the Far Right have been implicated in plots involving chemical weapons as well, as evidenced by the 2003 arrest of William Krar and his common-law wife, Judith Bruey. The sixty-three-year-old Krar kept a low profile, but it is believed he had associated with extremist groups. He first caught the attention of authorities in 1995, around the time of the Oklahoma City bombing, when the BATF investigated him and an unidentified man on weapons charges. In January 2002 Krar again raised suspicion after a package he had sent to a militiaman in New Jersey—containing five false identification documents, including a Defense Intelligence Agency ID card—was inadvertently delivered to a wrong address in Staten Island, New York. The unintended recipient promptly notified authorities. Not long after, federal authorities launched another investigation of Krar. A US Attorney's statement claimed that Krar had accumulated dangerous chemical weapons, a reference to a January 2002 stop of Krar's auto in which Tennessee Highway Patrol officers discovered dangerous chemicals and a note that appeared to be instructions for carrying out a covert operation. Soon authorities began to connect the dots. In April 2003 FBI agents raided his home and rented storage units in East Texas and discovered a large quantity of sodium cyanide and other substances, such as hydrochloric, nitric, and acetic acid, as well as a large cache of guns and ammunition—and a copy of *The Turner Diaries*. Consequently Krar was charged with possessing sodium cyanide and other chemicals for the purpose of creating a dangerous weapon, for which he pleaded guilty and received a 135-month prison sentence in November 2003. His codefendant, Bruey, pleaded guilty to conspiring to possess illegal weapons, for which she received a 57-month sentence. The Krar case was one of the most extensive domestic terrorism investigations since the 1995 Oklahoma City bombing.[82]

Civil chaos would be one of the most serious consequences of terrorism involving chemical weapons. Although it would be difficult to contaminate water supplies such as reservoirs because dilution would soon render contaminants inactive, such an attack could cause widespread public panic.[83] Allegedly the Covenant, the Sword, and the Arm of the Lord, the group discussed in Chapter 2, planned to contaminate a water supply with cyanide, but even if they had carried out their plot, it would have failed.[84] Although killing a few persons is feasible with poison, there are logistical limits to the number of people who can be killed in this way. In 1982, cyanide-laced Tylenol pills, sold in packages that had been tampered with, killed seven persons in the Chicago area.[85] Other methods could cause large-scale casualties. In the United States there are approximately fifteen thousand chemical plants, refineries, and other sites that store hazardous materials.[86] Conventional explosives could disperse dangerous chemicals, thus injuring nearby people and contaminating property.[87] In December 1984, a leak at the Union Carbide chemical plant in Bhopal, India, resulted in the deaths of over three thousand people in the local area. This represents another concern: the vulnerability of infrastructure to sabotage.

The Threat to Infrastructure

Here is an ominous proposition: infrastructure relied on by masses of people in their day-to-day lives might be targeted, attacked, and greatly disrupted. By attacking vital systems, terrorists could destabilize increasingly complex modern societies and wreak economic and political havoc. Market forces have resulted in the agglomeration of infrastructure in large urban areas in order to maximize economies of scale that create greater efficiency.[88] With cities as the hubs of modern economies, their infrastructures are prime targets for systems sabotage and their vulnerability ought to be of great concern. Disrupting key nodes could cause a catastrophic failure of a network.[89] One consequence of an advanced industrial-technological infrastructure is that it highly vulnerable to nonconventional operations of a sort used by terrorist organizations.[90] Contemporary terrorists could exploit vulnerabilities in networks in a number of ways. For example, civil air transportation and the mail delivery system were turned into mechanisms for terrorism on and after September 11, 2001.[91] Some computers seized from al Qaeda by US forces in Afghanistan contained information about ways to access and gain control of computers that run electrical, water, and transportation systems in the United States.[92]

The power industry, in particular, is vulnerable to system disruption.[93] Since electrical power networks are so interconnected, disrupting one could cause a cascade of failures throughout the system, as evidenced by a chain of events that occurred in August 2003, when 263 power plants shut down within seven minutes after three sagging power lines came into contact with the tops of overgrown trees in Ohio.[94] After the blackout, some elements of al Qaeda claimed responsibility for the incident, though in hindsight the boast seemed spurious. Nevertheless, such "effects-based operations" (EBO), as David A. Deptula called them, could cause huge disruptions in a complex system.[95]

Similarly, pipelines are vulnerable to sabotage since most are located aboveground, run through remote areas, and are largely unprotected. In 1977 saboteurs bombed the then-new Trans-Alaska pipeline, and although no oil was lost because the blast did not penetrate the pipeline wall, a shutdown was still required. A year later, however, the pipeline was bombed again, spilling fifteen thousand barrels of oil and shutting down the pipeline for twenty-one hours.[96] More recently, in an effort to undermine the economies in the Middle East, al Qaeda and its affiliates have struck oil pipelines. These attacks have resulted in hundreds of millions of dollars in lost revenue for the fledgling Iraqi government.[97] Low-cost operations carried out by saboteurs could inflict high-cost damage on a targeted country. As one observer speculated, if such sabotage techniques were even lightly employed in the target-rich West, "we could see a rapid onset of economic and political chaos unmatched since the advent of blitzkrieg."[98]

Ports are another potential target for terrorists. According to Stephen E. Flynn, a retired US Coast Guard officer and an authority on homeland security, it would not be difficult for terrorists to load a WMD into a container at its point of origin or anywhere en route to a marine terminal. He estimated that the current monitoring system would have a 10 percent chance of detecting a nuclear warhead surrounded by shielding material. Furthermore, the cost to lease such a container is only $3,000–$5,000, and these containers can be circulated around the globe. The economic fallout of an attack on a port could be substantial. If the United States closed its ports after a terrorist attack, it could have a cascading effect and send the entire system into gridlock. With maritime transportation so highly concentrated in a few major ports, shipping is a vulnerable pressure point.[99]

The information sector is another vulnerable part of national infrastructure, as evidenced by its traditional significance in war. For example, Britain's ULTRA program managed to break German codes early in the Second World War and this contributed to the Royal Air Force's great success in the Battle of Britain. Likewise, thanks to MAGIC—the US decipherment of Japanese codes—the US Navy won a major victory at Midway Island despite being outnumbered.[100] Sometimes referred to as information warfare, cyberterrorism targets information systems and computer networks. To meet the challenge of cyberwarfare, in 2004 the Department of Homeland Security announced the creation of the National Cyber Alert System, which is designed to detect and destroy cyberattacks. There is a much larger potential pool of cyberterrorists than terrorists wielding WMD. Furthermore, carrying out a cyberattack presents no immediate physical threat to the perpetrator. What is particularly worrisome about the prospect of cyberterrorism is that it could be used against technological infrastructure from a great distance, by a few persons, at low personal risk.[101] A strike could be launched from a remote location, offering anonymity. Moreover, because of the relatively simple equipment and low level of skill required, an individual could act alone, without the support of a terrorist network.[102] To date, the incidents of cybersabotage have been modest in scale.[103] Although computer viruses can do tremendous damage, they are not precise in their targeting. Conceivably, though, terrorists might launch attacks on computer networks to disrupt infrastructure.

Despite the concern about WMD and "superterrorism," the tactics used by terrorists have changed little over the last few decades, the terrorism analyst Ariel Merari points out. This stagnation is remarkable considering the massive changes that have taken place in conventional warfare during this period. Merari argues that despite the increasing availability of weapons of potentially greater lethality than ever, terrorists have been reluctant to use them for a variety of reasons, including the psychological, social, and political contexts within which terrorists operate. The most important factor limiting the use of WMD, as he sees it, is the need of terrorist organizations to maintain secrecy, which in turn dictates a compartmentalized organizational structure that limits the capability to carry out terrorist attacks. According to Merari's research, terrorist groups employing variants of WMD would need a high level of organizational complexity and members with considerable skills. But the clandestine nature of terrorism militates against this, except in the case of state-sponsored terrorism. As Merari points out, state sponsors would hesitate to give terrorists such capability, for fear that the sponsor could be held accountable and would face retribution by an aggrieved state.[104] Finally, as another observer noted, committing mass acts of destructive terrorism would require a long period of training and conditioning in a closed environment impervious to outside standards of morality. Such insular environments are harder and harder to maintain in today's increasingly interconnected world. As a result, early warning signs are more likely to be noticed and brought to the attention of law enforcement and intelligence authorities long before threats can be carried out.[105] Acquiring WMD is a more technologically challenging and expensive proposition than acquiring conventional weapons and would also entail greater health hazards for those who would handle them.[106] In sum, the technical challenges involved in developing effective WMD are daunting and thus may not yield results commensurate with the difficulties.[107] Despite these obstacles, some observers fear that terrorist groups informed by radical eschatologies would have no compunction about using them.

Radical Eschatologies and WMD

One worrisome development is the emergence of terrorist groups with radical beliefs about the end of the world and the destiny of humankind. According to the US National Security Strategy, "the gravest danger [the United States] faces lies at the crossroads of radicalism and technology."[108] In a seminal article on terrorism and WMD, written in 1975, Brian Jenkins argued that terrorists are basically rational and use a type of cost-benefit analysis in their calculations. At that time terrorists were seen as rational actors, and even if they would occasionally mount attacks, it was generally believed that they were reluctant to inflict mass casualties, or else they would risk losing international sympathy. Based on this reasoning, terrorists wanted just enough drama to get their message across. What is more, terrorists risked serious reprisals from the countries or communities they targeted. Pragmatic in their demands, they did not really seek to destroy the enemy; rather, they just wanted a seat at the negotiating table—or at least a voice. Thus, publicity was the paramount concern.[109]

By the late 1990s, however, Jenkins came to believe that radical religious terrorists were not swayed by the same deterrents that had constrained secular terrorists of the past. This may sound paradoxical, since one might think that a religious person would be more reluctant to inflict casualties, especially among innocent people. The presumption is that ethical constraints would inhibit terrorists from killing indiscriminately, but according to Jenkins, religion-inspired terrorists believe that

God is on their side, and as a consequence they are more self-assured in their mission and thus *more* likely to cause mass casualties. Once their enemy is demonized and labeled godless, such terrorists believe that nearly all measures are justified to bring about the enemy's defeat.[110] Presumably, groups with amorphous constituencies are less likely to worry about the opprobrium that would accompany their use of WMD. Echoing Jenkins, the esteemed terrorism scholar Walter Laqueur observed a nihilistic trend among contemporary terrorists, and he believes that the reluctance to use WMD is loosening. As he observes, "Not only have the arms become far more lethal, the targets have become much softer."[111]

Trends suggest that religiously inspired terrorists often demonstrate a willingness to use weapons of greater lethality and appear to have less compunction about inflicting heavy casualties.[112] Ominously, the past few decades suggest a shift in this direction, away from secular terrorism. In 1980 the US State Department roster of international terrorist groups listed scarcely a single religious organization. By 1998, over half of the thirty most dangerous groups were religious.[113]

What accounts for the resurgence of religious violence? According to the scholar Mark Juergensmeyer, various trends set in motion by globalization have led to a reassertion of religion as a public force. Disaffection with the values of modern Western civilization, he argues, has occasioned a loss of faith in the secular form of nationalism, or "the principle that the nation is rooted in a secular compact rather than a religious or ethnic identity." To some people, this model appears as an "alien cultural construction" closely linked with the "project of modernity." In this atmosphere, religious alternatives to secular ideologies have greater resonance and appeal.[114]

For religious terrorists, as Bruce Hoffman has pointed out, "violence is viewed first and foremost as a sacramental act in direct response to some theological demand or imperative."[115] Furthermore, secular and religious terrorists differ in their constituencies. Whereas the former tend to see themselves as appealing to a constituency of actual or potential sympathizers, the latter are at once activists and constituents involved in a total war. Unlike secular terrorists, religious terrorists who seek the approval of some higher deity are not constrained by a desire to appeal to a human constituency. Religious terrorists see themselves as "outside the system" and thus have no stake in preserving it. This profound sense of alienation and moral disengagement enables religious terrorists to contemplate far more destructive types of terrorist operations and carry out mass-casualty attacks. The lethality of religiously inspired terrorism since the 1990s lends credence to this theory.[116] As the noted Harvard law professor Alan Dershowitz observed in his study *Why Terrorism Works*, terrorists motivated by apocalyptic ideologies may not be subject to rational cost-benefit calculations.[117] He expounds on this proposition and the challenges it presents to governments:

> It seems to me that if you are right that we are getting fewer nations [supporting terrorism] and fewer centralized [terrorist] organizations and more

. . . little offshoots that are community based or based on small [constituencies that] have allegiance to each other, [then] I think one has to seriously think about some degree of collective accountability. I mean, you don't want to go to the extreme. The only way that you can deter terrorists is by threatening to impose punishment on people whom they deeply care about and on their cause. Now, we don't accept punishment of kin. But broadening the concept of individual responsibility somewhat, with fair warning and fair notice, may be at least one possible issue that has to be explored more. [The] other possibility, of course, is that you are not going to get significant deterrence, and you really have to move much more toward infiltration and preemption, but . . . it's even harder to infiltrate the smaller disorganized organizations like this.

[For example], Hamas has a political wing and a terrorist wing. When you think about it, it's really not two, it's a continuum. They have people who voted for them, people who support them financially, people who support them religiously, people who are part of their political unit. I try to introduce in my writing the concept of a continuum of "civilianality," or a continuum of accountability. And we ought to think hard on how they use that continuum with legal consequences.[118]

A common apocalyptic thread and an ethos of martyrdom run through several extremist movements. Robert Jay Lifton, the noted psychiatrist who studies political violence, argues that a pervasive sense of anomie has caused many people to believe that only extreme measures can restore virtue and righteousness in society. Radical groups often seek to decipher hermetic messages in order to understand the contemporary world, and believe that society is under siege by stealthy evildoers. Small and often ostracized from the larger society, they believe they "must destroy the world to save it." A period of apocalyptic tribulation is thought to have redemptive value, because it is seen as cleansing the corrupt world and ushering in a new era. Lifton sees a similar pattern to Aum Shinrikyo's in the brand of Islam practiced by Osama bin Laden and al Qaeda, in that they seek to destroy a world they see as defiled and to create a new Islamic caliphate in its stead.[119] To that end, the organization has made numerous attempts to acquire WMD, including nuclear weapons, anthrax, plague, ricin, and the botulinum toxin. Furthermore, several sympathetic Muslim clerics have issued fatwas condoning the use of WMD.[120]

Ideology is thus an important predictor in a group's proclivity to use WMD. According to the terrorism analyst Adam Dolnik, ideology is the most important factor in predicting terrorist group innovation, insofar as it frames a group's worldview and determines its core objectives and the strategy for how to achieve them. Furthermore, ideology determines the identification of the "enemy" and the means by which to defeat it. On the other hand, as Dolnik point out, the most extreme and apocalyptic groups that would seem most inclined to use WMD are also those least likely to possess the necessary technology to mount such attacks. Because of their radicalism, such groups are also more likely to be identified beforehand by authorities. As a consequence, Dolnik believes, "the likelihood of a successful mass-casualty WMD attack remains comparatively low.[121] Furthermore, even terrorist groups with radical eschatologies, such as al Qaeda, may be deterrable. These groups must factor the prospect of massive retaliation into their strategic calculations and may thus be reluctant to resort to WMD. Even al Qaeda must consider possible fallout from the Muslim community in the event of catastrophic terrorism. However, smaller affiliated groups with limited local support and extreme goals may not follow the dictates of the more strategically minded leadership of al Qaeda.[122]

WMD could be employed strategically by cunning terrorists. Frederick Iklé, a former Defense Department official and ex-director of the US Arms Control and Disarmament Agency, explored such a scenario in his study *Annihilation from Within: The Ultimate Threat of Nations*. He argues that the technological revolution has weakened the power of the state over the people. Some individuals can now project unprecedented power. He presages two likely scenarios in this new environment. First, lethal "last resort" weapons could fall into the hands of armed groups. Second, emerging, futuristic, "dual use" technology, such as biotechnology, robotics, nanomachines (microscopic machines), and artificial intelligence could be modified by nonstate actors into WMD. Ominously, he predicts that nonstate individuals and groups will find the means of harnessing new technology for use as weapons of mass destruction.[123]

Iklé speculates on the prospect of a charismatic leader who gains control of a WMD. The greatest threat to international order he sees is "an aspiring dictator who is utterly ruthless, brilliantly cunning, and possessed of strategic vision." By launching just a few WMD against carefully chosen targets, such a person could paralyze the national leadership and foster such panic that a central government would not hold. Out of this chaos, such a plotter could seize control and impose a dictatorship. Just as Adolf Hitler was able to exploit the Reichstag fire and use it as a pretext for a power grab in 1930s Germany, so could an unscrupulous opportunist use WMD to foment a crisis to wrest control of a national government and invoke emergency rule.[124] In such a scenario, a state sponsor would not be needed, nor would training camps. With WMD a ruthless leader could wreak havoc without a large logistical network and base of support.

Such a scenario is unlikely in the United States currently, but Iklé argues that some countries in central Asia could be vulnerable. Furthermore, he counsels that if the US immigration problem is left unsolved, the political strength of the country could "melt away" as assimilation becomes less feasible. This "disuniting of America," as Arthur Schlesinger warned about, could undermine the cohesion of the country and thus make it more vulnerable to political radicalism.[125] Still, Iklé believes that such an ambitious undertaking is beyond the reach of domestic lone wolves in the United States at present.[126]

The US government has taken seriously the prospect of WMD falling into the hands of nonstate actors and has sought to limit the proliferation of potentially dangerous materials. For example, the Antiterrorism and Effective Death Penalty

Act of 1996 criminalizes the use of chemical or biological weapons and regulates the distribution of pathogenic microorganisms and toxins. Similarly, the Defense Against Weapons of Mass Destruction Act of 1996 links programs to combat terrorism with efforts abroad to stem the proliferation of weapons of mass destruction and increases US domestic preparedness for WMD terrorism.[127] The prospect of a "rogue" state conveying a WMD to a terrorist group was one of the principal arguments George W. Bush used to justify the invasion of Iraq. As already noted, Osama bin Laden had unequivocally expressed his intention of acquiring WMD. An examination of the evolution of the network he fostered is in order.

CHAPTER 7

The Global Islamic Resistance Movement

The global Islamic resistance movement has endured despite a multinational effort to eradicate it after 9/11. To some observers, militant Islam, or Islamism, is a retrograde phenomenon, a rearguard action against the inexorable march of modernity and globalization.[1] To its supporters, however, it represents an effort to return humankind to the righteous guidance of Allah as expressed in the Koran. Islamists seek to revitalize the universalistic fervor of early Islam and repackage it as viable political ideology. Islamism offers a vanguard philosophy with a complete program to improve people and remake society. It is an Islamic attempt to come to terms with the challenge of modernity.[2] Even with the death of its key figurehead—Osama bin Laden—militant Islam continues to inspire disaffected Muslims around the world.

Background

In the second half of the nineteenth century, the impact of Western ideas in the Middle East brought new definitions of identity there, and consequently new aspirations and allegiances. Western notions of freedom and political participation gained currency, first largely among Christians and other minorities, and later among the Muslim majority. At the same time, pan-Islamism emerged as a movement. An early proponent, Jamal al-Din al-Afghani (1839–1897), urged his co-religionists to apply the European concept of nationhood to the Muslim world so that it could develop into a major global power.[3] Afghani, along with his student Mohammed Abdu, led an intellectual movement to modernize Islam. Together they sought to create a moderate synthesis of Islam and modernity for the Muslim world.

After World War I, a secularizing trend swept parts of the Middle East, exemplified by the Turkish leader Mustafa Kemal Atatürk, who saw Islam as a hindrance to the modernization of Turkey. Blaming the religion for his nation's defeat in World War I, he derided Islam as "the absurd theology of an immoral Bedouin." To distance Turkey from the Arab world, he adopted the Latin alphabet, abolished the Koranic system of education, and declared religion to be a matter of individual concern only.[4] Today Atatürk is considered the bête noire of Islamists, as the collapse of the Ottoman Empire is generally recognized as the genesis of the crisis in the contemporary Muslim world. Secularization engendered a backlash against Westernization and modernization, and as a result, intensified the fledgling Islamist movement.

The Muslim Brotherhood

The collapse of the caliphate troubled much of the Islamic world. Many Muslims were aghast as they witnessed how Atatürk had transformed Turkey into a secular state, and feared that such a development might spread to their nations. With the fall of Turkey, Egypt assumed the fulcrum position in the Islamic world. The most enduring institution of Islamism—the Muslim Brotherhood (Al-Ikhwan Al-Muslimun)—was founded by Hassan al-Banna in Egypt in 1928, and the movement it spawned spread rapidly throughout the Islamic world. The Egyptian branch also served as a vehicle of national liberation by seeking to extricate Egypt from Western control and non-Islamic influences.[5]

Eventually al-Banna ran afoul of the regime, and he was assassinated in 1949 on the orders of King Farouk. However, Farouk's days as the leader of Egypt were numbered. Arab nationalism proved to be a dynamic force the monarch could not squelch. When a coup by the army colonel Gamal Adbel Nasser and his Free Officers deposed Farouk in 1952, the Muslim Brotherhood initially supported Nasser and its relations with him were amicable. By 1956, Nasser had taken over full control of the state, and not long into his tenure some Islamic fundamentalists began to criticize his regime. Relations broke down irrevocably between the government and the Muslim Brotherhood in 1954 when a member, Mahmud Abd al-Latif, attempted to assassinate Nasser while he gave a speech in Alexandria. Soon thereafter, the regime fiercely repressed the Brotherhood, imprisoning many members and driving the movement underground. Yet rather than silencing the group, these measures only emboldened it. Chief among the Brotherhood's critics of the regime was Sayid Qutb.

Sayid Qutb and *Milestones*

The ideological roots of al Qaeda can be traced to Egypt's prisons of the 1960s and 1970s, where some of the most prominent Islamist thinkers were detained.[6] The chief ideologist of Islamism, Sayid Qutb (1906–1966) inspired some of Islam's most prominent leaders, including Osama bin Laden and Ayatollah Khomeini. Early in his career, Qutb gained prominence as a literary critic. From 1948 to 1950 he lived in the United States as part of a mission to acquire information on US education curricula for the Egyptian Education Ministry. Initially a moderate, Qutb believed that Islam could be revised to meet the challenges of modernity, but his time in the United States shifted his ideological orientation. In 1951 he wrote a three-part essay based on his experiences, titled "The America I Have Seen." Apparently Qutb was aghast by what he had witnessed during his stay in the United States and was especially taken aback by the licentiousness of some Americans. As he would lead his readers to believe, the experience in the United States changed his outlook and he became a born-again Muslim of sorts.[7]

Although he grudgingly admired the nation's industrial and economic might, Qutb was highly critical of US secular society. Furthermore, he criticized US capitalism, describing it as overly competitive and devoid of spiritual meaning. The United States, he believed, was inherently aggressive and sought to enlist the Arab world for its struggle against the Soviet Union.[8] Although he conceded that the West, and the United States in particular, had made great accomplishments in science and technology, Qutb believed that these societies had become morally and spiritually bankrupt, and that the West had no dynamic principles remaining with which to guide the world.[9] Through Islam, he argued, human beings would reach heir highest stage of development. As Qutb saw things in the early 1950s, human history was at a crossroads. All types of government and human organizing systems—including communism, capitalism, democracy, and nationalism—were human constructs and thus woefully inadequate in comparison to the divine administration revealed in the Koran. In their stead, Islam would provide a religiopolitical ideology to lead humanity out of its current crisis. For Qutb, the Koran constituted a complete system of life—no additions were necessary.

In Qutb's analysis, the societies of the contemporary Muslim world were not authentically Islamic. Rather, they still existed in a state of *jahiliyya*—a Koranic term designating a pre-Islamic state of barbarism and ignorance. To Qutb, *jahiliyya* amounted to one person's lordship over another. Therefore, it was the duty of Muslims to implement *sharia*, or Islamic law, so that God alone would rule. For Qutb, the only places on earth that could genuinely be called Dar-al-Islam (the abode of Islam) were those countries and territories in which an Islamic state had been established, where *sharia* was recognized as the law, and where Muslims administered state affairs with mutual consultation (*shura*). The rest of the world was Dar-al-Harb (home of hostility). Based on this reasoning, Qutb argued that Muslims could have only two possible relations with Dar-al-Harb: peace with a contractual agreement, or war.[10] Qutb predicted that one day Islam would be engaged in a war with the United States.[11]

According to Qutb's reading of history, the universal quality of Islam and the potency of its faith had enabled its believers to prevail in the past.[12] He followed in the tradition of Ibn Taymiyya, a thirteenth-century Islamic purist who had castigated the Mongols of his day for not (as he saw it) following the Koranic guidelines laid down by the prophet Muhammad. In effect, Qutb used Taymiyya's doctrine to justify his struggle against the secular regime of Nasser.[13] According to some accounts, Qutb was instrumental in planning Nasser's coup in 1952.[14] Anwar Sadat, who succeeded Nasser as Egypt's president, once conceded that Qutb was the main ideologist of the Free Officers revolution.[15] Reportedly, Nasser admired Qutb's writings and even offered him a cabinet position.[16] But Qutb was not one to compromise when it came to applying Islamic principles, refusing to adulterate Islam with other concepts such as nationalism, democracy, and socialism, and he disapproved of Nasser's attempts to apply these systems in Egypt.[17] His criticism and oppositional activities landed Qutb in prison in the wake of Nasser's crackdown on the Muslim Brotherhood in 1954. While incarcerated, he wrote *Milestones*, a book that became the manifesto of the Islamist movement, a work tantamount to a declaration of war on the rulers of Muslim countries, including Nasser.

Perhaps Qutb's most significant contribution to Islamism was his exegesis on jihad. In order to bring about the new Islamic order, Qutb averred that the Islamists had to wage jihad, yet there were doctrinal strictures in Islam that discouraged revolution. For example, the Islamic notion of *fitna* refers to the disunity in the Islamic community within a half century of the prophet Muhammad's death, which resulted in the Sunni-Shiite split. The Sunni tradition strongly condemns *fitna* within the *umma* (worldwide community of Muslims), and even bad Sunni leadership is considered better than *fitna*.[18] Therefore, Qutb searched for a way to legitimize his revolt, invoking the concept of jihad against Arab regimes that were, he claimed, Muslim in name but *jahiliyya* in practice. Only through jihad could *jahiliyya* be combated.[19] Not unlike the Bolsheviks, Qutb argued that only a vanguard of the *umma* could lead the masses in a revolution. Qutb counseled that every Muslim, male and female, had the personal responsibility to undertake jihad against non-Islamic regimes. Anticipating the notion of leaderless resistance, he exhorted Muslims to assume their individual duties to "execute the will of Allah" as they saw fit, regardless of whether they could coordinate their actions through a single organization.[20] Thus, to create a genuine Islamic society, good Muslims needed to wage jihad against their local governments.[21] This theme would be taken up by subsequent Islamists. Like Soviet strategic theoreticians who believed that the laws of dialectical materialism assured the eventual victory of socialism, Qutb imparted to Islamists the certainty of victory if only they would follow the dictates of the Koran, thus giving them a sense of omnipotence in their struggle against the West and Zionism.

Qutb's authorship of *Milestones* was not without great cost, as it would eventually be used against him in a trial that concluded with a death sentence. Until the end of his life, he would serve as the supreme guide of the Muslim Brotherhood, yet the group was sharply divided on how to achieve power.[22] One faction favored a legal approach, while the other favored revolutionary violence. On August 29, 1966, Qutb was executed by the Egyptian state, and according to legend went to the gallows with a smile on his face. Through death he attained the status of *shaheed* (martyr), but in his absence Islamism entered a period of dormancy.[23] Facing formidable state repression, Islamism lost support among the political elite in the Middle East. By the early 1970s, however, events redounded to the movement's favor.

The Resurgence of Militant Islam

The Six-Day War in June 1967 between Egypt and Israel set the stage for the revival of the Islamist movement, as Egypt's defeat shocked the entire Muslim world and acted as a catalyst for change. The Arab population discussed the loss in apocalyptic terms, calling it "the second *Naqbah*" (holocaust).[24] The humiliating defeat at the hands of Israel bolstered the position of Islamists at the expense of the Arab nationalists and ushered in the Islamist awakening.[25] Islamic revivalism was in large part a reaction to failed nationalist programs. As the journalist and foreign affairs analyst Robin Wright explains, the Six-Day War was viewed as a catastrophe in the Arab world, and as a result, Arabs turned inward to look for an alternative to Nasserism, "and inward they found Islam."[26]

The 1973 Yom Kippur War further bolstered the stature of the Islamists. At the time of the conflict, a heightened sense of Islamic identity crystallized in the Arab world, as expressed in the rallying cry "*Allah akbar*" (God is great). Increasingly Islamism seemed a better vehicle through which to lead the Arab world out of its inferior position in relation to the West.

A rapprochement between Israel and Egypt further antagonized the Islamists, and their ranks continued to grow. With the signing of the Camp David Peace Accords in March 1979, the Egyptian president, Anwar Sadat, sealed his fate. His acceptance of a diplomatic solution to the Arab-Israel conflict alienated many of the Islamists and made him a marked man. On October 6, 1981, Islamists calling themselves Jama At al-Jihad (Sacred Combat) carried out a spectacular assassination as Sadat reviewed a military parade.[27] Although Sadat was killed, the subsequent putsch was quelled.

Sadat's assassins were greatly inspired by Muhammad Faraj's book *The Neglected Duty*. Faraj had left the Muslim Brotherhood because of its reluctance to engage in armed struggle against the government, and he would eventually emerge as the chief ideologist for Jama At al-Jihad. According to Faraj, any means were justified to overthrow apostate regimes, which were sometimes referred to as the "near enemy." This struggle even took precedence over the war against Jews and Israel, the "far enemy."[28] Leading by example, Faraj was executed in 1982 for his role in the assassination of Sadat.[29]

In the wake of the assassination, the Egyptian government brutally repressed the Islamists. A major trial, which included twenty-four defendants, followed in 1982. Five of the defendants were sentenced to death. One of the conspirators, Dr. Ayman al-Zawahiri, received a three-year sentence. Though he was convicted only on weapons charges, his role in the assassination was far more extensive.[30] He would go on to become the mentor of Osama bin Laden.[31]

The year 1979 was a landmark in the development of militant Islam, as it set in motion many trends of great importance today. Egypt signed a historic peace treaty with its longtime foe, Israel. The Soviet Union invaded Afghanistan. Perhaps most important, Ayatollah Ruhollah Khomeini seized power in Iran and created an Islamic republic. Arguably no other individual had more impact on the Islamic revival than Khomeini. Before the Iranian Revolution, Islamism was still a marginal heterodoxy.[32] The success of the Iranian Revolution and the creation of an Islamic theocratic regime further strengthened the legitimacy of militant Islam and added to its appeal as a means of effecting change in the Middle East. Sunni clerics had been regarded as the chief proponents of the Islamist movement, but the revolution in Iran demonstrated that Islamism resonated with Shiites too.

Khomeini's rise coincided with a further decline in the potency of Arab nationalism. As Khomeini was not hesitant to point out, Arab nationalism had failed to defeat Israel in every single military confrontation. In his view, only Islam could be an effective alternative to the ideology of nationalism.[33] Once his Islamic republic was firmly established, Khomeini believed it would become a beacon of inspiration for all Muslims. He cited his own government as one that could defy the dictates of the United States. In some ways the rise of Khomeini was a harbinger of a more radical strain of Islam that was incubating in the Middle East. As one observer remarked, Khomeini was the "Henry Ford of Islamic terrorism" in the sense that his "assembly-line" model of revolutionary indoctrination, which included training manuals and videos, religious indoctrination, and paramilitary training, became a template for other Islamist movements. Khomeini unequivocally identified the United States and Israel as the two principal enemies of Islam, demonizing them as the "Great Satan" and "Little Satan," respectively. Osama bin Laden would echo this theme in the 1990s.[34]

One drawback to Ayatollah Khomeini's ecumenism was the Shiite nature of his militant Islam. He insisted that his brand of radical Shiism dominate Islam, but Iran reportedly supported several Sunni Islamist causes despite the historical animosities between the denominations.[35] Although Khomeini's rhetoric was full of vitriol and fury, with minor exceptions his version of Islamism failed to inspire many Sunnis to fight to the death against the Great Satan. His influence did not reach far beyond southern Lebanon and other areas dominated by his minority Shiites.[36] Nevertheless, Khomeini's success in establishing an Islamic state in defiance of the West had a potent effect on all Islamists, Shiite and Sunni. By the early 1990s, Sunni radicals would once again occupy the forefront of radical Islamism.

Osama bin Laden and al Qaeda

The military origins of al Qaeda came out of the jihad against the Soviet army in Afghanistan.[37] The 1979 Soviet invasion of Afghanistan resulted in calls throughout the Islamic world for jihad. The subsequent Soviet-Afghan War stimulated Islamic terrorism in three ways. First, it provided terrorism-related skills to non-Afghan volunteers (the so-called Afghan Arabs) who came to Afghanistan to fight in the jihad. Second, the war provided the opportunity for Muslims from many different nationalities to create a truly global network, as veterans of the war traveled back to their countries to wage jihad against apostate regimes.[38] Estimates of the total number of Afghan Arab fighters range from 14,000 to 22,000.[39] Finally, Afghanistan has tremendous symbolic and emotive importance for the jihadist movement because it was where the mujahideen defeated the Soviet army. This victory restored the belief of Sunni Muslims that if they persevered, then anything was possible, God willing. As such, Afghanistan remains a powerful locus of recruitment for al Qaeda and other Islamist insurgent groups.[40] By defeating a superpower, Islamists developed an enormous sense of self-confidence that they could wage jihad successfully in other parts of the world as well.[41] After a series of humiliating defeats at the hands of Israel, the victory in Afghanistan harked back to an earlier era in which their forebears, under the banner of Islam, had been a potent force in world history.[42]

The Soviet war in Afghanistan internationalized radical Islamists and allowed them to distance themselves from the influence of Arab nationalism, both as a doctrine and as a factor dividing them.[43] Out of this struggle, a more ecumenical brand of Islamism would emerge. The war would prove to have long-term repercussions, as Afghanistan would become the incubator of the major jihadist organizations that would bedevil the United States in years to come.

While working on the war effort on the Afghan-Pakistan border, Osama bin Laden came under the influence of his former professor Abdullah Azzam, who became his spiritual mentor. Azzam's most important contribution to jihadist doctrine was his emphasis on self-sacrifice and martyrdom.[44] Together, Azzam and bin Laden were instrumental in creating MaK, the Afghan Services Bureau, which raised funds for the mujahideen's jihad against the Soviets. Eventually a split developed between them as the two competed for control of the movement. Azzam preferred to focus on supporting the mujahideen's struggle in Afghanistan and creating a base of operations for the next stage of jihadist resistance. He harbored no illusions about overturning Arab regimes at that point in the struggle and was well aware of the government repression and brutality that Islamists faced in places such as Egypt. Instead, he preferred to concentrate exclusively on liberating former Muslim countries and the periphery of the Muslim would, such as the Philippines, central Asia, Kashmir, and Palestine.[45] For his part, bin Laden wanted to export jihad to "apostate" Arab regimes and eventually take on their chief sponsor, the United States. He reasoned that to bring down these regimes, the Islamists needed to eventually curtail the political and economic influence of the United States. By 1988 bin Laden had completely split from Azzam, and MaK had established a separate guesthouse for the mujahideen in Pakistan.

Ultimately bin Laden's vision prevailed. On November 24, 1989, Azzam and his two sons were killed by a bomb as they traveled a mountainous route in Afghanistan. Although rumors circulated that bin Laden was connected to the assassination, he consistently denied these allegations, and no conclusive evidence of his involvement has ever surfaced.[46] The principal lesson bin Laden learned from Azzam was that real power lies in forming a pan-Islamic, rather than a pan-Arab, organization. By reaching out to Muslims outside the Middle East, such as in Asia and the Far East, he could attract extensive support and build a broad-based operational infrastructure.[47]

The event that drove bin Laden to the point of no return was the first Gulf War. To many Muslims, the Saudi government is viewed as the custodian of the two most sacred places in Islam—Mecca and Medina. Not long after Saddam Hussein's August 1990 invasion of Kuwait, tens of thousands of US troops began deploying in Saudi Arabia as part of a buildup for what would ultimately become Operation Desert Storm. The presence of foreign troops on Saudi soil appalled bin Laden, who had recently returned to the country after his tour of duty in Afghanistan. The Saudi government's decision to allow the US military on the holiest soil of Islam galled him. Fresh from victory in Afghanistan, he approached the royal family and offered to raise an army of five thousand veteran mujahideen volunteers to thwart any aggression by Iraq. Not wanting to risk the fate that had befallen Kuwait, the Saudi royal family declined his offer and instead accepted US military assistance.[48]

The overwhelming military superiority the United States demonstrated during the first Gulf War sent shock waves throughout the Middle East. Despite its large size and relative strength compared with its neighbors, Iraq was no match for the United States and its coalition. The example of Iraq was a stark lesson for the Islamists that it was unwise to challenge the United States directly. Irregular warfare was the only viable strategic choice. In light of the awesome power brought to bear against Iraq, future foes in the region began adopting an asymmetric approach when confronting the United States and its allies.[49] What is more, with the defeat of Saddam Hussein's Iraq, the last major bastion of pan-Arabism dissolved.

That US forces failed to withdraw after the war only deepened bin Laden's sense of betrayal. He began to openly lecture against the Saudi royal family, and audio-cassettes of his sermons were widely distributed in Saudi Arabia. Further, he financially supported Saudi opposition groups based in London.[50] Crossing his own ideological Rubicon, he dispatched al Qaeda cells into Saudi Arabia to establish a presence, and they remain there to this day.[51] All of this was too much for the Saudi government, which would brook no opposition to its rule, not even from a national hero like bin Laden. He was effectively placed under house arrest, and his travel was limited to the city of Jeddah.[52] Despite these measures, he managed to escape to Kabul in 1992, where he sought to stop the internecine fighting among Afghan resistance factions. Not long after, he flew to Khartoum, the Sudanese capital.[53]

By the early 1990s, security services in the Middle East demonstrated that they were able to contain the radical Islamist movements in their countries.[54] Into this void Osama bin Laden reached. The marginalization of jihadist groups in Arab nations produced a large number of recruits for al Qaeda.[55] With the connections and moral authority established by his exploits in Afghanistan, bin Laden found sanctuary in Sudan, where he was welcomed by Hassan al-Turabi, a charismatic cleric who led the ruling National Islamic Front. Together, the Sudanese government and bin Laden launched a number of business and development projects.[56] From this secure base, bin Laden intensified his operations, expanded his terrorist network, and planned attacks against the United States.

But bin Laden eventually became too much of a liability for the Sudanese government, which came under increasing US pressure. He was forced to leave Sudan in 1996, but he found safe haven in Afghanistan, where he established headquarters in 1996.[57] Around that time, the Taliban, a militant Islamic group led by Mullah Mohammed Omar, achieved decisive victories in its battles against rival mujahideen groups, thus establishing control over most of the Afghan territory. The Taliban's rapid success in Afghanistan was facilitated by Pakistan's ISI, which supplied assault rifles, ammunition, training, logistics, and even combat support.[58] By the spring of 1996, the Taliban had conquered most of Afghanistan and brought a semblance of peace and security to a land beset with tribal warfare. With their strict interpretation of Islam, the Taliban forces were the only thing that could hold the country together and overcome the divisive tendencies of tribalism. Still, the Taliban was more an ideological movement than a functioning government apparatus.[59]

Bin Laden soon established a strategic alliance with Omar. This occurred for several reasons. First, bin Laden was attracted to the Taliban's conservative Islamic ideology. Second, bin Laden offered significant financial aid to the Taliban. Finally, the Afghan Arabs were known for their role in the jihad against the Soviets and thus their Afghan hosts trusted them.[60] To show his appreciation, bin Laden organized the 055 Brigade—an integrated army consisting of both al Qaeda and Taliban fighters—to battle the Northern Alliance, a resistance movement confined to a small area in northeastern Afghanistan that was led by Ahmed Shah Massoud. The assistance from al Qaeda was crucial. In exchange, Omar offered al Qaeda free movement in the country. At times the relations between the two were strained, as Omar thought that bin Laden's use of Western media to publicize his hatred of the United States was dangerous and could provoke retaliation.

In August 1996, Osama bin Laden formally proclaimed himself an enemy of the United States with a formal declaration of war.[61] Over the years, his fatwas denouncing the United States became more strident. At a press conference in Khost, Afghanistan, in May 1998, he announced the creation of "the Islamic Front for the Struggle against Jews and the Crusaders" (later called the World Islamic Front), exhorting Islamists leaders to forge a coalition with which to confront the United States. Initially he cited three major reasons why the United States should be targeted: the presence of US troops in Saudi Arabia, the sanctions regime imposed on Iraq and the consequent suffering of its population, and US support for Israel and what bin Laden saw as apostate regimes in the Middle East.[62]

The new organization strengthened existing ties between groups such as Ayman al-Zawahiri's Egyptian Islamic Jihad, which in June 2001 effectively merged with al Qaeda.[63] Zawahiri imparted to bin Laden a revolutionary jihadist ideology and surrounded him with some of the most important members of the jihadist movement.[64] For many years he was an advocate of the "near enemy" strategy, believing it was first necessary to bring down authoritarian regimes in the Middle East before taking on Israel and its chief sponsor, the United States. By first confronting the internal enemy, Islamists could consolidate power and then be in a better position to take on the external enemy. But events occasioned a change in Zawahiri's strategy. Fawaz Gerges argues that the decision to strike the far enemy arose from the strategic defeat of religious nationalists on their home fronts.[65] While they were together in Afghanistan, Zawahiri persuaded bin Laden to switch from his Salafist preacher approach to more of a jihadist fighter approach.[66]

Ensconced in Afghanistan, bin Laden resumed his war against the United States. On August 7, 1998, the seventh anniversary of the first US soldiers setting foot in Saudi Arabia, he launched a spectacular attack. A suicide truck bombing of the US embassy in Nairobi, Kenya, killed 224 people—including twelve Americans—and injured many more. Minutes later, another truck bomb exploded thirty-five feet from the US embassy in Dar es Salaam, Tanzania, killing twelve persons and seriously wounding eighty-five. The Clinton administration responded with Operation Infinite Reach, a secret attack on August 20, 1998, which launched cruise missiles toward a Sudanese factory believed to be manufacturing deadly VX nerve gas (it turned out to be only a pharmaceutical factory) and al Qaeda training camps in Afghanistan. Bin Laden had left the training camps not long before the attack, narrowly escaping injury. The US retaliation deepened the bond between bin Laden and Omar.[67] Another major attack took place on October 12, 2000, when a small ship navigated by two reputed al Qaeda operatives attacked the USS *Cole* as it floated in a port in Aden, Yemen, for refueling. Seventeen US sailors were killed and many more were injured.[68]

The September 11, 2001, attacks on the World Trade Center and the Pentagon were apparently the culmination of al Qaeda's terrorist campaign against the United States. Through spectacular acts of terrorism, bin Laden sought to polarize the Islamic world between the faithful *umma* and the regimes that ally themselves with the United States. As one observer has noted, bin Laden's attack on the United States was designed to overcome the weakness of political Islam, in that he succeeded in striking a blow against the universal enemy—the United States—which all Salafist movements around the world can recognize as their own.[69] The attacks against the United States resonated deeply with many of the more radically inclined Muslims around the world and also some secular groups in Arab countries. By his terrorist actions, bin Laden reinforced the belief that the *umma* constitutes one political community.[70]

Al Qaeda 2.0

Initially Islamists were adversely affected by the 9/11 attacks, which provoked a massive response from the United States and its allies. The ensuing backlash provided the political elite in the Middle East with the opportunity to suppress the

Islamists and other oppositional voices in the name of fighting terrorism.[71] Even Islamist groups not affiliated with al Qaeda found themselves caught in the new dragnet. According to some estimates, by early 2003 roughly two-thirds of al Qaeda's leadership had been killed or captured since 9/11, including many at the very top.[72] As a result, Osama bin Laden received considerable criticism in Islamist circles for having grossly underestimated the US response. In the wake of 9/11, no country could afford to be accused of harboring terrorists. The strategic environment had drastically changed to the detriment of the Islamists.[73] When Operation Enduring Freedom began in October 2001, al Qaeda initially lost its sanctuary in Afghanistan. Consequently the organization was deprived of vital resources and much of its financial assets were confiscated.[74] Although al Qaeda has skillfully employed terrorism in the past, some observers believe that the leadership gravely miscalculated by provoking a ferocious response for which the organization was unprepared.[75]

Nevertheless, al Qaeda quickly reformulated from a centralized organization into a series of autonomous organizations driven by local concerns, allowing the network to endure. Even before 9/11, al Qaeda was an insurgent group in exile without a popular base of support. The organization attracted a pan-Islamist global army of fighters financed by sympathizers around the world. Graduates of training camps operated worldwide and al Qaeda planned attacks without geographical limitation. New communications technology amplified this trend and enabled the movement to survive and continue operations without popular support in the classic sense of the term.[76]

Al Qaeda 2.0, as defined by Peter Bergen, suggests a decentralized alliance of terrorists spread throughout the world.[77] Since Operation Enduring Freedom, al Qaeda has been transformed into a more diffuse network that can still strike US targets abroad.[78] The organization has no single center of gravity, but multiple ones. The flexibility enables al Qaeda to effectively prosecute asymmetric warfare.[79] In some ways al Qaeda has become an "imagined jihadist community" or a "state of mind" organization. Although the core of the network has a rather hierarchical structure, the periphery is amorphous. Lacking a bureaucratic element and a concrete chain of command to provide strategic directives, the global Salafist community conducts strategic and operational discourse on jihadist web-based discussion groups.[80] Evidence suggests that disparate individuals and groups inspired by al Qaeda's ideology are coordinating and conducting attacks on their own initiative—a genuine form of leaderless resistance in practice. This has allowed the organization to persist despite efforts to destroy it. Once al Qaeda cells are established, they may require little direction from their superiors. Rather, they can act on their own initiative when the opportunity presents itself.[81] Significantly, nearly all Islamist terrorist attacks since 2002 have been conducted by either a franchised or an unaffiliated group.[82] In short, jihadists are exhorted to think globally but act locally.

By late 2002, al Qaeda appeared to have switched tactics, moving away from spectacular acts of terrorism to an attrition-style campaign, as evidenced by numerous bombings in Tunisia, Bali, Kenya, Pakistan, Morocco, Saudi Arabia, and Spain. Rohan Gunaratna, an authority on al Qaeda who has interviewed members of the organization, explains the transition of the group:

> Leaderless resistance or homegrown individuals or cells emerged due to sustained law enforcement and intelligence operations against structured threat groups. With the increase in threat from governments to terrorist groups, al Qaeda developed a strategy to radicalize the Muslim community by ideologically indoctrinating Muslims. Although the operational infrastructures of threat groups have suffered, the conceptual infrastructures of threat groups remain intact. As a direct result of the failure of governments to counter ideological extremism, the threat from homegrown terrorism and extremism has increased. This is largely due to the huge investment al Qaeda and its likeminded groups have made in propaganda.[83]

According to Michael Scheuer, a former CIA employee who served as chief of the Bin Laden Issue Station, al Qaeda's strength can be explained in large part by the spiritual preparation of its members. Al Qaeda's members are instructed to accept the notion that victory will come only when a sufficient number of Muslims return to Allah's path, abandon their fear of death, and embrace jihad. The most exceptional trait Scheuer finds in al Qaeda is its success in forging a united, global movement that has eliminated animosity among members of a variety of nationalities. The genius of bin Laden was that he was able to create an overarching political ideology into which the agendas of other groups could be subsumed. Despite its heterogeneous membership, the movement has remained cohesive. Furthermore, that it has remained a united and disciplined fighting force in a war against the United States is significant.[84]

The US invasion of Iraq in 2003 breathed new life into the jihadist movement. Scheuer describes the war against Iraq as a "gift" to bin Laden, which validated much of what he had previously said about US intentions. Moreover, the war presented the prospect of a classic defensive jihad, turning Iraq into a "jihad magnet" attracting Islamic fighters from around the region.[85] With the invasion of Iraq, Scheuer believes the United States committed a grave strategic error—diverting resources from the global war on terror as it became mired in an internecine, sectarian conflict.[86] During and immediately after Operation Enduring Freedom in Afghanistan, the al Qaeda network was systematically dismantled, as many important leaders and key operatives were killed or captured. The Iraq War, though, gave the organization new vitality, enabling the network to be successfully transformed into a broader social movement. Evidence suggests that groups and individuals with no organizational connection to al Qaeda, inspired by the group's ideology, are coordinating and conducting attacks on their own initiative.

The Iraqi insurgency developed without a center of gravity. No rigid hierarchy or leadership structure exists. Rather, it exemplifies the fluid nature of modern terrorist networks. The Iraqi insurgency consists of a shifting network of disparate entities and actors without the organizational and ideological cohesion of the classic Maoist insurgency. Despite a lack of centralization, insurgents have demonstrated an ability to coordinate their efforts. Furthermore, they all share the same goal: to expel the foreign occupiers. The insurgency has several factions, the most important of which are indigenous to Iraq. The major factions include former regime loyalists, Iraqi nationalists with Islamist leanings, tribal bands and criminal gangs, and foreign Sunni Islamists who exploit Iraq's porous borders to make their contribution to jihad. Although the foreign fighters represent a relatively small segment of the entire insurgency—an estimated 5–10 percent of the total—they nevertheless concern coalition military authorities. Overall, at its peak, the insurgency was estimated to number between ten thousand and thirty thousand fighters.[87]

The Iraqi insurgency differs from the classic Maoist insurgency in a number of significant ways. First, in the Iraqi case there was no preliminary political mobilization. Second, rather than ideological cohesion, the Iraqi insurgency is a variegated movement. Also, unlike communist insurgents, the Iraqi rebels do not conduct large-scale guerrilla operations. Instead they mount small-scale asymmetrical ones. For the most part too, the Iraqi insurgents do not seek to control territory, at least not for a sustained period of time. One lesson they learned from the Fallujah campaign in 2004 was that they could not fight effectively in a static position. Rather than endeavoring to win a conventional military victory, they seek to destroy an enemy's political will. The Iraqi insurgents also differ from Maoists with respect to bases of support, as they often live with their families. Therefore they do not require the same level of logistical support as the communist insurgents, who often controlled territory far from their homes. Thus one major advantage of the Iraqi insurgents is that they do not have to rely as much on the population as previous insurgents did.[88] As Loretta Napoleoni has observed, far from following the classic model of Cold War era insurgency, Iraq resembles more the outbreak of violence that plagued the Balkans in the 1990s.[89] On the one hand, the large number of groups suggests a political weakness. On the other hand, it made it difficult for US forces to unravel or understand the insurgency or to decapitate a centralized leadership structure, because no such structure exists. The Iraqi insurgency includes a mix of both centralized and decentralized networks. The former regime elements tend to affiliate with the more hierarchical networks. By contrast, the tribal and neighborhood insurgents tend to be more decentralized.[90] Drawing terminology from the world of commerce, John Robb sees the Iraq insurgency as having a "long tail" in the sense that it is not made of a single army with one goal but composed of hundreds of small groups.[91] Nevertheless, the divided insurgency is not unprecedented.[92]

Despite its persistence and durability, the Iraqi insurgency has several disadvantages that limit its effectiveness. Its chief weakness is that it has no unified platform of the sort that the Vietcong and the Algerian FLN had.[93] With the Iraqi insurgency composed primarily of Sunnis who are a minority in Iraq (about 20 percent of the entire population), its struggle cannot attain the status of a popular war of national liberation.[94] Relatedly, the vast majority of Iraqis do not want to see the Baath Party return to power.[95] Finally, the insurgents lack a unifying creed to rally behind, other than the immediate aim of expelling the coalition forces from Iraq. With that feat accomplished, the competing groups are fighting one another. After the US withdrawal, violence and political instability have escalated in Iraq.

After several years of frustration for coalition forces, stabilization has occurred, in large measure because of the surge of US troops in early 2007 under the direction of army general David Petraeus. Crucial to creating a stable Iraq was securing Baghdad and ensuring the safety of its residents. Prior to the surge, US military forces concentrated on seeking out and killing enemy combatants. This approach was problematic, however, because of the nature of guerrilla warfare. When outnumbered, insurgents usually melt into a crowd and wait to fight another day. Petraeus's new strategy sought primarily to protect the population and gain their trust and cooperation. Eventually, the so-called Anbar Awakening resulted in Sunni tribes making common cause with coalition and Iraqi government forces. Rather than a top-down development, it occurred more from the bottom up, with more and more local sheikhs supporting security efforts. Al Qaeda's atrocities and lack of respect for tribal sensibilities eventually precipitated a backlash, making tribes more amenable to the coalition forces and the fledgling Iraqi government. To stave off this development al Qaeda responded with horrendous reprisals, but these served only to further alienate the tribes. What was crucial for Petraeus's strategy was having enough boots on the ground to provide security for the population so that it could resist al Qaeda and related militants.[96]

One of the most worrisome propositions from the perspective of the US government and its coalition allies is that the insurgents will apply their knowledge of urban guerrilla warfare to other theaters after the Iraq War is over. As Peter Bergen and Alec Reynolds observed, the insurgents are testing themselves against what is perhaps the best army in history. The skills developed in the war, including car bombings and assassinations, would be more applicable to urban guerrilla warfare than knowledge the Afghan Arabs acquired in the Soviet-Afghan War.[97] Just as the Soviet war served as an incubator for subsequent jihadists, so could the Iraq War have a comparable effect on the contemporary global jihadist movement, as Paul Pillar, a veteran CIA counterterrorism official, explains:

> We already have seen . . . this in the form of Iraqi-based jihadists conducting attacks in places such as Jordan. But as with Afghanistan, most of the effects will be felt years in the future. In some respects, the aftereffects of Iraq are more worrisome than the ones from [the Soviet-Afghan War]. With regard to the skill-development issue, more of the conflict in Iraq has been in the form of urban guerrilla warfare, which is closer in the relevant skill sets to terrorism than was the more rural-based insurgency in Afghanistan.[98]

The jihadist violence could have an impact on other political movements as well. The ongoing wars in the Middle East might inspire oppositional groups compelled toward violent confrontation with states, not unlike what happened during the Vietnam War when radical left-wing groups within the United States adopted and adapted the tactics of guerrilla warfare based on practices in Vietnam, Cuba, Algeria, and elsewhere.[99] Some elements of the Far Left have defended radical Islam based on a shared anti-Americanism.[100] More counterintuitively, some elements of the extreme Right have lauded Islamic radicals based on a shared hatred of Israel and Jews.[101]

Much is at stake in Iraq. If the United States fails, it would give jihadists an enormous sense of self-confidence, as after the Soviet-Afghan War. The credibility and reliability of the United States would be in serious doubt, with great consequences for US interests and those of Middle East allies. On the other hand, if the United States can help Iraq form a viable government and revive the economy, this model could prove to be a great threat to antidemocratic and extremist forces in the region. Some observers fear that a precipitous US military withdrawal could trigger a full-scale Sunni-Shiite civil war.[102] If Iraq should break into pieces, it could lead to the destabilization of much of the surrounding region. What the United States sought to destroy in Afghanistan could be effectively re-created in Iraq.[103] Arguably, the diversion of US troops from Afghanistan to Iraq enabled the resurgence of the Taliban.

In the opening stages of Operation Enduring Freedom, US forces squared off against the Taliban, which was arrayed as a conventional fighting force. Unsurprisingly, US forces quickly routed the Taliban. Despite the initial victory in the conventional stage of the war, though, the 101st Airborne and 10th Mountain Divisions did not have an adequate number of troops on the ground, enabling Osama bin Laden to escape encirclement during the battle for Tora Bora in December 2001. After Operation Anaconda, the scattered elements of the Taliban and al Qaeda regrouped in the rugged border region in the North-West Frontier Province of Pakistan. Rather than decisively defeating al Qaeda and the Taliban, the United States and its coalition merely pushed the core of their leadership out of Afghanistan and into Pakistan. This failure to finish the job would have serious consequences, as it allowed the mujahideen to develop into a viable insurgency. After the conventional phase of the war, the Taliban left the urban areas and reverted to being a rural insurgent movement. In such an environment, massive firepower has strict limitations, as targets became less defined and better dispersed.[104]

As Seth G. Jones, an analyst at the Rand Corporation, explained, the "light footprint" military approach worked well during the conventional phase of the conflict, resulting in a quick overthrow of the Taliban regime, but this approach did not suffice for the peacekeeping phase that followed. And while a large occupation force can often trigger the growth of an insurgency that seeks to eject foreign troops, in the absence of a functioning, competent government, a light occupation can fail to provide the security essential to establishing order.[105] Jones argues that the main factor in the rebirth of the Taliban was weak governance. The second factor he sees as the religious ideology of the Taliban, "a well-articulated cause from insurgent leaders." Other factors contributed, including a mountainous terrain and low per capita incomes that can compound the grievances of a restive population. Moreover, the Afghan insurgents were able to tap into an array of resources from neighboring governments and the international jihadist network. Together, the supply of rural villagers disaffected with a failing government and the demand for recruits by ideologically motivated leaders provided the factors necessary for developing the Afghan insurgency.[106]

After the US invasion of Afghanistan in October 2001, the epicenter of international terrorism shifted to tribal Pakistan, located along the rugged 1,520-mile border separating the country from Afghanistan. This isolated region, known as the Federally Administered Tribal Areas (FATA), has emerged as the most important terrorist sanctuary in recent history. Virtually all terrorist and militant groups active in Afghanistan during the Taliban reign have reconstituted and maintain a robust presence in the FATA. As early as July 2002, remnants of the Taliban and al Qaeda, which reestablished themselves in the safe portions of Pakistan's semiautonomous tribal regions, began to move back into Afghanistan. By the summer of 2003, the Taliban had regrouped to fight a guerrilla-style war against US troops and the coalition, just as the mujahideen had fought the Soviet army two decades before. By 2004 it was estimated that the Taliban controlled roughly one-third of Afghan territory. Like insurgents in Iraq, Afghan insurgents have sought to destabilize the country by attacking key government officials, police officers, and NGO representatives. As the Taliban pursued an asymmetrical strategy, the relevance of conventional war diminished as a viable strategy for the US military. By 2010 the Taliban were estimated to have twenty-five thousand fighters.[107]

Al Qaeda remains the vanguard organization providing crucial knowledge and methodology to mobilize jihadist groups. Although the central organization's numbers are quite small—in June 2010, CIA director Leon Panetta estimated the figure to be between fifty and one hundred—al Qaeda still exerts a substantial influence: the group's ideology and tactics have spread throughout the Islamic world.[108] Ensconced in the FATA, much of the core leadership of al Qaeda survived, but several key leaders were captured or killed when they ventured elsewhere in Pakistan.[109] Nevertheless, al Qaeda central manages to plan key operations and terrorist attacks, not only in Pakistan and Afghanistan, but also through affiliated groups and migrant populations in the West.[110]

Jihadist Networks in the West

The global jihad has penetrated regions far removed from the Middle East. A third of the world's Muslims now live as minorities in the countries in which they reside.[111] According to some estimates, 80 percent of known jihadists reside in diasporic communities and are often physically disconnected from one another.[112] Europe's estimated twenty-three million Muslims represent 5 percent of the continent's total population, as well as the world's largest Muslim diaspora and the continent's largest religious minority.[113] Following the loss of al Qaeda's central base in Afghanistan, Europe has become even more important to the organization. Nearly every major attack carried out by al Qaeda throughout the world has had some link to Europe. For example, the 9/11 attacks were partially planned in Hamburg.[114] Although the United States and Israel are considered the far enemy, Europe is—besides being something of a base for jihadists—often targeted, because it is easy to move and organize freely in democratic societies.[115]

In his study *Globalized Islam: The Search for a New Ummah*, the French scholar of Islam Olivier Roy argued that Muslims in the West often experience a trauma of "deterritorialization," because they feel estranged from their native lands. To overcome their anomie and alienation, young Muslims in particular find solace in a new, purified Islam and attach themselves to a "virtual ummah" built on the World Wide Web.[116] Much of the new Muslim consciousness is formed from the Internet. Prior to the widespread diffusion of the Internet, terrorism was based primarily on face-to-face interactions. New technology enabled a movement to develop based on a loose, decentralized global network. The network plays the same role that "imagined communities" played in the development of feelings of nationalism.[117] However, the virtual community is not tied to any particular country. The Internet can help bridge the gap for an isolated person to connect with the global jihad.[118]

Social networks are vital to terrorism. A former CIA employee who was based in Islamabad during the late 1980s, Marc Sageman has had much direct interaction with jihadists. According to Sageman, the principal threat the West faces is not from a revived al Qaeda that straddles the lawless border of Afghanistan and Pakistan, but rather from loose-knit cells of Western-born Muslims and Muslim immigrants residing in the West. He maintains that al Qaeda's leadership has been greatly diminished, and, as such, exercises little operational control over contemporary jihadist groups. More troublesome today is the "third wave" of jihadists, a leaderless hodgepodge of what Sageman calls "terrorist wannabes," for whom ideology is less important.[119] These jihadists tend to be disaffected youths who are more like urban gang members than Islamic fanatics. Like Roy, Sageman found a strong link between the Muslim diaspora and terrorism, as the majority of subjects in his sample had joined the global Islamist terror network in a country where they did not grow up.[120] It is their lack of assimilation in their ambient society that has spurred them to join a virtual network.[121]

What Western jihadists seem to share is the urgent belief that Muslims are under attack by non-Muslims. Furthermore, the allure of joining a seemingly empowered social network should not be discounted.[122] The radicalization of Muslims in Europe and in the United States appears to differ markedly, much of the difference stemming from national identity. Whereas in the United States national identity is based largely on a creed grounded in the American Dream, democracy, individualism, and equality before the law, in Europe national identity is often based on an essence, including ethnicity, language, culture, and shared history. Thus assimilation is much easier in the United States than in Europe. A high concentration of Muslim immigrants in some European cities has produced communities where Islamists can spread their message. In such areas, radical Islam has become a sort of counterculture. By contrast, Muslims in the United States tend to be geographically dispersed.[123] Further, the American Dream, which entails such precepts as equality and individualism, encourages the desire for social mobility. This ideology makes it more difficult to blame external factors for lack of success. Europe's more generous welfare policies allow Muslims the time to engage in radicalization by browsing websites and attending mosques in which radical imams hold sway. By contrast, Sageman believes, in the United States would-be jihadists are too tired from a long day at work to seriously entertain such notions.[124] However, a spate of Islamist terrorist plots over the past few years suggest that radical Islam has made inroads in the United States.

In his initial study, *Understanding Terrorist Networks*, Sageman found that membership growth in jihadist networks was essentially bottom-up and self-selecting rather than based on recruitment. Generally he found his subjects middle-class, sane, well informed, and formally educated.[125] Jihadists in the West tend to spontaneously self-organize through "bunches of guys" joining groups with which they have a contact, such as a friend or relative.[126] Sageman rejects the theory that they are brainwashed or coerced into joining. He argues that it is a three-pronged process, consisting first of social affiliation with the jihad, accompanied by friendship, kinship, and discipleship (spreading the religious faith). Second, it includes a progressive intensification of beliefs and faith, leading to the acceptance of the global Salafist jihadist ideology. Finally, through an encounter with someone linked to the jihad, a prospective member gains acceptance into the group. By affiliating with a clique, a person may begin to identify with larger causes, as activists transform their sense of themselves and their relationships with others. Furthermore, as they become members, they can develop strong bonds of loyalty and emotional intimacy that can discourage their departure.[127] As Sageman points out, once someone has joined, group loyalties make leaving difficult. A member's comrades become best friends and a substitute family.[128] Although the personal jihad may be presented as an individual struggle, in reality, Sageman found, it is a social one. Faith and commitment are usually grounded and sustained within a group context, as friends and peers provide support and guidance.[129] Thus jihadists "follow kin and colleagues more than they do orders from afar."[130] Religion and a shared ideology foster social capital—that is, a sense of shared trust. But al Qaeda's media outreach is instrumental in this regard.

The Media Strategy

The Internet is an important aspect of al Qaeda's campaign. Ayman al-Zawahiri once said: "We are in a battle, and more than half of this battle is taking place in the battlefield of the media. We are in a media battle for the hearts and minds of our *umma*."[131] To that end, al Qaeda has a media committee, which was first led by a jihadist with the nom de guerre Abu Reuter. At present, the committee operates as something of a communications company, producing occasional videotapes rather than terrorist acts.[132] Al Qaeda has become the strategic communicator for the global Salafist movement, having stepped up its media operations over the years.[133] Those most susceptible to its propaganda are Muslims in or near conflict zones, as well as Muslims in diasporic communities.[134]

Apparently the Iraq War was the catalyst for the general surge in the number of jihadist online media outlets observed since 2003. In the media age, what may before have been isolated local insurgencies now have the potential to capture the attention of a worldwide audience. The late Abu Musab al-Zarqawi, the recognized leader of the foreign insurgents and al Qaeda in Iraq, mobilized computer-savvy allies to fight the US occupation.[135] In the Iraq War, he embraced the video camera as a weapon and encouraged militant groups to videotape their operations so they could later be broadcast as propaganda.[136] Using camcorders and the Internet, he was able to mount international media events at the tactical level, which had a tremendous strategic impact. He pioneered a new method of communication and even employed an online press secretary. An online jihadist—"Irhabi007"—was responsible for posting many of his pronouncements on the web and played a central role in Zarqawi's public relations network. It turned out that Irhabi007 was Younis Tsouli, a twenty-two-year-old West London resident of Moroccan descent.[137] His example illustrates how a distant audience can take an active role in conflicts around the world.

In 2005 al Qaeda's media outreach suffered a setback when the television network al Jazeera stopped airing the organization's videos in their entirety. Meanwhile, the US government and its allies pressured Internet service providers to shut down Islamist websites. Furthermore, many key online jihadists were captured, including Younis Tsouli.[138] In May 2008, Senator Joseph Lieberman (I-CT), the chair of the Senate Homeland Security Committee, wrote to Google officials and urged them to take down videos produced by al Qaeda and other terrorist groups.[139] Despite these measures, the web presence of al Qaeda has been resilient.

The researcher Brynjar Lia has observed a shift in jihadist websites from noninteractive, more or less official ones toward a much more multilayered and redundant media production and distribution system.[140] A thorough study that scanned the Internet revealed that more than forty-three hundred websites served terrorists and their supporters.[141] Moreover, there are now Islamist sites that target a Western audience.[142] By late 2007, West Point's Combating Terrorism Center estimated that as many as one hundred English-language websites offered militant Islamic views. In addition, sites are available in languages other than English and Arabic, enabling jihadists to reach a new audience.[143]

According to US and European intelligence sources, al Qaeda's media committee—as-Sahab (The Clouds)—established a secure base in the ungoverned tribal areas of western Pakistan. Despite his diminished operational stature in the final years of his life, Osama bin Laden continued to use the media. To maintain security, typically when he wanted to deliver a speech a trusted cameraman would meet him at a safe house in Pakistan and shoot the video. The footage was then edited, stored on a small computer memory stick, given to a courier, and passed through several hands to disguise its route. Finally, an operative in an Internet café would save the data to a password-protected website.[144] Likewise, bin Laden's chief lieutenant, Zawahiri, maintains a robust presence on the web. In December 2007 he announced in a web forum that he would answer questions on virtually any topic. His offer resulted in 1,888 written queries from journalists and the public.[145] Al Qaeda's appropriation of the new media is not without drawbacks, however, as it has taken some control out of the leadership's hands. As a result of the democratization and decentralization of the media, would-be leaders may find it increasingly difficult to control the debate in their ideological circles.[146]

According to Brynjar Lia, the "e-jihad" depends significantly on free web hosting, anonymous access to web storage, and file sharing.[147] Web sites on which large video files can be uploaded for free are invaluable to the online jihadists, allowing them to disseminate high-quality material. Lia identified several categories of jihadist websites, suggesting a division and specialization of labor.[148] It is now possible for terrorist movements to control the entire communications process, so that they can now they determine the content and context of their messages and how to convey them to specific audiences.[149] By doing so, al Qaeda reaches several target audiences, including both supporters and enemies. Thus the Internet is an important contributing factor that makes jihadist terrorism more global in scope, as it reduces the need for physical contact and makes possible the coordination of decentralized autonomous groups sharing the same ideology. The anonymity of the Internet enables extremists to interact more freely with fewer constraints than in a real-world setting in which monitoring is almost ubiquitous.[150]

Resources for would-be terrorists are now available online. For example, al Qaeda's online *Encyclopedia of Jihad* offers religious guidance as well as instructions on terrorism and insurgency. This Internet library allows scattered jihadists unaffiliated with al Qaeda to train at their leisure in their own homes and plan operations with less chance of being detected and interdicted.[151] To date, the Internet serves primarily as a resource bank of training manuals and handbooks maintained and accessed largely by self-radicalized sympathizers rather than a "virtual training camp" operated by al Qaeda. Jihadists use the Internet as an interactive forum to discuss training-related issues, convey personal experiences, and ask online "trainers" for advice and clarification on related subjects. Much of the instructional materials are derived from English-language open sources, including US Army field manuals and various explosives "cookbooks." Advanced technology enables the production of high-quality instructional videos that can be uploaded online. So far, the Lebanese group Hezbollah has produced the highest-quality videos on explosives manufacturing. Some Salafist sites have appropriated these videos and modified them for Sunni audiences. According to the terrorism researcher Anne Stenersen, the Internet can best be viewed as a kind of "pre-school of jihad" rather than a "university," since jihadists tend to use Internet manuals as a preparation for real-life training rather than a substitute for it.[152]

Leaderless Jihad

Sustained law enforcement and intelligence operations against structured terrorist groups forced a tactical shift to leaderless resistance. To meet this challenge, al Qaeda developed a strategy to radicalize the Muslim community by ideologically indoctrinating Muslims through the Internet. Owing to al Qaeda's decentralized orientation, there is no overarching training doctrine. Several prominent theoreticians, including Abdullah Azzam, Abdel Aziz al-Muqrin, Ayman al-Zawahiri, Abu Bakr Naji, Sayyid Imam al-Sharif, and Abu Musab al-Suri, have propounded jihadist strategies, but they have often differed in their approaches.[153] Nevertheless, they all agree on the importance of ideological indoctrination and spiritual preparation, and think this should take precedence over physical and military training. Osama bin Laden counseled Muslims that jihad was an "individual duty" for every one of them capable of going to war, declaring that "no other priority, except faith, could be considered before [jihad]."[154] He encouraged Muslims around the world to view their regional conflicts not as isolated, parochial struggles but as theaters of a larger war to defend Islam against the West and Zionism. Over the years, his video pronouncements suggested a change in al Qaeda's strategy. Al Qaeda has effectively been transformed from a centralized hierarchy to a communications hub that exhorts jihadist cells and Islamist lone wolves to commit acts of terrorism and resistance on their own initiative without central al Qaeda direction.

Since the US war in Afghanistan commenced in October 2001, al Qaeda has been moving toward a more decentralized approach to terrorism, in which loosely affiliated groups with slight connections to the central organization commit acts of terrorism on their own. Such groups tap into bin Laden's "franchise" and adopt al Qaeda's brand name.[155] Leaderless resistance has caught on in the jihadist movement. Radical Islamists with only tenuous affiliations to terrorist organizations have demonstrated the capacity to form ad hoc amalgamations of like-minded individuals and converge to conduct acts of violence, representing what Bruce Hoffman once dubbed the "amateurization of terrorism."[156] Al Qaeda has mastered the new terrorist paradigm that researchers at the Rand Corporation have referred to as swarming—an operational innovation whereby dispersed nodes of a network of forces converge on a target from multiple directions to accomplish a task, then disperse immediately. This tactical flexibility allows al Qaeda to seize advantage of opportunities.[157]

Even without much direct communication or collaboration, and without guidance from Osama bin Laden since his death in May 2011, small jihadist outfits around the world now claim to be part of al Qaeda and commit acts of terrorism on their own. By doing so they bring attention to their local grievances and gain the prestige of belonging to an international movement, often resulting in the United States racing out to fight them.[158] Islamist cells with tenuous connections to al Qaeda receive a green light from the parent organization, but the targets and specific operational details are left under the control of the cells. The March 2004 train bombings in Madrid are believed to have followed this model. The attack killed 191 people and wounded roughly 1,800 others.[159] The common thread in almost all terrorist attacks after 9/11 is their having been launched by local groups. This presents a challenge to law enforcement and intelligence agencies since it is generally easier to spot and stop foreign agents than to detect locals who can blend in.[160] Islamic terrorism in western Europe usually occurs in a small-group context. In contrast, jihadist lone wolves feature prominently in the United States.[161]

Marc Sageman has written the definitive study on the "leaderless jihad." After Operation Enduring Freedom in Afghanistan, Sageman believes, al Qaeda has been largely isolated in the Waziristan region of northwest Pakistan and exercises little to no operational direction over affiliate groups that use its name. According to Sageman, the Internet is central to the evolution of contemporary terrorism. Specifically, the vast communications systems that include e-mail, electronic mailing lists, and chat rooms are essential in forging networks. Operationally, the Internet allows al Qaeda to post its informational and intelligence requirements, and to ask Muslims to help meet these requests. Most respondents are not al Qaeda members and are thus more likely to avoid police attention.[162] The Internet has undermined the traditional hierarchy of terrorist organizations, paving the way for leaderless jihad. Sageman argues that al Qaeda's new modus operandi is to advertise demands for terrorist operations on the Internet in hopes that local networks will conduct terrorist activities on their own without guidance from the central organization. In a sense, it is like the marketplace governed by an "invisible hand." In many cases, al Qaeda merely telegraphs its desire for attacks.[163] Each small terrorist organization may pursue terrorist activities for its own local reasons, but by doing so it promotes al Qaeda's grand strategy. Often the local group receives recognition from al Qaeda only after the fact.[164]

A few examples illustrate this tactical approach. On August 1, 2007, an al Qaeda website promised that a big surprise would soon occur. Although the message did not specify its precise nature, the accompanying visual displayed a montage of President George W. Bush with then-visiting Hamid Karzai (president of Afghanistan) and Pervez Musharraf (then president of Pakistan) against a backdrop of the White House in flames, suggesting they should be targeted. On August 5 another video followed in which Adam Gadahn, an al Qaeda spokesman, warned that US embassies would be attacked. Such threats have become commonplace in the organization's discourse, but, as the terrorism analyst Brian Jenkins observes, they highlight its communications strategy. Gadahn's videotape threatened no specific action. Rather, it identified targets that ought to be attacked and left it to jihadists to act on their own. Not long after, Gadahn appeared in another video in which he seemingly commanded sleeper agents to attack nuclear power plants inside the United States. Although no such attacks occurred, Jenkins believes it is still possible for terrorist groups to wreak nuclear terror, characterizing al Qaeda as the first "nuclear terrorist organization." By instilling a sense of nuclear anxiety through bin Laden's pronouncements on the suitability of acquiring nuclear weapons, al Qaeda has managed to induce nuclear terror in the United States.[165]

More threats would follow. In March 2010, al Qaeda's media army—as-Sahab—released a videotape in which Gadahn commended Major Nidal Malik Hasan, the army psychologist suspected of killing thirteen people and wounding twenty-nine others at Fort Hood, calling him an "ideal role model" whose lone wolf terrorism should be a model for other jihadists in the United States and elsewhere in the West.[166] And in June 2011, Gadahn appeared in video titled "Do Not Rely on Others, Take the Task upon Yourself," in which he urged Muslims in the United States to take advantage of lax firearm laws to purchase guns and carry out attacks on their own.[167]

The increasing role of Gadahn, the terrorism analyst Peter Bergen observes, suggests the Americanization of the Qaeda leadership.[168] Gadahn, also known as "Azzam the American," has emerged as one of al Qaeda's leading spokesmen. Amazingly, the young native of California and convert to Islam was able to ingratiate himself into the highest echelons of al Qaeda. A seemingly alienated youth, he underwent a radicalization process and made his way to Pakistan, where he was recruited and served as translator for the organization. He has emerged as somewhat of an Internet celebrity on websites such as YouTube.[169] Another important figure was Anwar al-Awlaki, a Yemeni cleric who grew up in New Mexico. Awlaki played a key operational role for al Qaeda in the Arabian Peninsula and reached out to several American jihadists. He exerted a strong influence on Major Hasan, with whom he exchanged e-mails several times before the attack at Fort Hood. Awlaki also met with Umar Farouk Abdulmutallab, the Nigerian man who attempted to blow up a Detroit-bound flight on Christmas Day in 2009. Awlaki's sermons inspired Faisal Shahzad, who attempted to set off a car bomb in New York's Times Square in May 2010, and Zachary Chesser, a Fairfax, Virginia, man who was arrested in July 2010 on charges of trying to join the Somali Islamic terrorist group al-Shabab. Once characterized as the "bin Laden of the Internet," Awlaki's pronouncements are still broadcast on sites such as YouTube.[170] On September 30, 2011, a US military drone attack in Yemen killed Awlaki. Just two weeks later, another strike in Yemen killed his sixteen-year-old son.[171]

Threats conveyed through the new media are an integral part of al Qaeda's grand strategy. In 2010, an al Qaeda affiliate based in Yemen launched an English-language online magazine, *Inspire*, which contained a foreword by Osama bin Laden encouraging "individual jihad" against Americans and other Westerners. One article suggested random shooting rampages in crowded restaurants in Washington, D.C., at lunch hour, while another instructed readers how to weld blades to the front of a pickup truck so that it could be used as a mowing machine, not to mow grass but to "mow down the enemies of Allah." A similar tactic was employed in 2006 by Mohammed Taheri-azar, an Iranian-born US citizen who injured nine persons with a sports utility vehicle on the campus of the University of North Carolina at Chapel Hill.[172] Over the past few years, Islamic lone wolf attacks have become frequent. In that vein, one al Qaeda strategist in particular advanced the idea of leaderless resistance.

Abu Musab al-Suri

A senior member of al Qaeda, Abu Musab al-Suri propounded an operational strategy of decentralization to fit contemporary conditions. He first gained notoriety in the West in late 2004, when Spanish investigators referred to him as a possible mastermind of the Madrid train bombings that year. In November, the US State Department announced that it was offering $5 million for information leading to his arrest.[173] Perhaps sensing that the net was closing in on him, Suri posted many of this books, lectures, and letters on the Internet.[174]

The Syrian-born Suri is well traveled both in the Middle East and Europe. Fair-skinned with red hair, he could "easily pass for an Irish pub patron," one observer notes.[175] Suri holds a history degree and styles himself as an intellectual who has endeavored to formulate a grand strategy for global jihad in the modern world. To that end, in his writings—which have a penchant for satire and ridicule—he draws on Western sources pertaining to guerrilla warfare. In a milieu that tends toward conformity rather than self-criticism, he favors a thorough, dispassionate analysis, reassessing earlier terrorist campaigns so jihadists can learn from their mistakes. He discards traditional jihadist rhetoric about God's promised victory and instead puts forth analysis based on brutal honesty and hard-nosed realism.[176]

Mustafa bin Abd al-Qadir Setmariam Nasar was born into a middle-class family in the city of Aleppo in northwestern Syria in October 1958. Years later he assumed the name Abu Musab al-Suri. His family traces its ancestry back to Hasan, son of the fourth caliph, and Fatima, the prophet Mohammed's daughter.[177] Little is known about his childhood. Suri studied engineering at the University of Aleppo for four years, but he abandoned his studies to join Syria's Islamist opposition.[178] On June 11, 1980, as a twenty-one-year-old student, Suri enlisted in the Combat Vanguard, launching his career as a militant. Soon after, he left Syria for Jordan, where he stayed off and on until mid-1983.

Despite Suri's departure from Syria, early on his home country was his overriding concern. The nucleus of the opposition was the Syrian Muslim Brotherhood, which had been banned by the government at the end of the 1950s but remained active underground. Together with the affiliated Combat Vanguard, the Syrian Muslim Brotherhood launched an armed campaign against the Syrian government in the late 1970s. The insurrection culminated in 1982, when the Syrian Muslim Brotherhood led a rebellion in the city of Hama. The government responded forcefully, killing between ten thousand and thirty thousand people in nearly two weeks of fighting.[179] Many of Suri's companions were killed during the crackdown in Hama. Suri blamed the Syrian Muslim Brotherhood for the failure of the revolt that had resulted in such horrific casualties.[180] During this period, he visited Baghdad and received military training, which allowed him to meet well-known figures in the Islamist movement, in particular Abu Usama al-Misri, an important figure in the Egyptian Muslim Brotherhood's military wing, or "Special Apparatus." He also befriended such prominent Islamist leaders as Ayman al-Zawahiri, Omar Abdel Rahman, and Abdullah Azzam. A quick learner, Suri served as a military instructor at Muslim Brotherhood military camps in both Jordan and Iraq.[181]

In 1983, Suri left the Middle East for France, where he enrolled to study engineering at a university after having taken French language courses. Apparently physically fit and well built, he earned a black belt in judo while in France in 1984.[182] He left France in 1985 and arrived in Spain that year as an illegal immigrant. Settling in Madrid, he sought to legalize his residency, marrying a Spanish woman, Elena Moreno Cruz, and eventually fathering four children. A left-wing student of philology, Cruz converted to Islam. Through his marriage, Suri obtained Spanish citizenship. While in Madrid, he earned a living selling secondhand furniture at a flea market and later opened up a gift shop.[183] In 1984 or 1985 Suri enrolled at Beirut University's branch in Amman, where he took correspondence courses and obtained his BA in history in 1991. For nearly ten years he stayed in Spain, but from 1987 to 1992 he spent much time in Afghanistan and traveled widely throughout the Middle East and North Africa. During his time in Spain, Suri authored several books and tracts that analyzed jihadist campaigns in which he sought to develop a broad theory on how to integrate his own personal experiences and guerrilla warfare theory into a comprehensive jihadist war-fighting strategy. In 1991 he wrote a thirty-five-page tract titled *Communiqué to the Islamic Nation in Order to Establish a Global Islamic Resistance*, in which he introduced the term "individual action," which would later become a cornerstone of his strategy. He became more and more wary of the feasibility of so-called *tanzims* or secret organizations, such as the Muslim Brotherhood, to mount effective resistance.[184]

While in Afghanistan, Suri expanded his contacts with, and knowledge of, jihadist groups around the world. For years he was primarily concerned about the Syrian jihad. However, after his arrival in Afghanistan in 1987, Suri adopted the doctrine of global jihad, while remaining an advocate of focusing on the "near enemy." Suri's most important activity was lecturing at jihadist training camps, through which he developed an acquaintance with Abu Musab al-Zarqawi, who operated his own training camp in the country.[185] Like Zarqawi, Suri had an abiding antipathy for Shiites.[186] Suri also retained a close relationship with Ayman al-Zawahiri.[187] By the early 1990s he had left Afghanistan, returning to Spain before moving to London.

When Suri arrived in London in 1994, the city was quite tolerant of radical Islam.[188] He served as a spokesman for the Algerian Groupe Islamique Armé (GIA) and published an Islamist newsletter. During this period he was intensely interested in the Algerian jihad. At first he supported the GIA, but by 1995 the group's indiscriminate violence led him to disavow it.[189] Following his split from the GIA in Europe, he departed for Afghanistan again with his family. While there, he swore *bayat* (loyalty) to the Taliban leader Mohammed Omar, worked for the Taliban Ministry of Defense, and established the al-Ghurba training camp.[190]

His ideas took a while to take hold in jihadist circles, but they were eventually endorsed by al Qaeda's leadership. His relationship with bin Laden is hard to pin down. Suri claimed to have first met bin Laden in 1988. If true, that would make Suri a founding member of the organization. During the late 1990s he served as intermediary between bin Laden and the Western media, securing international interviews for the al Qaeda leader. Reportedly he took pride in his contacts with both al Jazeera and other media outlets. In 1997 he is believed to have organized a CNN interview for bin Laden with Peter Arnett and Peter Bergen.[191] At times the relationship between the two was strained, however. Suri once criticized bin Laden as a "pharaoh"—a highly derisive term in Islamist circles—for the way in which he managed al Qaeda.[192] He was also wary of bin Laden and other Saudi jihadists because he thought they might be tempted by their government's standing offer to let them return home if they repented.[193] Yet Suri named one of his sons Osama, presumably in honor of the al Qaeda leader.[194]

In sharp contrast to Osama bin Laden, who cultivated an image of piety and humility, Suri often comes across as gruff, sarcastic, and not very religious. In fact he has often chided the Salafist elements for their inflexible dogmatism and narrow-mindedness.[195] He has been described as intelligent and intellectually curious.[196] This appeals to well-educated, young Westernized Muslims who seem to be motivated more by a mixture of leftist radicalism and militant pan-Islamic nationalism than by religiosity.[197] According to Suri, Muslims will not risk their lives for some abstract notion of an Islamic utopian state, but they will die for more concrete objectives, such as a chance to liberate Palestine or fight against the occupation of Afghanistan or Iraq. As he keenly observed, Muslims are deeply offended by anything that smacks of foreign domination.[198]

In 1997 Suri relocated to Taliban-controlled Afghanistan, which he described as "the best example of the Islamic state on earth today."[199] Strategically, he saw that the period of temporary safe havens in the West was drawing to a close because of the increased international antiterrorism efforts led by the United States. Moreover, Arab governments were stepping up their efforts to get European governments to hand over fugitives to face charges. Finally, Suri believed that a geopolitical alliance was forming against the Taliban, consisting of Russia, Iran, the United States, and

US "colony states" in central Asia, all of which had geostrategic incentives to contain Islamism in the region. By this time Suri had come to agree with bin Laden that the United States was now the primary enemy.[200]

Suri took issue with many of bin Laden's activities in Afghanistan. In particular, he was critical of bin Laden for not respecting the rules of conduct set by the Taliban. Because of this, Suri argued, bin Laden endangered the Arab presence in Afghanistan. Bin Laden acted unilaterally in reiterating his declaration of war against the United States when he announced the creation of the "World Islamic Front for Jihad against Jews and Crusaders" in 1998. The much-heralded media event was highly embarrassing to the Taliban.[201] The Taliban leader Mullah Mohammed Omar thought that bin Laden's use of the Western media to publicize his enmity for America was dangerous and could provoke retaliation. As a consequence, Suri feared that the Arab jihadists would lose their Afghan sanctuary.

The US military's precision raids in August 1998 on al Qaeda training camps in Afghanistan left a deep impression on Suri. The lesson was that it would be folly for al Qaeda to rely on fixed training camps in an era of US hegemony and total air dominance. After 9/11, Suri questioned bin Laden's "Tora Bora" mentality, arguing that it was necessary to develop a decentralized jihadist struggle that used autonomous cells without fixed bases or traceable organizational ties. Rather than a formal organization, he favored "a call, a reference, a methodology." From 2002 onward he devoted all his time to studying and writing, completing research for a book he claims was for the "third generation" of the mujahideen.[202]

His 1,600-page online tome, *The Global Islamic Resistance Call*, seeks to inspire a worldwide Islamic uprising led by autonomous cells and individual jihadists. In his book he argues that it is senseless for the Islamist movement to fight from fixed locations, because units could be trapped where Western forces could eventually destroy them. Furthermore, he saw the traditional hierarchical model of a terrorist group as outdated: if authorities could capture one member, it could put the whole organization at risk. Taking into account these factors, Suri proposed a "jihad of individual terrorism" in which self-contained cells implement their own terrorist template to start their own jihad. What is critical is a shared ideology that creates a feeling of common cause and unity of purpose. In his model, which is akin to the open software movement, autonomous cells learn from the mistakes and successes of others, thus improving their collective action.[203] Rather than traveling to a distant guerrilla theater of war, Suri counsels that Islamic youth should strike enemy targets in their own countries.[204] This model fosters adaptability and creativity in the realm of terrorism. When the actions of local jihadist groups are examined, targeting often appears to be a function of local access and local grievances.[205]

In order to work in unison, Suri believes, jihadists need a system that instills common purpose and identity. To bring that about, Suri provides a name—the Global Islamic Call—around which they can rally. The movement also requires a political program, a common doctrine, and an oath to God committing to the struggle. Finally, it requires shared goals: in this case, resisting the United States and its allies, and working to establish a new caliphate. What unites these jihadists is not a formal organization, but "a program of beliefs, a system of action, a common name, and a common goal."[206] There would be no formal organizational links between cells. Like Mao, Suri emphasizes the need for propagandizing and education.

Suri's model encompasses two forms of jihad. First, the mujahideen still fight on "open fronts" around the world, such as Iraq, Afghanistan, and Chechnya. Second, their efforts should be augmented by individual jihadists in other countries, who commit acts of terrorism on their own initiative. He finds it unfeasible in the post-9/11 world to operate by the methods of the "old model": "secret—regional—hierarchical organizations." Thus he proffers an individual, secret jihad that takes place globally, which lets any Muslim take part in the battle against the United States and contribute to jihad. Still, Suri believes that a central authority needs to guide the movement. Thus operations can be coordinated in order to give meaning to the various acts of terrorism so that they serve broader strategic ends.[207]

Also reminiscent of Mao, Suri calls for a three-stage phase of resistance. In the first stage, jihadists exhaust the enemy through small acts of resistance, such as assassinations, raids, and ambushes. In the second stage—equilibrium—the guerrillas move to mount larger, strategic attacks and carry out operations in which they temporarily control some areas. Finally, in the third stage, guerrillas establish solid control over some areas from which they launch operations to liberate the rest of a country.[208]

Suri's treatise contains case studies of twenty-five movements from which he derives lessons about guerrilla warfare theories, principles, and models for an Islamist global struggle. These are divided into four broad categories. First are "errors in the curriculum and ideology." This is his most critical subject, because he believes that they define ultimate objectives and identify possible roads to take toward this goal. To be effective, he argues, Islamists must develop a comprehensive revolutionary ideology and a proper political-strategic framework for action. Second are errors in structure and organization. Suri argues that Islamist revolutionary organizations' pyramid structure makes them highly vulnerable to state infiltration, because one compromised cell can bring down the whole organization. The third category is errors in developmental methods, errors that include the failure of the Islamist movement to achieve unity of effort, problems of strategic financing, flaws in planning and decision making, and failure to follow relevant operational security principles. Finally, the fourth category encompasses miscellaneous issues such as a lack of ideological education among Islamists, the low quality of personnel in their ranks, poor decision making, and an absence of total commitment to the Islamist cause.[209]

The power of the Internet is integral to Suri's strategy of individual terrorism, in that it serves as a mobilization tool. Suri's writing might not come across as particularly tech-savvy, but conjoining his theory with the web created an effective composite.[210] To make leaderless resistance orderly, Suri recognized, it is necessary to direct such actions through strategic guidance from al Qaeda's leaders so that they have a unity of purpose. In that regard, al Qaeda's leaders have taken his advice, as demonstrated by the cases in which locally recruited cells carry out attacks under the guidance of the parent organization, such as in the Madrid attacks.[211]

Like bin Laden, Suri makes references to WMD, arguing that the use of "dirty bombs" is appropriate against "a dirty people" (Americans). He seems, however, to be naïve about the ease with which nuclear weapons can be acquired: "They are quick and easy and can be obtained from most mafias in the world. Nuclear weapons have become mafia merchandise. They are sold. They are sold in Uzbekistan and in Pakistan." He tends to gloss over the enormous difficulties of attaining, smuggling, storing, deploying, and detonating such weapons.[212]

Suri's assessment of the 9/11 attacks was ambivalent. On the one hand, he wrote that the global jihadist movement had not been prepared for the maelstrom that followed the attacks, as many were swallowed up or decimated. He argues that the United States used the attacks to launch a crusade against the Muslim world. Nevertheless, he concedes that 9/11 had a strong mobilizing effect on the global jihadist movement.[213] He categorically denied any involvement or foreknowledge of the 9/11 attacks, but he praised them and called them "honorable." Likewise, he denied any connection to the Madrid train bombings, but lauded them and called those responsible martyrs.[214] As proof of their effectiveness, he noted, the 2004 Madrid attacks prompted Spain to withdraw its forces from Iraq and weakened the Euro-American alliance. In his post-9/11 analysis, he counseled bin Laden not to attempt to re-create the old al Qaeda organization.[215]

There was similarity between Suri's doctrine and locally initiated recruitment for the Madrid attacks. According to some sources, al Qaeda also had a role in supporting the locally recruited cell that carried out the July 7, 2005, suicide bombings of London's transit system, which killed fifty-two people and injured over seven hundred more. In a 2004 tract, Suri instructed how a leader should form cells and recruit from individuals who are able to influence a wide circle of friends. Still, those involved in the Madrid and London attacks reached out to more experienced jihadists or al Qaeda operatives for help and guidance. The important point is that the cells were formed autonomously, following Suri's model.[216]

Suri's assessment of the contemporary geopolitical equation is simply the "new world order versus the armed jihadist current." As he has written, with the dissolution of the Soviet Union and the emergence of a unipolar era, smaller countries could no longer play the superpowers off against each other. Increasingly they were following the dictates of the United States. As a consequence, Islamist groups could no longer expect to find safe havens as they did during the Cold War.[217] Moreover, the four countries that have provided secure bases to al Qaeda—Afghanistan, Pakistan, Saudi Arabia, and Yemen—have become highly inhospitable and dangerous.[218] Suri believes that jihadists should take advantage of weak states and semiautonomous tribal areas to establish a presence, but he believes that even these countries are now precarious because the United States has given high priority to controlling them in the aftermath of 9/11. Consistent with other advocates of engaging the "far enemy," Suri argues that once the United States is defeated, the Arab regimes will fall. To reach this goal, he calls for striking targets including missionaries, foreign corporations, security services, diplomats, military personnel, and tourists. In order to precipitate an economic collapse of these regimes and also hurt the US economy, Suri counsels jihadists to strike at the oil industry, calling it the "life-artery of our enemies."[219]

On October 31, 2005, police in the Goualmandi district of Quetta, Pakistan, raided a local store. Volleys of gunfire ensued, and when the smoke cleared, one man was dead and several others were arrested, including Suri. For a few years after his arrest, his writings did not circulate far beyond the Arab-speaking jihadist community, though they were discovered on computers belonging to jihadist terrorists in Europe, including the Madrid cell.[220] Suri's hard-hitting realism differs greatly from much jihadist literature. He is rarely quoted in the wider-spread and more religiously oriented Salafist jihadist literature. Nevertheless, Suri's writings have become popular with a limited but important audience among the more intellectually oriented jihadists.[221]

In recent years it appears that al Qaeda's leadership has endorsed Suri's approach, as suggested by the online magazine *Inspire*, which first appeared in 2010. Echoing Suri, some al Qaeda strategists, such as Atiyah Abd al-Rahman, a second-tier leader of the organization's central group, have counseled would-be jihadists that traveling to Pakistan is too perilous and poses a serious security risk for the travelers and al Qaeda. Rahman recommended that jihadists fight where they are.[222]

Al Qaeda's Grand Strategy

From the 1970s to the late 1990s, jihadists focused primarily on targeting the "near enemy"—the so-called apostate regimes in the Middle East they believed were inadequately Islamic. This struggle took precedence over the war against the United States and Israel, the "far enemy."[223] By the late 1990s, however, security services in the Middle East demonstrated that they could quell the various Islamist movements, thus leading to a repositioning of jihadist strategy. A faction in the jihadist movement—with Osama bin Laden in its vanguard—determined that by attacking the "Zionist-Crusader alliance" and their collaborators, they could revitalize their movement and reverse its decline.[224] By striking at the head of the snake, they believed, they could ultimately bring down the apostate regimes in the Middle East. Walid Phares has argued that al Qaeda employs a "world strategy," in that the organization seeks to exploit global conflicts so that they serve its long-term goal of reestablishing the caliphate.[225]

Early in his political career, even Ayman al-Zawahiri advocated first bringing down the regime in Cairo, but later he moved toward a "far enemy" strategy. Written in 2001, his *Knight under the Prophet's Banner* identifies and prioritizes the goals of his movement. First he advises that it is imperative to achieve ideological coherence and organization. Once that is achieved, jihadists can wage an effective struggle against the regimes of the Arab world, to be followed by the establishment of genuinely Muslim states. However, since the terrain in key Arab countries is unsuitable for guerrilla war, he argues that Islamists should conduct political action among the masses, combined with an urban terrorism campaign against apostate regimes and supplemented with attacks against the far enemy. He and his fellow radical Salafists do not intend to defeat the United States in a physical sense, but to use spectacular acts of terrorism to galvanize the Muslim world, thus attracting mass support for their struggle against the near enemy.[226]

As some observers have commented, al Qaeda is mounting a global version of fourth-generation warfare against the United States and its allies. As described in Chapter 1, fourth-generation warfare is an evolved form of insurgency in which combatants use all available networks—political, social, and military—to convince enemy decision makers that their strategic goals are unattainable or not worth the cost. Based on this reasoning, bin Laden's strategic approach has viability. In an essay posted on an al Qaeda website not long after 9/11, Abu Ubayd al-Qurashi, identified as a bin Laden aide, made no fewer than nine references to fourth-generation warfare and indicated that al Qaeda intended to use this approach to wage a global insurgency against the United States.[227] Bin Laden was greatly influenced by his experiences in the Soviet-Afghan War of the 1980s, and he even went so far as to take credit for the downfall of the Soviet Union, as that war set in motion various developments that ultimately contributed to the Soviet dissolution. It is a foundational belief of al Qaeda leaders that a major setback in the Middle East could usher in a similar scenario for the United States. Mounting costs in the global war on terror have already taken their toll on the US economy, calling the sustainability of the conflict into question. Paul Kennedy's notion of "imperial overstretch" may be applicable to the United States today, as its military is committed to numerous hot spots around the world.[228]

Although al Qaeda's terrorist attacks may appear reckless, a close examination reveals that their planners may have an informed and nuanced understanding of the politics in the areas where they occur. An instructive case is the Madrid train station bombings on March 11, 2004, which killed 190 persons and wounded more than 1,800. After these attacks, a document titled "Jihadi Iraqi Hopes and Dangers" appeared on several Islamist websites. A draft was prepared in September 2003, but it was not published until December of that year. The document was prepared by "the Media Committee for the Victory of the Iraqi People," believed to have been an arm of al Qaeda. The main thesis was that the United States could not be forced to leave Iraq by military and political means alone, and that the Islamic resistance could succeed only if the US occupation was made as economically costly as possible. To this end, the document recommended that resistance fighters target coalition countries such as England, Spain, and Poland, so that the United States would be forced to bear almost the entire cost of the occupation. The author or authors evinced a sophisticated knowledge of the domestic politics of these countries, most notably Spain. Presciently, the document predicted that painful blows inflicted on that country near its general election could force the Spanish government to withdraw forces from Iraq.[229] Staged on the eve of the Spanish parliamentary elections, the attack had considerable political fallout. The governing People's Party led by Prime Minister José Maria Aznar was favored to win despite its unpopular support for US policy in Iraq, but after the attack, the opposition Socialist Party, led by Jose-Luis Rodriguez Zapatero, scored a surprising victory.[230] Less than a month later, Zapatero announced the withdrawal of Spanish troops from Iraq.

There are basically two schools of thought on how the 9/11 attacks fit into al Qaeda's grand strategy. One theory posits that al Qaeda and the Taliban were caught unawares by the massive US military response in Afghanistan. According to this view, the al Qaeda leadership had believed the US response would be limited, as it had been in the past after incidents of terrorism.[231] The other theory asserts that the attacks on 9/11 were intended to provoke a ferocious response from the United States. For nearly a decade prior to 9/11, al Qaeda had struck US targets overseas on numerous occasions. The US response to each of these incidents was limited. However, 9/11 could not be ignored. This event and its aftermath call to mind Walter Laqueur's observation that the chief danger of international terrorism is usually not the terrorist act per se, but an incident's potential to trigger a wider and more dangerous conflict—the "Sarajevo effect."[232]

Bin Laden was under no illusions that his al Qaeda network could single-handedly defeat the United States and Israel. Rather, he saw al Qaeda as a vanguard movement that exhorted the Islamic *umma* to join the global *jihad*. By this reasoning, once the United States was drawn into a major regional conflict in the Middle East, it could be worn down by attrition in a guerrilla war. This could engender a civilizational struggle and ultimately make the Middle East ungovernable. Such a scenario could precipitate a severe global economic downturn, and, by doing so, dramatically alter the geopolitical balance of the world.[233] In the past, bin Laden had exhorted his followers to "concentrate on hitting the U.S. economy through all possible means." This admonition has become a mantra in contemporary jihadist discourse.[234] The cost to carry out the 9/11 attacks was estimated to have been between $200,000 and $500,000.[235] The ensuing global war on terror has meant a vastly greater fiscal cost for the US government, calling into question the war's sustainability. According to a Congressional Research Office report, as of late 2010, the estimated total cost of the global war on terror had reached $1.121 trillion.[236]

Al Qaeda appears to be attempting to drive a wedge between parties in the United States. On the eighth anniversary of 9/11, al-Sahab released a twelve-minute audiotape in which Osama bin Laden addressed US citizens. He asserted that the main reason for the 9/11 attacks was US support for Israel as well as "some other injustices." In a conciliatory gesture, he claimed the war between the United States and the Islamic *umma* could end if the White House eliminated the "Israel lobby." Although US support for Israel has been a long-standing grievance by al Qaeda, the announcement was unique in that it placed the issue front and center in al Qaeda's strategic communications. Bin Laden even endorsed books, including

John Perkins's *Confessions of an Economic Hit Man* and John Mearsheimer and Stephen Walt's *The Israel Lobby*, commenting that the two "will give you [the American people] the truth." He urged Americans to free themselves of the neoconservatives and the Israel lobby, or al Qaeda would continue its war of attrition against the United States. According to some analysts, by singling out the issue of US-Israel relations, the message was calculated to put the new Obama administration under pressure to let go of its alliance with Israel.[237]

David Kilcullen, a retired Australian army officer who was the senior counterinsurgency adviser to General David Petraeus, views the war on terror as a series of small wars within the context of a larger global insurgency, with al Qaeda in the vanguard. As he sees it, what is unique about the war on terror is that it involves a complex interaction between local and global forces that includes both tribal and postmodern insurgent groups and both preindustrial and globalized cultures. Globalization has connected geographically distant groups that could not previously coordinate their actions. This development enables transnational groups to mount operations worldwide. In this protracted global war, a serious weakness for the United States is asymmetry of cost. To prosecute the wars in Iraq and Afghanistan, the United States must spend over $120 billion a year. In contrast, US adversaries deliberately adopt low-cost methods to sustain their operations over the long haul. As Kilcullen points out, al Qaeda's grand strategy appears aimed at bleeding the United States to exhaustion and bankruptcy, and, in doing so, forcing the United States to withdraw from the Middle East. Achieving this will cause US regional allies to collapse, while simultaneously inciting a mass Islamic uprising in the Arab world.[238]

Kilcullen characterizes al Qaeda as the "inciter-in-chief" seeking to exploit regional tensions. He uses the metaphor of an infection to explain how the organization takes advantage of hot spots in the Islamic world and establish a local presence from which to attack US and other Western interests. In the infection stage, al Qaeda inserts itself into remote areas and creates alliances with local communities. Once ensconced, a contagion stage begins in which the group's influence spreads. By exporting violence, al Qaeda prompts a Western response, thus leading to the third stage, intervention. The organization then exploits this backlash against the intervention to generate support for its Islamist agenda, which finally results in the emergence of local insurgents, or "accidental guerrillas." These insurgents fight to evict the foreign occupiers, not so much based on radical Islamist ideology, but more elementally to resist a foreign body, like antibodies fighting an infection.[239]

An important question is this: can militant Islamists sustain momentum? As Walter Laqueur has pointed out, messianic movements are subject to "routinization, to the circulation of generations, to changing political circumstances, and to sudden or gradual changes in the intensity of religious belief." Furthermore, fanaticism is difficult to transfer from one generation to the next.[240] Still, according to some sources, al Qaeda may have a presence in ninety or more countries. This is not a sign of weakness.[241]

Much of al Qaeda's efforts are directed toward winning a war of ideas. Fawaz Gerges has explored internal debate within the Islamist movement, which to outsiders often appears monolithic. As Gerges points out, Osama bin Laden and Ayman al-Zawahiri have not been without their critics in the global jihadist movement. The crux of the critique against them is that they diverted the jihad caravan from its correct historical path—the near enemy—into difficult foreign terrain. By doing so they plunged the movement into an uneven fight with the most powerful country in the world. The global coalition now arrayed against the movement has taken a heavy toll on its followers. In some respects, the 9/11 attacks had the effect of uniting the world, including much of the *umma*, against global jihad. Gerges believes al Qaeda's tactics were reckless and have made many enemies, both internal and external. In 2005, a series of terrorist attacks in Egypt that left eighty-five people dead and the London suicide bombings occasioned widespread condemnation in the Arab and Muslim worlds, with considerable soul-searching. There is an intense internal struggle within the movement that is shaking its foundation, as it faces a two-front war, one front internal and the other external.[242]

Despite setbacks, including the death of key leaders such as Osama bin Laden, Atiyah Abd al-Rahman, and Anwar al-Awlaki, al Qaeda has proven to be highly adaptable, as it has delegated to regional affiliates much of the responsibility for waging global jihad with little centralized planning. Its presence in countries such as Saudi Arabia, Yemen, Jordan, and Pakistan—where al Qaeda has its most important local affiliates—is rapidly shrinking because of efforts by security services and substantial US assistance.[243] Nevertheless al Qaeda remains formidable.[244] The movement simultaneously inspires and motivates radicalized Muslims around the world to join the global jihad. Moreover, al Qaeda central still exercises command-and-control capabilities by directing the implementation of terrorist attacks. The organization's malleability is part of its strength; Bruce Hoffman likens it to a shark in the water that must keep moving forward, no matter how slowly or incrementally, or die. Because of its resiliency, the organization cannot be defeated solely by a single tactical military engagement or series of engagements. To counter al Qaeda, Hoffman argues, it will be necessary to employ a "hard" or kinetic component—i.e., a "kill and capture" approach—along with a broader, "softer" effort to break the cycle of terrorist recruitment that allows it to replenish its ranks.[245]

One reason al Qaeda has been so resilient is because it is embedded in a larger ideological movement that gives it sustenance. Daniel Pipes, a noted authority on militant Islam, shares these thoughts on al Qaeda's transition to an increasingly leaderless social movement:

> The notion that somehow al Qaeda is the leader of the Islamist movement struck me as an odd one. I think the US government, for example, pays much too much attention to al Qaeda and how many al Qaeda operatives it has knocked out as a signal of progress in the war on terror. This is a very large-

scale ideological movement, comparable, say, to the communist movement, and has many different cadres, many different organizations, some violent, some not. . . . It's not really useful to see it as an organized whole. There are elements that are organized. But there is no clear leadership. . . . So, leaderless is one way of putting it, but I would [characterize] it as a large ideological movement with many different prongs or organizations, individuals, theorists, funders, lawyers, teachers, and the like.

What [the Islamist movement] can do is not [conduct] a war of attrition, but more broadly . . . challenge us in many different ways, from conversion, immigration, [and] what's called "creeping *sharia*" on the one hand, to developing means of violence, in some cases terrorism, weapons of mass destruction, conceivably conventional arms. . . . They count because they are part of a much larger enterprise. If you took a small ideology, [that of] the Basque terrorists [for example], they are limited by the fact of geography and demographics and the appeal of their ideology. They can't go very far. [Likewise for] the Palestinians, the Tamil Tigers, [Sendero] Luminoso (Shining Path)—but this ideology [Islamism] is huge. It's potentially universal. It has over a billion adherents that are prospects. Therefore, it has means and potential far beyond those others. I think radical Islam is a major threat to the West. And one component is terrorism and potentially WMD terrorism. These are very significant factors, but they are all the more significant because they are tied to a movement that is also nonviolent that has lots of influence over politicians, the media, the school systems, and so forth. I think it's a mistake to isolate the one from the other.[246]

Despite al Qaeda's extremist ideology, its message resonates with many Muslims around the world. The organization's acts of spectacular terrorism have made it appear as the leader of the Islamic resistance movement. Its acts of violence have provoked severe countermeasures from the United States, and al Qaeda is now at front and center in the confrontation between Islam and the West and in the global war on terror. This position gives al Qaeda tremendous prestige and bolsters its recruiting efforts. Affiliated organizations get the al Qaeda brand name and some corporate know-how.[247] The unification of jihadist groups under the al Qaeda banner suggests that the organization has gained recruits as a result of the global war, creating a united front.[248] Furthermore, the US invasions of Afghanistan and Iraq demonstrate the organization's power to provoke a superpower while also seemingly confirming its propaganda that the United States is waging a war against Islam. Nevertheless, al Qaeda's appeal has limitations. Although surveys indicate the movement still has much sympathy from Muslims all over the Middle East, only a small proportion would actually have wanted Osama bin Laden as their ruler.[249] Another self-limiting quality of the movement is that it has many enemies, as Edward Luttwak, an authority on strategy, explains:

The Islamists are fighting everybody. Every single non-Muslim culture in touch with every single Muslim culture, whether it's Thailand, or North Africa, or Mauritania, or Nigeria, or Indonesia . . . anywhere in the world where you have any contact with the Muslims and non-Muslims: that's the frontier of war, which means that they don't fight just us, they fight the world. At the present time, the enemies include the Russian federation, China, and the Indian Union. . . . And therefore they are losing.[250]

On April 29, 2011, President Barack Obama instructed the CIA to conduct a raid in the Pakistani town of Abbottabad, where Osama bin Laden was believed to be living in a compound. On May 2, two teams of twelve navy SEALs carried out the action, dubbed Operation Neptune Spear. The SEALs stormed a compound, and killed bin Laden in a firefight. A month later, al Qaeda announced that Ayman al-Zawahiri had been appointed leader of the organization. In the final years of his life, Osama bin Laden served mainly as an inspirational figure, not as an actual commander. This lack of command and control actually made it more difficult for authorities to monitor al Qaeda and its affiliates and supporters.[251] Globally dispersed and united by an ideology, al Qaeda could presage a fifth generation of warfare.

Conclusion

Fifth-Generation Warfare
and Leaderless Resistance

Throughout history, various political, social, and technological factors have influenced the development of conflict and warfare. Whereas first-generation warfare involved the amassment of huge forces on the battlefield, the latest generation of warfare—the fifth generation—involves small cells and individuals linked by ideology. The current long-term trend is a miniaturization of forces. Just as technological developments such as the machine gun made large troop formations untenable on the battlefield in second-generation warfare, so do surveillance capabilities, databases, US military dominance, and the changing political environment contribute to the rise of leaderless resistance and the emergence of fifth-generation warfare.

By some measures, war and organized violence have declined over the last two decades. Ted Robert Gurr found that fatalities resulting from conflicts have steadily decreased. One reason for this trend is the movement away from wars involving major powers, which have historically been the kind of conflicts to result in massive casualties, because states have enormous destructive capacities typically beyond the reach of nonstate actors. Modern technology has rendered obsolete the total war that was practiced in the early twentieth century.[1] Moreover, attitudes on the appropriateness of armed conflict as an instrument of foreign policy and as a way to settle international disputes have fundamentally shifted.[2]

Over the past few decades, the occurrence of state-to-state armed conflicts has steadily declined. Rupert Smith, a retired general in the British army, asserts that the industrial era of warfare between states is being replaced by war among people, in which political and military developments go hand in hand. War now involves a continuous crisscrossing between political confrontation and armed conflict, with no predefined sequence.[3] Although state-to-state conflicts are declining in frequency, much conflict persists within states.[4] Since World War II ended, civil wars have become the most frequent kind of war, accounting for roughly two-thirds of all conflicts.[5] Although the average lethality of war has declined, civilian fatalities have increased. It is estimated that between eighteen million and twenty-five million civilians have died in civil, international, and colonial wars since 1945.[6]

Fifth-generation warfare is a kind of "unrestricted warfare" encompassing a full spectrum of mechanisms, conventional and unconventional. A distinguishing characteristic is its leaderlessness. Whereas fourth-generation warfare presupposed a cohesive vanguard that would lead a movement to victory in guerrilla war, fifth-generation warfare relies on individuals acting with minimum or no direction from a central organization. Two contemporaneous, but contradictory, trends in global politics—integration and fragmentation—are shaping the contours of contemporary global conflict and give rise to leaderless resistance, the viability of which, as a strategic approach, is still a matter for debate.

Fifth-Generation Warfare

William S. Lind conceptualized a progression of warfare encompassing four generations. Building on this framework, Thomas X. Hammes now believes that a fifth generation of warfare is upon us, driven mainly by technology. He notes major changes since the end of World War II that have influenced contemporary international conflict. For instance, there are now many more actors—both state and nonstate. This proliferation of international players has the cumulative effect of diminishing the power of states.[7]

Unique to Hammes's thesis is its consideration of the emergence of new forms of human networks—political, economic, social, and military—and how they can be used to influence a state's involvement in a conflict. Another important feature in Hammes's analysis is the elevation of the transnational element. New technology, including cell phones and the Internet, makes networking across state boundaries easier and cheaper than in the past.[8] One important social trend that Hammes observes is a change in how communities are formed. Today, many people are shifting allegiances from countries to causes, a development being accelerated by the connectivity of the Internet. Although small groups and individuals espousing extremist and violent views may seem inconsequential, they have the potential to generate destructive power that was previously exclusive to states, as anthrax-laden letters demonstrated in October 2001. According to Hammes, the main characteristics of fifth-generation warfare are the increasing power and capabilities of smaller and smaller entities. He succinctly describes fifth-generation warfare as "nets and jets": networks that distribute key information, provide necessary resources, and constitute a field from which to recruit prospective volunteers; and airplanes to provide the global, inexpensive, effective means to travel and smuggle weapons.[9] In this framework, individuals and small cells will predominate as the primary agents of terrorism.

There is no widely agreed-upon definition of fifth-generation warfare, although Donald J. Reed of the US Northern Command once described it as warfare waged by coalitions, which could include nation-states, nonstate entities, and individuals, that recognize a fundamental precept that force is no longer restricted to the kinetic but can take other forms as well. In that sense, fifth-generation warfare is unique because it does not rely solely, or even primarily, on defeating one's opponents militarily, as in first- through third-generation warfare, or politically, as in fourth-generation warfare.[10]

Lind's litmus test to determine whether a new generation of warfare has truly arrived is that, unless there is a vast disparity in size, an army from a previous generation could not defeat a force from a new generation.[11] Fifth-generation warfare could be seen as a strategic approach that exploits a full spectrum of mechanisms against an adversary. Two Chinese Army officers have written about what such warfare might look like.

Unrestricted Warfare

In their book *Unrestricted Warfare*, published in 1999, Colonels Qiao Liang and Wang Xiangsui of the People's Liberation Army (PLA) advocated unorthodox methods for confronting US power asymmetrically. The book's initial publication by PLA Literature and Arts Publishing in Beijing suggests that at least some PLA leaders endorsed its release.[12] The two published a sequel, *China's Grand Strategy: A Blueprint for World Leadership*, but it was recalled and banned by Chinese authorities, who worried that its bellicosity would provoke fears of a "China threat" abroad.[13]

The Gulf War of 1991 left an indelible impression on Qiao and Wang, who believed it changed the future of warfare. They noted the rise of precision-kill (or "smart") weapons and nonlethal weapons as a turning point in arms development. These new weapons allow for "surgical" strikes and avoidance of collateral damage that can hurt public relations (more important than ever in a time of globalized media). The quick military victory, Qiao and Wang believed, deluded US military leaders, giving them a false sense of superiority. For example, not long after the first Gulf War, the US military failed to subdue the Somali warlord General Mohamed Farrah Aidid. Furthermore, the authors speculated that the escalating costs of the US military's advanced weaponry could lead to national bankruptcy. Although US and coalition combat fatalities in the Gulf War were relatively low (392 dead), the fiscal cost—$61 billion—was substantial.[14] With Americans so enamored of technology, Qiao and Wang reasoned that this orientation would likely remain. In their view, the major advances in weapons development drove the "revolution in military affairs," suggesting that modern technology was drastically altering US armed forces.

Although there has been a discernible reduction of military violence in recent decades, Qiao and Wang saw an increase in "political, economic, and technological violence." Their notion of "unrestricted warfare" encompasses many forms of conflict, in areas including finance, economics, culture, media, technology, cyberspace, natural resources, drugs, psychology, international law, and even the natural environment. Qiao and Wang frequently invoked the financier George Soros and characterized his currency manipulations as a type of financial warfare that ravaged the economies of Asia during the financial crisis in the late 1990s. They maintained that such financial warfare could be even more destructive than a conventional, regional war. Osama bin Laden was heralded as a new type of nonstate warrior who posed a serious challenge to US interests in the Middle East. Qiao and Wang predicted a world of conflict in which the battle lines would be blurred and where soldiers would no longer have a monopoly on war: "For bin Laden who hides under the hills of Islamic fundamentalism, Soros who conceals himself within the forests of free economics, and the computer hackers who hide themselves in the green curtains of networks, no national boundaries exist, and borders are also ineffective. What they want to do is carry out wanton destruction within a regulated sphere and act wildly and run amuck within an unregulated sphere."[15]

When asked "Where is the battlefield?," Qiao and Wang answered simply that it is now everywhere.[16] Two contemporaneous and contradictory trends are discernible in world politics today. On the one hand, there is greater integration of nations than ever. On the other hand, fragmentation appears to be taking place within many countries, not only in the developing world but in the North and West as well. A general trend in the post–World War II era has been expansion in the number of states, as more and more countries have been created by seceding from others. As of 2011, the United Nations had 193 member nations.[17] Despite this seeming fragmentation, some observers are sanguine about the integrative power of globalization.

Global Integration

In a sense, Qiao and Wang's advocacy of unrestricted warfare on multiple dimensions is similar to Thomas P. M. Barnett's notion of "war within the context of everything else." A former Pentagon defense analyst, Barnett argues that in the contemporary world security must encompass several different dimensions, including economics, politics, trade, international law, and, most important, connectivity. His major study, *The Pentagon's New Map*, advanced a grand strategy for the United States. In Barnett's scheme, the world is divided into two broad regions. Countries in the "Functioning Core" are integrated into a world system and operate under "rule sets." They arbitrate their differences through international bodies, such as the United Nations and the World Trade Organization, and are less likely to go to war against other countries in the core.[18] In contrast, countries in the "Non-Integrating Gap" do not follow these rule sets and are the setting for most of the problems that bedevil the world today.

The real enemy, according to Barnett, is disconnectedness, the separation of people—especially globally. Life in the Gap is, to paraphrase Thomas Hobbes, poor, nasty, short, and brutal, he says.[19] An unabashed economic determinist, he believes that people integrated into the global economy are far less likely to succumb to radicalism. As he puts it, the only viable exit strategy for the US military in countries such as Iraq and Afghanistan is to leave those countries with more jobs than when the operations began.[20] With no reservoir of discontent, extremist and terrorist groups will find few recruits and pose no existential challenge to the system.

Although Muslim rage may be fueled by issues such as the status of the Palestinians and US foreign policy, Barnett argues that it really stems from the Middle East being one of the most disconnected parts of the world. In short, Barnett's long-term strategic goal is the integration of all into the global economy, to drain the reservoir for international terrorism. Multilateral efforts could eliminate the Gap altogether, making globalization truly global.[21] Barnett sees globalization as inevitable, because it is the ultimate "non-zero-sum game"—meaning that all sides win. The entire world will benefit from greater connectedness, he believes, through economic growth and higher standards of living.[22]

Lending credence to Barnett's thesis, researchers at the Center for International Development and Conflict Management at the University of Maryland have discovered that countries that are more tightly integrated into the global economy experience less instability.[23] Nearly 80 percent of all international crises in the post–Cold War era have involved at least one unstable or failing state.[24] The physical security of the United States is now threatened not so much by the strength of other states, but by their weakness, since weak and failed states often serve as sanctuaries for transnational terrorist groups.[25] Despite current global problems, Barnett is optimistic about the future and believes that the terrorist threat can be managed effectively:

> I don't see the Salafist threat as particularly profound. It has not done well, particularly in the last several years by my calculations. . . . I see them more as a friction. I expect to see more of it as globalization more extensively penetrates the Middle East at a much faster pace. The Salafists are a response to globalization, a reflection. . . .
>
> If we pursue the strategy [of expanding "the core" and shrinking "the Gap"], I don't see how it could fail. If we pursue the strategy, then we can participate in it more and we can shape the process and shape the regimes and the global pillars that arise from the process.[26]

According to Barnett, economics got ahead of politics during the 1990s, and technology got ahead of security, causing the world to become too connected too quickly.[27] New technology has led to the emergence of "superempowered individuals," who Barnett believes have the potential to wreak unprecedented damage or "system perturbation."[28] Although the United States cannot be defeated at the nation-state level, Barnett points out that it can still be humbled and even defeated at a system level if the US government is induced to disengage from the Middle East, through acts of terrorism in the style of 9/11.[29] Another terrorist attack on that scale could further destabilize financial markets and have a negative ripple effect throughout the economy. Nevertheless, he believes that modern societies have advanced precisely because they have mastered network complexity, usually in response to disasters and scandals that have periodically perturbed their systems and exposed vulnerabilities.[30]

The encroaching process of globalization, Barnett avers, will undoubtedly engender opposition from those who feel threatened with a loss of identity and culture. The goal of such actors is a "civilizational apartheid"—removal of their areas from the process of globalization. In some ways, though, greater connectivity could increase the number of terrorists. For instance, inasmuch as the "virtual *umma*" is built on the Internet, increasing access to the medium would increase the potential to radicalize a large number of disaffected Muslims.[31]

Despite disruptions along the way, Barnett believes that globalization, if managed effectively, is a force for good that improves the life conditions of many people. In order for his grand strategy to become a reality, the United States must take a leading role, with other "great powers" pitching in.[32] Some observers, though, presage an end to US hegemony. What is more, some fear that centrifugal forces could actually tear the United States apart.

Fragmentation

Despite the increasing economic power of other countries, the United States maintains a staggering military advantage. The US military budget accounts for over half of the aggregate global spending on defense.[33] Still, some observers warn that societal fragmentation could undermine the security of countries in the West, including the United States. In 2006, Rear Admiral Chris Parry, a British senior military strategist, raised eyebrows when he announced at a conference that the West faced peril from third-world hordes, just as Ancient Rome was endangered by barbarian invasions. In an era of globalization, Parry reasoned, large immigrant communities in the West reject assimilation, seeing it as "redundant and old-fashioned." Instead diasporic populations stay connected to their homelands through the Internet and cheap airline flights. Moreover, porous borders render some areas beyond governmental control. This process has resulted in a "reverse colonization" that could have severe implications for the West.[34] In a similar analysis, in 2007 Walter Laqueur predicted the demographic diminution and displacement of native Europeans in his book *The Last Days of Europe: Epitaph for an Old Continent*.[35] Some fear that the transformation of Europe into "Eurabia" could pose a serious security challenge to the United States. Originally advanced by Bat Ye'or, the argument goes that an Islamicized Europe could be used as a launching pad for jihad against the United States.[36] Europe, ravaged by two world wars in the last century, experienced a drastic decline in civilizational self-confidence, so the argument goes, enfeebling the continent and making it vulnerable to demographically dynamic Islam. This "denationalization" of Europe accelerated with trends such as multiculturalism, which was favored by European elites but found less support among its masses.[37]

Similar trends are at play in the United States. More than a decade ago, Robert Kaplan said in his influential article "The Coming Anarchy" that it was not clear whether the United States could survive in its present form: as a multiethnic nation-state it is more fragile than homogeneous ones. As he pointed out, during the 1960s "America began a slow but unmistakable process of transformation," resulting in a more fragmented country.[38] This theme was taken up in 2004, when the political scientist Samuel Huntington's book *Who Are We: The Challenges to America's National Identity* argued that massive Hispanic (primarily Mexican) migration to the United States would constitute the greatest challenge to national unity. The United States became even more multiracial, multilingual, and multicultural after enactment of the Immigration and Nationality Act of 1965. The rise of multiculturalism and the demise of the assimilationist ethic have contributed to a predicament, Huntington believes, that could conceivably divide the nation "into two peoples, two cultures, and two languages."[39] The rise of various group identities based on race and ethnicity threatens to diminish the larger national identity, which Huntington believes is essential for the long-term survival of the country as a unified political entity. Paradoxically, as Huntington points out, leaders among the elite in US politics, business, media, and academia have been in the forefront to deconstruct the nation, a situation he believes is possibly "without precedent in human history." Eventually these trends, Huntington predicts, will engender a backlash in the form of a new white nativism.[40]

Similarly, the conservative US political commentator Patrick J. Buchanan sees massive immigration and multiculturalism as posing an existential threat to Western nations.[41] According to his analysis, several trends, including aging native populations, low native birthrates, large-scale Third World immigration, declining religiosity, political correctness, divisive politics, a major chasm between elite and mainstream opinion, and a declining sense of civilizational self-confidence, are fragmenting Western societies.[42] Like Huntington, Buchanan believes that multicultural societies are fragile. He takes issue with the idea that the United States is even an authentic nation, a country with a shared creed. An authentic nation, he maintains, results from shared history, heritage, language, traditions, and customs, and cannot be artificially created by constitutions, no matter how eloquently written or well intentioned.[43] According to his reading of history, multicultural states can be held together only by an authoritarian regime or a dominant ethnocultural core; otherwise their breakup is inevitable.[44] Faced with this predicament, Buchanan believes, the United States is experiencing an existential crisis that has been largely orchestrated by elites whose vision is radically different from that of the country's mainstream.[45]

Years before Huntington's and Buchanan's books on social disintegration, Donald Horowitz argued in *Ethnic Groups in Conflict* that ethnic and religious differences were the main factors fueling violent internal conflicts during the 1980s. He found that multiethnic and multireligious societies had difficulty establishing political identities accepted by all their citizens.[46] Thus ethnic and religious conflict tends to emerge in divided societies where ethnic communities are linked by little more than geography and repressive police power.[47]

Could Western countries experience fragmentation and disintegration, like countries in the developing world? Serious strategic thinkers have considered these trends. In his 1991 book *The Transformation of War*, the military historian Martin van Creveld predicted that the Clausewitzian style of war had all but been replaced by a new type of conflict that threatens the continued survival of countries as cohesive political entities. He saw a crisis of legitimacy for many states, as they were being pulled apart by "centrifugal forces." Van Creveld predicted that the wave of the future would be low-intensity warfare between ethnic and religious groups. In his estimation, the United States is vulnerable because of its multiracial composition, the wide availability of weapons, and a tradition of internal violence. Rampant crime in some urban areas could even develop into low-intensity conflicts "by coalescing along racial, religious, social, and political lines." Van Creveld predicted that future wars would be fought not by professional armies but by "terrorists, guerrillas, bandits, and robbers," motivated not by "professionalism" but by "fanatical, ideologically-based loyalties."[48]

A nation-state that cannot safeguard its citizens, van Creveld said, is unlikely to command their loyalty or to survive long, because people will turn elsewhere for protection. With the spread of low-intensity conflict, the distinction between soldiers and citizens, and between "front" and "rear," will progressively break down. The spread of small-scale sporadic warfare will cause regular armed forces to "change form, shrink in size, and wither away." In short, war in the future "will be protracted, bloody, and horrible."[49] This development is related to the ongoing trend of urbanization, not only in the United States but also worldwide. According to US military and intelligence sources, urban environments will be the locus of future conflicts. "Global cities"—overcrowded slum areas—have become autonomous zones and islands of instability within which state authority has diminished and militants, criminal networks, and terrorists flourish.[50] So-called feral cities, such as Mogadishu, Bogotá, and Ciudad Juárez, in which the government has lost the ability to maintain the rule of law can have an almost magnetic appeal for terrorist organizations and transnational criminal syndicates and thus present a security challenge to the United States.[51]

Since conventional war will disappear, so will strategy, van Creveld argued, at least in Clausewitz's sense of the term. "Trinitarian" war in the Clausewitzian framework consists of a close bond between citizens, government, and army. In van Creveld's view, nontrinitarian war will come to predominate in the twenty-first century. What is more, he counsels that many developed countries could be involved in such conflicts since they contain sizable immigrant minorities—Muslims in European countries and Hispanics in the United States—who identify with struggles in their countries of origin and may resort to violence to protest social and economic discrimination. "To believe one is safe from nontrinitarian war one has to be either very foolish or blind," van Creveld wrote. He pointed out that the United States is the most violent developed country and has frequently had some type of internal conflict resembling nontrinitarian war, adding that organized violence is seldom politically motivated and is usually classified as crime.[52] Nevertheless, he acknowledged that leaderless resistance could be troublesome in the future:

> If you commit leaderless resistance and terrorism, there's a good chance that you could throw society into chaos. You could pull your society apart....
>
> Back in 1994, I think, I was invited to give a talk to the CIA. This was not long after the Cold War and they were desperate to look for somebody else to spy on. So they asked the working group, including myself, what ... was the most dangerous country to the United States? And I said Mexico. So they asked the question, "Why Mexico?" And I said, "Look, suppose Mexico deteriorates, and as a result, millions of Mexicans come across the border to the United States. Once they are in the southwestern United States, they start organizing an army so as to take part in a civil war." This could develop in the United States very much like Pakistan with Nepal. If there is ... anything that could really demolish the United States it would be Mexico. This is the only thing that I see that could pull the United States apart.[53]

William S. Lind predicted a similar scenario. Lind lamented what he saw as the decline of Western civilization brought about by numerous wars between the great powers in the twentieth century. According to Lind, the most immediate challenge the West faces is from radical Islam, but even more threatening is its internal subversion—in the form of what he calls "cultural Marxism," which seeks to undermine traditional Judeo-Christian culture and replace it with multiculturalism characterized by social fragmentation based on identity politics. Lind predicted that the United States could fragment and implode. As a consequence, he believed, "the next real war we fight is likely to be on American soil."[54] Like van Creveld, Lind also believes that Western nations could lose their legitimacy in the future and face the prospect of internal war. He once recalled a conversation he had had with van Creveld, who had remarked that everyone could see this development "except the people in the capital cities." Lind believes that the current insurgencies in the Middle East are small parts of a much larger challenge that includes massive immigration into the West, which threatens to erode national unity.[55]

Could al Qaeda exploit division in the West? Osama bin Laden once called the United States a "gathering of nations," meaning that it was not a true nation. As Walid Phares observed, part of al Qaeda's strategy is to foment ethnic and racial discord in the United States as a way to undermine national security. According to Phares, al Qaeda's grand strategy along these lines could include sniper activities and dirty bombs, which would cause a repressive government reaction and engender an "ethnic crumbling" of the country. Bin Laden's pronouncements suggested that he believed the United States, despite its superpower status, was internally weak because of its heterogeneous population. By exacerbating ethnic and racial hostilities in the United States, al Qaeda might be able to detonate an "ethnic bomb" and provoke crises such as the riot that convulsed Los Angeles in 1992, causing the social and legal order to disintegrate further.[56] Phares fears that a breaking point could someday be reached when urban mayhem will explode across the country. Europe, he warns, is already close to that, as the 2005 riots in the Paris suburbs demonstrated.[57]

In the spring of 2007, Ayman al-Zawahiri announced in a four-minute video titled "To Black Americans" that al Qaeda was fighting for African Americans and other people of color, even invoking Malcolm X.[58] As he stated,

> al Qaeda is not merely for the benefit of Muslims. That's why I want blacks in America, people of color, American Indians, Hispanics, and all the weak and oppressed in North and South America, in Africa and Asia, and all over the world to know that when we wage jihad in Allah's path, we aren't waging jihad to lift oppression from Muslims only; we are waging jihad to lift oppression from all mankind, because Allah has ordered us never to accept oppression, whatever it may be. . . . This is why I want every oppressed one on the face of the earth to know that our victory over America and the Crusading West—with Allah's permission—is a victory for them, because they shall be freed from the most powerful tyrannical force in the history of mankind.[59]

In a similar vein, in an essay titled "A Lesson in War," the al Qaeda ideologist Abu-Ubayd al-Qurashi invoked the Clausewitzian principle of attacking the enemy's "center of gravity," and argued that the US center of gravity is its economy. In many of his pronouncements, Osama bin Laden exclaimed that al Qaeda's terrorist attacks on the United States saddled the country with enormous economic costs.[60] Echoing bin Laden, Qurashi referred to the "Disunited States of America" and described the country as "a mixture of nationalities, ethnic groups, and races united only by the 'American Dream,' or, to put it more correctly, worship of the dollar, which they openly call 'the Almighty Dollar.'"[61]

A socially and politically polarized United States could create a reservoir of terrorists. Christopher Hewitt, an authority on domestic terrorism in the United States, predicted that societal fragmentation could lead to increased terrorism:

> I think the diversity . . . works two ways. When you think about it, what are the two dangers? The Islamist extremists and the Far Right. And the Islamist extremist can hide because of the diversity. Imagine in the 1960s if somebody tried to do 9/11. In the 1960s, a group of Muslims would have stood out. But in America now, even in small towns, you have some people who look like they could be Middle Eastern, or what have you, so it's very easy for them to blend in. . . . And on the other side, the Far Right, the diversity is what they are against. My point has been that what triggers ethnic violence—nativist violence—is being overwhelmed. It's sort of the tipping point. And if you look at Northern Ireland or Lebanon or other countries, what happens is when a

majority either has just become a minority, or sees that it's going to become a minority, and they are going to lose their majority status, that really inspires a resort to violence.[62]

Immigration and diversity appear to have been the proximate causes that impelled Anders Behring Breivik to carry out his attacks in Norway in July 2011. According to his online political testament, his ideology was eclectic, invoking conservative political theorists such as Thomas Hobbes, John Stuart Mill, John Locke, Adam Smith, Edmund Burke, Ayn Rand, and William James. He shared some traits of the extreme Right—xenophobia, anticommunism, cultural conservatism, and opposition to multiculturalism. Nevertheless, some of his ideas and actions differed considerably from extreme Right views. For example, he expressed solidarity with Jews and Israel, and he targeted innocent white youths. He supported gay rights and feminism as well. Immigration and multiculturalism, which so concerned Breivik, received more attention in Europe after his attacks. Ominously, his sentiments appear not to be confined to a small, lunatic fringe. Prior to Breivik's attacks, leading European politicians—including Chancellor Angela Merkel of Germany, Prime Minister David Cameron of England, and President Nicolas Sarkozy of France—had declared in speeches that multiculturalism in Europe had failed. Electorally, in recent years, Far Right parties espousing immigration restrictions have made significant gains in Europe.[63] As these parties are quick to make clear, large-scale Muslim immigration, together with low fertility rates for European women, could portend the demographic displacement of native Europeans as early as this century.

In the United States, the gradualness of demographic change has dampened conflict. However, if the change intensifies during the current economic downturn, it will not be hard to imagine increased social strife.[64] The rise of the Tea Party movement in 2009 suggested a growing political polarization in America.[65] In such an environment political extremism could flourish.

The Viability of Leaderless Resistance

Societal fragmentation could increase the frequency of small-scale violence and the prevalence of lone wolf terrorism. But some observers believe the threat of leaderless resistance is overstated. Thomas Barnett finds the discussions about fourth-generation and fifth-generation warfare to be overwrought, depicting, as they sometimes do, a future in which Mad Max–like warriors roam a wasteland. Far from seeing al Qaeda as winning, Barnett sees a movement in retreat, as time and time again it has shifted its center of gravity from one locale to another in response to evictions and military reprisals. Likewise he sees little future for terrorism in "the core." As he points out, terrorism in core countries tends to be sporadic and unsupported by the populace. Perpetrators are often disaffected loners, such as Timothy McVeigh and

Ted Kaczynski, who "we see shuffling in orange jump suits and chains . . . on their way to a court appearance." Rather than representing a "political storm," they become a social nuisance. This is in contrast to terrorists in the Gap who often thrive in a "wild frontier" environment.[66]

Some observers argue that leaderless resistance indicates the growing weakness of radicalism, not its strength. In the United States, documented cases consist mainly of sporadic crimes whose body count over several years is dwarfed by that of one year of urban gang warfare.[67] The infrequency of terrorist acts suggests to some observers just how unwilling US Muslims are to kill for Allah.[68]

When a movement adopts leaderless resistance, the researcher Simson L. Garfinkel argues, this is a tacit admission of failure since it suggests a last-ditch effort to keep a struggle alive in the face of overwhelming opposition.[69] Defining a lone wolf strictly as an individual terrorist with no connections to any movement, Fred Burton and Scott Stewart argue that this species is extremely rare. Moreover, many reported cases of lone wolves could be more aptly described as "lone nuts," such as the Virginia Tech shooter Seung-Hui Cho, who evinced mental illness. Burton and Stewart believe it unlikely that terrorists will self-radicalize. As they point out, radicalization tends to occur in a like-minded group in which individuals receive ideological education and support. What is more, terrorist attacks often require careful planning and skills, which few individuals can carry out alone. A lone wolf who reaches out for assistance often comes to the attention of law enforcement. Finally, in order to survive over a period of time, lone wolves require detection-avoidance ability. Eric Rudolph excelled at operational security and had good bomb-making and wilderness survival skills, but he was ultimately caught because of his lack of street smarts: his suspicious behavior caused a fellow citizen to follow him to his truck and then report the vehicle's license plate number to police.[70]

Regarding Islamist terrorism, some observers believe that the notion of leaderless jihad is overstated. For instance, Bruce Hoffman publicly took issue with Marc Sageman's thesis, arguing that al Qaeda central is still functioning in the tribal areas near the Pakistan-Afghanistan border and quite capable of planning attacks. Likewise, the terrorism analyst Daveed Gartenstein-Ross argues that although al Qaeda lost its safe haven in Pakistan, the organization has established a new one in the FATA. Moreover, efforts by the Pakistani military to flush out the militants have repeatedly been beaten back by al Qaeda and its tribal allies. To Gartenstein-Ross, characterizing attacks perpetrated by affiliates as leaderless "is a bit off the mark." Islamist terrorists who are self-financed and unconnected to international networks have a much spottier record of success.[71] It remains to be seen whether al Qaeda central can continue to operate effectively in light of the deaths of Osama bin Laden and other key Qaeda leaders in 2011.

Even Sageman conceded that the current wave of "leaderless" Islamist terrorists is inherently self-limiting since gathering and training makes them vulnerable to monitoring and arrest.[72] As he points out, the shape and dynamics of networks affect their survivability, flexibility, and success.[73] He adds that the leaderless approach lacks a firm overarching strategy. With the al Qaeda movement so dispersed, its leaders could find it increasingly difficult to exert control, beyond offering mere inspiration. Moreover, the movement has become a magnet for the world's most backward and frustrated radicals, which could limit its appeal to the broader masses.[74] Unlike those of the 1980s and 1990s, many jihadist recruits today have little or no practical experience in fighting.[75] A final strategic drawback to leaderless jihad is that without direction it is difficult for scattered jihadists to coalesce into a political organization capable of governing a state.[76] Some observers believe that al Qaeda's endorsement of leaderless jihad proves the organization's infrastructure is under pressure.[77] Nevertheless, al Qaeda endures, in large measure because it has adopted a more leaderless orientation. Michael V. Hayden expressed his thoughts on this:

> I think it's instructive to remember the literal translation of "al Qaeda"—"the base." That conjures up in my mind questions of facilitation, questions of enabling, which might play into . . . leaderless resistance. Perhaps not leaderless resistance, but maybe [a blend of that and] homegrown terrorism or spontaneous groups springing up. . . . Folks without that absolutely definable clear linkage back to some sort of command structure still go out and do things of great harm and great evil.[78]

The US government appears to be taking leaderless resistance more seriously than in the past. For example, the Domestic Security Enhancement Act of 2003 (DSEA) gives law enforcement authorities even greater powers than those outlined in the USA Patriot Act of 2001. Previously, under the Foreign Intelligence Surveillance Act of 1978 (FISA), before conducting surveillance authorities had to show probable cause that an individual was acting on behalf of a "foreign power," but the DSEA changes this to include all individuals involved in suspected terrorism, regardless of whether they are affiliated with a foreign power or terrorist group. Likewise, the Intelligence Reform and Terrorism Prevention Act of 2004 contains a "lone wolf" provision that makes it easier to conduct surveillance on individuals who either act in sympathy with the aims of international terrorist groups, but are not officially affiliated, or whose link with an international terrorist group can be demonstrated.[79]

The movements examined in this book—the US extreme Right, the radical environmental and animal liberation movements, and radical Islamism—increasingly attract individuals who see their struggles in global terms. For each of these movements, it is the eleventh hour, demanding that they act quickly lest the forces of modernity and globalization destroy what they see as their communities. The radical environmentalist movement sees the entire planet imperiled by the ravages of industrialization. And just as Osama bin Laden encouraged Islamists worldwide to view their regional conflicts not as isolated, parochial battles but as theaters of a war to defend Islam against the West and Zionism, some on the extreme Right view their individual nationalist movements as part of a larger struggle for white survival against a rising tide of nonwhite demographic expansion, said to be orchestrated by the forces of globalization and international Jewry. Here the Internet has been crucial, allowing disparate groups to spread their messages and exchange ideas. With a global pool of potential recruits, they can take advantage of the "long-tail" phenomenon, just as firms such as Amazon can profit by selling previously hard-to-find items to a larger number of customers instead of selling a smaller variety of popular items in large quantities.

As Thomas Rid and Marc Hecker observed in their study *War 2.0: Irregular Warfare in the Information Age*, a similar logic applies to extremist groups and terrorism in that a large popular following is not required. A relatively low number of highly motivated, partly self-recruited, and geographically dispersed followers can share an extremist cause without broad appeal, thus making niche terrorism possible. (According to some estimates, before 9/11 al Qaeda had only an estimated two hundred sworn members.)[80] The number of people needed for an established, enduring terrorist group has been drastically lowered, but this development makes it more difficult for such a group to attain power. Although it is easier for insurgents and terrorists to enter the game, it is more difficult for them to evolve into a viable global insurgency because they lack the broad popular support necessary to take over a state. As modern terrorist groups tend to move away from popular appeal, it becomes less likely that they could consolidate and assume political power. They cannot reasonably be expected to defeat their conventional and democratic opponents who have much more military, economic, and political power, but they probably cannot be totally defeated.[81]

The current incarnation of leaderless resistance recalls the anarchist movement in the late nineteenth century that sometimes used bombs and assassination to disrupt governments in the West. With new technology, however, terrorist groups could evolve into more resilient entities as transnational crime syndicates have over the past two decades. A significant international trend is the growing connection between terrorism and organized crime.[82] Their aims differ considerably—terrorists pursue political goals while mobsters seek financial profit—but some terrorist groups, desperate for cash, have resorted to criminal enterprises to fund their operations, resulting sometimes in a "hybridization" of terrorist and criminal networks.[83] For example, the al Qaeda cell that carried out the Madrid attacks included drug traffickers who used their proceeds to finance the operation.[84] So far, transnational crime syndicates appear to have adapted better to globalization, as they thrive on mobility.[85]

Terrorism in the West appears to be moving in the direction of leaderless resistance and lone wolf attacks despite the limitations of this approach. Rather than there being a clear dichotomy between lone wolves and large, established groups, the trend is more aptly seen as a continuum, with more and more terrorist activities committed by those at the lone wolf end of the spectrum.[86] Major terrorist attacks prior to 9/11—such as the 1993 World Trade Center bombing and the attack at the 1972 Summer Olympics in Munich—were carefully planned, financed, and carried out by functioning organizations. In the wake of 9/11 and the resultant government repression, a new pattern has emerged, characterized by attacks that are more frequent yet less complex. At least in the short term, increased scrutiny by law enforcement and intelligence agencies will continue to make major coordinated terrorist activities extremely difficult, but not impossible.[87] Although the state's capacity to monitor is substantial, individuals can still operate covertly and commit violence with little predictability. Leaderless resistance can serve as a catalyst spurring others to move from thought to action, in effect inspiring copycats.[88] Extraordinary examples of leaderless resistance serve to recruit new members to networks.[89]

Several factors make leaderless resistance a potentially effective strategy. One is that the work of aboveground groups to raise ideological consciousness can also motivate unaffiliated underground movement radicals. Moreover, lone wolves do not require expensive or sophisticated equipment, as evidenced by the snipers who used a semiautomatic rifle and a 1990 Chevrolet Caprice to terrorize the Washington, D.C., area. Leaderless resistance makes the penetration of terrorist movements difficult because such perpetrators work alone and have no information on other activists. Further, the mass media can amplify the exploits of lone wolves. Finally, open societies make leaderless resistance easier to carry out because there are so many soft targets.[90]

To date, most episodes of leaderless resistance have been ill planned and haphazard. Some perpetrators of terrorist acts could be aptly described as insane.[91] Proponents of leaderless resistance may believe that lone wolves are calculating and carefully plot their operations, but instances of this have been exceptional. Some advocates of leaderless resistance like to point out that history is replete with examples of political organizations that began with modest numbers—a small, committed core of activists—but eventually developed into powerful mass movements. Stealthy lone wolves who are disciplined in their operations, the argument goes, have the potential to carry out acts of sabotage as the number of soft targets in society increases. As the lone wolf concept becomes more visible, and with the increasing availability of weapons of mass destruction, it is conceivable that a new breed of more dangerous lone wolves could emerge. The case of Anders Behring Breivik illustrates this danger.

According to his online political manifesto and diary, Breivik spent nine years methodically planning his attacks. His writings explain in detail how he procured firearms, tons of fertilizer, and caches of weapons while evading suspicion from authorities. He rented a farm as a cover for his large fertilizer purchases. During his shooting spree, he dressed as a police officer, deceiving some of his victims, who approached him, presumably hoping he would save them. In the attack, he used dumdum bullets, maximizing internal damage to those he shot. The first part of his attack—the bombing at the offices of the prime minister—was intended to send a message to the government that he disapproved of Norway's liberal immigration policies. The second part of his attack—a shooting spree at a summer camp where some liberal party leaders sent their children—presumably was intended to send a message to the ruling elite that not only they but also their children were no longer safe from retribution.

The new media figured prominently in Breivik's campaign of terror. Shortly before his attacks, he uploaded his 1,500-page electronic book—*2083: A European Declaration of Independence*—to the Internet. In addition, he uploaded a video on YouTube titled "The Knight Templar 2083," which contained numerous references to the threat of Islam interspersed with iconic images of crusaders. Whereas Ted Kaczynski implored major newspapers to publish his manifesto (from which Breivik plagiarized) to ensure maximum exposure of his ideas, Breivik was able to take advantage of the Internet, bypassing the traditional mass media. Notoriety stemming from his attacks, he predicted, would serve as "marketing" for his manifesto, assuring that there would be substantial interest in its contents. He expected to be either arrested or killed, and if arrested, he planned to use his subsequent trial as a forum to voice his ideological views. Claiming to be a member of the Knights Templar—a medieval order that protected pilgrims in the Holy Land after the First Crusade in the eleventh century—he saw himself as part of an unorganized and leaderless vanguard that would awaken Europe to the perils of Islamicization brought about by the immigration policies engineered by Europe's liberal parties.[92] Thus the seemingly senseless shootings at the youth camp were meant to punish Norway's ruling party for its "treasonous acts against Europe and Europeans."

Less than a week after Breivik's attacks, US military authorities announced that an AWOL soldier was in custody for planning an attack on Fort Hood, the same base Nidal Hasan had struck nearly two years before. Explosives and weapons were said to have been found in the suspect's motel room that he had rented near the base. A conscientious objector who had begun questioning the legitimacy of the wars in Iraq and Afghanistan after studying Islamic teachings about war and peace, Private First Class Naser Abdo admitted to planning an attack on the base.[93] As this plot and others suggest, terrorism from Islamic radicals will continue. Not long after the death of Osama bin Laden in the spring of 2011, the CBS correspondent Lara Logan warned that his demise could "speed up the trend of recent years which has seen al Qaeda become increasingly decentralized, and therefore even harder to stop."[94]

Though some observers were quick to declare victory over al Qaeda after the death of bin Laden, the campaign against him and the movement he inspired have come with great costs. As of May 2012, 6,438 US soldiers and Defense Department civilian workers have died and over 40,000 have been wounded in the global war on terror.[95] According to one estimate, the financial cost of fighting bin Laden's network has reached $3 trillion when "economic consequences" are taken into account.[96] Over time these costs have taken a devastating toll on the US economy and are unsustainable in the long term. As the national debt continues to increase, inevitable cuts in defense spending will make it more difficult for the US military to counter al Qaeda in those countries—Somalia, Pakistan, and Yemen—in which the movement maintains a significant foothold.[97] Although it is more difficult than ever for terrorists to mount a spectacular attack in the United States today because security measures have been significantly strengthened, sporadic smaller attacks persist. As part of a strategy of attrition, leaderless resistance is becoming the modus operandi of contemporary terrorist movements. Episodes of lone wolf terrorism in news headlines suggest that leaderless resistance has become the most common tactical approach of political violence in the West. Meanwhile, sophisticated tools with uses that are not always benevolent continue to be developed and made widely available. A few angry people now have the potential to cause unprecedented destruction.

Notes

Introduction

1. Sean D. Hamill, "Man Accused in Pittsburgh Killings Voiced Racist Views Online," *New York Times*, April 7, 2009.
2. Peter Slevin, "Slaying Raises Fears on Both Sides of Abortion Debate," *Washington Post*, June 2, 2009.
3. The FBI was aware of von Brunn before the attack—he sometimes voiced extremist views on websites—but was not tracking him. Gary Fields and Evan Perez, "FBI Seeks to Target Lone Extremists," *Wall Street Journal*, June 15, 2006. Abraham Foxman, the director of the Anti-Defamation League, announced that the shooting reflected a broader "wave of hate" against Jews. According to Foxman, several lone wolf incidents over the preceding months were fueled in part by anti-Semitism. "Shooting at U.S. Holocaust Museum Part of a 'Wave of Hate' against Jews," press release, Anti-Defamation League, June 11, 2009.
4. According to acquaintances, Hasan felt conflict between his role in the US military and his Muslim religion. April Castro and Devlin Barrett, "Army Psychiatrist Kills 12 at Fort Hood," *Times News* (Kingsport, TN), November 6, 2009, 1–2.
5. Alan Levin, "In Austin Plane Crash, an Echo of Terrorism," *USA Today*, February 19, 2010.
6. Scott Schifrel and Jose Martinez, "Times Square Terror Suspect Faisal Shahzad Admits Plot to Use Weapon of Mass Destruction," *New York Daily News*, June 21, 2010; J. M. Berger, *Jihad Joe: Americans Who Go to War in the Name of Islam* (Washington, DC: Potomac Books, 2011), 161.
7. Although characterized as a Far Rightist, Anders Behring Breivik does not seem to fit the classic profile. From his own pronouncements, his ideology consists of European nationalism, cultural Christianity, support for Zionism, Austrian School economics, and freemasonry. He identified Islam as the greatest threat to Europe.
8. Associated Press, "Suspected Norway Gunman/Bomber Reportedly Has Extreme Right-Wing Views, but No Links to Radical Groups," July 23, 2011.
9. According to a 2010 study conducted at the University of Maryland, "since 1995, a much higher percentage of terrorist attacks in the United States have been conducted by unaffiliated individuals, rather than by organized groups. In the period 1995 (post–Oklahoma City) through 2007, 43 out of 131 incidents with attributed perpetrators were committed by individuals—33% of all attacks in the United States in this period." National Consortium for the Study of Terrorism and Responses to Terrorism, *Background Report: On the Fifteenth Anniversary of the Oklahoma City Bombing*, April 2010, *www.start.umd.edu/start/ announcements/2010April_OklahomaCityAnniversary.pdf*, 1. While thorough, this study probably underestimates the percentage of lone wolf attacks since such incidents are often not classified as terrorism but treated as standard criminal acts by authorities. For obvious reasons, attacks conducted by organized terrorist groups are more likely to be noticed and classified as terrorism.
10. Kevin Johnson, "Feds Try to Detect 'Lone Offenders,'" *USA Today*, August 12, 2009.

11. Fields and Perez, "FBI Seeks to Target Lone Extremists."

12. As described in Jeffrey Kaplan, "Leaderless Resistance," *Terrorism and Political Violence* 9, no. 3 (1997): 80.

13. Jeremy Pressman, "Leaderless Resistance: The Next Threat?," *Current History*, December 2003, 423.

14. Author interview with Darren Mulloy, June 13, 2008. Mulloy is a keen observer of the Far Right in the United States and the author of *American Extremism: History, Politics and the Militia Movement* (London: Routledge, 2008).

15. Adam Elkus, "Future War: The War on Terror after Iraq," *Athena Intelligence Journal* 2, no. 1 (2007): 18.

16. Barak Mendelsohn, *Combating Jihadism: American Hegemony and Interstate Cooperation in the War on Terrorism* (Chicago: University of Chicago Press, 2009).

17. Since the late 1980s, states have been getting out of the business of terrorism. That the US State Department has maintained a list of state sponsors has probably discouraged states from this practice. Symbolically it helps keep counterterrorism high on the policy agenda and provides a handy frame of reference for international cooperation on counterterrorism. Paul R. Pillar, *Terrorism and U.S. Foreign Policy* (Washington, DC: Brookings Institution Press, 2001), 152.

18. Michael Teague, "New Media and the Arab Spring," *Al Jadid*, n.d., *www.aljadid.com/content/new-media-and-arab-spring*.

19. Howard Rheingold, *Smart Mobs: The Next Social Revolution* (Cambridge, MA: Basic Books, 2002), 157–62.

20. Ian Urbina, "Mobs Are Born as Word Grows by Text Message," *New York Times*, March 24, 2010.

21. Fareed Zakaria, "Terrorists Don't Need States," in *Annual Editions Violence and Terrorism 07/08*, 10th ed., ed. Thomas J. Badey (New York: McGraw Hill, 2007), 29. Thomas Friedman first advanced the notion of the "super-empowered individual." See Friedman, *The Lexus and the Olive Tree: Understanding Globalization* (New York: Anchor, 2000). Thomas Barnett applied this concept to the field of terrorism in Barnett, *Great Powers: America and the World after Bush* (New York: Putnam, 2009), 295.

22. John Robb, *Brave New War: The Next Stage of Terrorism and the End of Globalization* (Hoboken, NJ: Wiley, 2007).

23. US Department of State, *Country Reports on Terrorism 2005* (Washington, DC: Government Printing Office, 2005), chap. 2; *www.state.gov/documents/organization/65465.pdf*.

24. Martin J. Muckian, "Structural Vulnerabilities of Networked Insurgencies: Adapting to the New Adversary," *Parameters*, Winter 2006–2007, 15.

25. William S. Lind et al., "The Changing Face of War: Into the Fourth Generation," *Marine Corps Gazette*, October 1989, 22–26.

26. "Fifth Generation Warfare," *Federal Patriot*, n.d., *64.203.107.114/papers/05-10_paper.asp* (website discontinued). Accessed November 3, 2008.

Chapter 1

1. Vauban's early writings on warfare favored fortification, but his thinking evolved in the direction of developing a flexible army as the linchpin of a strong defense. Henry Guerlac, "Vauban: The Impact of Science on War," in *Makers of Modern Strategy: from Machiavelli to the Nuclear Age*, ed. Peter Paret (Princeton, NJ: Princeton University Press, 1986), 64–90.

2. Machiavelli correctly saw that the medieval society based on agriculture was giving way to a new economy based on money and commerce, which presented greater opportunity for recruiting armies. He counseled that a national militia composed of a cross section of all citizens would be far more effective then mercenaries, believing they would fight more enthusiastically. His prescription presaged the *levée en masse* so effectively implemented by

Napoleon. The new laws of war he wanted to introduce were actually old laws that he had inferred from his reading of the history of Roman military order.

3. Lind et al., "Changing Face of War," 22–26.

4. Thomas X. Hammes, *The Sling and the Stone: On War in the 21st Century* (St. Paul, MN: Zenith Press, 2004), 12–13.

5. The system had many downsides, however, including high cost, slow speed of communication, and vulnerability to sabotage, disruption, and interception of messages. The cost of the system made it available only to states—and only for the most urgent political and military matters. Thomas Rid and Marc Hecker, *War 2.0: Irregular Warfare in the Information Age* (Westport, CT: Praeger Security International, 2009), 14–15.

6. Martin van Creveld, *The Transformation of War* (New York: Free Press, 1991), 39.

7. John A. Nagl, *Learning to Eat Soup with a Knife: Counterinsurgency Lessons from Malaya and Vietnam* (Chicago: University of Chicago Press, 2005), 16.

8. Greene, *The 33 Strategies of War* (New York: Penguin, 2007), 93.

9. Gunther E. Rothenberg, *The Napoleonic Wars* (New York: Collins, 2006), 26.

10. Rupert Smith, *The Utility of Force: The Art of War in the Modern World* (New York: Knopf, 2007), 37.

11. Peter Paret, "Napoleon and the Revolution in War," in *Makers of Modern Strategy: From Machiavelli to the Nuclear Age*, ed. Peter Paret (Princeton, NJ: Princeton University Press, 1986), 129.

12. Hammes, *The Sling and the Stone*, 16–22.

13. Smith, *The Utility of Force*, 35, 36.

14. Rothenberg, *The Napoleonic Wars*, 19.

15. Anthony James Joes, *Resisting Rebellion: The History and Politics of Counterinsurgency* (Lexington: University Press of Kentucky, 2004), 63.

16. Peter Paret, "Clausewitz," 188, 191.

17. Anatol Rapoport, introduction to *On War*, by Carl von Clausewitz (London: Penguin Books, 1982), 23.

18. "Introduction by Col. F. N. Maude," in Clausewitz, *On War*, 83–97.

19. Martin van Creveld, *The Art of War: War and Military Thought* (London: Collins, 2000), 108.

20. Van Creveld, *The Transformation of War*, 34; Jon Tetsuro Sumida, *Decoding Clausewitz: A New Approach to 'On War'* (Lawrence: University Press of Kansas, 2008), 9.

21. John Keegan, *A History of Warfare* (New York: Alfred A. Knopf, 1993), 19.

22. Clausewitz, *On War*, 101, 119.

23. Richard H. Shultz Jr. and Andrea J. Dew, *Insurgents, Terrorists, and Militias: The Warriors of Contemporary Combat* (New York: Columbia University Press, 2006), 4.

24. Van Creveld, *The Art of War*, 112.

25. Rapaport, introduction to *On War*, 25.

26. Paret, "Clausewitz," 200.

27. Clausewitz, *On War*, 173.

28. T. X. Hammes, "Fourth Generation Warfare Evolves, Fifth Emerges," *Military Review*, May/June 2007, 20.

29. Rapoport, introduction to *On War*, 21, 24.

30. Clausewitz, *On War*, 117, 123, 276, 393.

31. Ibid., 117, 259.

32. Sumida, *Decoding Clausewitz*, 3.

33. Clausewitz, *On War*, 274.

34. Van Creveld, *The Art of War*, 111.

35. Van Creveld, *The Transformation of War*, 108.

36. Rapoport, introduction to *On War*, 17.

37. Keegan, *A History of Warfare*, 354.

38. Rapoport, introduction to *On War*, 25.

39. Sumida, *Decoding Clausewitz*, xi.

40. Nagl, *Learning to Eat Soup with a Knife*, 18.

41. Rid and Hecker, *War 2.0*, 15–16.

42. Hammes, *The Sling and the Stone*, 16–22, and Smith, *The Utility of Force*, 70–73.

43. Hajo Holborn, "The Prusso-German School: Moltke and the Rise of the General Staff," in Paret, *Makers of Modern Strategy*, 283.

44. Rothenberg, *The Napoleonic Wars*, 175.

45. Smith, *The Utility of Force*, 53.

46. Greene, *The 33 Strategies of War*, 75.

47. Smith, *The Utility of Force*, 99.

48. Van Creveld, *The Art of War*, 133.

49. Martin van Creveld, *The Changing Face of War: Lessons of Combat, from the Marne to Iraq* (New York: Ballantine Books, 2006), 70.

50. Thomas P. M. Barnett, *Blueprint for Action: A Future Worth Creating* (New York: Berkley Books, 2005), 19.

51. Bruce Berkowitz, *The New Face of War: How War Will Be Fought in the 21st Century* (New York: Free Press, 2003), 4.

52. Hammes, *The Sling and the Stone*, 18–22.

53. Van Creveld, *The Changing Face of War*, 25.

54. As John Keegan observed, by 1914 a cultural ethos pervaded Europe that accepted the right of the state to demand the duty of every fit male for military service, which was viewed as a necessary training in civic virtue. During that period, the United States was the least militarized Western society. Keegan explains that the US Civil War had "inoculated several generations of Americans against the false romanticism of uniforms and training camps." Keegan, *History of Warfare*, 356–57.

55. Smith, *The Utility of Force*, 127.

56. Keegan, *A History of Warfare*, 313, 365, 368.

57. Van Creveld, *The Art of War*, 176–78.

58. Sumida, *Decoding Clausewitz*, 25–26.

59. Germany employed such tactics in World War I when Captain Willy Rohr relied on the initiative of small units—assault detachments—to penetrate the enemy's trenches and then rapidly exploit those breaches in enemy lines. His commander, General Gaede, gave him simple, mission-focused orders that allowed for tactical flexibility. Hammes, *The Sling and the Stone*, 27.

60. Hy S. Rothstein, *Afghanistan and the Troubled Future of Unconventional Warfare* (Annapolis, MD: Naval Institute Press, 2006), 47–48.

61. Hammes, *The Sling and the Stone*, 287.

62. The late US Air Force colonel John Boyd described the heart of maneuver warfare as consisting of "people, ideas, and hardware"—in that order. To perform effectively in maneuver warfare, combatants have to master operating inside the OODA (observe, orient, decide, act) loop. The essence of maneuver warfare is deception so that one's opponents never obtain a clear picture of action or intentions unless one is trying to convey a message. Chet Richards, *Neither Shall the Sword: Conflict in the Years Ahead* (Washington, DC: Center for Defense Information, 2005), 2–4.

63. Lind et al., "Changing Face of War," 22–26.

64. Clay Shirky, *Here Comes Everybody: The Power of Organizing without Organizations* (New York: Penguin Press, 2008), 172, 173.

65. Michael Geyer, "German Strategy in the Age of Machine Warfare, 1914–1945," in Paret, *Makers of Modern Strategy*, 579, 582.

66. Van Creveld, *The Changing Face of War*, 263.

67. The word "guerrilla" is Spanish for "small war." Rothenberg, *The Napoleonic Wars*, 156.

68. Van Creveld, *The Art of War*, 113.
69. Clausewitz realized that since partisans usually faced superior forces, they had to avoid danger whenever possible lest their units quickly be eliminated.
70. Rothenberg, *The Napoleonic Wars*, 154.
71. Nagl, *Learning to Eat Soup with a Knife*, 16.
72. Walter Laqueur, *Guerrilla Warfare: A Historical and Critical Study* (New Brunswick, NJ: Transaction Publishers, 1998), xviii.
73. Matthew J. Morgan, "An Evolving View of Warfare: War and Peace and the American Military Profession," *Small Wars and Insurgencies* 16, no. 2 (June 2005): 151. A corollary argument was that because great powers were ponderously prepared for big wars, they left themselves vulnerable to the tactics of revolutionary warfare. John Shy and Thomas W. Collier, "Revolutionary War," in Paret, *Makers of Modern Strategy*, 818.
74. Hammes, *The Sling and the Stone*.
75. Dennis M. Drew and Donald M. Snow, *Making Twenty-First Century Strategy: An Introduction to Modern National Security Processes and Problems* (Maxwell Air Force Base, Alabama: Air University Press, 2006), 143.
76. Robert M. Cassidy, C*ounterinsurgency and the Global War on Terror: Military Culture and Irregular War* (repr., Stanford, CA: Stanford University Press, 2008), 25.
77. Laqueur, *Guerrilla Warfare*, 7.
78. Edward N. Luttwak, *Strategy: The Logic of War and Peace* (Cambridge, MA: Belknap Press of Harvard University Press, 2003), 152–53.
79. Joes, *Resisting Rebellion*, 17.
80. Bard E. O'Neill, *Insurgency and Terrorism: Inside Modern Revolutionary Warfare* (Dulles, VA: Brassey's, 1990), 55.
81. Joes, *Resisting Rebellion*, 18.
82. Quoted in Rid and Hecker, *War 2.0*, 130.
83. Ibid., *War 2.0*, 1, 43.
84. O'Neill, *Insurgency and Terrorism*, 74–85.
85. Ibid., 112.
86. For example, moral support includes both private and public statements of sympathy for the insurgents in general terms. Political support goes a step further and is marked by explicit and active backing of the insurgents and their aims in the diplomatic arena. Material support includes tangible resources provided to the insurgents. Sanctuary can be provided as well to insurgents who seek to temporarily flee and regroup, offering a location for training, arms stockpiling, and operational planning. O'Neill, *Insurgency and Terrorism*, 114–16.
87. Jeffrey Record, *Beating Goliath: Why Insurgencies Win* (Washington, DC: Potomac Books, 2007).
88. Furthermore, during the brief Soviet occupation of Manchuria near the end of the war and afterward, the Soviet army established external communist control over an area where the Chinese Communist Party was politically and militarily weak. Ibid., 38–39.
89. Ibid., 60.
90. Ninety percent of the composition of the rebel groups, the Malayan Communist Party and the Malayan Races Liberation Army, were Chinese, who represented less than 40 percent of the country's population. Ibid., 63.
91. Timothy Naftali, *Blind Spot: The Secret History of American Counterterrorism* (New York: Basic Books, 2005), 1–11; Perry Biddiscombe, *Werewolf! The History of the National Socialist Guerrilla Movement, 1944–1946* (Toronto: University of Toronto Press, 1998). Decades later the Werewolves were a source of inspiration for neo-Nazi proponents of leaderless resistance in Germany, Russia, and the United States. Perry Biddiscombe, *The Last Nazis: Werewolf Guerrilla Resistance in Europe 1944–1947* (Stroud, Gloucestershire, UK: Tempus,

2006), 9–10; Walter Laqueur, *Fascism: Past, Present, Future* (Oxford: Oxford University Press, 1996), 191.

92. The first constant factor in war is the moral law, which causes people to follow their ruler faithfully and resolutely. Second is heaven, which signifies conditions such as night and day, weather, time of day, and seasons. The third factor, Earth, comprises variables such as distances, dangers, topography, and the "chances of life and death." Fourth, the commander stands for the "virtues of wisdom, sincerity, benevolence, courage, and strictness." Finally, method and discipline refer to the organization of the army and the logistics involved in supporting it. Sun Tzu, *The Art of War* (New York: Barnes and Noble Classics, 2003).

93. Ibid., 18.

94. Van Creveld, *The Art of War*, 38.

95. Jonathan R. White, *Terrorism and Homeland Security*, 5th ed. (Belmont, CA: Wadsworth Thomson Learning, 2006), 271–73.

96. Mao Tse-tung, *On Guerrilla Warfare* (Urbana: University of Illinois Press, 2000), 23, 41.

97. Nagl, *Learning to Eat Soup with a Knife*, 20.

98. Mao, *On Guerrilla Warfare*, 12–14.

99. Laqueur, *Guerrilla Warfare*, 246.

100. Hammes, *The Sling and the Stone*, 47.

101. Ibid., 51.

102. Mao, *On Guerrilla Warfare*, 27.

103. Ibid., 20–21.

104. O'Neill, *Insurgency and Terrorism*, 39.

105. Robert Taber, *War of the Flea* (Washington, DC: Brassey's, 2002), 152.

106. Shy and Collier, "Revolutionary War," 823.

107. Nagl, *Learning to Eat Soup with a Knife*, 25.

108. Mao, *On Guerrilla Warfare*, 24.

109. Daniel Moran, *Wars of National Liberation* (London: Collins, 2006), 22–23.

110. Laqueur, *Guerrilla Warfare*, 265.

111. Shy and Collier, "Revolutionary War," 848.

112. Laqueur, *Guerrilla Warfare*, 263.

113. Shy and Collier, "Revolutionary War," 849.

114. Joes, *America and Guerrilla Warfare*, 217.

115. Hammes, *The Sling and the Stone*, vii–ix, 69.

116. Joes, *Urban Guerrilla Warfare*, 99, 102.

117. Rid and Hecker, *War 2.0*, 22.

118. Joes, *Urban Guerrilla Warfare*, 91.

119. Rid and Hecker, *War 2.0*, 22–23.

120. Greene, *The 33 Strategies of War*, 152–55.

121. Joes, *Urban Guerrilla Warfare*, 107.

122. Rothstein, *Afghanistan and the Troubled Future*, 182.

123. Taber, *War of the Flea*, 29.

124. Joes, *Resisting Rebellion*, 21.

125. Moran, *Wars of National Liberation*, 158–59.

126. Taber, *War of the Flea*, 8.

127. Shy and Collier, "Revolutionary War," 850.

128. For more on the life of Guevara, see Marc Becker, introduction to *Guerrilla Warfare*, by Che Guevara (Lincoln: University of Nebraska Press, 1998), v–xvii.

129. Guevara, *Guerrilla Warfare*, 7.

130. Laqueur, *Guerrilla Warfare*, 334.

131. Moran, *Wars of National Liberation*, 162.

132. Shy and Collier, "Revolutionary War," 850.

133. Walter Laqueur, *The Age of Terrorism* (Boston: Little, Brown, 1987), 23–24.

134. Joes, *Urban Guerrilla Warfare*, 1–2.

135. Thomas P. Raynor, *Terrorism: Past, Present, Future* (New York: Franklin Watts, 1982), 51.

136. Joes, *Urban Guerrilla Warfare*, 6.

137. Ibid., 76.

138. For the most part the Tupamaros confined their activities to Montevideo, for several reasons. First, the group was too small to mount a guerrilla campaign because it did not have a broad-based constituency, as most members were middle-class students. Second, the countryside of Uruguay was not conducive to guerrilla war because unrest tended to be most pronounced in the urban areas. Third, the peasants were unwilling to provide popular support for the guerrilla forces. Finally, Montevideo was the nerve center of Uruguay. The Tupamaros reasoned that if they could strike the infrastructure in Montevideo, they could bring down the whole government. In 1968 the Tupamaros launched a massive campaign of decentralized terrorism. For a good synopsis of the Tupamaros' campaign, see Jonathan R. White, *Terrorism: An Introduction*, 3rd ed. (Belmont, CA: Wadsworth Thomson Learning, 2002), 125–31.

139. As Anthony Joes explains, guerrilla operations in the city can be problematic for several reasons. First, whereas the state is often absent in the countryside, the state is heavily present in cities, so guerrillas run a great risk of being captured there by police. Second, by establishing safe houses and the like, urban guerrillas lose their mobility and make themselves vulnerable to neighborhood cordons and house-to-house searches. Third, because of their geographic locations, cities are usually not positioned in such a way as to establish cross-border sanctuaries or receive outside assistance. Joes, *Urban Guerrilla Warfare*, 87.

140. According to some accounts, Zbigniew Brzezinski, then national security adviser, instigated the crisis so that the Soviets would fall into the "Afghan Trap." Months before the Soviet invasion, he publicly admitted that the Carter administration was helping the mujahideen subvert the Taraki government. For a synopsis of the Afghan political situation during this period, see Michael Parenti, *The Terrorism Trap: September 11 and Beyond* (San Francisco: City Lights Books, 2002), 56–59.

141. Cassidy, C*ounterinsurgency and the Global War on Terror*, 31.

142. Ibid., 65, 305.

143. Joes, *America and Guerrilla Warfare*, 305, 306.

144. Kenneth R. Timmerman, *Preachers of Hate: Islam and the War on America*. (New York: Crown Forum, 2003), 138.

145. Samuel Katz, *Relentless Pursuit: The DSS and the Manhunt for the al-Qaeda Terrorists* (New York: Forge, 2002), 52.

146. The Stingers proved enormously effective and are estimated to have downed more than 270 Soviet aircraft. Milton Bearden, "Graveyard of Empires," in *How Did This Happen? Terrorism and the New War*, ed. James F. Hoge Jr. and Gideon Rose (New York: Public Affairs, 2001), 87. Simon Reeve asserts that according to one source, US emissaries actually met directly with bin Laden, who reportedly first suggested that the mujahideen be provided with Stingers. Simon Reeve, *The New Jackals: Ramzi Yousef, Osama bin Laden, and the Future of Terrorism* (Boston: Northeastern University Press, 1999), 167.

147. Joes, *America and Guerrilla Warfare*, 300.

148. Ibid., 307, 311.

149. Greene, *The 33 Strategies of War*, 287.

150. Van Creveld, *The Changing Face of War*, 219.

151. Raymond Millen, "The Hobbesian Notion of Self-Preservation Concerning Human Behavior during an Insurgency," *Parameters*, Winter 2006–2007, 4–13.

152. Rid and Hecker, *War 2.0*, 49.

153. Andrew Mack, "Why Big Nations Lose Small Wars: The Politics of Asymmetric Conflict," in Record, *Beating Goliath*, 1–9. For example, in 1975 the government in Hanoi announced that communist forces during the "American period" of the Vietnam War had

sustained 1.1 million dead and also an estimated two million civilian dead. However, political will in and of itself is not a sufficient condition to prevail. For example, Adolf Hitler
demonstrated strong political will but nevertheless lost the Second World War.

154. Gil Merom, *How Democracies Lose Small Wars* (Cambridge: Cambridge University Press,
2003), 1–32, 230.

155. David C. Rapoport, "The Four Waves of Modern Terrorism," in *Attacking Terrorism: Elements of a Grand Strategy*, ed. Audrey Kurth Cronin and James M. Ludes (Washington,
DC: Georgetown University Press, 2004), 46–74.

156. Jeffrey Kaplan, *Terrorist Groups and the New Tribalism: Terrorism's Fifth Wave* (London:
Routledge, 2010).

Chapter 2

1. See, for example, Seymour Martin Lipset and Earl Raab, *The Politics of Unreason: Right
Wing Extremism in America, 1790–1970* (New York: Harper and Row, 1970).

2. Ted Robert Gurr, "Terrorism in Democracies: Its Social and Political Bases," in *Origins of
Terrorism: Psychologies, Ideologies, Theologies, States of Mind*, ed. Walter Reich (Washington,
DC: Woodrow Wilson Center Press, 1998), 91.

3. Benjamin Netanyahu, *Fighting Terrorism: How Democracies Can Defeat the International
Terrorist Network* (New York: Farrar, Straus and Giroux, 2001), 13.

4. Ultimately it is the minister of interior at the Lander level who decides whether to ban
a group, based on—among other things—data that the Office of the Protection of the
Constitution provides. Listing a group as "extremist" in the annual Reports of the Office
(Federal and/or Land Offices) can be seen as a "public recommendation" to ban them. For
more on the response to the German extreme Right, see George Michael and Michael
Minkenberg, "A Continuum for Responding to the Extreme Right: A Comparison between the United States and Germany," *Studies in Conflict and Terrorism* 30, no. 12 (2007):
1109–23.

5. Raphael Cohen-Almagor, "Combating Right-Wing Political Extremism in Israel: Critical
Appraisal," *Terrorism and Political Violence* 9, no. 4 (1997): 16–23.

6. FBI internal memorandum, File Number 438611424445, September 8, 1964.

7. Jessica Stern, *The Ultimate Terrorists* (Cambridge, MA: Harvard University Press, 1999),
149.

8. Michael A. Ledeen, *The War against the Terror Masters* (New York: St. Martin's Press,
2003), 71.

9. James Kirkpatrick Davis, *Spying on America: The FBI's Domestic Counterintelligence Program*
(Westport, CT: Praeger, 1992), 176.

10. A University of Florida study estimates that by 1999 there were approximately three
hundred such groups nationwide. This study was cited in Maria T. Padilla, "Race Violence
Leads to Rise in Anti-racism Groups," *Salt Lake Tribune*, August 22, 1999.

11. Anti-Defamation League, *The ADL Anti-paramilitary Training Statute: A Response to Domestic Terrorism* (New York: ADL, 1995).

12. James Oliphant, "Anti-gay Violence Bill Heads to White House after Senate Approval,"
Los Angeles Times, October 23, 2009.

13. "ADL Hails Long Overdue Enactment of Federal Hate Crime Law as a 'Monumental
Achievement for America,'" press release, Anti-Defamation League, October 28, 2009,
www.adl.org/PresRele/HatCr_51/5635_51.htm.

14. Morris Dees and Ellen Bowden, "Courtroom Victories: Taking Hate Groups to Court,"
Southern Poverty Law Center, *www.splcenter.org/pdf/static/courtroom_victories.pdf*.

15. The independent researcher Laird Wilcox has thoroughly examined various FBI and ADL
memoranda that indicate a close working relationship between the two entities. See Laird
Wilcox, *The Watchdogs: A Close Look at Anti-Racist "Watchdog" Groups* (Olathe, KS: Laird

Wilcox Editorial Research Center, 1999), 45–46. My review of Wilcox's archives on this subject confirms his assertion.

16. Morris Dees and Steven Fiffer, *Hate on Trial: The Case against America's Most Dangerous Neo-Nazi* (New York: Villard Books, 1993), 19. This seemingly backdoor relationship with law enforcement is not without critics, as some believe that it raises serious civil liberties issues.

17. Homeland Security Advisory Council, "Countering Violent Extremism (CVE) Working Group," Spring 2010, *www.dhs.gov/xlibrary/assets/hsac_cve_working_group_recommendations.pdf*.

18. In 1983 members of the Far Right underground group known as the Order drew up a list of prominent figures marked for assassination. At the top of the list was Morris Dees. See Kevin Flynn and Gary Gerhardt, *The Silent Brotherhood* (New York: Signet, 1990), 233. Authorities apprehended all Order members before they could carry out their plan.

19. Bill Stanton, *Klanwatch: Bringing the Ku Klux Klan to Justice* (New York: Mentor, 1991), 159–70.

20. Members of the now-defunct White Patriot Party were implicated in this plot. Repeated threats prompted the SPLC to improve the security of its facility. See "Upgraded Security System Protects Center Employees," *SPLC Report*, March 1997.

21. Robert H. Churchill, *To Shake Their Guns in the Tyrant's Face: Libertarian Political Violence and the Origins of the Militia Movement* (Ann Arbor: University of Michigan Press, 2009), 261.

22. Furrow confessed this to FBI authorities after his surrender. He had carried a map with both the Simon Wiesenthal Center and its Museum of Tolerance circled, indicating they were targets. For more on this episode, see "FBI: Wiesenthal Center Was Terrorist's Main Target," *Response* (Simon Wiesenthal Center) 20, no. 2 (1999): 2–3.

23. The federal government has demonstrated increased vigilance, as the remarks of the Department of Justice spokesman Bryan Sierra indicate: "The Department of Justice is also making every effort to shut down hate groups and homegrown terrorists before they, too, can act violently on their hatred." Maria Glod and Jerry Markon, "Tracking Hate Groups Aids Terrorism Fight," *Washington Post*, May 19, 2003.

24. For more on these arrests, see George Michael, *The Enemy of My Enemy: The Alarming Convergence of Militant Islam and the Extreme Right* (Lawrence: University Press of Kansas, 2006), 179–92, and Michael and Minkenberg, "A Continuum for Responding to the Extreme Right."

25. Glod and Markon, "Tracking Hate Groups."

26. Christopher Hewitt, Understanding Terrorism in America: From the Klan to Al Qaeda (London: Routledge, 2003), 78, 126.

27. James Corcoran, Bitter Harvest: Gordon Kahl and the Posse Comitatus; Murder in the Heartland (New York: Penguin Books, 1990).

28. Danny O. Coulson and Elaine Shannon, *No Heroes: Inside the FBI's Secret Counter-Terror Force* (New York: Pocket Books, 1999), 192–93.

29. The organization used several names, including "the Silent Brotherhood" and a German version of that name, the Brüder Schweigen.

30. James Aho, *The Politics of Righteousness: Idaho Christian Patriotism* (Seattle: University of Washington Press, 1990), 7.

31. Coulson and Shannon, *No Heroes*, 194.

32. James Coates, *Armed and Dangerous: The Rise of the Survivalist Right* (New York: Noonday Press, 1987), 67.

33. This is according to the statements of Danny O. Coulson, the founder of the FBI's Hostage Rescue Team, who was involved in the Order investigation. Coulson and Shannon, *No Heroes*, 195. According to one estimate, the investigation involved one-quarter of the total manpower resources of the FBI. Aho, *The Politics of Righteousness*, 61.

34. The prison addresses of the "POWs" are occasionally listed in the Far Right literature, and readers are encouraged to write and provide material and moral support to them and their families.

35. This observation is made in Betty A. Dobratz and Stephanie L. Shanks-Meile, *White Power, White Pride! The White Separatist Movement in the United States* (New York: Twayne Publishers, 1997), 193.

36. For more on the Order's donations to the White Patriot Party and WAR, see Glenn Miller, *A White Man Speaks Out* (G. Miller, 1999), 149–56. The White Patriot Party dissolved because of pressure from federal prosecutors and Morris Dees of the Southern Poverty Law Center. WAR continues operations to this day, but it has lost strength because of a civil suit initiated by Dees.

37. According to an account of Mathews's former lover Zillah Craig, Mathews stuffed a large amount of money in a paper bag. Later she saw Mathews hand the bag to Pierce. Kevin Flynn and Gary Gerhardt, *The Silent Brotherhood* (New York: Signet, 1990), 321–22. Soon after the meeting Pierce paid $95,000 in cash for a 346-acre plot in Hillsboro, West Virginia, on which the National Alliance encampment is headquartered. Kathy Marks, *Faces of Right Wing Extremism* (Boston: Branden, 1996), 59. The encampment has allowed the organization a good deal of privacy to go about its business away from the watchful eyes of its opponents. A 1987 FBI memorandum on the activities of the National Alliance lamented that the remoteness of the encampment made "physical surveillance nearly impossible." FBI internal memorandum, File Number 100-487473-53X.

38. *The Turner Diaries* has been linked to other right-wing terrorists for whom it may have been a source of inspiration, including the Aryan Republican Army, which committed approximately twenty bank robberies between 1992 and 1996; Dennis McGiffin, whom the FBI arrested for conspiracy for planning to bomb state capitols and poison water supplies; David Copeland, who conducted a one-man campaign of terror in London in 1999; and Timothy McVeigh, who was convicted of the 1995 bombing in Oklahoma City. Robert S. Griffin, *The Fame of a Dead Man's Deeds: An Up-Close Portrait of White Nationalist William Pierce* (Bloomington, IN: 1st Books, 2001), 5.

39. John Sutherland, "Gospels of Hate That Slip through the Net," *Guardian* (UK), April 3, 2000; David Segal, "The Pied Piper of Racism," *Washington Post* (January 12, 2000).

40. Andrew Macdonald, *The Turner Diaries* (Hillsboro, WV: National Vanguard Books, 1978).

41. This is how the FBI characterized the book. See FBI internal memorandum, File Number 100-487473-50, January 23, 1987, and FBI internal memorandum, File Number 100-487473-67, September 10, 1987. Robert Burnham, the FBI's section chief for domestic terrorism, remarked on the book's connection to acts and potential acts of terrorism. According to Burnham, FBI field offices have received numerous calls from local police departments reporting that they have found copies of *The Turner Diaries* with explosives and bomb-making materials. "Domestic Terrorism: The FBI View," MSNBC, July 5, 1999.

42. Associated Press, "'Turner Diaries' Puts FBI on Heightened Alert," December 31, 1999.

43. For more on the Order II, see William E. Barker, *Aryan America: Race Revolution and the Hitler Legacy* (St. Maries, ID: Falcon Ridge Publishing, 1993).

44. FBI, *Terrorism in the United States 1998* (Washington, DC: FBI, 1999), 5.

45. Coulson and Shannon, *No Heroes*, 212.

46. Ibid., 222.

47. Some of the alleged plots included an attempt to blow up a natural gas pipeline in Fulton, Arkansas; the explosive failed. Some CSA member allegedly planned to assassinate several public officials, including federal judges H. Franklin Waters and Jack Knox and US Attorney Asa Hutchinson. Ellison and Noble planned to bomb a gay church in Kansas City, Missouri, but Noble lost his nerve and failed to carry out the attack. Finally, according to Ellison and Noble, the CSA planned to use a thirty-gallon drum of cyanide that it had stockpiled to poison the water supplies of New York City and Washington, D.C. They had

hoped that this would foment urban unrest and precipitate their anticipated revolution. Kerry Noble, *Tabernacle of Hate: Seduction into Right-Wing Extremism*, 2nd ed. (Syracuse, NY: Syracuse University Press, 2010).

48. Brent L. Smith, *Terrorism in America: Pipe Bombs and Pipe Dreams* (Albany: State University of New York Press, 1994), 41.

49. Bruce Hoffman, *Inside Terrorism* (New York: Columbia University Press, 1998), 178–79. Martha Crenshaw sees terrorism as the final act in a sequence of choices that extremist groups make. According to her theory, terrorism is part of a learning process in which terrorists weigh their available resources and resort to violence when other means of opposition seem unfeasible. Crenshaw, "The Logic of Terrorism," in *The Origins of Terrorism*, ed. Walter Reich (Washington, DC: Woodrow Wilson Center Press, 1998), 7–24.

50. It took the Far Right quite a while to learn how vulnerable it could be when isolated in a rural setting. As Smith and Damphousse observed, the Far Left had widely publicized in their publications the failure of Che Guevara's similar strategy in Bolivia. Brent L. Smith and Kelly R. Damphousse, "Two Decades of Terror," in *The Future of Terrorism: Violence in the New Millennium*, ed. Harvey W. Kushner (Thousand Oaks, CA: Sage Publications, 1998), 142.

51. Hewitt, "Patterns of American Terrorism, 1955–1998: An Historical Perspective on Terrorism-Related Fatalities," *Terrorism and Political Violence* 12, no. 1 (2000): 11.

52. According to James Aho, roughly half of all right-wing homicides from 1980 to 1990 can be attributed to individuals acting alone. Aho, *The Politics of Righteousness*, 62.

53. In February 2007, Nichols claimed in a nineteen-page signed declaration that McVeigh had told him that he, McVeigh, was taking instructions from a former FBI official named Larry Potts. According to Nichols, McVeigh had been recruited in 1992, while he was still in the army, to carry out undercover missions. Nichols asserted that McVeigh acquired the bomb-making knowledge while traveling the gun-show circuit. Nichols claimed he knew in November 1994 that McVeigh was building a bomb, and so left for the Philippines to avoid being implicated in the plot. Geoffrey Fattah, "Nichols Says Bombing Was FBI Op," *Deseret Morning News*, February 21, 2007.

54. Brandon M. Stickney, *All-American Monster: The Unauthorized Biography of Timothy McVeigh* (Amherst, NY: Prometheus Books, 1996), 97–100, 158–59. One Michigan Militia member who was present at the meeting told me that McVeigh and Nichols were not well received, because of their "extreme racial feelings," and were asked to leave. Author interview with Norm Olson, September 8, 2000.

55. McVeigh claimed to have joined the Klan because he thought it was "fighting for the restoration of individual rights, especially gun rights." After more research he discovered that the Klan was "almost entirely devoted to the cause of racism." Lou Michel and Dan Herbeck, *American Terrorist: Timothy McVeigh and the Oklahoma City Bombing* (New York: Regan Books, 2001), 88–89. McVeigh's claimed naïveté regarding the nature of the Klan seems disingenuous since he was intelligent and intellectually curious. It is also worth mentioning that he appears to have been a seeker, willing to look anywhere for knowledge.

56. Kenneth S. Stern, *A Force upon the Plain: The American Militia Movement and the Politics of Hate* (New York: Simon and Schuster, 1996), 51, 192.

57. Robert S. Griffin, *The Fame of a Dead Man's Deeds: An Up-Close Portrait of White Nationalist William Pierce* (Robert S. Griffin, 2001), 7; *www.victoryforever.com/fameofadeadmansdeeds.pdf*.

58. Howard Pankratz, "'Turner Diaries' and Inspiration?," *Denver Post*, May 2, 1997.

59. McVeigh left several messages on the answering machine of Richard Coffman, an Arizona representative of the National Alliance. McVeigh claimed he called the National Alliance before the bombing to make a "serious request for a safe haven." Michel and Herbeck, *American Terrorist*, 205.

60. Griffin, *The Fame of a Dead Man's Deeds*, 165.

61. "Turner Diaries Author William Pierce," *Time.com*, June 1, 2000, *www.time.com/time/ community/transcripts/chattr060197.html* (web page discontinued). Accessed January 22, 2001.

62. Author interview with Pierce, July 12, 2000.

63. Statements by McVeigh indicate that *The Turner Diaries* may have determined his choice of target and his decision to carry out the attack. While in prison, McVeigh read a novel called *Unintended Consequences*, published by John Ross in 1996. It tells the story of Henry Bowman, a hunter and gun owner who is alarmed at government efforts to ban firearms. Bowman assembles a team that assassinates government officials and agents one by one. John Ross, *Unintended Consequences* (St. Louis: Accurate Press, 1996). Commenting on the book, McVeigh said: "If people say *The Turner Diaries* was my Bible, *Unintended Consequences* would be my New Testament. I [thought it] was a better book. It might have changed my whole plan of operations if I'd read that one first." Michel and Herbeck, *American Terrorist*, 304.

64. Jeffrey Kaplan, *The Encyclopedia of White Power: A Sourcebook on the Radical Racist Right* (Walnut Creek, CA: AltaMira Press, 2000), 182, 185.

65. Coulson and Shannon, *No Heroes*, 532, 533, 534.

66. McVeigh was calling for Andreas Strassmeir, a German national he had met at a gun show. Strassmeir's grandfather was an early Nazi Party member during Hitler's quest for power in Germany. Rumors circulated on the Far Right that Strassmeir was a German intelligence agent conspiring with US authorities to bomb the Murrah Federal Building and blame innocent people in their movement. David Hoffman, *The Oklahoma City Bombing and the Politics of Terror* (Venice, CA: Feral House, 1998), 121–26.

67. See, for example, Stephen Jones and Peter Israel, *Others Unknown: The Oklahoma City Bombing Case and Conspiracy* (New York: Public Affairs, 1998), and Hoffman, *The Oklahoma City Bombing*. This theory is based on the fact that accomplice Terry Nichols visited the Philippines twice and the suspicion that he and his wife had consorted with Islamic extremists there who might have been linked to Ramzi Yousef, the mastermind of the 1993 World Trade Center bombing.

68. Michel and Herbeck, *American Terrorist*, 286–87.

69. This view was expressed by John Trochman, a leader of the Militia of Montana. Author interview with Trochman, October 6, 2000.

70. Partin's report is reprinted in Hoffman, *The Oklahoma City Bombing*, 461–69.

71. Partin lost some credibility when in his first report to Congress he attributed the attack to a communist conspiracy (of the "Third Socialist International"). Ibid., 23. Many theorists of the bombing still give credence to his report although they disagree with his allegation that communists were responsible for the attack.

72. Editorial, *WAR*, July 1997, 1.

73. Mark S. Hamm, *In Bad Company: America's Terrorist Underground* (Boston: Northeastern University Press, 2001); Langan material from page 293.

74. Martin Durham, *White Rage: The Extreme Right and American Politics* (London: Routledge, 2007), 103–4.

75. I borrow much of the analysis in this section from Jeffrey Kaplan, "Leaderless Resistance," *Terrorism and Political Violence* 9, no. 3 (1997): 80–95.

76. James Mason, *Siege* (Denver: Storm Books, 1992), 37.

77. Kaplan, "Leaderless Resistance," 81–82. For more on Tomassi and the NSLF, see Mason, *Siege*. A longtime neo-Nazi, Mason is a former associate of Tomassi. His book contains many reprinted articles on revolution and leaderless resistance from a neo-Nazi perspective.

78. The terms "extreme Right" and "Far Right" are generally interchangeable and are used that way in this book. "Extreme Right" usually implies a more racialist orientation not found in some Far Right organizations, such as the John Birch Society.

79. *The John Franklin Letters* (New York: Bookmailer, 1959). Robert Griffin, the biographer of William Pierce, believes that Revilo P. Oliver was the book's author. See Griffin, *The Fame of a Dead Man's Deeds*, 143.

80. *The John Franklin Letters.*

81. Robert B. DePugh, *Blueprint for Victory*, 4th ed. (Norborne, MO: Salon, 1978).

82. Kaplan, "Leaderless Resistance," 83.

83. Kaplan refers to several themes, including the idea of a period of tribulation, right-wing terrorists' belief that they must engage in violent struggle before achieving victory, which will result in a period of millennial bliss. Kaplan also sees a Manichaean theme to this struggle: denizens of the Far Right see themselves as a righteous remnant and their enemies as the embodiment of evil. Kaplan argues that as the Far Right was banished beyond respectability it abandoned any reformist ambitions it once had: "The state ZOG was increasingly seen as not worth claiming, and with this conclusion, the movement's dreams became increasingly chiliastic. With this too, the pattern of violence emanating from the fringes of the movement began to shift from vigilantism to anti-state terrorism." Jeffrey Kaplan, "Right Wing Violence in North America," in *Terror from the Extreme Right*, ed. Tore Bjorgo (London: Frank Cass, 1995), 85–87.

84. Durham, *White Rage*, 104.

85. Stern, *A Force upon the Plain*, 35–36.

86. Kaplan, "Leaderless Resistance," 85.

87. Louis Beam, "Leaderless Resistance," *Seditionist*, no. 12 (February 1992), *www.louisbeam.com/leaderless.htm.*

88. Beam's essay was first published in the *Inter-Klan Newsletter and Survival Alert* in the early 1980s. Durham, *White Rage*, 103.

89. For example, the Anti-Defamation League issued a report on Beam titled "Louis Beam: Dedicated to Hate," which alerted people to his assassination "point system" posting on the Aryan Nation's Liberty Net computer network.

90. Andrew Macdonald, *Hunter* (Hillsboro, WV: National Vanguard Books, 1989).

91. Author interview with Pierce, July 12, 2000.

92. Quoted in Durham, *White Rage*, 108.

93. Several scholars have cited *Hunter* as influencing the development of the leaderless resistance concept in the Far Right underground. See, for example, Hoffman, *Inside Terrorism*, 118, and Kaplan, "Leaderless Resistance," 85.

94. Brad Whitsel, "'The Turner Diaries' and Cosmotheism: William Pierce's Theology of Revolution," *Nova Religio* 1, no. 2 (April 1998), *home.alphalink.com.au/~radnat/usanazis/cosmotheism.html.*

95. Wotan is another name for the god Odin of the Norse pantheon. He is considered to be a complex figure, both intellectually contemplative and a fierce warrior.

96. Quotes from Kaplan, "Leaderless Resistance," 89.

97. "Alex Curtis: Lone Wolf of Hate Prowls the Internet," ADSL, 2000, *www.adl.org/curtis/default.asp.*

98. "Alex Curtis," in *Extremism in America*, ADL, *www.adl.org/learn/ext_us/.*

99. Alex Curtis, "Biology for Aryans," *Nationalist*, no. 21 (June 2000): 1.

100. "Alex Curtis," in *Extremism in America.*

101. Quoted in "Alex Curtis: Lone Wolf of Hate Prowls the Internet."

102. The alleged offenses include placing racist stickers at offices of some of the victims; putting a snakeskin in the mail slot of Congressman Filner's office; spray-painting anti-Semitic words and symbols on a synagogue; and placing an inactive hand grenade outside Mayor Madrid's residence. For more on this investigation, see FBI, "Operation Lone Wolf," *www.fbi.gov/sandiego/history/operation-lone-wolf.*

103. "Alex Curtis," in *Extremism in America.*

104. See Liberty Lobby, *Survival and Leaderless Resistance* (Washington, DC: Liberty Lobby,

1999). While not specifically calling for terrorism, the publication reprints an early version of Beam's "Leaderless Resistance" essay and offers tips on survival, physical fitness, creating resistance units, and so on.

105. Eric Hollyoak, "The Fallacy of Leaderless Resistance," *Resistance*, no. 10 (Winter 2000): 14–18.

106. Barry is the founder of the Special Forces Underground, a covert right-wing organization composed of active duty and retired Special Forces soldiers. Barry was sometimes referred to as the "military adviser" to the National Alliance.

107. Crenshaw discusses some of the preparatory work that must go into effective terrorist campaigns in "The Logic of Terrorism," 17.

108. Quoted in Durham, *White Rage*, 108.

109. Author interview with William Pierce, July 12, 2000.

110. "Advice for 'Lone Wolves,'" Aryan Nations, *www.aryan-nations.org/adviceforwolves*.

111. Jefferson Mack, *Invisible Resistance to Tyranny* (Boulder, CO: Paladin Press, 2002).

112. See, for example, Harold Covington, *The March Up Country* (Reedy, WV: Liberty Bell Publications, 1987).

113. For more on the Greensboro Massacre, see Elizabeth Wheaton, *Codename Greenkil: The 1979 Greensboro Killings* (Athens: University of Georgia Press, 1987). For a brief biographical sketch of Covington, see "Little Big Man," *Intelligence Report*, Winter 2008, *www.splcenter.org/*.

114. Covington claimed that these allegations stemmed from Elizabeth Wheaton's book, *Codename Greenkil*. According to Covington, Wheaton was affiliated with a left-leaning organization called the Institute for Southern Studies, and thus had an ax to grind. Author interview with Covington, July 24, 2000.

115. Harold A. Covington, *The Hill of the Ravens* (Bloomington, IN: 1st Books, 2003); Covington, *A Distant Thunder* (Bloomington, IN: authorHouse, 2004); Covington, *A Mighty Fortress* (New York: iUniverse, 2005); and Covington, *The Brigade* (Philadelphia: Xlibris, 2008).

116. Presumably the law was named after Morris Dees, whose Southern Poverty Law Center has won several large lawsuits resulting in the dissolution of right-wing groups. For more on the SPLC, see George Michael, *Confronting Right-Wing Extremism and Terrorism in the USA* (New York: Routledge, 2003).

117. Presumably this law was named after Senator Charles Schumer (D-NY), a staunch advocate of gun control.

118. Michael O'Meara, "The Defeat of the Jewnited States as Imagined by H. A. Covington," *Vanguard News Network*, July 9, 2007, *www.vanguardnewsnetwork.com/?p=1936*.

119. Author interview with Covington, June 4, 2008.

120. Ibid.

121. Jack Kay, "Communicating through Electronic Bulletin Boards in the White Supremacy Movement: Creating Culture via Computer," paper presented at the International Communication Association Conference, Mass Communication Division, New Orleans, June 1988.

122. Previously Black had been affiliated with the National Socialist White People's Party, the successor to George Lincoln Rockwell's American Nazi Party. Later he joined the Knights of the Ku Klux Klan, at the time led by David Duke. The two developed an enduring friendship. Black even married Duke's ex-wife and helped raise his two daughters. In 1981 Black was arrested for his role in a bizarre plot to invade the Caribbean island of Dominica and overthrow its government. The plan was to spark a coup led by black and white mercenaries who would lead disgruntled black soldiers against the island nation's seventy-man police force. Black spent 1982 to 1985 in a federal prison in Texas, during which time he studied computers and became proficient in using them. He settled in Palm Beach,

Florida, in 1987. David Schwab Abel, "The Racist Next Door," *New York Times*, February 19, 2008.

123. Lorraine Bowman-Grieve, "Exploring 'Stormfront': A Virtual Community of the Radical Right," *Studies in Conflict and Terrorism* 32 (2009): 996–97.

124. Jeffrey Kaplan and Leonard Weinberg, *The Emergence of a Euro-American Radical Right* (New Brunswick, NJ: Rutgers University Press, 1998).

125. The program also has a "redirect" feature, which allows users who try to access a blocked site the chance to link directly to the ADL or a related watchdog site to access educational material. HateFilter runs on Mattel's CyberPatrol, a software-blocking program that has been distributed to approximately fifteen thousand schools and libraries, public and private. Matt Isaacs, "Spy vs. Spite," *Sfweekly.com*, February 2–8, 2000.

126. For example, Prodigy removed offensive messages from a bulletin board it hosted after receiving a complaint from the ADL. "Anti-Semitism Detoured on the Information Highway," press release, ADL, February 24, 1999. The ADL persuaded Amazon.com and Barnes and Noble to insert statements warning about the extremist content of certain books they offered for sale, such as *The Protocols of Zion*. "Amazon.com and Barnes & Noble.Com Respond to ADL's Concerns on *Protocols* Book," press release, ADL, March 28, 2000. Finally, the ADL persuaded the Internet auction site eBay to refrain from listing items bearing extremist symbols. "ADL Applauds eBay for Expanding Guidelines to Prohibit the Sale of Items That Glorify Hate," press release, ADL, May 4, 2001.

127. David W. Hulvey, "Neo-Nazis on the Net: Representations of a Cyberspace Reich," unpublished paper, May 12, 1999.

128. Hamm, *In Bad Company*, 248.

129. Mike German, "Behind the Lone Terrorist, a Pack Mentality," *Washington Post*, June 5, 2005.

130. Katie Nelson, "Attorney: FBI Trained NJ Blogger to Incite," Associated Press, August 18, 2009.

131. Noam Cohen, "Traces of Gunman's Life Begin to Vanish," *New York Times*, June 10, 2006; Brett Zongker and Calvin Woodward, "White Supremacist Charged with Murder," *Denver Post*, June 12, 2009; Anti-Defamation League, "James Von Brunn: An ADL Backgrounder," Anti-Defamation League, *adl.org/*; and Daryl Fears and Marc Fisher, "A Suspect's Long History of Hate, and Signs of Strain," *Washington Post*, June 11, 2009.

132. This is consistent with Roger Griffin's notion of the palingenetic myth, which permeates the fascist ideology (i.e., process of death and rebirth). See Roger Griffin, *The Nature of Fascism* (New York: Routledge, 1993).

133. "Assessing White Supremacist Groups in the U.S.," National Public Radio, October 30, 2008, *www.npr.org/*.

134. Barton Gellman, "The Secret World of Extreme Militias," *Time*, October 11, 2010, 24–33.

135. Nicholas Köhler, "America Is Angry," *Maclean's*, April 19, 2010, 30.

136. Mark Potok, "Rage on the Right," *Intelligence Report*, Spring 2010, *www.splcenter.org/*.

137. US Department of Homeland Security, *Rightwing Extremism: Current Economic and Political Climate Fueling Resurgence in Radicalization and Recruitment*, April 2009, IA-0257-09, *www.fas.org/irp/eprint/rightwing.pdf*.

138. Katie Engelhart, "The Return of Hitler," *Maclean's*, April 26, 2010, 30–34.

139. Stuart P. Wright, "Strategic Framing of Racial-Nationalism in North America and Europe: An Analysis of a Burgeoning Transnational Network," *Terrorism and Political Violence* 21 (2009): 199.

Chapter 3

1. Walter Laqueur, *The New Terrorism: Fanaticism and the Arms of Mass Destruction* (New York: Oxford University Press, 1999), 200.

2.   Donald R. Liddick, *Eco-Terrorism: Radical Environmental and Animal Liberation Movements* (Westport, CT: Praeger, 2006), 13.

3.   See Laqueur, *The New Terrorism*, 199, for origin of term "ecology."

4.   For a short but excellent exegesis on the religion of nature, see Jeffrey Kaplan, "Religion of Nature," in *The Encyclopedia of White Power: A Sourcebook on the Radical Racist Right* (Walnut Creek, CA: AltaMira Press, 2000), 253–58.

5.   Neopaganism is popular in the radical environmental movement, and some elements of the extreme Right follow a variant of neopaganism known as Asatru or Odinism. Nevertheless, according to the researcher Bron Taylor's fieldwork, the two movements are unlikely to collaborate. As he points out, radical environmentalists tend to stridently criticize even the most remotely politically incorrect racial sentiments. In fact, environmentalists with racialized worldviews are likely to be "biased against persons with European ancestry for presumed imperialist predispositions." Bron Taylor, "Diggers, Wolves, Ents, Elves and Expanding Universes: Bricolage, Religion, and Violence from Earth First! And the Earth Liberation Front to the Antiglobalization Resistance," in *The Cultic Milieu: Oppositional Subcultures in an Age of Globalization*, ed. Jeffrey Kaplan and Heléne Lööw (Walnut Creek, CA: AltaMira Press, 2002), 26–74.

6.   Liddick, *Eco-Terrorism*, 14–15.

7.   Ibid., 13–15.

8.   Sean P. Eagan, "From Spikes to Bombs: The Rise of Eco-Terrorism," *Studies in Conflict and Terrorism* 19, no. 1 (1996): 4.

9.   Liddick, *Eco-Terrorism*, 15–16.

10.   Ibid., 1, 17–18. Liddick cites Lawrence Finsen and Susan Finsen, *The Animal Rights Movement in America: From Compassion to Respect* (New York: Twayne Publishers, 1994).

11.   Edward Abbey, *The Monkey Wrench Gang* (New York: Avon Books, 1975).

12.   Taylor, "Diggers, Wolves, Ents, Elves," 31.

13.   Paul Josse, "Leaderless Resistance and Ideological Inclusion: The Case of the Earth Liberation Front," *Terrorism and Political Violence* 19, no. 3 (September 2007): 351–67.

14.   According to Rik Scarce, they made their decision while they were drunk. Martha F. Lee, "Violence and the Environment: The Case of 'Earth First!,'" *Terrorism and Political Violence* 7, no. 3 (Autumn 1995): 112; Lee cites two sources for the story: Christopher Manes, *Green Rage* (Boston: Little Brown, 1990), 65–69, and Rik Scarce, *Eco-Warriors* (Chicago: Noble Press, 1990), 58–61.

15.   Kelly Stoner and Gary Perlstein, "Implementing 'Justice' through Terror and Destruction: Ecoterror's Violent Agenda to 'Save' Nature," *Terrorism: Research, Readings, and Realities*, ed. Lynne L. Snowden and Bradley Whitsel (Upper Saddle River, NJ: Pearson Prentice Hall, 2005), 92.

16.   Eagan, "From Spikes to Bombs," 6–7.

17.   Liddick, *Eco-Terrorism*, 19.

18.   Eagan, "From Spikes to Bombs," 3.

19.   Liddick, *Eco-Terrorism*, 19–21.

20.   Gary A. Ackerman, "Beyond Arson? A Threat Assessment of the Earth Liberation Front," *Terrorism and Political Violence* 14, no. 4 (Winter 2003): 159n41.

21.   W. Seth Carus, "R.I.S.E.," in *Toxic Terror: Assessing Terrorist Use of Chemical and Biological Weapons*, ed. Jonathan B. Tucker (Cambridge, MA: MIT Press, 2000), 55–70.

22.   Stefan H. Leader and Peter Probst, "The Earth Liberation Front and Environmental Terrorism," *Terrorism and Political Violence* 15, no. 4 (Winter 2003): 42.

23.   James J. F. Forrest, "Terrorist Use of WMD," in *The World's Most Threatening Terrorist Networks and Criminal Gangs*, ed. Michael T. Kindt, Jerrold Post, and Barry R. Schneider (New York: Palgrave Macmillan, 2009), 100.

24.   Lee, "Violence and the Environment," 112.

25.   Liddick, *Eco-Terrorism*, 55–57, 61.

26. The group was named ironically after the impeached former governor of Arizona, Evan Mecham. Ibid., 4.

27. Lee, "Violence and the Environment," 122.

28. Bron Taylor, "Religion, Violence and Radical Environmentalism: From Earth First! to the Unabomber to the Earth Liberation Front," *Terrorism and Political Violence* 10, no. 4 (Winter 1998): 6.

29. Eagan, "From Spikes to Bombs," 7.

30. Lee, "Violence and the Environment," 120–22.

31. Liddick, *Eco-Terrorism*, 113.

32. Ibid., 64.

33. Leader and Probst, "Earth Liberation Front," 38.

34. Liddick, *Eco-Terrorism*, 4–5, 67.

35. Josse, "Leaderless Resistance and Ideological Inclusion," 352.

36. Stoner and Perlstein, "Implementing 'Justice,'" 95.

37. Anti-Defamation League, "Ecoterrorism: Extremism in the Animal Rights and Environmentalist Movements," *www.adl.org/learn/ext_us/ecoterrorism.asp*.

38. Jean-Marc Flükiger, "The Radical Animal Liberation Movement: Some Reflections on Its Future," *Journal for the Study of Radicalism* 2, no. 2 (2009): 122.

39. Anti-Defamation League, "Ecoterrorism."

40. Liddick, *Eco-Terrorism*, 75.

41. Anti-Defamation League, "Ecoterrorism."

42. Eagan, "From Spikes to Bombs," 9.

43. Josse, "Leaderless Resistance and Ideological Inclusion," 352.

44. Anti-Defamation League, "Ecoterrorism."

45. Liddick, *Eco-Terrorism*, 3.

46. In 1985 an environmental group calling itself the Peace Conqueror claimed responsibility for an attack on a Frankfurt airport that killed three people. Gerry Nagtzaam and Pete Lentini, "Vigilantes on the High Seas? The Sea Shepherds and Political Violence," *Terrorism and Political Violence* 20 (2008): 117. In November 2002 Andrew McCrae, a twenty-three-year-old college student, killed a police officer outside Red Bluff, California, to protest what he viewed as corporate irresponsibility against the environment. Gary A. Ackerman, "Beyond Arson? A Threat Assessment of the Earth Liberation Front, *Terrorism and Political Violence* 14, no. 4 (Winter 2003): 167n41.

47. Taylor, "Religion, Violence and Radical Environmentalism," 9–26.

48. Bruce Barcott, "From Tree Hugger to Terrorist," *New York Times*, April 7, 2002.

49. Rosebraugh's strategy appears in Michelle Malkin, "Eco-terrorists Declare War," *Washington Times*, March 24, 2003.

50. Anti-Defamation League, "Ecoterrorism."

51. Craig Rosebraugh, *The Logic of Political Violence: Lessons in Reform and Revolution* (Portland, OR: Arissa Media Group, 2004), 8, 10.

52. Ibid., 2–3.

53. Ackerman, "Beyond Arson?," 149.

54. Rosebraugh, *The Logic of Political Violence*.

55. Ibid., 13–16, 202.

56. Ibid., 6.

57. Craig Rosebraugh, former press officer of Earth Liberation Front, *Ecoterrorism and Lawlessness on the National Forests*, testimony given before the House Committee on Resources, Subcommittee on Forests and Forest Health, 107th Cong., 2nd sess., February 12, 2002, in Liddick, *Eco-Terrorism*, 134–48.

58. Stoner and Perlstein, "Implementing 'Justice,'" 98.

59. "From Push to Shove," Intelligence Report, Fall 2002, *www.splcenter.org/*.

60. Stoner and Perlstein, "Implementing 'Justice,'" 99–100.

61. Liddick, *Eco-Terrorism*, 28–29.
62. Anti-Defamation League, "Ecoterrorism."
63. Stoner and Perlstein, "Implementing 'Justice,'" 100–101.
64. Ibid., 102.
65. Liddick, *Eco-Terrorism*, 3, 25.
66. Leader and Probst, "The Earth Liberation Front," 38.
67. Liddick, *Eco-Terrorism*, 40–43.
68. Those guidelines are: (1) To liberate animals from places of abuse, i.e., laboratories, factory farms, fur farms, etc.; (2) to inflict economic damage on those who profit from the misery and exploitation of animals; (3) to reveal the horror and atrocities committed against animals; (4) to take all necessary precautions against harming any animal, human and nonhuman. Stoner and Perlstein, "Implementing 'Justice,'" 104.
69. Although liberating animals from facilities may initially seem high-minded, often the animals that are turned loose die from exposure, lack of food, dehydration, car collisions, and other animals that prey on them. Stoner and Perlstein, "Implementing 'Justice,'" 105–8.
70. For example, the NAALPO spokesman Dr. Jerry Vlasak once defended the actions of Walter Bond, who was arrested in July 2010 for the arson of a Glendale, Colorado, business called the Sheepskin Factory, at which a variety of sheepskin products were sold. Vlasak opined that such actions have "gotten concrete results as opposed to lobbying our congressmen and writing letters to editors." Quoted in Scott Stewart, "Escalating Violence from the Animal Liberation Front," STRATFOR, July 29, 2010, *www.stratfor.com/*.
71. Liddick, *Eco-Terrorism*, 40–43, 44.
72. "From Push to Shove."
73. Bron Taylor, "Threat Assessments and Radical Environmentalism," *Terrorism and Political Violence* 15, no. 4 (Summer 2010): 180.
74. In 1992, Van der Graaf and his friend Sjoerd van de Wouw founded the Association Environmental Offensive, an organization that challenged permits awarded to fur and cattle farmers in court in order to force them out of business. *Lone-Wolf Terrorism* (The Hague: Instituut voor Veiligheids en Crisismanagement, 2007), 24, 35, 53.
75. Liddick, *Eco-Terrorism*, 44-48.
76. Ibid., 34–35.
77. Jean-Marc Flükiger, "The Radical Animal Liberation Movement," 126.
78. Liddick, *Eco-Terrorism*, 48–52, 70–71.
79. For more on the SSCS, see Nagtzaam and Lentini, "Vigilantes on the High Seas?," 110–33.
80. Eagan, "From Spikes to Bombs," 4–5.
81. Taylor, "Religion, Violence and Radical Environmentalism," 18.
82. Leader and Probst, "The Earth Liberation Front," 38.
83. Flükiger, "The Radical Animal Liberation Movement," 122.
84. Taylor, "Religion, Violence and Radical Environmentalism," 8.
85. Anti-Defamation League, "Ecoterrorism."
86. Laqueur, *The New Terrorism*, 205; Liddick, *Eco-Terrorism*, 75.
87. Rebecca Trounson and Joe Mozingo, "Chancellor Taking Steps to Protect UCLA," *Seattle Times*, August 27, 2006.
88. "Operation Backfire Press Conference," speech by FBI director Robert S. Mueller III, January 20, 2006, *www.fbi.gov/news/speeches/operation-backfire-1*.
89. Alston Chase, *Harvard and the Unabomber: The Education of an American Terrorist* (New York: Norton, 2003), 371.
90. Taylor, "Religion, Violence and Radical Environmentalism," 7.
91. Chase, *Harvard and the Unabomber*, 12, 207–50.
92. Ibid., 12.
93. Ibid., 39, 81.

94. *Lone-Wolf Terrorism* (The Hague, 2007), 27–28.

95. Taylor, "Religion, Violence and Radical Environmentalism," 32.

96. Chase, *Harvard and the Unabomber*, 24, 84–85, 93–94.

97. Taylor, "Religion, Violence and Radical Environmentalism," 16.

98. Liddick, *Eco-Terrorism*, 104. The article listed Burson-Marsteller. Lending credence to the charge is the fact that his name was misspelled "Burston-Marsteller" in *Live Wild or Die!* as well as in a letter written by Kaczynski. Taylor, "Religion, Violence and Radical Environmentalism," 28–29.

99. Liddick, *Eco-Terrorism*, 104–8.

100. Chase, *Harvard and the Unabomber*, 99.

101. Liddick, *Eco-Terrorism*, 1–2, 63, 99–100.

102. Testimony of John Lewis, deputy assistant director, Federal Bureau of Investigation, *Oversight on Eco-terrorism Specifically Examining the Earth Liberation Front ("ELF") and the Animal Liberation Front ("ALF")*, statement given to the Senate Committee on Environmental and Public Works, 109th Cong., 1st sess., May 18, 2005, cited in Liddick, *Eco-Terrorism*, 127–30. By 2008, the American Legislative Exchange Council, a group of conservative state legislators, blamed ecoterrorists for more than $200 million in property damages. Brent Baldwin, "Wade's War," *Style Weekly*, February 6, 2008, *www.styleweekly.com/*.

103. Laqueur, *The New Terrorism*, 204.

Chapter 4

1. Frank Anderson, "International Terrorism and International Cooperation," in *Countering Suicide Terrorism* (New York: International Policy Institute for Counter-Terrorism and the Anti-Defamation League, 2002), 53.

2. Claire Sterling, *The Terror Network* (New York: Berkley Books, 1984).

3. Walter Laqueur, *The New Terrorism: Fanaticism and the Arms of Mass Destruction* (New York: Oxford University Press, 1999), 161.

4. Substantial documentary evidence suggests that terrorism was an important instrument of Soviet statecraft. Paul R. Pillar, *Terrorism and U.S. Foreign Policy* (Washington, DC: Brookings Institution, 2001), 42–51.

5. Francis Fukuyama, "Their Target: The Modern World," *Newsweek* special edition, December 13, 2001.

6. John Lewis Gaddis, "And Now This: Lessons from the Old Era for the New One," in *The Age of Terror: America and the World after September 11*, ed. Strobe Talbott and Nayan Chanda (New York: Basic Books, 2001), 11.

7. Paul Kennedy, "Maintaining American Power: From Injury to Recovery," in Talbott and Chanda, *The Age of Terror*, 59.

8. In 2004 the Libyan government turned over two suspects for trial who were implicated in the 1988 Pan Am 103 bombing over Lockerbie, Scotland. Anderson, "International Terrorism and International Cooperation," 56. As Philip C. Wilcox Jr., a former US ambassador at large and coordinator of counterterrorism summarized, by the early 1990s state-sponsored terrorism declined for a number of reasons, including the dissolution of the Soviet Union, the beginning of the Israeli-Palestinian peace process, and a growing condemnation of terrorism in the international community. Philip C. Wilcox Jr., "United States," in *Combating Terrorism: Strategies of Ten Countries*, ed. Yonah Alexander (Ann Arbor: University of Michigan Press, 2002), 29–30.

9. Daniel Patrick Moynihan, *Pandemonium: Ethnicity in International Politics* (Oxford: Oxford University Press, 1993).

10. Samuel P. Huntington, *The Clash of Civilizations and the Remaking of World Order* (New York: Touchstone, 1996), 20, 256–57. As Paul Pillar opined, "If bin Laden or someone of

his ilk were to read Huntington's work, the reaction would not be surprise or shock but rather acknowledgement that this indeed is the conflict in which they believe themselves engaged." Pillar, *Terrorism and U.S. Foreign Policy*, 65.

11. Fareed Zakaria, "The Return of History," in *How Did This Happen? Terrorism and the New War*, ed. James F. Hoge Jr. and Gideon Rose (New York: Public Affairs, 2001), 307–17.

12. Patrick J. Buchanan, *Death of the West: How Dying Populations and Immigrant Invasions Imperil Our Country and Civilization* (New York: Thomas Dunne Books, 2002), 120.

13. In his "end of history" treatise, Fukuyama conceded that even in the posthistorical world, terrorism and wars of liberation would continue for some time. He acknowledged that militant Islam could pose a threat to the stability of world order, conceding that there is a fundamental clash between the West and hard-core Islamist groups and that much of the Islamic world has problems with US foreign policy. Author interview with Fukuyama, June 30, 2008.

14. Zakaria, "The Return of History," 315.

15. Norman Podhoretz, *World War IV: The Long Struggle against Islamofascism* (New York: Doubleday, 2007), 2. The term "World War IV," coined by Eliot Cohen and popularized by Podhoretz, has come to mean a crusade against recalcitrant regimes in the Middle East (the Cold War, in Podhoretz's analysis, is World War III). For more on this concept, see George Michael, *The Enemy of My Enemy: The Alarming Convergence of Militant Islam and the Extreme Right* (Lawrence: University Press of Kansas, 2006), 247–48.

16. For example, in 1995 President Clinton issued Presidential Decision Directive (PDD) 39, which was the first directive to make terrorism a top national priority and which concluded that the United States was threatened from within. This directive further articulated and defined the roles of members of the US counterterrorism community. The FBI was designated as the chief government agency responsible for investigating and preventing domestic terrorism. Robert M. Blitzer, "FBI's Role in the Federal Response to the Use of Weapons of Mass Destruction: Statement of Robert M. Blitzer, Chief Domestic Terrorism/Counter-terrorism Planning Section FBI before the U.S. House of Representatives Committee on National Security," November 4, 1997; "Fact Sheet: Combating Terrorism: Presidential Decision Directive 62," White House, Office of the Press Secretary, May 22, 1998.

17. The new laws and initiatives nearly doubled the amount of money spent on counterterrorism, to $11 billion a year. Jim Redden, *Snitch Culture* (Venice, CA: Feral House, 2000), 71. Much of the money went to the FBI, whose annual antiterrorism budget jumped from $78 million to $609 million. Furthermore, between fiscal years 1993 and 2000, the number of FBI special agents assigned to counterterrorism programs rose from 550 to 1,669—an increase of approximately 224 percent. "Statement for the Record of Dale L. Watson, Executive Assistant Director Counterterrorism and Counterintelligence Federal Bureau of Investigation on the Terrorist Threat Confronting the United States, before the Senate Select Committee on Intelligence," February 6, 2002; and Pillar, *Terrorism and U.S. Foreign Policy*, 80.

18. Timothy Naftali, *Blind Spot: The Secret History of American Counterterrorism* (New York: Basic Books, 2005), 285.

19. For example, in the Senate by a vote of 98–0, and in the House of Representatives by a vote of 420–1, Congress passed a joint resolution authorizing President Bush to use "all necessary and appropriate force" against those responsible for the 9/11 terrorist attacks.

20. Barry Rubin and Judith Colp Rubin, eds., *Anti-American Terrorism and the Middle East: A Documentary Reader* (Oxford: Oxford University Press, 2002), 339–43.

21. Dan Eggen and Jim McGee, "FBI Rushes to Remake Its Mission: Counterterrorism Focus Replaces Crime Solving," *Washington Post*, November 12, 2001.

22. Kurt M. Campbell and Michèle A. Flournoy, *To Prevail: An American Strategy for the Campaign against Terrorism* (Washington, DC: CSIS Press, 2001), 15. Actually, an interagency

effort to combine US government information and analysis began in the late 1980s, when the CIA created the Counterterrorist Center to coordinate the intelligence collection and evaluation of many government agencies involved in counterterrorism issues. Amos A. Jordan, William J. Taylor, and Michael J. Mazarr, *American National Security*, 5th ed. (Baltimore: Johns Hopkins University Press, 1999), 167. In August 2004, President Bush renamed it the National Counterterrorism Center (NCTC) by an executive order. Naftali, *Blind Spot*, 318–19. The NCTC is located in an unmarked office complex in Northern Virginia and has become the centerpiece of reform efforts to integrate the various intelligence agencies in the United States. Most of the work focuses on analysis. NCTC analysts from the CIA, FBI, and National Security Agency monitor unfolding plots and investigations and produce continually updated reports called "Threat Threads" on cases that are potentially most dangerous. Kevin Whitelaw, "The Eye of the Storm," in *Annual Editions Violence and Terrorism 08/09*, ed. Thomas J. Badey (New York: McGraw-Hill, 2009), 192–95.

23.   Ronald Kessler writes that Bill Clinton stopped CIA morning briefings six months after he became president. Ronald Kessler, *The Terrorist Watch: Inside the Desperate Race to Stop the Next Attack* (New York: Crown Forum, 2007), 87.

24.   Ibid., 67–68.

25.   Josh Meyer, "Ashcroft Rethinks Domestic Spying," *Los Angeles Times*, December 1, 2001.

26.   As discussed in Chapter 2, numerous NGOs work to monitor the extreme Right. Authorities now also rely on recently created private groups that monitor radical Islam, including JihadWatch.org, the Middle East Media Research Institute (MEMRI), and the Investigative Project on Terrorism (IPT). Founded by the prominent terrorism analyst Steven Emerson, the IPT is the largest nongovernmental repository of information related to Islamic radicalism in the United States and is indicative of a broader trend whereby private organizations augment government efforts in certain policy areas, including intelligence collection and analysis. George Michael, "Steven Emerson: Combating Radical Islam," *Middle East Quarterly* 17, no. 1 (Winter 2010): 15–25.

27.   Barak Mendelsohn, *Combating Jihadism: American Hegemony and Interstate Cooperation in the War on Terrorism* (Chicago: University of Chicago Press, 2009), 177.

28.   Among the most notable captured was Abu Zubaydah. Apprehended in March 2002, he is believed to have been the chief of external operations for al Qaeda. Exactly one year after the 9/11 attacks, Pakistani authorities arrested Ramzi Binalshibh, who disclosed that he was the principal organizer of the attacks. His colleague and co-conspirator Khalid Sheikh Mohammed was arrested in Rawalpindi, Pakistan, on March 1, 2003. Khalid Sheikh Mohammed, the uncle of Ramzi Yousef, had been indicted years earlier for his role in "Operation Bojinka," which planned, among other things, to blow up US airliners over the Pacific Ocean. Yosri Fouda and Nick Fielding, *Masterminds of Terror: The Truth behind the Most Devastating Terrorist Attack the World Has Ever Seen* (New York: Arcade Publishing, 2003), 88, 140.

29.   Author interview with Hayden, October 21, 2009.

30.   For example, the NSA operates a satellite surveillance program called Echelon, which collects and analyzes vast amounts of data on electronic information all over the world. Redden, *Snitch Culture*, 39–41. Likewise, the National Geospatial-Intelligence Agency (NGA), part of the National Imagery and Mapping Agency within the Department of Defense, analyzes and interprets images created by satellites and spy planes. Kessler, *The Terrorist Watch*, 175–76. These agencies are augmented by private institutions. For example, the University of Arizona, Tucson, houses the Dark Web Forum Portal, a system of computers that store web data from roughly fifteen hundred terrorist and extremist groups with roots in the Middle East. The project, which is supposed to be the largest collection of online terrorist data in the world, has developed algorithms for assessing threats associated with various websites and forums. It seeks to measure the "infectiousness" of ideas on

web forums and, by doing so, to give indications of future terrorist attacks. "The Future of Terrorism," *Discover*, July 2006, 32–34.

31. Phillip B. Heymann, *Terrorism and America: A Commonsense Strategy for a Democratic Society* (Cambridge, MA: MIT Press, 1998), 138.

32. Redden, *Snitch Culture*, 43.

33. Michele Anini and Sean J. A. Edwards, "The Networking of Terror in the Information Age," in *Networks and Netwars: The Future of Terror, Crime, and Militancy*, ed. John Arquilla and David Ronfeldt (Santa Monica, CA: Rand, 2001), 39.

34. Mendelsohn, *Combating Jihadism*, esp. 188–89.

35. Quoted in John Mueller, "Is There Still a Terrorist Threat? The Myth of the Omnipresent Enemy," *Foreign Affairs* (September/October 2006), 6.

36. Kessler, *The Terrorist Watch*, 9.

37. Bob Woodward, *Bush at War* (New York: Simon and Schuster, 2002), 330, 332, 346.

38. Ibid., 349.

39. "US Public Thinks Saddam Had Role in 9/11," *Observer* (UK), September 7, 2003.

40. Mendelsohn, *Combating Jihadism*.

41. Ibid.

42. Ibid., 116–17, 119, 123–24.

43. Yonah Alexander, conclusion to *Combating Terrorism: Strategies of Ten Countries* (Ann Arbor: University of Michigan Press, 2002), 375–77.

44. Ian O. Lesser, "Counter the New Terrorism: Implications for Strategy," in *Countering the New Terrorism* (Santa Monica, CA: Rand, 1999), 113.

45. As John Mueller and Karl Mueller pointed out, "The irony is that in contrast to the others, this device—economic sanctions—is deployed frequently by large states rather than small ones, and may have contributed to more deaths during the post–Cold War era than all weapons of mass destruction throughout history." John Mueller and Karl Mueller, "Sanctions of Mass Destruction," in *Asymmetrical Warfare: Today's Challenge of U.S. Military Power*, ed. Roger W. Barnett (Washington, DC: Brassey's, 2003), 2.

46. The Group of Eight is a forum created in France in 1975 for the governments of the strongest economies of the world to discuss issues of mutual or global concern. Originally it was the Group of Six—France, Germany, Italy, Japan, the United Kingdom, and the United States. Canada and Russia were added in 1976 and 1997, respectively.

47. Senator Richard Lugar (R-IN) once put the probability of a nuclear attack on US soil within ten years to be around 29 percent. To avert such a scenario, he sponsored the Nunn-Lugar Cooperative Threat Reduction Program. "The Future of Terrorism," *Discover*, July 2006, 37–38.

48. Mendelsohn, *Combating Jihadism*, 149–53.

49. Campbell and Flournoy, *To Prevail*, 5–6.

50. First, Russia resents that the United States has fostered the eastward expansion of NATO and the West's increasing influence in Ukraine. Furthermore, Russia was frustrated by the Western attitude toward the Serbs and the defense of Muslims in the Balkans. The deployment of antiballistic missiles in Europe aimed at potential Iranian, and possibly Syrian, intercontinental missiles caused consternation in Russia as well. For its part, the United States resents that Russia sells weapons to Iran, Syria, and Sudan. Furthermore, Russia resisted the US war in Iraq in 2003. Walid Phares, *The Confrontation: Winning the War against Future Jihad* (New York: Palgrave Macmillan, 2008), 87, 97.

51. Ibid., 97.

52. Campbell and Flournoy, *To Prevail*, 273.

53. Phares, *The Confrontation*, 96. The SCO arrangement was paralleled by the Collective Security Treaty Organization (CSTO), essentially a Kremlin-led version of NATO with embryonic joint armed forces. An immediate aim is to force NATO to recognize the

CSTO as counterpart, mostly on issues such as narcotics, Afghanistan, and counter-terrorism. In recent years, however, the CSTO has adopted a sharply anti-Western and anti-interventionist tone. Edward Lucas, *The New Cold War: Putin's Russia and the Threat to the West* (New York: Palgrave Macmillan, 2008), 135, 205.

54.   Marc Sageman, *Understanding Terror Networks* (Philadelphia: University of Pennsylvania Press, 2004), 52, 54.

55.   Dmitry Orlov, *Reinventing Collapse: The Soviet Example and American Prospects* (Gabriola Island, BC: New Society Publishers), 37. Although the US Army has a long tradition of fighting small wars, the experiences of both World War I and World War II reinforced the primacy of fighting large-scale conventional wars. John A. Nagl, *Learning to Eat Soup with a Knife: Counterinsurgency Lessons from Malaya and Vietnam* (Chicago: University of Chicago Press, 2005), 6.

56.   Benjamin Netanyahu advocated these initiatives prior to 9/11. See Netanyahu, *Fighting Terrorism: How Democracies Can Defeat the International Terrorist Network* (New York: Farrar, Straus and Giroux, 2001), 129–48.

Chapter 5

1.   Mark Juergensmeyer once referred to dispersed people connected culturally via the Internet as "email ethnicities." Mark Juergensmeyer, *Terror in the Mind of God: The Global Rise of Religious Violence* (Berkeley: University of California Press, 2000), 194.

2.   As Benedict Anderson observed, most members of a national community may never meet or get to know one another, but they nevertheless come to identify themselves as a unified nation. In that sense, they are an "imagined community," or fictive kin. Mohammed M. Hafez, "Dying to Be Martyrs: The Symbolic Dimension of Suicide Terrorism," in *Root Causes of Suicide Terrorism: The Globalization of Martyrdom*, ed. Ami Pedazhur (London: Routledge, 2006), 73; Benedict Anderson, *Imagined Communities: Reflections on the Origins and Spread of Nationalism* (London: Verso, 1991).

3.   Clay Shirky, *Here Comes Everybody: The Power of Organizing without Organizations* (New York: Penguin Press, 2008), 200.

4.   Michele Anini and Sean J. A. Edwards, "The Networking of Terror in the Information Age," in *Networks and Netwars: The Future of Terror, Crime, and Militancy*, ed. John Arquilla and David Ronfeldt (Santa Monica, CA: Rand, 2001), 35–36.

5.   Bruce Berkowitz, *The New Face of War: How War Will Be Fought in the 21st Century* (New York: Free Press, 2003), 71–72.

6.   Peter Jepson, "Tackling Hate on the Internet," September 24, 1998. (Accessed January 28, 1999. The article is no longer on the Internet.)

7.   Internet Software Consortium, 2008. *www.isc.org/*. The organization now goes by the Internet Systems Consortium.

8.   "Internet Usage Statistics," Internet World Stats, *www.internetworldstats.com/stats.htm*.

9.   John A. Bargh and Katelyn Y. A. McKenna, "The Internet and Social Life," *Annual Review of Psychology* 55 (2004): 577.

10.   Gabriel Weimann, *Terror on the Internet: The New Arena, the New Challenges* (Washington, DC: United States Institute of Peace, 2006), 24–25. Michael Whine, "The Use of the Internet by Far Right Extremists," International Institute for Counter-Terrorism, August 30, 1999, *www.ict.org.il/Articles/tabid/66/Articlsid/720/currentpage/28/Default.aspx*.

11.   Nayan Chanda and Strobe Talbott, introduction to *The Age of Terror: America and the World after September 11* (New York: Basic Books, 2001), xiii.

12.   Norman J. Ornstein and Shirley Elder, *Interest Groups, Lobbying and Policymaking* (Washington, DC: Congressional Quarterly Press, 1978), 17.

13.   Political scientists have explained how interest groups come about. Peter B. Clark and

James Q. Wilson proposed a threefold typology of incentives, which entice members to join groups: (1) material—tangible rewards such as economic ones, which members enjoy from belonging to groups (such as labor unions and trade associations); (2) "solidary"—personal intangible rewards that members receive, such as the camaraderie of interacting with other members or the prestige of being associated with certain groups; and (3) purposive—benefits that are widely diffused, such as good government, clean air, and so on. (Common Cause is a good example of a group that seeks this type of goal.) Peter B. Clark and James Q. Wilson, "Incentive Systems: A Theory of Organizations," *Administrative Science Quarterly* 6 (September 1961): 129–66. Robert Salisbury added that the key element in interest group formation is the organizer or entrepreneur of the group. His "exchange theory" is based on mutual incentives that exist between members and leaders of groups. Robert H. Salisbury, "An Exchange Theory of Interest Groups," in *Interest Group Politics in America*, 3rd ed., ed. Ronald J. Hrebenar (New York: M. E. Sharpe, 1997), 20.

14. Rheingold, *Smart Mobs: The Next Social Revolution* (Cambridge, MA: Basic Books, 2002), 31.

15. Shirky, *Here Comes Everybody*, 20–21.

16. Rheingold, *Smart Mobs*, xviii.

17. Don Tapscott and Anthony D. Williams, *Wikinomics: How Mass Collaboration Changes Everything* (New York: Portfolio, 2008), 55–56.

18. Shirky, *Here Comes Everybody*, 46–47.

19. Bargh and McKenna, "The Internet and Social Life," 573–90.

20. Rheingold, *Smart Mobs*, 114.

21. Walter Laqueur, *The New Terrorism: Fanaticism and the Arms of Mass Destruction* (New York: Oxford University Press, 1999), 40.

22. Jonathan R. White, *Terrorism: An Introduction*, 3rd ed. (Belmont, CA: Wadsworth Thomson Learning, 2002), 32–33.

23. A study by Chris Hewitt found that the use of informants was the single most important factor leading to the capture of terrorists. Christopher Hewitt, *Understanding Terrorism in America: From the Klan to Al Qaeda* (London: Routledge, 2003), 89–90.

24. White, *Terrorism*, 37–40.

25. Jessica Stern, *Terror in the Name of God: Why Religious Militants Kill* (New York: HarperCollins, 2003), 278.

26. According to Crenshaw, when a radical organization's outlook contains a combination of optimism and urgency, it is more likely to resort to terrorism, especially if the regime it is fighting appears vulnerable. Martha Crenshaw, "The Logic of Terrorism: Terrorist Behavior as a Product of Strategic Choice," in *Origins of Terrorism: Psychologies, Ideologies, Theologies, States of Mind*, ed. Walter Reich (Washington, DC: Woodrow Wilson Center Press, 1998), 12–13.

27. Amazon generates most of its sales revenue from items outside its 130,000 top-selling items. John Robb, *Brave New War: The Next Stage of Terrorism and the End of Globalization* (Hoboken, NJ: Wiley, 2007), 71–74.

28. Thomas Rid and Marc Hecker, *War 2.0: Irregular Warfare in the Information Age* (Westport, CT: Praeger Security International, 2009), 31.

29. Brian M. Jenkins, "The Organization Men: Anatomy of a Terrorist Attack," in *How Did This Happen? Terrorism and the New War*, ed. James F. Hoge Jr. and Gideon Rose (New York: Public Affairs, 2001), 11.

30. Audrey Kurth Cronin, "Sources of Contemporary Terrorism," in *Attacking Terrorism: Elements of a Grand Strategy*, ed. Audrey Kurth Cronin and James M. Ludes (Washington, DC: Georgetown University Press, 2004), 29.

31. John Arquilla, David Ronfeldt, and Michele Zanini, "Networks, Netwar, and Information-Age Terrorism," in *Countering the New Terrorism*, by Ian Lesser et al. (Santa Monica, CA: Rand, 1999), 49–51.

32. Luther P. Gerlach, "The Structure of Social Movements: Environmental Activism and Its Opponents," in *Networks and Netwars: The Future of Terror, Crime, and Militancy*, ed. John Arquilla and David Ronfeldt (Santa Monica, CA: Rand, 2001), 289–310.

33. In their study, Brafman and Beckstrom identify eight major principles of decentralization. First, when attacked, a decentralized organization tends to become even more open and decentralized. Second, it is easy to mistake "starfish" for "spiders." Third, an open system does not have central intelligence; rather, the intelligence is spread throughout the system. Fourth, open systems can easily mutate. Fifth, the decentralized organization can sneak up quickly and take over an industry, in contrast to spider organizations that slowly amass resources over a period of years and become centralized. Sixth, as industries become decentralized, overall profits therein diminish. Seventh, when people are placed in an open system, they will automatically want to contribute to it. Eighth, when attacked, centralized organizations tend to become even more centralized. Ori Brafman and Rod A. Beckstrom, *The Starfish and the Spider: The Unstoppable Power of Leaderless Organizations* (New York: Portfolio, 2006).

34. Ibid., 88–90.

35. Ibid., 92–94, 95, 122–25.

36. Martin J. Muckian, "Structural Vulnerabilities of Networked Insurgencies: Adapting to the New Adversary," *Parameters* (Winter 2006–2007), 15. To that end, Jessica Stern found several factors that enhance cohesion in terrorist organizations. First, the group must identify an enemy and create an atmosphere in daily life of "Us versus Them." Second, the group must have "a story" that inspires and guides its membership, a narrative developed over time. Third, the group needs its own language or symbolic words to demonize the enemy. Stern, *Terror in the Name of God*.

37. A. L. Kavanaugh and C. J. Patterson, "The Impact of Community Computer Networks on Social Capital and Community Involvement," *American Behavioral Scientist* 45, no. 3 (November 2001): 496–509, cited in Bargh and McKenna, "The Internet and Social Life," 585.

38. As Seth Godin observed, new technology allows "microleaders" more leverage in influencing their groups. New technology is designed to "connect tribes and amplify their work." A tribe, as he defines it, consists of a shared interest and a way to communicate among its members. What has changed is the ability to communicate. Seth Godin, *Tribes: We Need You to Lead Us* (New York: Portfolio, 2008), 6.

39. The software engineer Ward Cunningham created the first wiki in 1995. One of his fundamental assumptions was that people who collaborate tend to trust one another. His user-editable website became the model for subsequent wikis. Tapscott and Williams, *Wikinomics*, 111. As of 2008, Wikipedia had approximately 2.2 million entries—twenty-three times the amount of entries in the *Encyclopaedia Britannica*. Jeff Howe, *Crowdsourcing: Why the Power of the Crowd Is Driving the Future of Business* (New York: Crown Business, 2008), 61.

40. Shirky, *Here Comes Everybody*, 121–22, 239.

41. Howe, *Crowdsourcing*, 52–55.

42. Tapscott and Williams, *Wikinomics*, 67.

43. According to Wikipedia's founder, Jimmy Wales, approximately 50 percent of edits are made by less than 1 percent of users. This suggests that behind the legion of users there is a small, committed core of regular users who do most of the work. Ibid., 73.

44. Howe, *Crowdsourcing*, 19. By 2000, roughly 63 percent of all US high school graduates pursued some type of higher education. Ibid., 37.

45. Ibid., 29.

46. Tapscott and Williams, *Wikinomics*, 70.

47. Howe, *Crowdsourcing*, 15.

48. Mark Earls, *Herd: How to Change Mass Behavior by Harnessing Our True Nature* (West Sussex, UK: Wiley, 2007), 268.

49. James Surowiecki, *The Wisdom of Crowds* (New York: Anchor Books, 2005), 10.

50. Tapscott and Williams, *Wikinomics*, 70.

51. Ibid., 1, 12, 20.

52. Tom Whipple, "Scientology: The Anonymous Protestors," *The Times* (United Kingdom), June 20, 2008.

53. "'Anonymous' Hackers Arrested in US Sweep," *Herald Sun*, July 20, 2011, *www.heraldsun. com.au/*; Andy Greenberg, "Fourteen Anonymous Hackers Arrested for 'Operation Avenge Assange,' LulzSec Leader Claims He's Not Affected," *Forbes* July 19, 2011, *www.forbes. com.*

54. Robb, *Brave New War*, 4.

55. Ibid., 135–37.

56. Author interview with Robb, June 3, 2008.

57. John Arquilla and David Ronfeldt, "Afterword (September 2001): The Sharpening Fight for the Future," in *Networks and Netwars: The Future of Terror, Crime, and Militancy* (Santa Monica, CA: Rand, 2001), 367.

58. Arquilla and Ronfeldt, "The Advent of Netwar (Revisited)," in ibid., 6.

59. Arquilla and Ronfeldt, "Summary," in ibid., ix.

60. Arquilla, Ronfeldt, and Zanini, "Networks, Netwar, and Information-Age Terrorism," 45.

61. David Ronfeldt and John Arquilla, "Emergence and Influence of the Zapatista Social Netwar," in Arquilla and Ronfeldt, *Networks and Netwars*, 171–99.

62. Arquilla and Ronfeldt, "The Advent of Netwar (Revisited)," 12.

63. Paul de Armond, "Netwar in the Emerald City: WTO Protest Strategy and Tactics," in Arquilla and Ronfeldt, *Networks and Netwars*, 210, 232.

64. John P. Sullivan, "Gangs, Hooligans, and Anarchists—the Vanguard of Netwar in the Streets," in Arquilla and Ronfeldt, *Networks and Netwars*, 121, 123.

65. De Armond, "Netwar in the Emerald City," 204, 209.

66. In contradistinction to other variants of Marxism, autonomist Marxism posits that the working class can effect change in the capitalist system independent of the state, trade unions, or political parties. The autonomist movement favors self-organized action outside traditional organizational structures.

67. Michael Hardt and Antonio Negri, *Multitude: War and Democracy in the Age of Empire* (New York: Penguin Press, 2004).

68. Adam Elkus, "Future War: The War on Terror after Iraq," *Athena Intelligence Journal* 2, no. 1 (2007): 19.

69. Hardt and Negri, *Multitude*, 3–95.

70. Ibid., 218.

71. Ibid., 285–88.

72. Jim Redden, *Snitch Culture* (Venice, CA: Feral House, 2000), 151.

73. Hardt and Negri, *Multitude*, 305.

74. Such intangibles, including media, culture, and ideology, contrast with tangible resources such as military and economic might. Joseph Nye, "The Changing Nature of World Power," *Political Science Quarterly* 105, no. 2 (Summer 1990): 7.

75. This figure was derived from survey data collected from the Internet World Stats website, *www.internetworldstats.com/*.

76. Kara-Jane Lombard, "Gen E (Generation Extremist): The Significance of Youth Culture and New Media in Youth Extremism," in *Recent Advances in Security Technology*, ed. Priyan Mendis, Joseph Lai, Ed Dawson, and Hussein Abass (Melbourne: Research Network for a Secure Australia, 2007), *seit.unsw.adfa.edu.au/staff/sites/dcornforth/Papers/Cornforth_Intel-ligentEvacuationModels.pdf*.

77. Henry Jenkins, *Convergence Culture: Where Old and New Media Collide* (New York: New York University Press, 2006), 3–4.

78. Rid and Hecker, *War 2.0*, 7.

79. Tapscott and Williams, *Wikinomics*, 38.

80. Peter Turchin, *War and Peace and War: The Rise and Fall of Empires* (New York: Plume, 2006), 352.

81. Tapscott and Williams, *Wikinomics*, 40.

82. Shirky, *Here Comes Everybody*, 17.

83. Jenkins, *Convergence Culture*, 135–36.

84. Rid and Hecker, *War 2.0*, 5.

85. The story was presented by Dan Rather and centered on allegations that George W. Bush used friends in high places to secure him a position in the Texas Air National Guard in 1968 so that he could avoid the draft and evade military service in Vietnam. Bloggers charged that the alleged memos written by Lieutenant Colonel Jerry Killian were fabricated. CBS was forced to retract the story and not long after that Rather retired. Turchin, *War and Peace and War*, 353.

86. Shirky, *Here Comes Everybody*, 106.

87. Jenkins, *Convergence Culture*, 2, 11.

88. Howe, *Crowdsourcing*, 104.

89. Jenkins, *Convergence Culture*, 14.

90. John A. Nagl, *Learning to Eat Soup with a Knife: Counterinsurgency Lessons from Malaya and Vietnam* (Chicago: University of Chicago Press, 2005), 24.

91. Gabriel Weimann, "Terror on Facebook, Twitter, and Youtube," *Brown Journal of World Affairs* 16, no. 2 (Spring/Summer 2010): 52–53.

92. Shirky, *Here Comes Everybody*, 20–21.

93. Justin Sharrock, "Right-Wing Extremists Organize and Promote Violence on Facebook—Should the Feds Bust Them or Leave Them Alone?," AlterNet, June 3, 2010, *www.alternet.org/*.

94. Rid and Hecker, *War 2.0*, 208.

95. Encryption transforms electronically transmitted information so that it is unreadable by anyone except someone with a password that allows the message to be decrypted. Internet Relay Chat is a form of real-time Internet text messaging, mainly designed for group communication in discussion forums but also allowing one-to-one communication. Steganography is the practice of embedding hidden messages within other messages or images. An anonymous remailer is a server computer that receives messages with embedded instructions on where to send them next, and then forwards them without revealing the original source. Web-based bulletin boards are areas on websites where users can leave and messages so that other people can read them.

96. Linda Garrison and Martin Grand, eds., *National Infrastructure Protection Center Highlights*, no. 10-01, November 10, 2001.

97. Carol M. Swain, *The New White Nationalism in America: Its Challenge to Integration* (New York: Cambridge University Press, 2002), 309.

98. Juergensmeyer, *Terror in the Mind of God*, 142, and "Anti-abortion Web Site Goes on Trial," *USA Today*, January 7, 1999.

99. Shirky, *Here Comes Everybody*, 23, 27–28, 45.

100. Stern, *Terror in the Name of God*, 271–72.

101. Frank Anderson, "International Terrorism and International Cooperation," in *Countering Suicide Terrorism* (New York: International Policy Institute for Counter-Terrorism and the Anti-Defamation League, 2002), 58.

102. Arquilla, Ronfeldt, and Zanini, "Networks, Netwar, and Information-Age Terrorism," 53–55.

Chapter 6

1.   Martha Crenshaw, "The Logic of Terrorism: Terrorist Behavior as a Product of Strategic Choice," in *Origins of Terrorism: Psychologies, Ideologies, Theologies, States of Mind*, ed. Walter Reich (Washington, DC: Woodrow Wilson Center Press, 1998), 13–15.

2.   Francis Fukuyama, *America at the Crossroads: Democracy, Power, and the Neoconservative Legacy* (New Haven, CT: Yale University Press, 2006), 66–94.

3.   "The Future of Terrorism," *Discover*, July 2006, 37.

4.   Michael T. Osterholm and John Schwartz, *Living Terrors: What America Needs to Know to Survive the Coming Bioterrorist Catastrophe* (New York: Random House, 2000), 36–37.

5.   Challenges for those who seek to produce or acquire nuclear weapons are still great, but design and construction problems are being mitigated by advances in computers and commercial equipment. Also, the spread of centrifuge technology and advances in centrifuge design create potentially greater capacity to produce nuclear weapons. (Centrifuges are used to enrich uranium for nuclear weapons.) Finally, the technology used to produce delivery systems such as cruise missiles, line source attacks, and covert attacks is becoming more readily available as well. Anthony Cordesman, *The War after the War: Strategic Lessons of Iraq and Afghanistan* (Washington, DC: CSIS Press, 2004), 21–23.

6.   Jessica Stern, *The Ultimate Terrorists* (Cambridge, MA: Harvard University Press, 1999), 8–10.

7.   Author interview with Fukuyama, June 30, 2008.

8.   David E. Sanger and William J. Broad, "Leaders Gather for Nuclear Talks as New Threat Is Seen," *New York Times*, April 11, 2010.

9.   Barry R. Schneider, "Al Qaeda's Modus Operandi: Anticipating Their Target Selection," in *The World's Most Threatening Terrorist Networks and Criminal Gangs*, ed. Michael T. Kindt, Jerrold Post, and Barry R. Schneider (New York: Palgrave Macmillan, 2009), 38–39.

10. Benjamin Netanyahu, *Fighting Terrorism: How Democracies Can Defeat the International Terrorist Network* (New York: Farrar, Straus and Giroux, 2001), 126.

11. The terrorism analyst Jessica Stern identified several indicators of a terrorist group's ability to overcome technical hurdles to the development of WMD: previous use of high-tech weapons; state sponsorship; access to significant financial resources; a relatively large, well-educated membership; and ties with corrupt government officials, scientists, or organized crime. Stern, *The Ultimate Terrorists*, 77.

12. As Osama bin Laden said in one interview: "Acquiring weapons for the defense of Muslims is a religious duty. If I have indeed acquired these weapons [WMD], I am carrying out a duty. It would be a sin for Muslims not to try to possess the weapons that would prevent the infidels from inflicting harm on Muslims." Quoted in Rohan Gunaratna, *Inside Al Qaeda: Global Network of Terror* (New York: Columbia University Press, 2002), 48. Not long thereafter he remarked: "At a time when Israel stocks hundreds of nuclear warheads and when the Western crusaders control a large percentage of this [type of] weapon, we do not consider this an accusation but a right, and we reject anyone who accuses us of this. We congratulated the Pakistani people when they achieved this nuclear weapon, and we consider it the right of all Muslims to do so." "Interview with Usama bin Ladin (December 1998)," in *Anti-American Terrorism and the Middle East: A Documentary Reader*, ed. Barry Rubin and Judith Colp Rubin (Oxford: Oxford University Press, 2002), 154–55.

13. Kenneth R. Timmerman, "Fear of a Nuclear D-Day," *Newsmax*, May 2010, 59–60.

14. In February 2004, Abdul Qadeer Khan, the founder of Pakistan's nuclear program, confessed to selling equipment related to centrifuges to several nations, including Iran, Libya, and North Korea. See Gordon Corera, *Shopping for Bombs: Nuclear Proliferation, Global Insecurity, and the Rise of the A. Q. Khan Network* (New York: Oxford University Press, 2006), and William Langewiesche, *The Atomic Bazaar: Dispatches from the Underground World of Nuclear Trafficking* (New York: Farrar, Straus and Giroux, 2008).

15. David Albright, *Peddling Peril: How the Secret Nuclear Trade Arms America's Enemies* (New York: Free Press, 2010), 169–84.

16. Sultan Bashiruddin Mahmood dedicated much of his time to providing social services to needy people in Afghanistan. Despite these laudable efforts, he has consorted with various Islamist groups and reportedly met with Osama bin Laden at least once. He is strongly suspected of having offered al Qaeda the expertise to construct a so-called dirty bomb. Yosri Fouda and Nick Fielding, *Masterminds of Terror: The Truth behind the Most Devastating Terrorist Attack the World Has Ever Seen* (New York: Arcade Publishing, 2003), 48. The researcher Paul Williams claims that as US armed forces combed the tunnels of a Qaeda base in Kandahar, they discovered low-grade uranium-238 in a canister. If this report is true, conceivably such material could suffice to create a dirty bomb and was presumably in al Qaeda's possession before the group withdrew from the base. Paul L. Williams, *Al Qaeda: Brotherhood of Terror* (Indianapolis: Alpha, 2002), 75; and Burt Herman, "Experts Worry Terrorists Have Nuke Plans," Associated Press, February 4, 2004.

17. Rolf Mowatt-Larssen, "Al Qaeda's Religious Justification of Nuclear Terrorism," Belfer Center for Science and International Affairs, Harvard University, November 12, 2010, *belfercenter.ksg.harvard.edu/publication/20518/al_qaedas_religious_justification_of_nuclear_terrorism.html*.

18. Jack Kelley, "Terrorists Courted Nuclear Scientists," *USA Today*, November 5, 2001.

19. "Status of Nuclear Forces," Federation of American Scientists, *www.fas.org/programs/ssp/nukes/nuclearweapons/nukestatus.html*.

20. Netanyahu, *Fighting Terrorism*, 125.

21. Richard A. Falkenrath, Robert D. Newman, and Bradley A. Thayer, *America's Achilles' Heel: Nuclear, Biological, and Chemical Terrorism and Covert Attack* (Cambridge, MA: MIT Press, 2001), 141. This scenario was featured in *The Sum of All Fears*, a popular movie released in 2002 and based on a Tom Clancy novel. The plot centers on a global cabal of neofascists that acquires the materials and expertise to construct a nuclear weapon and ultimately detonates it in a terrorist attack on Baltimore's harbor.

22. In the gun-assembly type of nuclear weapon, two pieces of weapons-grade uranium are rapidly combined to produce a nuclear chain reaction that results in a release of a tremendous amount of energy. In the implosion-style design, the pit of the bomb contains a subcritical density of weapons-grade nuclear material—either plutonium or uranium—surrounded by conventional explosives. When the conventional explosives are detonated, the blast squeezes the nuclear material to a supercritical density that results in the chain reaction. The implosion device is more efficient in that it produces a greater yield for the amount of fissile material used, but its design is considerably more complicated.

23. Michael Levi, *On Nuclear Terrorism* (Cambridge, MA: Harvard University Press, 2007), 73–85.

24. Charles D. Ferguson et al., *The Four Faces of Nuclear Terrorism* (Monterey, CA: Center for Nonproliferation Studies, 2004), 48.

25. Graham Allison, *Nuclear Terrorism: The Ultimate Preventable Catastrophe* (New York: Times Books, 2004), 130.

26. Levi, *On Nuclear Terrorism*.

27. Alexander Glaser and Frank N. von Hippel, "Thwarting Nuclear Terrorism," *Scientific American*, February 2006, 58.

28. Joseph Cirincione, *Bomb Scare: The History and Future of Nuclear Weapons* (New York: Columbia University Press, 2008), 91.

29. Richard Rhodes, *The Twilight of the Bombs: Recent Challenges, New Dangers, and the Prospects for a World without Nuclear Weapons* (New York: Knopf, 2010), 141–55.

30. Kenneth R. Timmerman, *Preachers of Hate: Islam and the War on America* (New York: Crown Forum, 2003), 121.

31. Stern, *The Ultimate Terrorists*, 60; Allison, *Nuclear Terrorism*, 43.

32. Stanislav Lunev and Ira Winkler, *Through the Eyes of the Enemy* (Washington, DC: Regnery, 1998).

33. Glen E. Schweitzer and Carole C. Dorsch, *Superterrorism: Assassins, Mobsters, and Weapons of Mass Destruction* (New York: Plenum Trade, 1998), 55.

34. Allison, *Nuclear Terrorism*, 10.

35. Brian Michael Jenkins, *Will Terrorists Go Nuclear?* (Amherst, NY: Prometheus Books, 2008), 247.

36. See, for example, Paul L. Williams, *Osama's Revenge: The Next 9/11* (Amherst, NY: Prometheus Books, 2004).

37. Allison, *Nuclear Terrorism*, 3.

38. Simon Reeve, *The New Jackals: Ramzi Yousef, Osama bin Laden, and the Future of Terrorism* (Boston: Northeastern University Press, 1999), 214.

39. Allison, *Nuclear Terrorism*, 27.

40. "Bin Laden Claims to Have Nuclear Weapons," *USA Today*, November 10, 2001.

41. Jenkins, *Will Terrorists Go Nuclear?*, 84.

42. Ferguson et al., *The Four Faces of Nuclear Terrorism*, 197–231.

43. Allison, *Nuclear Terrorism*, 196–97.

44. The radiation stemming from the accidental explosion in the reactor caused an estimated $300 billion in economic damage and will likely lead to tens of thousands of cancer deaths among those exposed to the fallout. Ibid., 7.

45. Philip Henshall has written that in April 1945 a German U-boat—U-234—set sail toward Japan, possibly with cargo that contained highly radioactive material, but surrendered to the United States in May after learning of Germany's surrender. According to Henshall, the radioactive material was to be delivered to the Japanese for construction of a dirty bomb that might have been transported to the United States in an aircraft-carrying submarine. Once the submarine neared the west coast of the United States, a plane might have been launched to deliver the payload. Philip Henshall, *Vengeance: Hitler's Nuclear Weapon: Fact or Fiction?* (Stroud, Gloucester, UK: Alan Sutton, 1995), 148–58.

46. Noam Herold, "Nuclear Terrorism: A 21st Century Threat," *Counter Terrorist*, May/June 2008, 12.

47. In August 2007, Jose Padilla was convicted on charges related to supporting overseas terrorism, but not on charges related to planning to build a dirty bomb. Peter Whoriskey, "Jury Convicts Jose Padilla of Terror Charges," *Washington Post*, August 17, 2007.

48. John Stone, "Al Qaeda, Deterrence, and Weapons of Mass Destruction," *Studies in Conflict and Terrorism* 32 (2009): 768.

49. Cummings never had a chance to carry out his plot. His wife, Amber, shot and killed him with a Colt .45 revolver on December 9, 2008. Reportedly there was evidence that she had suffered years of domestic abuse. She told authorities of her husband's ambition to kill President-elect Barack Obama. Previously James Cummings had filled out an application to join the National Socialist Movement, a neo-Nazi group that attained notoriety during the first decade of the twenty-first century after several contentious public demonstrations. Barton Gellman, "The Secret World of Extreme Militias," *Time*, October 11, 2010, 29–31.

50. "The Future of Terrorism," *Discover*, July 2006, 38.

51. Osterholm and Schwartz, *Living Terrors*, 15–19.

52. Although smallpox was effectively eradicated through a global inoculation effort, most people in the world are no longer vaccinated against the deadly disease. Vaccinations ceased in the 1970s. The disease still exists in laboratories. It would take considerable effort to reintroduce the vaccine in the wake of another global outbreak. In the previous century, wiping out the disease involved the efforts of 150,000 people working over an eleven-year period. Ibid., 108.

53. Anthony Lake, *Six Nightmares: Real Threats in a Dangerous World and How America Can Meet Them* (Boston: Little, Brown, 2000), 13.

54. Falkenrath, Newman, and Taylor, *America's Achilles' Heel*, 112.

55. Walter Laqueur, *The New Terrorism: Fanaticism and the Arms of Mass Destruction* (New York: Oxford University Press, 1999), 67.

56. W. Seth Carus, "The Rajneeshees," in *Toxic Terror: Assessing Terrorist Use of Chemical and Biological Weapons*, ed. Jonathan B. Tucker (Cambridge, MA: MIT Press, 2000), 115–37.

57. FBI, *Terrorism in the United States 1996* (Washington, DC: FBI, 1997), 9.

58. Jonathan B. Tucker and Jason Pate, "The Minnesota Patriots Council," in Tucker, *Toxic Terror*, 159–83.

59. Osterholm and Schwartz, *Living Terrors*, 162.

60. Bob Coen and Eric Nadler, *Dead Silence: Fear and Terror on the Anthrax Trail* (Berkeley, CA: Counterpoint, 2009), 15–16.

61. The American Type Culture Collection (ATCC), a private nonprofit scientific organization in Northern Virginia, has been a focal point for the acquisition of biological cultures. The firm maintains a vast library of microbial cultures for scientific use. Falkenrath, Newman, and Thayer, *America's Achilles' Heel*, 115.

62. Schweitzer and Dorsch, *Superterrorism*, 117.

63. Jessica Eve Stern, "Larry Wayne Harris," in Tucker, *Toxic Terror*, 227–46.

64. Coen and Nadler, *Dead Silence*, 8.

65. The five dead were Robert Stevens, a photo editor at the *Sun*, a tabloid in Boca Raton, Florida; Kathy Nguyen, a stockroom worker in Manhattan; Thomas Morris, a postal worker in Washington, D.C.; Joseph Curseen, also a postal worker in Washington, D.C.; and Ottilie Lundgren, the last known victim, the ninety-four-year-old widow of a prominent judge from Oxford, Connecticut.

66. Fred Charles Iklé, *Annihilation from Within: The Ultimate Threat of Nations* (New York: Columbia University Press, 2006), 63.

67. Coen and Nadler, *Dead Silence*, 4, 5, 9.

68. In 1990 the United Nations Special Commission on Iraq was established to inspect Iraqi WMD facilities.

69. Coen and Nadler, *Dead Silence*, 31, 227–28, 124–25; Richard Spertzel, "Bruce Ivins Wasn't the Anthrax Culprit," *Wall Street Journal*, August 2, 2008.

70. Stern, *The Ultimate Terrorists*, 53.

71. Osterholm and Schwartz, *Living Terrors*, 12.

72. Ibid., 8.

73. Author interview with Robb, June 3, 2008.

74. As H. G. Wells once noted, "in the country of the blind, the one-eyed man is king." Robert Jay Lifton, *Destroying the World to Save It: Aum Shinrikyo, Apocalyptic Violence, and the New Global Terrorism* (New York: Metropolitan Books, 1999).

75. Falkenrath, Newman, and Thayer, *America's Achilles' Heel*, 19.

76. Lake, *Six Nightmares*, 28.

77. Schweitzer and Dorsch, *Superterrorism*, 85.

78. Jonathan B. Tucker, introduction to *Toxic Terror*, 6.

79. Stern, *The Ultimate Terrorists*, 51.

80. Falkenrath, Newman, and Thayer, *America's Achilles' Heel*, 98.

81. Stone, "Al Qaeda, Deterrence, and Weapons of Mass Destruction," 768.

82. For more on the Krar case, see "Feds: What Did Texas Couple Plan to Do with Cyanide?," *USA Today*, January 30, 2004; "Prison Sentence for Possessing Chemical Weapons," *ATF News*, May 4, 2004, *www.atf.org/*; Camille Jackson, "Terror, American Style," *Intelligence Report*, Spring 2004, *www.splcenter.org/*; "Fighting Fire on the Right," *U.S. News and World Report*, August 15–22, 2005, 24; and Michael Reynolds, "Homegrown Terror," in *Annual Editions Violence and Terrorism 07/08*, ed. Thomas J. Badey (New York: McGraw Hill, 2007), 86–91.

83. Stern, *The Ultimate Terrorists*, 54.

84. Members of the CSA believed Armageddon was imminent. At the Aryan Nations Congress in July 1983, James Ellison, Richard Butler, Robert Miles, and Louis Beam developed an elaborate plan to overthrow the US government. Through terrorism they believed they could precipitate a societal breakdown that would spark a revolution, raising the likelihood of achieving their goal of creating a whites-only bastion in the Pacific Northwest. James Ellison, the leader of the CSA, testified at a trial that Robert K. Miles gave him a thirty-gallon barrel of cyanide and once suggested that the water system of Washington, D.C., would be a good possible target, opining that "the ones who would be killed would not really matter. It would be a good cleansing." See Jessica Eve Stern, "The Covenant, the Sword, and the Arm of the Lord," in Tucker, *Toxic Terror*, 139–57; and Brent L. Smith, *Terrorism in America: Pipe Bombs and Pipe Dreams* (Albany: State University of New York Press, 1994), 45.

85. Falkenrath, Newman, and Thayer, *America's Achilles' Heel*, 28–33.

86. Flynn, *America the Vulnerable: How Our Government Is Failing to Protect Us from Terrorism* (New York: HarperCollins, 2004), 118.

87. Schneider, "Al Qaeda's Modus Operandi," 41.

88. Sean P. Gorman, *Networks, Security and Complexity: The Role of Public Policy in Critical Infrastructure Protection* (Cheltenham, UK: Edward Elgar, 2005), 127.

89. John Robb, *Brave New War: The Next Stage of Terrorism and the End of Globalization* (Hoboken, NJ: Wiley, 2007), 108.

90. According to the research of Ely Karmon, the most developed parts of the industrialized world (the United States, western Europe, and Japan) were the main sites of nonconventional terrorist attacks and threats. Karmon includes in his analysis threats to use WMD, threats against WMD facilities, attempts to acquire WMD, possession of WMD, attempted use of WMD, action against facilities of WMD, and the actual use of WMD. Ely Karmon, "Trends in Contemporary International Terrorism," in *Countering Suicide Terrorism* (New York: International Policy Institute for Counter-Terrorism and the Anti-Defamation League, 2002), 40, 46.

91. R. James Wollsey, foreword to *Combating Terrorism: Strategies of Ten Countries*, ed. Yonah Alexander (Ann Arbor: University of Michigan Press, 2002), vi.

92. Anti-Defamation League, *Jihad Online: Islamic Terrorists and the Internet* (Washington, DC: Anti-Defamation League, 2002), 11.

93. In the US electric power industry, there are 3,500 utility companies, 11,000 power-generating facilities, and 365,000 miles of overhead electrical lines of 66,000 volts or more. A well-coordinated attack on several substations could knock out power in a large region of the country. With power systems so interconnected, disrupting one can cause a cascade of failures. S. F. Tomajczyk, *US Elite Counter-Terrorist Forces* (Osceola, WI: MBI , 1997), 22–23.

94. Flynn, *America the Vulnerable*, 86.

95. According to a study titled "Structural Vulnerability of the North American Power Grid," Reka Albert, Istvan Albert, and Gary L. Nakarado estimated that if only 2 percent of the high-load nodes in the system were disabled, 60 percent of the power grid could shut down. Robb, *Brave New War*, 106–7.

96. Tomajczyk, *US Elite Counter-Terrorist Forces*, 22–23.

97. For example, in 2004 one attack on a pipeline in Iraq, conducted by a small team of saboteurs for an estimated $2,000, resulted in a loss of more than $500 million in lost oil revenue for the Iraqi government. Robb, *Brave New War*, 6.

98. Robb, *Brave New War*, 5.

99. Flynn, *America the Vulnerable*, 83, 88, 96. Approximately 70 percent of the eight million containers that arrived in US ports in 2002 originated or moved through four overseas terminal operators. As Stephen Flynn points out, in 2002 "over 400 million people, 122 million cars, eleven million trucks, 2.4 million rail freight cars, approximately eight million

maritime containers, and 59,995 vessels entered the United States at more than 3,700 and 301 ports of entry." Ibid., 93. Moreover, if ports in Houston, Charleston, Norfolk, and New York were incapacitated, it would be difficult for the United States to send military materiel overseas to a region of conflict. Jonathan R. White, *Terrorism and Homeland Security: An Introduction* (Belmont, CA: Wadsworth, 2004).

100. Bruce Berkowitz, *The New Face of War: How War Will Be Fought in the 21st Century* (New York: Free Press, 2003), 185.

101. Laqueur, *The New Terrorism*, 75.

102. Lake, *Six Nightmares*, 40.

103. For example, in 1997 some members of the Tamil Tigers sought to crash computer systems of Sri Lankan embassies by flooding them with e-mails. Lake, *Six Nightmares*, 45. According to some observers, Russia employed a form of cyberwarfare against Estonia by disrupting government websites, such as that of the foreign ministry, that were needed to counter the Kremlin's propaganda offensive in April 2007, when the Kremlin reacted to an Estonian government decision to move a Soviet war memorial and some nearby graves from central Tallinn to a military cemetery. The highly charged incident inflamed nationalist sentiments on both sides. Edward Lucas, *The New Cold War: Putin's Russia and the Threat to the West* (New York: Palgrave Macmillan, 2008), 150–55. Examples of previous cyberwarfare include hacking financial systems to hinder financial transactions of firms supporting terrorist groups, and sabotaging nuclear, chemical, and biological weapons development programs in countries such as North Korea and Iran. Amos A. Jordan, William J. Taylor, and Michael J. Mazarr, *American National Security*, 5th ed. (Baltimore: Johns Hopkins University Press, 1999), 168. Israel may have employed information warfare against Syria. Richard Clarke speculates that just prior to the Israeli Air Force's September 6, 2007, raid on a Syrian complex believed to have been a nuclear weapons plant, the Syrian air defense system was disabled by hackers, allowing Israeli bombers to target the facility unscathed. Richard A. Clarke and Robert K. Knake, *Cyber War: The Next Threat to National Security and What to Do about It* (New York: HarperCollins, 2010), 1–11.

104. Ariel Merari, "Terrorism as a Strategy of Struggle: Past and Future," in Taylor and Horgan, *The Future of Terrorism*, 52–65.

105. Ronald D. Crelinsten, "Terrorism and Counter-Terrorism in a Multi-Centric World: Challenges and Opportunities," in Taylor and Horgan, *The Future of Terrorism*, 183.

106. Falkenrath, Newman, and Thayer, *America's Achilles' Heel*, 57.

107. James J. F. Forrest, "Terrorist Use of WMD," in Kindt, Post, and Schneider, *The World's Most Threatening Terrorist Networks*, 99.

108. Quoted in Schneider, "Al Qaeda's Modus Operandi," 38.

109. Jenkins, *Will Terrorists Go Nuclear?*, 101.

110. In 2001 Brian Jenkins pointed out that of the more than ten thousand incidents of international terrorism recorded since 1968, only fourteen had resulted in one hundred or more fatalities. However, a fundamental shift in terrorists' proclivities to inflict casualties occurred during the 1990s, as more and more terrorists were inspired by apocalyptic ideologies. Brian M. Jenkins, "The Organization Men: Anatomy of a Terrorist Attack," in *How Did This Happen? Terrorism and the New War*, ed. James F. Hoge Jr. and Gideon Rose (New York: Public Affairs, 2001), 5.

111. Walter Laqueur, *No End to War: Terrorism in the Twenty-First Century* (New York: Continuum, 2003), 209–10.

112. For example, although religious terrorists carried out only 25 percent of the recorded international terrorist attacks in 1995, they were responsible for 58 percent of terrorist casualties that year. Bruce Hoffman, *Inside Terrorism* (New York: Columbia University Press, 1998), 199–205.

113. Mark Juergensmeyer, *Terror in the Mind of God: The Global Rise of Religious Violence* (Berkeley: University of California Press, 2000), 6.

114. Ibid., 227.

115. Hoffman, *Inside Terrorism*, 94.

116. Bruce Hoffman cites numerous examples, including the 1995 Aum Shinrikyo cult attack in the Tokyo subway, the 1995 assassination of Prime Minister Yitzhak Rabin of Israel, the 1993 bombing of the World Trade Center in New York by Islamic extremists, and the 1996 campaign of Hamas suicide bombings. See ibid., 92–93.

117. Alan M. Dershowitz, *Why Terrorism Works* (New Haven, CT: Yale University Press, 2002).

118. Author interview with Dershowitz, July 1, 2008. On "civilianality," see, for example, Dershowitz, "'Civilian Casualty'? It Depends: Those Who Support Terrorists Are Not Entirely Innocent," *Los Angeles Times*, July 22, 2006.

119. For more on Lifton's analysis of apocalyptic groups, see Lifton, *Destroying the World to Save It*. For his analysis of bin Laden and al Qaeda, see Peter Benesh, "Terrorism Expert Points to Bin Laden's Utopian Vision," *Investor's Business Daily*, September 26, 2001.

120. For example, in 2002 a Kuwaiti-born cleric, Suleiman Abu Ghaith, posted a statement on the Internet to the effect that al Qaeda had the right to kill four million Americans in retaliation for US attacks against Muslims. Noam Herold, "Nuclear Terrorism: A 21st Century Threat," 11. In 2003 a Bahraini cleric, Sheikh Nasir bin Hamid al-Fahd, issued a fatwa titled "A Treatise on the Legal Status of Using Weapons of Mass Destruction on the Infidels," in which he condoned such methods. He reasoned that since the United States had killed "millions" of Muslims, it was appropriate to respond in kind. James J. F. Forrest, "Terrorist Use of WMD," in Kindt, Post, and Schneider, *The World's Most Threatening Terrorist Networks and Criminal Gangs*, 109. After Fahd was arrested by Saudi authorities he recanted the fatwa on Saudi television. However, according to a letter he wrote in prison, he claimed that Saudi authorities had coerced his retraction. Mowatt-Larssen, "Al Qaeda's Religious Justification of Nuclear Terrorism."

121. Adam Dolnik, *Understanding Terrorist Innovation: Technology, Tactics and Global Trends* (London: Routledge, 2007).

122. Stone, "Al Qaeda, Deterrence, and Weapons of Mass Destruction," 770.

123. Adam Elkus, "Future War: The War on Terror after Iraq," *Athena Intelligence Journal* 2, no. 1 (2007): 19–20.

124. Iklé, *Annihilation from Within*, 72.

125. In a well-established democracy, an aspiring dictator would more likely have to build up a lawful political role by advancing a seemingly benign new ideology that was not exclusionary, so that it could appeal to a significant number of people. Such a person could seek to recruit from the ranks of "restless minorities." In the United States, Iklé believes, illegal Spanish-speaking immigrants or unassimilated legal ones make up a potential pool for such recruitment. The person could attempt to appear as a "compassionate, liberal 'anti-racist' who cares about the welfare of *all* minorities [italics in original]," and during an election campaign promise to protect the country from nuclear terrorism. Near election time, the prospective dictator could order followers to detonate a low-yield nuclear bomb in the capital. In the aftermath, media would give positive coverage to the person (who, after all, had warned of such a possible scenario). If the aspiring dictator won the election, a secret police could be organized to intimidate political opponents. Iklé, *Annihilation from Within*, 77.

126. Iklé explains: "These individuals or groups are not likely to have the most lethal weapons. They couldn't make them. They couldn't manage them. You need some people with knowledge who can operate these things. The United States is not a country that is open to extremism. I made a point in [*Annihilation from Within* that] the US is one of the least likely countries to experience annihilation from within. It would more likely be a central Asian country, where all the power is in one place. . . . Individuals can only do so much. You need a substantial organization to do great damage, unless you lose all control of all these weapons in the extreme case." Author interview with Iklé, June 2, 2008.

127. Schweitzer and Dorsch, *Superterrorism*, 262–63. For the fiscal year 1999–2000, the Clinton
       administration requested that roughly 28 percent of the $10 billion counterterrorism
       budget be dedicated specifically to countering chemical and biological terrorism as well as
       cyberterrorism, and to preparing to deal with the outcomes of such possible attacks. David
       Claridge, "Exploding the Myths of Superterrorism," in Taylor and Horgan, *The Future of
       Terrorism*, 134.

Chapter 7

1.   See, for example, Thomas P. M. Barnett, *Great Powers: America and the World after Bush*
      (New York: Putnam, 2009).
2.   Daniel Pipes, *Militant Islam Reaches America* (New York: Norton, 2002), 38–44.
3.   Yossef Bodansky, *Islamic Anti-Semitism as a Political Instrument* (Houston: Ariel Center for
      Policy Research, 1999), 19.
4.   Amir Taheri, *Holy Terror: Inside the World of Islamic Terrorism* (Bethesda, MD: Adler and
      Adler, 1987), 199.
5.   Ibid., 48.
6.   Thomas Rid and Marc Hecker, *War 2.0: Irregular Warfare in the Information Age* (Westport,
      CT: Praeger Security International, 2009), 185.
7.   John Zimmerman argues that Qutb's animus toward the United States predated his stay
      there. Moreover, he believes that many of Qutb's anecdotes about the United States are
      probably apocryphal. Most notable is Qutb's allegation that while traveling on an ocean
      liner, a drunken American woman attempted to seduce him. He was particularly affronted
      by this experience. Zimmerman suspects that this experience was probably contrived.
      Qutb also expressed outrage over a putative incident in which employees at the George
      Washington Hospital in Washington, D.C., upon hearing of the assassination of Hasan al-
      Banna, began celebrating. Subsequent research revealed no record of Qutb receiving treat-
      ment there. Moreover, few Americans had even heard of Banna, much less had enough
      interest in him to celebrate his death. John C. Zimmerman, "Sayyid Qutb's Influence
      on the 11 September Attacks," *Terrorism and Political Violence* 16, no. 2 (Summer 2004):
      222–52.
8.   Youssef Aboul-Enein, "Sheik Abdel-Fatah al-Khalidi Revitalizes Sayid Qutb" (West
      Point, NY: United States Military Academy, Combating Terrorism Center, n.d.), guest
      commentary.
9.   Ahmad S. Moussalli, *Radical Islamic Fundamentalism: The Ideological and Political Discourse
      of Sayyid Qutb* (Beirut: American University of Beirut, 1992), 26.
10.   Sayid Qutb, *Milestones* (Cedar Rapids, IA: Mother Mosque Foundation, n.d.), 9, 118.
11.   One of his contemporary admirers, Sheikh Abdel-Fatah al-Khalidi, portrayed Qutb as a
      great prognosticator and quasi-Nostradamus who predicted the so-called clash of civiliza-
      tions between the United States and Islam. In 1985 Khalidi compiled Qutb's unpublished
      writings in a book titled *Amreeka Kamaa Ra'aytu*. Aboul-Enein, "Sheik Abdel-Fatah al-
      Khalidi Revitalizes Sayid Qutb."
12.   Qutb, *Milestones*, 160.
13.   Jane Corbin, *Al Qaeda: In Search of the Terror Network That Threatens the World* (New York:
      Thunder's Mouth Press, 2002), 10–11.
14.   This is according to the statements of one of the Free Officers. See Moussalli, *Radical
      Islamic Fundamentalism*, 32.
15.   "Do Not Call Jihad a Defense, from 'Milestones,' the Book That Killed Its Authors," in
      Adam Parfrey, *Extreme Islam: Anti-American Propaganda of Muslim Fundamentalism* (Los
      Angeles: Feral House, 2001), 63.
16.   Kenneth R. Timmerman, *Preachers of Hate: Islam and the War on America* (New York:
      Crown Forum, 2003), 121.

17. Moussalli, *Radical Islamic Fundamentalism*, 42.

18. Marc Sageman, *Understanding Terror Networks* (Philadelphia: University of Pennsylvania Press, 2004), 8.

19. Qutb had drawn from the writings of an Indian Muslim, Mawlana Abu al-Ala Mawdudi, to formulate his theory of jihad. Actually Mawdudi had resurrected the *jahiliyya* discourse before Qutb. Mawdudi had used the term "jahiliyya" in an abstract way to describe the system of beliefs and ideas in India during the early twentieth century. But Qutb took Mawdudi's ideas out of context and applied them to his own theories of jihad and *jahiliyya*. See Sageman, *Understanding Terror Networks*, 6–9.

20. Taheri, *Holy Terror*, 57.

21. Qutb, *Milestones*, 70.

22. Taheri, *Holy Terror*, 264.

23. Gilles Kepel, *Muslim Extremism in Egypt: The Prophet and Pharaoh* (Berkeley: University of California Press, 1993), 34.

24. The creation of the state of Israel in 1948 is considered the first *Naqbah*.

25. Aboul-Enein, "Sheik Abdel-Fatah al-Khalidi Revitalizes Sayid Qutb," 4.

26. Robin Wright, *Sacred Rage: The Wrath of Militant Islam* (New York: Touchstone, 2001), 65.

27. Kepel, *Muslim Extremism in Egypt*, 192.

28. Walter Laqueur, *No End to War: Terrorism in the Twenty-First Century* (New York: Continuum, 2003), 37; and Sageman, *Understanding Terror Networks*, 17–18.

29. Mark Juergensmeyer, *Terror in the Mind of God: The Global Rise of Religious Violence* (Berkeley: University of California Press, 2000), 81.

30. Samuel Katz, *Relentless Pursuit: The DSS and the Manhunt for the al-Qaeda Terrorists* (New York: Forge, 2002), 49.

31. A former colleague, Montasser al-Zayyat, claimed that under the duress of torture Zawahiri was forced to testify against his fellows during the trial. The shame he felt prompted him to leave Egypt after he was released from prison in the mid-1980s. He first went to Saudi Arabia and then left for Afghanistan in 1987. Zawahiri was born into an aristocratic Egyptian family in 1951. Although he had strong opinions, he was described as humble and avoided the limelight of leadership. He went on to earn medical degrees from Cairo University and, while he was living in Peshawar, a university in Pakistan. Zawahiri has been described as very effective in individual persuasion and in recruiting new cadres because he articulates his aims clearly. Montasser al-Zayyat, *The Road to Al-Qaeda: The Story of Bin Laden's Right-Hand Man* (London: Pluto Press, 2004).

32. Ladan Boroumand and Roya Boroumand, "Terror, Islam, and Democracy," *Journal of Democracy* 13, no. 2 (April 2002): 9.

33. Bodansky, *Islamic Anti-Semitism as a Political Instrument*, 86.

34. Michael A. Ledeen, *The War against the Terror Masters* (New York: St. Martin's Press, 2003), 12, 23.

35. For example, during the mid-1980s Iran supported Gulbuddin Hekmatyar's Hizb-i Islami in its struggle against the Soviets in Afghanistan. By 1991 Iran had also consolidated a strategic alliance with Sudan. Yossef Bodansky, *Bin Laden: The Man Who Declared War on America* (Rocklin, CA: Forum, 1999), 22. Hekmatyar would later make peace with his erstwhile rival Mullah Mohammed Omar. Reportedly, Hekmatyar met with Omar, bin Laden, and Ayman al-Zawahiri in early 2003 to form an alliance to resist the US occupation in Afghanistan. Paul L. Williams, *Osama's Revenge: The Next 9/11* (Amherst, NY: Prometheus Books, 2004), 110–11.

36. Michael Scheuer, *Imperial Hubris: Why the West Is Losing the War on Terror* (Washington, DC: Brassey's, 2004), 210–11.

37. Rid and Hecker, *War 2.0*, 185.

38. Paul L. Williams, *Al Qaeda: Brotherhood of Terror* (Indianapolis: Alpha, 2002), 99–101.

39. Simon Reeve put the estimate at 14,000 to 17,000. Reeve, *The New Jackals: Ramzi Yousef,*

Osama bin Laden, and the Future of Terrorism (Boston: Northeastern University Press, 1999), 3; Adam Robinson put the figure at 15,000 to 22,000. Robinson, *Bin Laden: Behind the Mask of the Terrorist* (New York: Arcade Publishing, 2001), 114.

40. Scheuer, *Imperial Hubris*, 143.

41. Paul R. Pillar, *Terrorism and U.S. Foreign Policy* (Washington, DC: Brookings Institution Press, 2001), 46.

42. Yosri Fouda and Nick Fielding, *Masterminds of Terror: The Truth behind the Most Devastating Terrorist Attack the World Has Ever Seen* (New York: Arcade Publishing, 2003), 39.

43. Barry Rubin and Judith Colp Rubin, eds., *Anti-American Terrorism and the Middle East: A Documentary Reader* (Oxford: Oxford University Press, 2002), 43.

44. Brynjar Lia, "Doctrines for Jihadi Terrorist Training," *Terrorism and Political Violence* 20, no. 4 (2008): 520–24.

45. Sageman, *Understanding Terror Networks*, 3, 36.

46. Nearly a decade after the incident, a captured Pakistani al Qaeda member, Mohammed Saddiq Odeh, told his Pakistani and US interrogators that bin Laden had personally ordered the assassination of Azzam because he suspected that his former mentor had ties to the CIA. Rohan Gunaratna, *Inside Al Qaeda: Global Network of Terror* (New York: Columbia University Press, 2002), 24.

47. Corbin, *Al Qaeda*, 22–23.

48. Gunaratna, *Inside Al Qaeda*, 27–28.

49. See Hoffman, *Inside Terrorism*, 195.

50. Reeve, *The New Jackals*, 172.

51. Gunaratna, *Inside Al Qaeda*, 28–29. Eventually members of al Qaeda in Saudi Arabia coalesced into the group al Qaeda in the Arabian Peninsula (QAP), which in the early years of the twenty-first century was led by Abdel Aziz al-Muqrin. Muqrin authored a book—*A Practical Course for Guerrilla War*—that became popular in jihadist circles. In 2004 he was killed in a shootout with police in Saudi Arabia after he and other members were cornered in a gas station. After his death, he attained a cult status among jihadists in Saudi Arabia. For more on Muqrin, see Norman Cigar, *Al-Qa'ida's Doctrine of Insurgency: 'Abd Al-'Aziz Al-Muqrin's 'A Practical Course for Guerrilla War'* (Washington, DC: Potomac Books, 2009). An important regional commander based in Yemen, Anwar al-Awlaki, was born and raised in the United States and held dual citizenship. His sermons appear on Islamist websites and on social media sites such as YouTube. His death was considered a significant victory by the Obama administration in the global war on terror.

52. Robinson, *Bin Laden*, 132.

53. Sageman, *Understanding Terror Networks*, 39.

54. Paul R. Rich, "Introduction," *Small Wars and Insurgencies* 14, no. 1 (Spring 2003): 10.

55. Paul R. Rich, "Al Qaeda and the Radical Islamic Challenge to Western Strategy," *Small Wars and Insurgencies* 14, no. 1 (Spring 2003): 43.

56. Roland Jacquard, *In the Name of Osama bin Laden: Global Terrorism and the Bin Laden International* (Durham, NC: Duke University Press, 2002), 31.

57. Corbin, *Al Qaeda*, 60.

58. Seth G. Jones, *In the Graveyard of Empires: America's War in Afghanistan* (New York: Norton, 2009).

59. Robert D. Kaplan, *Imperial Grunts* (New York, Vintage Books, 2005), 187.

60. Zayyat, *The Road to Al-Qaeda*, 11.

61. Bin Laden, "Declaration of War (August 1996)," in Rubin and Rubin, *Anti-American Terrorism and the Middle East*, 137.

62. Bin Laden, "Statement: Jihad against Jews and Crusaders (February 23, 1998)," in Rubin and Rubin, *Anti-American Terrorism and the Middle East*, 149–51.

63. Sageman, *Understanding Terror Networks*, 51.

64. Zayyat, *The Road to Al-Qaeda*, 11.

65.   Fawaz A. Gerges, *The Far Enemy: Why Jihad Went Global* (New York: Cambridge University Press, 2005), 273.

66.   Zayyat, *The Road to Al-Qaeda*, 68.

67.   The Taliban reportedly struck a deal with Saudi officials in 1998 to hand over bin Laden in exchange for Saudi support and US recognition. However, following Operation Infinite Reach, the chief of Saudi intelligence, Prince Turki bin Faisal, met in Afghanistan with Omar, whereupon Omar rebuffed Saudi requests to hand over bin Laden. In September 1998, Omar convened a meeting of the Afghan Ulema Council to discuss bin Laden's status. The body decided that since bin Laden had been granted Afghani citizenship, only an Afghan court could legitimately determine his guilt or innocence and would thus not extradite him. Williams, *Osama's Revenge*, 58–59; Yossef Bodansky, *Bin Laden: The Man Who Declared War on America* (Rocklin, CA: Forum, 1999), 301–2.

68.   Katz, *Relentless Pursuit*, 270.

69.   The Salafists seek to emulate the venerable forefathers of Islam, the generation of Muslims who lived during the time of the prophet Muhammad. The Salafist tradition has spawned many other religiopolitical movements over the years, including the Muslim Brotherhood, Hamas, and a host of other voluntary organizations.

70.   Michael Scott Doran, "Somebody Else's Civil War," in *How Did This Happen? Terrorism and the New War*, ed. James F. Hoge Jr. and Gideon Rose (New York: Public Affairs, 2001), 44–45.

71.   Zayyat, *The Road to Al-Qaeda*, 4–5.

72.   "Al-Qaeda 'Extinct within a Year,'" *Australian*, October 9, 2003, *www.news.com.au/common/story_page/0,4057,7431422%5E1702,00.html*.

73.   Zayyat, *The Road to Al-Qaeda*, 95–99.

74.   Sageman, *Understanding Terror Networks*, 52.

75.   Thomas X. Hammes, *The Sling and the Stone: On War in the 21st Century* (St. Paul, MN: Zenith Press, 2004), 130–52.

76.   Rid and Hecker, *War 2.0*, 139.

77.   Bergen's definition is quoted in Jonathan White, Terrorism and Homeland Security, 5th ed. (Belmont, CA: Thomson Wadsworth, 2006), 101–2.

78.   Numerous "number three" al Qaeda leaders have been killed or captured since 9/11: Mohamed Atef, Abu Zubaydah, Khalid Sheikh Mohammed, and Saif al-Adel. Faye Bowers, "Al Qaeda's Profile: Slimmer but Menacing," *Christian Science Monitor*, September 9, 2003.

79.   Rich, "Al Qaeda and the Radical Islamic Challenge to Western Strategy," 47.

80.   Dima Adamsky, "Jihadi Operational Art: The Coming Wave of Jihadi Strategic Studies," *Studies in Conflict and Terrorism* 33 (2010): 12.

81.   Thomas R. Mockatis, "Winning Hearts and Minds in the 'War on Terrorism,'" *Small Wars and Insurgencies* 14, no. 1 (Spring 2003): 26.

82.   Barry R. Schneider, "Al Qaeda's Modus Operandi: Anticipating Their Target Selection," in *The World's Most Threatening Terrorist Networks and Criminal Gangs*, ed. Michael T. Kindt, Jerrold Post, and Barry R. Schneider (New York: Palgrave Macmillan, 2009), 34. Regarding "franchises," see, for example, Alfred De Montesquiou, "Official: Al-Qaeda Like a Fast Food Franchise 'for Terrorism,'" *USA Today*, June 7, 2009.

83.   Author interview with Gunaratna, May 28, 2008.

84.   Michael Scheuer, "Al-Qaeda Doctrine: Training the Individual Warrior," *Terrorism Focus* 3, no. 12 (March 28, 2006), *www.jamestown.org/*.

85.   Scheuer, *Imperial Hubris*, 182, 212–13.

86.   Michael A. Cohen and Maria Figueroa Küpçü, "Congress and the 'YouTube War,'" in *Annual Editions Violence and Terrorism 08/09*, ed. Thomas J. Badey (New York: McGraw Hill, 2009), 123.

87.   Kevin Whitelaw, "Blown Away," *U.S. News and World Report*, June 19, 2006, 24.

88. Martin J. Muckian, "Structural Vulnerabilities of Networked Insurgencies: Adapting to the New Adversary," *Parameters*, Winter 2006–2007, 16–21.

89. Loretta Napoleoni, *Insurgent Iraq: Al Zarqawi and the New Generation* (New York: Seven Stories Press, 2005), 189.

90. Ahmed S. Hashim, *Insurgency and Counter-Insurgency in Iraq* (Ithaca, NY: Cornell University Press, 2006), 55, 208.

91. John Robb, *Brave New War: The Next Stage of Terrorism and the End of Globalization* (Hoboken, NJ: Wiley, 2007), 71–74.

92. As the noted insurgency authority Anthony Joes pointed out: "The anti-Soviet struggle in Afghanistan was also seriously fragmented, with vicious internecine fighting throughout the conflict. This was the case with the IRA and in Nazi-occupied Poland as well. And to a lesser degree Colombia has had the same phenomenon at different periods." Author interview with Joes, June 25, 2008.

93. Christopher C. Harmon, "The Myth of the Invincible Terrorist," *Policy Review*, no. 142 (April/May 2007): 72.

94. Hashim, *Insurgency and Counter-Insurgency in Iraq*, 201.

95. Hammes, *The Sling and the Stone*, 184–85.

96. For more on the US troop surge, see David Kilcullen, *The Accidental Guerrilla: Fighting Small Wars in the Midst of a Big One* (New York: Oxford University Press, 2009), and Thomas E. Ricks, *The Gamble: General David Petraeus and the American Military Adventure in Iraq, 2006–2008* (New York: Penguin Press, 2009).

97. Peter Bergen and Alec Reynolds, "Blowback Revisited: Today's Insurgents in Iraq Are Tomorrow's Terrorists," *Foreign Affairs*, November/December 2005, 4. Similarly a CIA assessment leaked in June 2005 warned that Iraqi and foreign fighters were developing a broad range of skills that could be applied in other theaters, thus possibly destabilizing other countries after the war. Napoleoni, *Insurgent Iraq*, 13.

98. Author interview with Pillar, June 8, 2008.

99. Author interview with Darren Mulloy, June 13, 2008.

100. David Horowitz, *Radical Islam and the American Left* (Washington, DC: Regnery, 2004).

101. George Michael, *The Enemy of My Enemy: The Alarming Convergence of Militant Islam and the Extreme Right* (Lawrence: University Press of Kansas, 2006).

102. Seymour M. Hersh, "Up in the Air: Where Is the Iraq War Headed Next?," *New Yorker*, December 2, 2005, 54.

103. Joseph Scolnick, "Issues, Yes, but Too Much to Lose to Pull Out Troops," *Coalfield Progress*, August 8, 2005, 11.

104. Hy S. Rothstein, *Afghanistan and the Troubled Future of Unconventional Warfare* (Annapolis, MD: Naval Institute Press, 2006), 13–27.

105. Jones, *In the Graveyard of Empires*.

106. Ibid., xxviii–xxx.

107. Peter Bergen, "Why Bin Laden Still Matters," *Newsweek*, September 4, 2010, *www.thedailybeast.com/newsweek/*.

108. Ibid.

109. Sabir Shah, "Top al-Qaeda Leaders Captured or Killed on Pakistani Soil," *The News*, May 3, 2011, *www.thenews.com.pk/*.

110. Rohan Gunaratna, "Al-Qaedastan: The Terrorist Sanctuary of the Afghan-Pakistan Border," Special Operation Report, No. 14 (Singapore: International Centre for Political Violence and Terrorism Research, n.d.), 12.

111. Olivier Roy, *Globalized Islam: The Search for a New Ummah* (New York: Columbia University Press, 2004), 18.

112. Robert S. Leiken, *Bearers of Global Jihad? Immigration and National Security after 9/11* (Washington, DC: Nixon Center, 2004), cited in Scott Atram, "The Moral Logic and Growth of Suicide Terrorism," in Badey, *Annual Editions Violence and Terrorism 07/08*, 29.

113. Timothy M. Savage, "Europe and Islam: Crescent Waxing, Cultures Clashing," *Washington Quarterly* 27, no. 3 (Summer 2004): 25–50; Rid and Hecker, *War 2.0*, 196.

114. Lorenzo Vidino, *Al Qaeda in Europe: The New Battleground of International Jihad.* (Amherst, NY: Prometheus Books, 2006), 17, 80–81.

115. Walter Laqueur, *The Last Days of Europe: Epitaph for an Old Continent* (New York: Thomas Dunne Books/St. Martin's Press, 2007), 96. According to a July 2007 US National Intelligence Estimate, the "internal Muslim terror threat is not likely to be as severe [in the U.S.] as it is in Europe." Quoted in Schneider, "Al Qaeda's Modus Operandi," 34.

116. Olivier, *Globalized Islam.*

117. Benedict Anderson coined the phrase "imagined communities." Benedict Anderson, *Imagined Communities: Reflections on the Origins and Spread of Nationalism* (London: Verso, 1991).

118. Sageman, *Understanding Terror Networks*, 163.

119. Sageman explains that the first wave of contemporary jihadists gathered around Osama bin Laden in the late 1980s during the Soviet-Afghan War. They formed the core of al Qaeda central. The second wave of Islamist terrorists trained in camps in Afghanistan during the 1990s. This wave ended with the allied military invasion of Afghanistan after 9/11. The third wave arose in response to the US invasion of Iraq. Marc Sageman, *Leaderless Jihad: Terror Networks in the Twenty-First Century* (Philadelphia: University of Pennsylvania Press, 2008), 48–49.

120. Ibid., 65–66.

121. Sageman, *Understanding Terror Networks*, 151.

122. J. M. Berger, *Jihad Joe: Americans Who Go to War in the Name of Islam* (Washington, DC: Potomac Books, 2011), 204–7.

123. Lorenzo Vidino, "Homegrown Jihadist Terrorism in the United States: A New and Occasional Phenomenon?," *Studies in Conflict and Terrorism* 32 (2009): 11–12.

124. Sageman, *Leaderless Jihad*, 108.

125. Sageman's database contains information on five hundred jihadist terrorists. "The Future of Terrorism," *Discover*, July 2006, 36.

126. Sageman, *Understanding Terror Networks.*

127. Ibid., 135, 155.

128. Sageman, *Leaderless Jihad*, 87.

129. Marc Sageman, "Islam and Al Qaeda," in *Root Causes of Suicide Terrorism: The Globalization of Martyrdom*, ed. Ami Pedazhur (London: Routledge, 2006), 129.

130. Atram, "The Moral Logic and Growth of Suicide Terrorism," 29.

131. Hanna Rogan, "Abu Reuter and the E-jihad: Virtual Battlefronts from Iraq to the Horn of Africa," *Georgetown Journal of International Affairs*, Summer/Fall 2007, 89.

132. Fareed Zakaria, *The Post-American World* (New York: Norton, 2008), 13.

133. As Rohan Gunaratna found, "in the twelve-month period ending December 2007, al Qaeda produced a cassette, sermon, or video every three days." Gunaratna, "Al-Qaedastan: The Sanctuary of the Afghan-Pakistan Border," 12. In the six years following 9/11, Osama bin Laden appeared in more than twenty videos and audiotapes. His chief lieutenant, Ayman al-Zawahiri, appeared in more than forty such productions during that period. Brian Michael Jenkins, *Will Terrorists Go Nuclear?* (Amherst, NY: Prometheus Books, 2008), 247.

134. Author's interview with Rohan Gunaratna, May 28, 2008. According to a study of al Qaeda's media outreach efforts, important themes in the pronouncements of bin Laden and Zawahiri, in descending order of frequency, include the call to jihad, the clash of civilizations, "apostate" Muslim leaders who betray Islam, the US-Israel connection, the call for Muslim unity, the "weakening" of the United States, and the "theft" of Muslim oil. Carl J. Ciovacco, "The Contours of Al Qaeda's Media Strategy," *Studies in Conflict and Terrorism* 32 (2009): 858.

135. Rogan, "Abu Reuter and the E-jihad."

136. Michael Moss and Souad Mekhennet, "An Internet Jihad Aims at U.S. Viewers," *New York Times*, October 15, 2007.

137. Nadya Labi, "Jihad 2.0," *Atlantic Monthly*, July/August 2006, 102–8.

138. Craig Whitlock, "Al-Qaeda's Growing Online Offensive," *Washington Post*, June 24, 2008.

139. Although YouTube pulled some videos, others Lieberman had requested to be taken off were not removed, because they were not violent or did not qualify as "hate speech." Ibid.

140. Brynjar Lia, "Jihadi Web Media Production: Characteristics, Trends, and Future Implications," February 2007, *www.mil.no/multimedia/archive/00092/Jihadi_Web_Media_Pro_92100a.pdf*.

141. Gabriel Weimann, *Terror on the Internet: The New Arena, the New Challenges* (Washington, DC: United States Institute of Peace, 2006), 15.

142. Moss and Mekhennet, "An Internet Jihad Aims at U.S. Viewers."

143. Lia, "Jihadi Web Media Production."

144. Whitlock, "Al-Qaeda's Growing Online Offensive."

145. Zawahiri patiently responded to about one-fifth of the queries, some of which were even hostile postings condemning al Qaeda for harming innocent people and perverting Islam. Ibid.

146. Rid and Hecker, *War 2.0*, 204.

147. Brynjar Lia, "Al-Qaeda Online: Understanding Jihadist Internet Infrastructure," *Jane's Intelligence Review*, January 1, 2006, *www.mil.no/multimedia/archive/00075/Al-Qaeda_online__und_75416a.pdf*.

148. Jihadist website categories identified by Lia include first the official websites of jihadist groups. Second are distributors—websites that copy and upload material from multiple sites and direct the viewers to the most important ones. Finally, "producers" reformat and refashion raw material from the official websites into a sleeker and more attractive product. Ibid.

149. Bruce Hoffmann, introduction to Gabriel Weimann, *Terror on the Internet: The New Arena, the New Challenges* (Washington, DC: United States Institute of Peace, 2006), ix.

150. Lia, "Al-Qaeda Online."

151. Scheuer, *Imperial Hubris*, 81–82.

152. Anne Stenersen, "The Internet: A Virtual Training Camp," *Terrorism and Political Violence* 20, no. 2 (2008): 215–33.

153. Brynjar Lia, "Doctrines for Jihadi Terrorist Training," *Terrorism and Political Violence* 20, no. 4 (2008): 518–42. For more on Muqrin, see Cigar, *Al-Qa'ida's Doctrine of Insurgency*. For more on Naji, see Martin Hart, "Al Qaeda: Refining a Failing Strategy," *Joint Forces Quarterly*, no. 51 (4th Quarter 2008): 118–20.

154. Gerges, *The Far Enemy*, 3.

155. Adam Elkus, "Future War: The War on Terror after Iraq," *Athena Intelligence Journal* 2, no. 1 (2007): 20.

156. Bruce Hoffman, "Responding to Terrorism across the Technological Spectrum," *Terrorism and Political Violence* 6, no. 3 (Autumn 1994): 365–89.

157. John Arquilla and David Ronfeldt, "Afterword (September 2001): The Sharpening Fight for the Future," in *Networks and Netwars: The Future of Terror, Crime, and Militancy* (Santa Monica, CA: Rand, 2001), 367.

158. Zakaria, *The Post-American World*, 245.

159. On the morning of March 11, 2004, between 7:37 and 7:42 a.m., ten bombs exploded on commuter trains from the eastern suburbs of Madrid to the Spanish capital city, killing 191 persons and injuring more than fifteen hundred. Those involved in the attacks were Moroccan Islamists with a variety of affiliations, including local terrorist groups, remnants of the pre-9/11 al Qaeda network operating in Europe, jihadists linked to the late Abu Musab al-Zarqawi's network, and drug traffickers with a newly acquired sympathy for

radical Islam—an amalgamation that Lorenzo Vidino called "the new face of al Qaeda in Europe." The seven Maghreb Muslims who carried out the Madrid attacks were all part of a community of activists who were poorly integrated in Spanish society and held together by an extremist ideology. Some observers have characterized the Madrid bombings as an example of fifth-generation warfare. A small, networked terrorist group in one day was able to influence an election that brought a new Spanish government into office. The cell also reflected the increasing overlap between terrorism and crime, as the group obtained much of its finances from selling drugs. Vidino, *Al Qaeda in Europe*; Rogelio Alonso and Fernando Reinares, "Maghreb Immigrants Becoming Suicide Terrorists: A Case Study of Religious Radicalization Processes in Spain," in Pedazhur, *Root Causes of Suicide Terrorism*, 191; and "The Architect and Fifth Generation Warfare," *Strategist*, June 4, 2006, *www.thestrategist.org/archives/2006/06/the_architect_o.html*.

160. Zakaria, *The Post-American World*, 254.

161. Lorenzo Vidino, "Homegrown Jihadist Terrorism in the United States: A New and Occasional Phenomenon?," *Studies in Conflict and Terrorism* 32 (2009): 3.

162. Scheuer, *Imperial Hubris*, 83.

163. Paul Cruikshank and Mohanad Hage Ali, "Abu Musab Al Suri: Architect of the New Al Qaeda," *Studies in Conflict and Terrorism* 30, no. 1 (2007): 9.

164. Sageman, *Leaderless Jihad*.

165. Jenkins, *Will Terrorists Go Nuclear?*, 127–29.

166. "Al-Qaeda on Alleged Fort Hood Killer: 'Ideal Role Model,'" *USA Today*, March 7, 2010.

167. "American Al Qaeda Adam Gadahn's Chilling Video Shows How the Gun Lobby Hampers the War on Terror," *Daily News* (New York), June 4, 2011.

168. Bergen, "Why Bin Laden Still Matters."

169. For more on Gadahn, see George Michael, "Adam Gadahn and Al Qaeda's Internet Strategy," *Middle East Policy* 16, no. 3 (Fall 2009): 135–52.

170. Aamer Madhani, "Cleric al-Awlaki Dubbed 'bin Laden of the Internet,'" *USA Today*, August 25, 2010.

171. Mark Mazzetti, Eric Schmitt, and Robert F. Worth, "Two-Year Manhunt Led to Killing of Awlaki in Yemen," *New York Times*, September 30, 2011; Associated Press, "Al-Awlaki's Son among Al Qaeda Militants Killed in Yemen Air Strike," October 15, 2011.

172. Richard Spencer, "Al-Qaeda Magazine Teaches How to Kill Americans," *Telegraph* (UK), October 12, 2010; Shaun Waterman, "Jihad Abroad Discouraged," *Washington Times*, October 13, 2010.

173. Brynjar Lia, *Architect of Global Jihad: The Life of Al-Qaida Strategist Abu Mus'ad al-Suri* (New York: Columbia University Press, 2008), 1–2.

174. "The Brains behind the Bombs," *Economist*, November 3, 2007, 106.

175. Because of his light hair, Suri occasionally went by the alias "El Rubio" (Spanish for "the blond"). Lia, *Architect of Global Jihad*, 2.

176. Ibid., 2–4.

177. Adam Shatz, "Laptop Jihadi," *London Review of Books*, March 20, 2008, 14.

178. Lia, *Architect of Global Jihad*, 33.

179. Ibid., 35–37.

180. Michael V. Samarov, "Abu Musab al-Suri's Lessons Learned," unpublished paper, United States Marine Corps Command and Staff College, n.d., 2.

181. Lia, *Architect of Global Jihad*, 39–43, 88.

182. Ibid., 51, 81.

183. Shatz, "Laptop Jihadi," 15.

184. Lia, *Architect of Global Jihad*, 53, 54, 61, 102–4.

185. Ibid., 65, 89, 259–69.

186. Paul Cruickshank and Mohanad Hage Ali, "Abu Musab al Suri: Architect of the New Al Qaeda," *Studies in Conflict and Terrorism* 30, no. 1 (2007): 7.

187. Lia, *Architect of Global Jihad*, 279.

188. Cruickshank and Ali, "Abu Musab al Suri," 4.

189. Lia, *Architect of Global Jihad*, 158.

190. Evan Kohlmann, "Abu Musab al-Suri and His Plan for the Destruction of America: 'Dirty Bombs for a Dirty Nation,'" *Global Terroralert*, July 11, 2005, *www.globalterroralert.com/pdf/0705/abumusabalsuri.pdf*.

191. Lia, *Architect of Global Jihad*, 6, 30, 165–70, 199.

192. Henry Schuster, "The Mastermind," CNN, March 9, 2006.

193. Shatz, "Laptop Jihadi," 15.

194. Lia, *Architect of Global Jihad*, 233.

195. Ibid., 9.

196. Shatz, "Laptop Jihadi," 15.

197. Lia, *Architect of Global Jihad*, 27.

198. Brynjar Lia, "Al-Qaida's Appeal: Understandings Its Unique Selling Points," lecture at the "Treating Terrorism" conference, Dubai, United Arab Emirates, March 17–18, 2008.

199. Shatz, "Laptop Jihadi," 17.

200. Lia, *Architect of Global Jihad*, 231–32, 237–40.

201. Ibid., 281–86.

202. Ibid., 6–7, 318.

203. Elkus, "Future War," 19.

204. Lia, *Architect of Global Jihad*, 422.

205. Schneider, "Al Qaeda's Modus Operandi," 34.

206. Lia, *Architect of Global Jihad*, 419–22.

207. Ibid., 367–70, 391–93.

208. Ibid., 471–72.

209. Samarov, "Abu Musa al-Suri's Lessons Learned," 3, 5–10.

210. Rid and Hecker, *War 2.0*, 193.

211. Lia, *Architect of Global Jihad*.

212. Ibid., 306–7, 311–12.

213. Ibid., 313–14.

214. Kohlmann, "Abu Musab al-Suri and His Plan for the Destruction of America."

215. Lia, *Architect of Global Jihad*, 315, 415–16.

216. Cruickshank and Ali, "Abu Musab al Suri," 9, 10.

217. Lia, *Architect of Global Jihad*, 99, 358–59.

218. Gerges, *The Far Enemy*, 251.

219. Lia, *Architect of Global Jihad*, 395–97, 399–400, 461.

220. Ibid., 1, 20, 26.

221. Brynjar Lia, "Doctrines for Jihadi Terrorist Training," *Terrorism and Political Violence* 20, no. 4 (2008): 536.

222. Shaun Waterman, "Jihad Abroad Discouraged," *Washington Times*, October 13, 2010.

223. A chief ideologist in this regard was the Egyptian Muhammad Faraj, whose tract *The Neglected Duty* argued that any means necessary were justified in order to overthrow apostate regimes. Faraj was affiliated with Jama At al-Jihad and played an important role in the assassination of the Egyptian president Anwar Sadat. For more on Faraj, see Laqueur, *No End to War*, 37, and Sageman, *Understanding Terror Networks*, 17–18.

224. Gerges, *The Far Enemy*, 57.

225. See Walid Phares, *The Confrontation: Winning the War against Future Jihad* (New York: Palgrave Macmillan, 2008).

226. Christopher Henzel, "The Origins of al Qaeda's Ideology: Implications for US Strategy," *Parameters*, Spring 2005, 76–77.

227. Donald J. Reed, "Beyond the War on Terror: Into the Fifth Generation of War and Conflict," *Studies in Conflict and Terrorism* 31 (2008): 688.

228. Paul Kennedy recognized a pattern throughout the history of empires expanding beyond their capacity to maintain hegemony. At first an imperial domain may buttress an empire, but eventually the costs outweigh the benefits, leading to decline and disintegration. Kennedy, *The Rise and Fall of the Great Powers: Economic Change and Military Conflict from 1500 to 2000* (New York: Vintage Books, 1989).

229. This document was analyzed by the Norwegian Defense Research Establishment (FFI). See "FFI Explains al-Qaida Document, *Forsvarets forskningsinstitutt,* March 19, 2004.

230. Jeffrey Kaplan, *Terrorist Groups and the New Tribalism: Terrorism's Fifth Wave* (London: Routledge, 2010), 21–22.

231. Chief among those who hold this view is Rohan Gunaratna, arguably the most authoritative scholar on al Qaeda. He believes that al Qaeda never expected the United States to place ground troops in Afghanistan. Al Qaeda viewed the United States in light of previous attacks in Aden, Somalia, Lebanon, and so on, and therefore did not believe a ground response would come after 9/11. Author interview with Gunaratna, January 17, 2004. Marc Sageman suggests this position as well. Sageman, *Understanding Terror Networks,* 51. Thomas Hammes argues that al Qaeda committed a fundamental strategic error with the 9/11 attacks, which sent the message that it was attacking the United States in its homeland rather than in some faraway land in an act intended to compel the United States to leave the Middle East. Hammes, *The Sling and the Stone,* 148–49.

232. Walter Laqueur, *The Age of Terrorism* (Boston: Little, Brown, 1987), 321. Jonathan Wilkenfeld found that roughly half of all international crises in the post–Cold War era were precipitated by a violent act. Wilkenfeld, "Unstable States and International Crises," in *Peace and Conflict 2008,* ed. J. Joseph Hewitt, Jonathan Wilkenfeld, and Ted Robert Gurr (Boulder, CO: Paradigm Publishers, 2008), 69.

233. Decision Support Systems, *Al-Qaida's Endgame? A Strategic Scenario Analysis* (Decision Support Systems, 2001), *getpdf.info/Al-Qaida's-Endgame:-A-Strategic-Scenario-Analysis.*

234. Sean P. Gorman, *Networks, Security and Complexity: The Role of Public Policy in Critical Infrastructure Protection* (Cheltenham, UK: Edward Elgar, 2005), 21.

235. Reed, "Beyond the War on Terror," 711.

236. Amy Belasco, *The Cost of Iraq, Afghanistan, and Other Global War on Terror Operations since 9/11* (Washington, DC: Congressional Research Office, 2010).

237. Walid Phares, "Bin Laden: 'US Must Eliminate the Israel Lobby to End War,'" Counterterrorism Blog, September 14, 2009, *counterterrorismblog.org/,* and Daveed Gartenstein-Ross, "New OBL-Tape: Appeasement Talk and Cited Westerners," *Threat Matrix,* September 14, 2009, *longwarjournal.org/threat-matrix/.* John Perkins's book *Confessions of an Economic Hit Man* decried American economic imperialism. In their book *The Israel Lobby,* Mearsheimer and Walt asserted that the interest groups lobbying on behalf of Israel have subverted foreign policy in the Middle East to the detriment of US national interests.

238. To that end, al Qaeda employs four tactics: (1) provocation: by committing atrocities the radical Salafists cause their opponents to overreact; (2) intimidation: by killing collaborators, for example, the Salafists seek to prevent local populations from cooperating with government or coalition forces; (3) protraction: they seek to prolong the conflict so that it exhausts their opponents' resources and political will to continue the counterinsurgency campaign; (4) exhaustion: they seek to impose high costs on opponent governments, and by doing so to convince them that continuing the war is not worth the cost. Kilcullen, *The Accidental Guerrilla.*

239. Ibid.

240. Walter Laqueur, "The Terrorism to Come," in Badey, *Annual Editions Violence and Terrorism 07/08,* 213.

241. Scheuer, *Imperial Hubris,* 70.

242. Gerges, *The Far Enemy,* 226–49.

243. Ibid., 247, 249.

244. Hoffman conceptualizes four dimensions of the Qaeda movement. The first category—al Qaeda central—comprises the core leadership and remains in or near the Afghanistan-Pakistan border region. The second category—affiliates—includes groups such as al Qaeda in Mesopotamia and the Islamic Movement of Uzbekistan. The third category—locals—consists of dispersed cells of Qaeda adherents who have had some connection with al Qaeda, no matter how tenuous or brief. Examples include Ahmed Ressam, who was a planner of the year 2000 plot and one of four British Muslims responsible for the July 7, 2005, bombings of mass transit targets in London. The fourth category—the al Qaeda network—consists of homegrown Islamic radicals as well as converts who have no direct connection to the parent organization, but nevertheless gravitate toward each other to plan and mount terrorist attacks in solidarity with al Qaeda's global agenda. Bruce Hoffman, "From the War on Terror to Global Counterinsurgency," in Badey, *Annual Editions Violence and Terrorism 08/09*, 210.
245. Hoffman, "From the War on Terror to Global Counterinsurgency," 208, 212.
246. Author interview with Pipes, June 9, 2008.
247. De Montesquiou, "Official: Al-Qaeda Like a Fast Food Franchise 'for Terrorism.'"
248. Rita Katz and Josh Devon, "Five Years after 9/11, Al-Qaeda Remains the Vanguard of the Jihadist Movement," Site Institute, October 6, 2006.
249. Lia, "Al-Qaida's Appeal," 2–6.
250. Author interview with Luttwak, June 17, 2009.
251. Vidino, *Al Qaeda in Europe*, 79.

Conclusion

1. Matthew J. Morgan, "An Evolving View of Warfare: War and Peace and the American Military Profession," *Small Wars and Insurgencies* 16, no. 2 (June 2005): 148.
2. J. Joseph Hewitt, "Unpacking Global Trends in Violent Conflict, 1946-2005," in *Peace and Conflict 2008*, ed. J. Joseph Hewitt, Jonathan Wilkenfeld, and Ted Robert Gurr (Boulder, CO: Paradigm Publishers, 2008), 107–18.
3. Rupert Smith, *The Utility of Force: The Art of War in the Modern World* (New York: Knopf, 2007), xiii, 19.
4. The Center for International Development and Conflict Management at the University of Maryland reported that in 2005 there were twenty-five active conflicts in the world, the highest annual total since 2001. However, the long-term trend since the end of the Cold War has been a decline. J. Joseph Hewitt, "Trends in Global Conflict, 1946–2005," in Hewitt, Wilkenfeld, and Gurr, *Peace and Conflict 2008*, 21–26. Similarly, in his study of 164 armed conflicts that took place from 1945 to 1995, K. J. Holsti found that only 38 were of the state-state variety. K. J. Holsti, *The State, War, and the State of War* (Cambridge: Cambridge University Press, 1996), 6, cited in Richard H. Shultz Jr. and Andrea J. Dew, *Insurgents, Terrorists, and Militias: The Warriors of Contemporary Combat* (New York: Columbia University Press, 2006), 32.
5. Niall Ferguson, "Clashing Civilizations or Mad Mullahs: The United States between Informal and Formal Empire," in Strobe Talbott and Nayan Chanda, *The Age of Terror: America and the World after September 11* (New York: Basic Books, 2001), 133–34.
6. What accounts for these high figures? Paul Huth and Benjamin Valentino postulate that states often resort to genocidal policies in order to deprive guerrillas of a population to rely on for support, including food, shelter, supplies, and intelligence, as well as a form of "human camouflage" into which they can disappear for protection. If a government can effectively quell a guerrilla rebellion, it usually does not resort to genocide. Rather, it will first employ less violent strategies. In the twentieth century, guerrilla warfare has proven to be highly effective in forcing regime change. States that face a well-organized guerrilla movement with strong support from the people find they have few options for meeting this

threat and are more likely to respond with massive violence. Democracies are less likely to succumb to this approach than autocratic regimes. Paul Huth and Benjamin Valentino, "Mass Killings of Civilians in Time of War, 1945–2000," in Hewitt, Wilkenfeld, and Gurr, *Peace and Conflict 2008*, 79–92.

7.   Thomas X. Hammes, *The Sling and the Stone: On War in the 21st Century* (St. Paul, MN: Zenith Press, 2004), 37.

8.   Chet Richards, *Neither Shall the Sword: Conflict in the Years Ahead* (Washington, DC: Center for Defense Information, 2005), 22–24.

9.   T. X. Hammes, "Fourth Generation Warfare Evolves, Fifth Emerges," *Military Review*, May/June 2007, 14–23.

10. Donald J. Reed, "Beyond the War on Terror: Into the Fifth Generation of War and Conflict," *Studies in Conflict and Terrorism* 31 (2008): 697.

11. William S. Lind, "Fifth Generation Warfare?," Military.com, February 3, 2004, *www.military.com/*.

12. "Translator's Note," in Qiao Liang and Wang Xiangsui, *Unrestricted Warfare: China's Master Plan to Destroy America* (Panama City: Pan American, 2002), xvii.

13. Anthony Lake, *Six Nightmares: Real Threats in a Dangerous World and How America Can Meet Them* (New York: Little, Brown, 2000), 182.

14. Qiao and Wang, *Unrestricted Warfare*, 13, 14, 47; *2010 World Almanac and Book of Facts* (New York: World Almanac, 2009), 176.

15. Qiao and Wang, *Unrestricted Warfare*, xxi, 39, 114.

16. Ibid., 32.

17. United Nations, *secint24.un.org/en/members/growth.shtml*.

18. Barnett's "functioning core" consists of North America, eastern and western Europe (including Russia), Japan, China, India, Australia, New Zealand, South Africa, Argentina, Brazil, and Chile—with a combined population of roughly four billion out of a global population of over six billion in 2004. Thomas P. M. Barnett, *The Pentagon's New Map: War and Peace in the Twenty-First Century* (New York: G. P. Putnam's Sons, 2004), 131–32.

19. Ibid., 161–66.

20. Thomas P. M. Barnett, *Great Powers: America and the World after Bush* (New York: G. P. Putnam's Sons, 2009), 48. Similarly, Fareed Zakaria pointed out that when countries reach a per capita income in the range of $5,000 to $10,000, they usually develop into pluralist democracies and mass violence disappears. Once they attain that benchmark, it is almost certain that they will not slide back toward authoritarianism. Fareed Zakaria, *The Post-American World* (New York: Norton, 2008), 100–101.

21. Barnett, *The Pentagon's New Map*, 56, 217–24.

22. Thomas P. M. Barnett, *Blueprint for Action: A Future Worth Creating* (New York: Berkley Books, 2005), 302.

23. J. Joseph Hewitt, "Peace and Conflict Instability Ledger: Ranking States on Future Risks," in Hewitt, Wilkenfeld, and Gurr, *Peace and Conflict 2008*, 8.

24. Jonathan Wilkenfeld, "Unstable States and International Crises," in Hewitt, Wilkenfeld, and Gurr, *Peace and Conflict 2008*, 70.

25. Barnett, *The Pentagon's New Map*, 88. Rather than assuming complete control over a failed state, terrorists are more likely to acquire control over areas where they will be left alone. Governments of weak or failed states may also issue legitimate passports that allow terrorists to travel worldwide (and identification documents that allow them to disguise themselves). Ray Takeyh and Nikolas Gvosdev, "Do Terrorist Networks Need a Home?," *Washington Quarterly* 25 (Summer 2002).

26. Author interview with Barnett, May 20, 2008.

27. Barnett, *The Pentagon's New Map*, 29.

28. Barnett, *Great Powers*, 295. Thomas Friedman first advanced the notion of the "super-

empowered individual." See Thomas Friedman, *The Lexus and the Olive Tree: Understanding Globalization* (New York: Anchor, 2000).

29. Barnett, *The Pentagon's New Map*, 94.

30. Barnett, *Great Powers*, 305.

31. Thomas Rid and Marc Hecker, *War 2.0: Irregular Warfare in the Information Age* (Westport, CT: Praeger Security International, 2009), 137.

32. In particular, Barnett argues that it is imperative to include new market economies, mainly China, India, and Brazil, and also those countries that at times have an adversarial relationship with the United States, such as Russia and Iran. Barnett, *Great Powers*.

33. Although some observers question the sustainability of this trend, defense spending accounts for only about 3.2 percent of US Gross Domestic Product. Moreover, by historic standards, this figure is quite low—during the Cold War, the United States some years spent up to four times that much on defense. Lake, *Six Nightmares*, 181.

34. Peter Almond, "Beware: The New Goths Are Coming," *Times* (UK), June 11, 2006.

35. Walter Laqueur, *The Last Days of Europe: Epitaph for an Old Continent* (New York: Thomas Dunne Books/St. Martin's Press, 2007).

36. Tom Blankley, *The West's Last Chance: Will We Win the Clash of Civilizations?* (Washington, DC: Regnery, 2005), 21.

37. Tom Whitehead, "Labour Wanted Mass Immigration to Make UK More Multicultural, Says Former Adviser," *Telegraph* (UK), October 23, 2008. As Tom Blankley argues, Hitler's cult of Aryan superiority made subsequent claims of racial and cultural pride anathema in Europe. The destruction that the world wars wrought discredited nationalism, which was deemed to be dangerous and to lead to catastrophe. Blankley says this malaise has made the West less able to confront the challenge posed by militant Islam, which enjoys a growing cultural and religious assertiveness. Had Europe faced the Islamic threat earlier in the twentieth century, it could have countered it. However, lacking civilizational self-confidence, the continent puts up only a feeble defense. Blankley, *The West's Last Chance*.

38. Robert Kaplan, "The Coming Anarchy," *Atlantic Monthly*, February 1994, *www.theatlantic.com/politics.foreign/anarchy.htm/*.

39. Samuel Huntington, "The Hispanic Challenge," *Foreign Policy*, March/April 2004, 1.

40. Samuel Huntington, *Who Are We? The Challenges to America's National Identity* (New York: Simon and Schuster, 2004), 143, 310–13.

41. See, for example, Patrick J. Buchanan, *State of Emergency: The Third World Invasion and Conquest of America* (New York: Thomas Dunne Books, 2006).

42. Patrick J. Buchanan, *Death of the West: How Dying Populations and Immigrant Invasions Imperil Our Country and Civilization* (New York: Thomas Dunne Books, 2002).

43. Patrick J. Buchanan, *Day of Reckoning: How Hubris, Ideology, and Greed Are Tearing America Apart* (New York: Thomas Dunne Books, 2007), 143.

44. Buchanan, *State of Emergency*, 166.

45. These transnational elites, according to Huntington, make up less than 4 percent of the American people. Buchanan, *Day of Reckoning*, 162.

46. Donald Horowitz, *Ethnic Groups in Conflict* (Berkeley: University of California Press, 1985).

47. A competing view of ethnic conflict posits that opportunistic leaders in divided societies employ violence and divisive rhetoric to mobilize communities for the leaders' self-aggrandizement. Internal wars stem, the argument goes, not so much from inherent ethnic animosities as from elite conflicts over the distribution of resources. Einar Braathen, Morten Boas, and Gjermund Saether, *Ethnicity Kills?* (New York: St. Martin's Press, 2000), 8, cited in Richard H. Shultz Jr. and Andrea J. Dew, *Insurgents, Terrorists, and Militias: The Warriors of Contemporary Combat* (New York: Columbia University Press, 2006), 32–33. Counterintuitively, Paul Collier found that the more society is fractionalized into

different ethnic and religious groups, the less likely there will be conflict between these groups and the state. This is because no group with a sense of unity and common identity is large enough to mobilize the population to defeat the government, which can appeal to nationalism to rally its troops and defeat rebels. According to Collier a collective-action problem arises from three factors: (1) there is a human tendency to seek a free ride and let others do the fighting; (2) rebel groups usually start out very small—people are reluctant to join, from fear of punishment, until the groups become large enough that they seem to have a good chance of success; (3) people may not trust rebel leaders, and they may doubt these leaders will follow through on promises once they attain power. These factors pose formidable obstacles to rebellions based solely on grievance. Overcoming these obstacles requires building social capital. However, this is difficult to achieve in an ethnically and religiously fragmented society, Collier points out, since social capital building does not usually span ethnic and religious divides. Therefore, it is much more difficult to mobilize people in large numbers in heterogeneous societies than in homogeneous societies. Paul Collier, "Doing Well out of War: An Economic Perspective," in *Economic Agendas in Civil Wars, Greed, and Grievance*, ed. Mats Berdal and David M. Malone (Boulder, CO: Lynne Rienner, 2000), 91–111.

48. Martin van Creveld, *The Transformation of War* (New York: Free Press, 1991), ix, 5, 195–97.

49. Ibid., 198, 202–3, 205–12.

50. This long-term trend of urbanization could also presage an increase in terrorism. As Walter Laqueur observed, traditionally cities are inhabited by "dangerous classes," from which the ranks of terrorists have emerged. Walter Laqueur, *The New Terrorism: Fanaticism and the Arms of Mass Destruction* (New York: Oxford University Press, 1999), 250.

51. Richard J. Norton, "Feral Cities," *Naval War College Review* 56, no. 4 (Autumn 2003): 97–106.

52. Van Creveld, *The Transformation of War*, 60, 63, 225.

53. Author interview with van Creveld, May 28, 2008.

54. William S. Lind, John F. Schmitt, and Gary I. Wilson, "Islam vs. Western Civilization," *Marine Corps Gazette*, December 1994. Lind founded the Free Congress Foundation for Cultural Conservatism. He is highly critical of the so-called Frankfurt School, a group of mostly Jewish academics who fled Germany in the 1930s and taught at Columbia University.

55. William S. Lind, "Not Fourth Generation War," *On War*, no. 225 (July 11, 2007).

56. Walid Phares, *Future Jihad: Terrorist Strategies against America* (New York: Palgrave Macmillan, 2005), 119, 169, 229–34.

57. Walid Phares, *The Confrontation: Winning the War against Future Jihad* (New York: Palgrave Macmillan, 2008), 151.

58. Michael Moss and Souad Mekhennet, "An Internet Jihad Aims at U.S. Viewers," *New York Times*, October 15, 2007.

59. "Al-Qaeda No. 2 Mocks American 'failure,'" *USA Today*, May 5, 2007, and Raymond Ibrahim, "Seeking Sympathy from the Infidel: Zawahiri Invokes the Language of Social Justice," *National Review Online*, May 21, 2007, *www.nationalreview.com/*.

60. For example, according to Osama bin Laden, al Qaeda spent $500,000 on the 9/11 attacks, which he also claimed resulted in a $500 billion loss for the United States. Likewise, he saw the war in Iraq as an opportunity to bleed the United States to the point of bankruptcy. Barry R. Schneider, "Al Qaeda's Modus Operandi: Anticipating Their Target Selection," in Michael T. Kindt, Jerrold Post, and Barry R. Schneider, *The World's Most Threatening Terrorist Networks and Criminal Gangs* (New York: Palgrave Macmillan, 2009), 36–38.

61. Michael Scheuer, *Imperial Hubris: Why the West Is Losing the War on Terror* (Washington, DC: Brassey's, 2004), 101.

62. Author interview with Hewitt, July 7, 2008.

63. Mohammed Abbas, "Analysis: Norway Massacre Exposes Incendiary Immigration Issue," Reuters, July 24, 2011; Eben Harrell, "Norway Attacks: How a Once Moderate Region Became a Haven for the Far Rights," *Time*, June 25, 2011, *www.time.com/*.

64. Author interview with Laird Wilcox, July 27, 2009. Wilcox is an acute observer of political extremism in the United States. See John George and Laird Wilcox, *Nazis, Communists, Klansmen, and Others on the Fringe* (Buffalo: Prometheus Books, 1992).

65. According to a 2010 *USA Today*–Gallup poll, 28 percent of Americans believe that President Barack Obama should have the most influence on government policy, while 27 percent stated that the Tea Party standard bearers should. Susan Page, "Poll: Tea Party Support Grows; USA Divided," *USA Today*, November 22, 2010, *www.usatoday.com/*.

66. Barnett, *Blueprint for Action*, 21, 109–10, 119.

67. For example, in 1991 there were over seven hundred deaths in Los Angeles related to inter-gang violence. Jesse Katz, "Gang Killings in LA County Top a Record of 700," *Los Angeles Times*, December 8, 1991.

68. Jesse Walker, "The Jihad That Failed: 'Leaderless Resistance' Barely Dents the U.S.A.," *Reason.com*, June 19, 2006, *www.reason.com/news/show/116273.html*.

69. Simson L. Garfinkel, "Leaderless Resistance Today" *First Monday* 8, no. 3 (2003), *firstmonday.org/issues/issue8_3/garfinkel/index.html*; John Mueller, "Is There Still a Terrorist Threat? The Myth of the Omnipresent Enemy," *Foreign Affairs*, September/October 2006, 2–8.

70. Fred Burton and Scott Stewart, "The 'Lone Wolf' Disconnect," STRATFOR, January 30, 2008, *www.stratfor.com/weekly/lone_wolf_disconnect*.

71. As Gartenstein-Ross explains: "The second problem with that view [leaderless resistance] is that some of the successful terrorist attacks popularly described as 'leaderless resistance' are not in fact unambiguous examples of the phenomenon. For example, the 7/7 attacks in Britain [July 7, 2005] are generally described as the work of an autonomous and self-actuating cell—but are they really? At least two of the 7/7 bombers, Mohammad Sidique Khan and Shehzad Tanweer, trained in Pakistan. Al Qaeda's senior leaders had enough foreknowledge of 7/7 to send footage of Khan and Tanweer to al Jazeera after the attacks. Haroon Rashid Aswat, who helped set up a Qaeda training camp in Oregon, had telephoned the London bombers hours before the 7/7 attacks. Underscoring this point, al Jazeera aired a new video from Qaeda deputy Ayman al-Zawahiri on the first anniversary of the bombings, claiming that Khan and Tanweer had visited–a Qaeda camp in Pakistan 'seeking martyrdom.' I'm not saying that the 7/7 attacks were ordered by al Qaeda's senior leadership. Rather, I'm pointing out the presence of international networks in the attacks, such that describing them as leaderless resistance is a bit off the mark.

"The third problem is that we can now see the return of terrorist plots that are connected to networks. Most recently, the November 2008 Mumbai attacks have been connected to Lashkar-e-Taiba. Multiple intelligence agencies have linked operational command for the August 2006 transatlantic air plot—which Homeland Security Secretary Michael Chertoff said would have killed thousands—to top Qaeda leaders in Pakistan. Beyond that, British terrorists trained in Pakistan for at least half a dozen plots since 2003, while other European countries have likewise seen their extremists travel there for training—a trend dramatically illustrated by the plots disrupted on the same day in Germany and Denmark in September 2007.

"Fourth, terrorists who are self-financed, self-trained, and unconnected to international networks have a spottier record. For example, the 'Fort Dix Six' had terrible operational security, taking a video of themselves—firing weapons and yelling in a foreign tongue—to Circuit City to be transferred to DVD. Localized cells recognize that they need to link up with international networks. The Miami cell that allegedly wanted to destroy Chicago's Sears Tower reached out to al Qaeda because they doubted they could succeed on their own. According to the indictment in the June 2007 JFK airport plot, members of the conspiracy wanted to 'present the plan to contacts overseas who may be interested in purchasing or funding it.' Homegrown cells without links to outside networks have not come close to matching the success of al Qaeda and its affiliates." Author interview with Gartenstein-Ross, December 2, 2008.

72. David Ignatius, "The Fading Jihadists," *Washington Post*, February 28, 2008.

73. Marc Sageman, *Understanding Terror Networks* (Philadelphia: University of Pennsylvania Press, 2004), vii.

74. Rid and Hecker, *War 2.0*, 217.

75. J. M. Berger, *Jihad Joe: Americans Who Go to War in the Name of Islam* (Washington, DC: Potomac Books, 2011), 209.

76. Marc Sageman, *Leaderless Jihad: Terror Networks in the Twenty-First Century* (Philadelphia, PA: University of Pennsylvania Press, 2008).

77. This is according to Brian Fishman of the Combating Terrorism Center at the US Military Academy. Shaun Waterman, "Jihad Abroad Discouraged," *Washington Times*, October 13, 2010.

78. Author interview with Hayden, October 21, 2009.

79. *Lone-Wolf Terrorism* (The Hague: Instituut voor Veiligheids en Crisismanagement, 2007), 76–77.

80. Peter Bergen, "Why Bin Laden Still Matters," *Newsweek*, September 4, 2010, *www.thedailybeast.com/newsweek/*.

81. Rid and Hecker, *War 2.0*, 219–20.

82. Rather than there being cooperation between the two entities, some terrorist groups are acquiring more of the attributes of organized crime. Thomas M. Sanderson, "Transnational Terror and Organized Crime: Blurring the Lines," *SAIS Review* 24, no. 1 (Winter/Spring 2004): 49–61.

83. Chris Dishman, "The Leaderless Nexus: When Crime and Terror Converge," *Studies in Conflict and Terrorism* 28 (2005): 237–49.

84. Reed, "Beyond the War on Terror," 709.

85. Usually organized crime groups are more effective in maintaining internal discipline. What is more, their financial resources enable them to corrupt officials and avoid prosecution. Finally, because these groups often provide illicit goods and services that are socially acceptable to a substantial portion of the population, they provoke less repression than terrorist groups. This observation is made in John Ross, *Unintended Consequences* (St. Louis: Accurate Press, 1996), 716–17.

86. For example, using FBI data on terrorism, Smith and Damphousse found that before the attorney general's guidelines on investigating dissident and terrorist groups were implemented, the average size of right-wing terrorist groups whose members had been indicted was 9.4 persons. In the post-guidelines era (after 1976), that figure had dropped to 5.8 persons. A similar pattern was evident for international terrorist groups operating in the United States, with an average of six indicted members in the pre-guidelines era but just three in the post-guidelines era. Brent L. Smith and Kelly R. Damphousse, *American Terrorism Study: Patterns of Behavior, Investigation, and Prosecution of American Terrorists* (Rockville, MD: National Institute of Justice, 2002), 6. Similarly, according to the research of Christopher Hewitt, during the period 1955–1977, just 7 percent of all terrorist fatalities in the United States were attributed to individuals. For the period 1978–1999, the proportion had risen to 26 percent. Christopher Hewitt, *Understanding Terrorism in America: From the Klan to Al Qaeda* (London: Routledge, 2003), 78.

87. Berger, *Jihad Joe*, 210–13.

88. Jeremy Pressman, "Leaderless Resistance: The Next Threat?," *Current History*, December 2003, 422.

89. Garfinkel, "Leaderless Resistance Today."

90. Pressman, "Leaderless Resistance," 424.

91. Jonathan R. White, *Terrorism: An Introduction*, 3rd ed. (Belmont, CA: Wadsworth Thomson Learning, 2002), 33.

92. Bjoern Amland, "Suspect: Norway Attacks 'Marketing' for Manifesto," Associated Press, July 24, 2011.

93. Jamie Stengle, "Army: AWOL Soldier Admits to Fort Hood Plan," Associated Press, July 28, 2011.

94. Quoted in Tucker Reals, "What's Next for al Qaeda?," CBS News, May 2, 2011, *www.cbsnews.com/*.

95. "U.S. Military Casualties," US Department of Defense, *www.defense.gov/news/casualty.pdf*.

96. Tim Fernholz and Jim Tankersley, "The Cost of bin Laden: $3 Trillion over 15 Years," *National Journal*, May 6, 2011, *www.nationaljournal.com/*. In 2008 Linda J. Bilmes and the Nobel Prize–winning economist Joseph E. Stiglitz estimated that the invasion of Iraq would cost an estimated $3 trillion when the economic consequences and ancillary costs were taken into account (e.g., treating wounded veterans). Linda J. Bilmes and Joseph E. Stiglitz, *The Three Trillion Dollar War: The True Cost of the Iraq Conflict* (New York: Norton, 2008).

97. Spencer Ackerman, "Even Dead, Osama Has a Winning Strategy (Hint: It's Muhammad Ali's)," Wired.com, July 20, 2011, *www.wired.com/*.

Selected Bibliography

Abbey, Edward. *The Monkey Wrench Gang*. New York: Avon Books, 1975.

Aho, James. *The Politics of Righteousness: Idaho Christian Patriotism*. Seattle: University of Washington Press, 1990.

Albright, David. *Peddling Peril: How the Secret Nuclear Trade Arms America's Enemies*. New York: Free Press, 2010.

Alexander, Yonah. *Combating Terrorism: Strategies of Ten Countries*. Ann Arbor: University of Michigan Press, 2002.

Allison, Graham. *Nuclear Terrorism: The Ultimate Preventable Catastrophe*. New York: Times Books, 2004.

Almond, Peter. "Beware: The New Goths Are Coming." *Times* [London], June 11, 2006.

Alonso, Rogelio, and Fernando Reinares. "Maghreb Immigrants Becoming Suicide Terrorists: A Case Study of Religious Radicalization Processes in Spain." In Pedazhur, *Root Causes of Suicide Terrorism*, 179–98.

Anderson, Benedict. *Imagined Communities: Reflections on the Origins and Spread of Nationalism*. London: Verso, 1991.

Anini, Michele, and Sean J. A. Edwards. "The Networking of Terror in the Information Age." In Arquilla and Ronfeldt, *Networks and Netwars*, 29–60. Santa Monica, CA: Rand, 2001.

Anti-Defamation League. *The ADL Anti-paramilitary Training Statute: A Response to Domestic Terrorism*. New York: Anti-Defamation League, 1995.

———. "Ecoterrorism: Extremism in the Animal Rights and Environmentalist Movements." Anti-Defamation League, 2005.

———. "James Von Brunn: An ADL Backgrounder." Anti-Defamation League, n.d.

———. *Jihad Online: Islamic Terrorists and the Internet*. Washington, DC: Anti-Defamation League, 2002.

———. *Not the Work of a Day: The Story of the Anti-Defamation League of B'nai B'rith*. New York: Anti-Defamation League, 1965.

"The Architect and Fifth Generation Warfare." *Strategist*, June 4, 2006.

Arquilla, John, and David Ronfeldt. *Networks and Netwars: The Future of Terror, Crime, and Militancy*. Santa Monica, CA: Rand, 2001.

Arquilla, John, David Ronfeldt, and Michele Zanini. "Networks, Netwar, and Information-Age Terrorism." In Ian O. Lesser et al., *Countering the New Terrorism*, 39–84.

"Assessing White Supremacists Groups in the U.S." National Public Radio, October 30, 2008.

Badey, Thomas J., ed. *Annual Editions Violence and Terrorism 07/08*. New York: McGraw Hill, 2007.

———, ed. *Annual Editions Violence and Terrorism 08/09*. New York: McGraw Hill, 2009.

Baird, Robert Arthur. "Pyro-Terrorism—the Threat of Arson-Induced Forest Fires as a Future Weapon of Mass Destruction." *Studies in Conflict and Terrorism* 29 (2006): 419–21.

Bargh, John A., and Katelyn Y. A. McKenna. "The Internet and Social Life." *Annual Review of Psychology* 55 (2004): 573–90.

Barnett, Roger W. *Asymmetrical Warfare: Today's Challenge of U.S. Military Power*. Washington, DC: Brassey's, 2003.

Barnett, Thomas P. M. *Blueprint for Action: A Future Worth Creating*. New York: Berkley Books, 2005.

———. *Great Powers: America and the World after Bush*. New York: Putnam, 2009.

———. *The Pentagon's New Map: War and Peace in the Twenty-First Century*. New York: G. P. Putnam's Sons, 2004.

Beam, Louis. "Leaderless Resistance." *Seditionist*, no. 12 (February 1992). *www.louisbeam.com/leaderless.htm.*

Bearden, Milton. "Graveyard of Empires." In Hoge and Rose, *How Did This Happen?*, 83–95.

Bergen, Peter. *The Osama bin Laden I Know: An Oral History of al Qaeda's Leader*. New York: Free Press, 2006.

Bergen, Peter, and Alec Reynolds. "Blowback Revisited: Today's Insurgents in Iraq Are Tomorrow's Terrorists." *Foreign Affairs*, November/December 2005, 2–6.

Berger J. M. *Jihad Joe: Americans Who Go to War in the Name of Islam*. Washington, DC: Potomac Books, 2011.

Berkowitz, Bruce. *The New Face of War: How War Will Be Fought in the 21st Century*. New York: Free Press, 2003.

Biddiscombe, Perry. *The Last Nazis: Werewolf Guerrilla Resistance in Europe, 1944–1947*. Stroud, Gloucestershire, UK: Tempus, 2006.

———. *Werewolf! The History of the National Socialist Guerrilla Movement, 1944–1946*. Toronto: University of Toronto Press, 1998.

Bilmes, Linda J., and Joseph E. Stiglitz. *The Three Trillion Dollar War: The True Cost of the Iraq Conflict*. New York: Norton, 2008.

Blankley, Tom. *The West's Last Chance: Will We Win the Clash of Civilizations?* Washington, DC: Regnery, 2005.

Bodansky, Yossef. *Bin Laden: The Man Who Declared War on America*. Rocklin, CA: Forum, 1999.

———. *Islamic Anti-Semitism as a Political Instrument*. Houston: Ariel Center for Policy Research, 1999.

Boroumand, Ladan, and Roya Boroumand. "Terror, Islam, and Democracy." *Journal of Democracy* 13, no. 2 (April 2002): 5–20.

Braathen, Einar, Morten Boas, and Gjermund Saether. *Ethnicity Kills?* New York: St. Martin's Press, 2000.

Brafman, Ori, and Rod A. Beckstrom. *The Starfish and the Spider: The Unstoppable Power of Leaderless Organizations*. New York: Portfolio, 2006.

Brodie, Renee. "The Aryan New Era: Apocalyptic Realizations in the *Turner Diaries*." *Journal of American Culture* 21, no. 3 (Fall 1998): 13–22.

Buchanan, Patrick J. *Churchill, Hitler, and the Unnecessary War: How Britain Lost Its Empire and the West Lost the World*. New York: Crown Publishers, 2008.

———. *Day of Reckoning: How Hubris, Ideology, and Greed Are Tearing America Apart*. New York: Thomas Dunne Books, 2007.

———. *Death of the West: How Dying Populations and Immigrant Invasions Imperil Our Country and Civilization*. New York: Thomas Dunne Books, 2002.

———. *State of Emergency: The Third World Invasion and Conquest of America*. New York: Thomas Dunne Books, 2006.

Burton, Fred, and Scott Stewart. "The 'Lone Wolf' Disconnect." STRATFOR, January 30, 2008, *www.stratfor.com/weekly/lone_wolf_disconnect.*

Campbell, Kurt M., and Michele A. Flournoy. *To Prevail: An American Strategy for the Campaign against Terrorism*. Washington, DC: CSIS Press: 2001.

Carus, W. Seth. "The Rajneeshees." In Tucker, *Toxic Terror*, 115–37.

———. "R.I.S.E." In Tucker, *Toxic Terror*, 55–70.

Cassidy, Robert M. *Counterinsurgency and the Global War on Terror: Military Culture and Irregular War*. Stanford, CA: Stanford Security Studies, 2008.

Chase, Alston. *Harvard and the Unabomber: The Education of an American Terrorist*. New York: Norton, 2003.

Clark, Peter B., and James Q. Wilson. "Incentive Systems: A Theory of Organizations." *Administrative Science Quarterly* 6 (September 1961): 129–66.

Clarke, Richard A., and Robert K. Knake. *Cyber War: The Next Threat to National Security and What to Do about It*. New York: HarperCollins, 2010.

Clausewitz, Carl von. *On War*. London: Penguin Books, 1982.

Coen, Bob, and Eric Nadler. *Dead Silence: Fear and Terror on the Anthrax Trail*. Berkeley, CA: Counterpoint, 2009.

Cohen, Michael A., and Maria Figueroa Küpçü. "Congress and the 'YouTubeWar.'" In Badey, *Annual Editions Violence and Terrorism 08/09*, 122–25.

Cohen-Almagor, Raphael. "Combating Right-Wing Political Extremism in Israel: Critical Appraisal." *Terrorism and Political Violence* 9, no. 4 (1997): 16–23.

Collier, Paul. "Doing Well out of War: An Economic Perspective. In *Economic Agendas in Civil Wars, Greed, and Grievance*, edited by Mats Berdal and David M. Malone, 91–111. Boulder, CO: Lynne Rienner, 2000.

Corbin, Jane. *Al Qaeda: In Search of the Terror Network That Threatens the World*. New York: Thunder's Mouth Press, 2002.

Corcoran, James. *Bitter Harvest: Gordon Kahl and the Posse Comitatus; Murder in the Heartland*. New York: Penguin Books, 1990.

Cordesman, Anthony. *The War after the War: Strategic Lessons of Iraq and Afghanistan*. Washington, DC: CSIS Press, 2004.

Corera, Gordon. *Shopping for Bombs: Nuclear Proliferation, Global Insecurity, and the Rise of the A. Q. Khan Network*. New York: Oxford University Press, 2006.

Coulson, Danny O., and Elaine Shannon. *No Heroes: Inside the FBI's Secret Counter-Terror Force*. New York: Pocket Books, 1999.

Covington, Harold A. *The Brigade*. Philadelphia: Xlibris, 2008.

———. *A Distant Thunder*. Bloomington, IN: AuthorHouse, 2004.

———. *The Hill of the Ravens*. Bloomington, IN: 1st Books, 2003.

———. *The March Up Country*. Reedy, WV: Liberty Bell Publications, 1987.

———. *A Mighty Fortress*. New York: iUniverse, 2005.

Craig, Gordon A. "Delbrück: The Military Historian." In Paret, *Makers of Modern Strategy*, 326–53.

Crelinsten, Ronald D. "Terrorism and Counter-Terrorism in a Multi-Centric World: Challenges and Opportunities." In Taylor and Horgan, *The Future of Terrorism*, 170–96.

Crenshaw, Martha. "The Logic of Terrorism: Terrorist Behavior as a Product of Strategic Choice." In Reich, *Origins of Terrorism*, 7–24.

Cronin, Audrey Kurth, and James M. Ludes, eds. *Attacking Terrorism: Elements of a Grand Strategy*. Washington, DC: Georgetown University Press, 2004.

Cruikshank, Paul, and Mohanad Hage Ali. "Abu Musab Al Suri: Architect of the New Al Qaeda." *Studies in Conflict and Terrorism* 30, no. 1 (2007): 1–14.

Davis, James Kirkpatrick. *Spying on America: The FBI's Domestic Counterintelligence Program*. Westport, CT: Praeger, 1992.

Davis, Jayna. *The Third Terrorist: The Middle East Connection to the Oklahoma City Bombing*. Nashville: WND Books, 2004.

De Armond, Paul. "Netwar in the Emerald City: WTO Protest Strategy and Tactics." In Arquilla and Ronfeldt, *Networks and Netwars*, 201–35.

Decision Support Systems. *Al-Qaida's Endgame? A Strategic Scenario Analysis*. Decision Support Systems, 2001.

Dees, Morris, and Steven Fiffer. *Hate on Trial: The Case against America's Most Dangerous Neo-Nazi.* New York: Villard Books, 1993.

DePugh, Robert B. *Blueprint for Victory.* 4th ed. Norborne, MO: Salon, 1978.

Dobratz, Betty A., and Stephanie L. Shanks-Meile. *White Power, White Pride! The White Separatist Movement in the United States.* New York: Twayne, 1997.

Dolnik, Adam. *Understanding Terrorist Innovation: Technology, Tactics and Global Trends.* London: Routledge, 2007.

Doran, Michael Scott. "Somebody Else's Civil War." In Hoge and Rose, *How Did This Happen?*, 44–45.

Dorpalen, Andreas. *The World of General Haushofer.* New York: Farrar and Rinehart, 1942.

Drew, Dennis M., and Donald M. Snow. *Making Twenty-First Century Strategy: An Introduction to Modern National Security Processes and Problems.* Maxwell Air Force Base, AL: Air University Press, 2006.

Durham, Martin. *White Rage: The Extreme Right and American Politics.* London: Routledge, 2007.

Earls, Mark. *Herd: How to Change Mass Behavior by Harnessing Our True Nature.* West Sussex, UK: Wiley, 2007.

Falkenrath, Richard A., Robert D. Newman, and Bradley A. Thayer. *America's Achilles' Heel: Nuclear, Biological, and Chemical Terrorism and Covert Attack.* Cambridge, MA: MIT Press, 2001.

Fanon, Frantz. *The Wretched of the Earth.* New York: Grove Press, 1963.

Federal Bureau of Investigation. *Terrorism in the United States 1996.* Washington, DC: FBI, 1997.

Federal Bureau of Investigation. *Terrorism in the United States 1998.* Washington, DC: FBI, 1999.

Ferguson, Charles D., et al. *The Four Faces of Nuclear Terrorism.* Monterey, CA: Center for Nonproliferation Studies, 2004.

Ferguson, Niall. "Clashing Civilizations or Mad Mullahs: The United States between Informal and Formal Empire." In Talbott and Chanda, *The Age of Terror*, 113–41.

Flynn, Kevin, and Gary Gerhardt. *The Silent Brotherhood.* New York: Signet, 1990.

Flynn, Stephen. *America the Vulnerable: How Our Government Is Failing to Protect Us from Terrorism.* New York: Harper Collins, 2004.

Forrest, James J. "Terrorist Use of WMD." In Kindt, Post, and Schneider, *The World's Most Threatening Terrorist Networks and Criminal Gangs*, 93–119.

Fouda, Yosri, and Nick Fielding. *Masterminds of Terror: The Truth behind the Most Devastating Terrorist Attack the World Has Ever Seen.* New York: Arcade, 2003.

Friedman, Thomas. *The Lexus and the Olive Tree: Understanding Globalization.* New York: Anchor, 2000.

Fukuyama, Francis. *America at the Crossroads: Democracy, Power, and the Neoconservative Legacy.* New Haven, CT: Yale University Press, 2006.

———. "Their Target: The Modern World." *Newsweek* special edition, December 13, 2001.

Ganor, Boaz, ed. *Countering Suicide Terrorism.* New York: International Policy Institute for Counter-Terrorism and the Anti-Defamation League, 2002.

Gartenstein-Ross, Daveed. *My Year in Radical Islam: A Memoir.* New York: Jeremy P. Tarcher/Penguin, 2007.

George, John, and Laird Wilcox. *Nazis, Communists, Klansmen, and Others on the Fringe.* Buffalo: Prometheus Books, 1992.

Gerges, Fawaz A. *The Far Enemy: Why Jihad Went Global.* Cambridge: Cambridge University Press, 2005.

Gerlach, Luther P. "The Structure of Social Movements: Environmental Activism and Its Opponents." In Arquilla and Ronfeldt, *Networks and Netwars*, 289–310.

Geyer, Michael. "German Strategy in the Age of Machine Warfare, 1914–1945." In Paret, *Makers of Modern Strategy*, 527–97.

Gilbert, Felix. "Machiavelli: The Renaissance of the Art of War." In Paret, *Makers of Modern Strategy*, 11–31.

Godin, Seth. *Tribes: We Need You to Lead Us*. New York: Portfolio, 2008.

Greene, Robert. *The 33 Strategies of War*. New York: Penguin Books, 2007.

Griffin, Robert S. *The Fame of a Dead Man's Deeds: An Up-Close Portrait of White Nationalist William Pierce*. Robert S. Griffin, 2000.

Griffin, Roger. *The Nature of Fascism*. New York: Routledge, 1993.

Guerlac, Henry. "Vauban: The Impact of Science on War." In Paret, *Makers of Modern Strategy*, 64–90.

Guevara, Che. *Guerrilla Warfare*. Lincoln: University of Nebraska Press, 1998.

Gunaratna, Rohan. *Inside Al Qaeda: Global Network of Terror*. New York: Columbia University Press, 2002.

———. "Al-Qaedastan: The Terrorist Sanctuary of the Afghan-Pakistan Border." *Special Operation Report* 14 (n.d.): 12.

Gurr, Ted Robert. "Terrorism in Democracies: Its Social and Political Bases." In Reich, *Origins of Terrorism*, 86–102.

Hafez, Mohammed M. "Dying to Be Martyrs: The Symbolic Dimension of Suicide Terrorism." In Pedazhur, *Root Causes of Suicide Terrorism*, 54–80.

Hamm, Mark S. *In Bad Company: America's Terrorist Underground*. Boston: Northeastern University Press, 2001.

Hammes, Thomas X. "Fourth Generation Warfare Evolves, Fifth Emerges." *Military Review*, May/June 2007, 14–23.

———. *The Sling and the Stone: On War in the 21st Century*. St. Paul, MN: Zenith Press, 2004.

Hardt, Michael, and Antonio Negri. *Multitude: War and Democracy in the Age of Empire*. New York: Penguin Press, 2004.

Hashim, Ahmed S. *Insurgency and Counter-Insurgency in Iraq*. Ithaca, NY: Cornell University Press, 2006.

Henshall, Philip. *Vengeance: Hitler's Nuclear Weapon: Fact or Fiction?* Stroud, Gloucester, UK: Alan Sutton, 1995.

Henzel, Christopher. "The Origins of al Qaeda's Ideology: Implications for US Strategy." *Parameters* (Spring 2005): 69–80.

Hewitt, Christopher. "Patterns of American Terrorism, 1955–1998: An Historical Perspective on Terrorism-Related Fatalities, 1955–98." *Terrorism and Political Violence* 12, no. 1 (2000): 1–14.

———. *Understanding Terrorism in America: From the Klan to Al Qaeda*. London: Routledge, 2003.

Hewitt, J. Joseph, Jonathan Wilkenfeld, and Ted Robert Gurr. *Peace and Conflict 2008*. Boulder, CO: Paradigm Publishers, 2008.

Heymann, Phillip B. *Terrorism and America: A Commonsense Strategy for a Democratic Society*. Cambridge, MA: MIT Press, 1998.

Hitler, Adolf. *Mein Kampf*. Translated by Ralph Manheim. Boston: Houghton Mifflin, 1971.

Hoffman, Bruce. "From the War on Terror to Global Counterinsurgency." In Badey, *Annual Editions Violence and Terrorism 08/09*, 208–13.

———. *Inside Terrorism*. New York: Columbia University Press, 1998.

———. "Responding to Terrorism Across the Technological Spectrum." *Terrorism and Political Violence* 6, no. 3 (Autumn 1994): 365–89.

Hoffman, David. *The Oklahoma City Bombing and the Politics of Terror*. Venice, CA: Feral House, 1998.

Hoffman, Frank G. "Hybrid Threats: Reconceptualizing the Evolving Character of Modern Conflict." *Strategic Forum*, no. 240 (April 2009): 1–8.

Hoge, James F., Jr., and Gideon Rose. *How Did This Happen? Terrorism and the New War.* New York: Public Affairs, 2001.

Holborn, Hajo. "The Prusso-German School: Moltke and the Rise of the General Staff." In Paret, *Makers of Modern Strategy*, 281–95.

Hollyoak, Eric. "The Fallacy of Leaderless Resistance." *Resistance*, no. 10 (Winter 2000): 14–18.

Holti, K. J. *The State, War, and the State of War.* Cambridge: Cambridge University Press, 1996.

Horowitz, David. *Radical Islam and the American Left.* Washington, DC: Regnery, 2004.

Horowitz, Donald L. *Ethnic Groups in Conflict.* Berkeley: University of California Press, 1985.

Howe, Jeff. *Crowdsourcing: Why the Power of the Crowd Is Driving the Future of Business.* New York: Crown Business, 2008.

Hrebenar, Ronald J., ed. *Interest Group Politics in America.* 3rd ed. New York: M. E. Sharpe, 1997.

Huntington, Samuel P. *The Clash of Civilizations: Remaking of World Order.* New York: Touchstone, 1996.

———. *Who Are We? The Challenges to America's National Identity.* New York: Simon and Schuster, 2004.

Huth, Paul, and Benjamin Valentino. "Mass Killings of Civilians in Time of War, 1945–2000." In Hewitt, Wilkenfeld, and Gurr, *Peace and Conflict 2008*, 79–92.

Iklé, Fred Charles. *Annihilation from Within: The Ultimate Threat of Nations.* New York: Columbia University Press, 2006.

Jacquard, Roland. *In the Name of Osama Bin Laden: Global Terrorism and the Bin Laden International.* Durham, NC: Duke University Press, 2002.

Jenkins, Brian M. "The Organization Men: Anatomy of a Terrorist Attack." In Hoge and Rose. *How Did This Happen?*, 11.

———. *Will Terrorists Go Nuclear?* Amherst, NY: Prometheus Books, 2008.

Jenkins, Henry. *Convergence Culture: Where Old and New Media Collide.* New York: New York University Press, 2006.

Joes, Anthony James. *America and Guerrilla Warfare.* Lexington: University Press of Kentucky, 2000.

———. *Resisting Rebellion: The History and Politics of Counterinsurgency.* Lexington: University Press of Kentucky, 2004.

———. *Urban Guerrilla Warfare.* Lexington: University Press of Kentucky, 2007.

The John Franklin Letters. New York: Bookmailer, 1959.

Jones, Seth G. *In the Graveyard of Empires: America's War in Afghanistan.* New York: Norton, 2009.

Jones, Stephen, and Peter Israel. *Others Unknown: The Oklahoma City Bombing Case and Conspiracy.* New York: Public Affairs, 1998.

Jordan, Amos A., William J. Taylor, and Michael J. Mazarr. *American National Security.* 5th ed. Baltimore: Johns Hopkins University Press, 1999.

Josse, Paul. "Leaderless Resistance and Ideological Inclusion: The Case of the Earth Liberation Front." *Terrorism and Political Violence* 19, no. 3 (September 2007): 351–67.

Juergensmeyer, Mark. *Terror in the Mind of God: The Global Rise of Religious Violence.* Berkeley: University of California Press, 2000.

Kaplan, Jeffrey. *The Encyclopedia of White Power: A Sourcebook on the Radical Racist Right.* Walnut Creek, CA: AltaMira Press, 2000.

———. "Leaderless Resistance." *Terrorism and Political Violence* 9, no. 3 (1997): 80–95.

Kaplan, Jeffrey, and Leonard Weinberg. *The Emergence of a Euro-American Radical Right.* New Brunswick, NJ: Rutgers University Press, 1998.

Kaplan, Robert D. "The Coming Anarchy." *Atlantic Monthly*, February 1994, *www.theatlantic. com/*.

———. *Imperial Grunts.* New York: Vintage Books, 2005.

Karmon, Ely. "Trends in Contemporary International Terrorism." In *Countering Suicide Ter-*

rorism. New York: International Policy Institute for Counter-Terrorism and the Anti-Defamation League, 2002.

Katz, Samuel. *Relentless Pursuit: The DSS and the Manhunt for the al-Qaeda Terrorists*. New York: Forge, 2002.

Kavanaugh, A. L., and C. J. Patterson. "The Impact of Community Computer Networks on Social Capital and Community Involvement." *American Behavioral Scientist* 45, no. 3 (November 1, 2001): 496–509.

Keegan, John. *A History of Warfare*. New York: Knopf, 1993.

Kennedy, Paul. "Maintaining American Power: From Injury to Recovery." In Talbott and Chanda, *The Age of Terror*, 53–80.

———. *The Rise and Fall of the Great Powers: Economic Change and Military Conflict from 1500 to 2000*. New York: Vintage Books, 1989.

Kepel, Gilles. *Muslim Extremism in Egypt: The Prophet and Pharaoh*. Berkeley: University of California Press, 1993.

Kessler, Ronald. *The Terrorist Watch: Inside the Desperate Race to Stop the Next Attack*. New York: Crown Forum, 2007.

Khatchadourian, Raffi. "Azzam the American: The Making of an Al Qaeda Homegrown." *New Yorker*, January 22, 2007, *www.newyorker.com*.

Kindt, Michael T., Jerrold Post, and Barry R. Schneider. *The World's Most Threatening Terrorist Networks and Criminal Gangs*. New York: Palgrave Macmillan, 2009.

Kohlmann, Evan. "Abu Musab al-Suri and his Plan for the Destruction of America: 'Dirty Bombs for a Dirty Nation.'" *Global Terroralert*, July 11, 2005. *www.globalterroralert.com/pdf/0705/abumusabalsuri.pdf*.

Labi, Nadya. "Jihad 2.0." *Atlantic Monthly*, July/August 2006, 102–8.

Lake, Anthony. *Six Nightmares: Real Threats in a Dangerous World and How America Can Meet Them*. Boston: Little, Brown, 2000.

Langewiesche, William. *The Atomic Bazaar: Dispatches from the Underground World of Nuclear Trafficking*. New York: Farrar, Straus and Giroux, 2008.

Laqueur, Walter. *The Age of Terrorism*. Boston: Little, Brown, 1987.

———. *Fascism: Past, Present, Future*. Oxford: Oxford University Press, 1996.

———. *Guerrilla Warfare: A Historical and Critical Study*. New Brunswick, NJ: Transaction Publishers, 1998.

———. *The Last Days of Europe: Epitaph for an Old Continent*. New York: Thomas Dunne Books/St. Martin's Press, 2007.

———. *The New Terrorism: Fanaticism and the Arms of Mass Destruction*. Oxford: Oxford University Press, 1999.

———. *No End to War: Terrorism in the Twenty-First Century*. New York: Continuum, 2003.

———. "The Terrorism to Come." In Badey, *Annual Editions Violence and Terrorism 07/08*, 211–18.

Ledeen, Michael A. *The War against the Terror Masters*. New York: St. Martin's Press, 2003.

Lee, Martha F. "Violence and the Environment: The Case of 'Earth First!'" *Terrorism and Political Violence* 7, no. 3 (Autumn 1995): 109–27.

Lesser, Ian O. "Countering the New Terrorism: Implications for Strategy." In Ian O. Lesser et al., *Countering the New Terrorism*, 85–144.

Lesser, Ian O., Bruce Hoffman, John Arquilla, David Ronfeldt, and Michele Zanini. *Countering the New Terrorism*. Santa Monica, CA: Rand, 1999.

Levi, Michael. *On Nuclear Terrorism*. Cambridge, MA: Harvard University Press, 2007.

Lia, Brynjar. *Architect of Global Jihad: The Life of Al-Qaida Strategist Abu Mus'ad al-Suri*. New York: Columbia University Press, 2008.

———. "Jihadi Web Media Production: Characteristics, Trends, and Future Implications," February 2007, *www.mil.no/multimedia/archive/00092/Jihadi_Web_Media_Pro_92100a.pdf*.

Liberty Lobby. *Survival and Leaderless Resistance*. Washington, DC: Liberty Lobby, 1999.

Liddick, Donald R. *Eco-Terrorism: Radical Environmental and Animal Liberation Movements*. Westport, CT: Praeger, 2006.

Lifton, Robert Jay. *Destroying the World to Save It: Aum Shinrikyo, Apocalyptic Violence, and the New Global Terrorism*. New York: Metropolitan Book, 1999.

Lind, William S. "Fifth Generation Warfare?" Military.com, February 3, 2004, *military.com/*.

———. "Not Fourth Generation War." *On War*, no. 225 (July 11, 2007): *www.dnipogo.org/lind/lind_7_12_07.htm*.

Lind, William S., Keith Nightengale, John F. Schmitt, Joseph W. Sutton, and Gary I. Wilson. "The Changing Face of War: Into the Fourth Generation." *Marine Corps Gazette*, October 1989, 22–26.

Lind, William S., John F. Schmitt, and Gary I. Wilson. "Not Fourth Generation War." *Marine Corps Gazette*, December 1994, *www.dnipogo.org/lind/lind_7_12_07.htm*.

Lipset, Seymour Martin, and Earl Raab. *The Politics of Unreason: Right Wing Extremism in America, 1790–1970*. New York: Harper and Row, 1970.

Lone-Wolf Terrorism. The Hague: Instituut voor Veiligheids en Crisismanagement, 2007.

Lucas, Edward. *The New Cold War: Putin's Russia and the Threat to the West*. New York: Palgrave Macmillan, 2008.

Lunev, Stanislav, and Ira Winkler. *Through the Eyes of the Enemy*. Washington, DC: Regnery, 1998.

Luttwak, Edward N. *Strategy: The Logic of War and Peace*. Cambridge, MA: Belknap Press of Harvard University Press, 2003.

Macdonald, Andrew. *The Turner Diaries*. Hillsboro, WV: National Vanguard Books, 1978.

———. *Hunter*. Hillsboro, WV: National Vanguard Books, 1989.

Mack, Andrew. "Why Big Nations Lose Small Wars: The Politics of Asymmetric Conflict." *World Politics* 27, no. 2 (1975): 175–200.

Mack, Jefferson. *Invisible Resistance to Tyranny*. Boulder, CO: Paladin Press, 2002.

Malkin, Michelle. "Eco-terrorists Declare War." *Washington Times*, March 24, 2003.

Mao Tse-tung. *On Guerrilla Warfare*. Urbana: University of Illinois Press, 2000.

Marighella, Carlos. *Mini-manual of the Urban Guerrilla*. 1969. *www.latinamericanstudies.org/marighella.htm*.

Marks, Kathy. *Faces of Right Wing Extremism*. Boston: Branden, 1996.

Mason, James. *Siege*. Denver: Storm Books, 1992.

Mendelsohn, Barak. *Combating Jihadism: American Hegemony and Interstate Cooperation in the War on Terrorism*. Chicago: University of Chicago Press, 2009.

Merari, Ariel, "Terrorism as a Strategy of Struggle: Past and Future." In Taylor and Horgan, *The Future of Terrorism*, 52–65.

Merom, Gil. *How Democracies Lose Small Wars*. Cambridge: Cambridge University Press, 2003.

Michael, George. *Confronting Right-Wing Extremism and Terrorism in the USA*. New York: Routledge, 2003.

———. *The Enemy of My Enemy: The Alarming Convergence of Militant Islam and the Extreme Right*. Lawrence: University Press of Kansas, 2006.

Michael, George, and Michael Minkenberg. "A Continuum for Responding to the Extreme Right: A Comparison between the United States and Germany." *Studies in Conflict and Terrorism* 30, no. 12 (2007): 1109–23.

Michel, Lou, and Dan Herbeck. *American Terrorist: Timothy McVeigh and the Oklahoma City Bombing*. New York: Regan Books, 2001.

Miller, Glenn. *A White Man Speaks Out*. G. Miller, 1999.

Millen, Raymond. "The Hobbesian Notion of Self-Preservation concerning Human Behavior during an Insurgency." *Parameters*, Winter 2006–2007, 4–13.

Mockatis, Thomas R., "Winning Hearts and Minds in the 'War on Terrorism,'" *Small Wars and Insurgencies* 14, no. 1 (Spring 2003): 21–38.

Moran, Daniel. *Wars of National Liberation*. London: Collins, 2006.

Morgan, Matthew J. "An Evolving View of Warfare: War and Peace and the American Military Profession." *Small Wars and Insurgencies* 16, no. 2 (June 2005): 147–69.

Moussalli, Ahmad S. *Radical Islamic Fundamentalism: The Ideological and Political Discourse of Sayyid Qutb*. Beirut: American University of Beirut, 1992.

Moynihan, Daniel Patrick. *Pandemonium: Ethnicity in International Politics*. Oxford: Oxford University Press, 1993.

Muckian, Martin J. "Structural Vulnerabilities of Networked Insurgencies: Adapting to the New Adversary." *Parameters*, Winter 2006–2007, 15.

Mueller, John. "Is There Still a Terrorist Threat? The Myth of the Omnipresent Enemy." *Foreign Affairs*, September/October 2006, 2–8.

Mulloy, Darren. *American Extremism: History, Politics and the Militia Movement*. London: Routledge, 2008.

Naftali, Timothy. *Blind Spot: The Secret History of American Counterterrorism*. New York: Basic Books, 2005.

Nagl, John A. *Learning to Eat Soup with a Knife: Counterinsurgency Lessons from Malaya and Vietnam*. Chicago: University of Chicago Press, 2005.

Naím, Mosés. *Illicit: How Smugglers, Traffickers, and Copycats Are Hijacking the Global Economy*. New York: Random House, 2005.

Netanyahu, Benjamin. *Fighting Terrorism: How Democracies Can Defeat the International Terrorist Network*. New York: Farrar Straus Giroux, 2001.

Neumann, Sigmund, and Mark von Hagen. "Engels and Marx on Revolution, War, and the Army in Society." In Paret, *Makers of Modern Strategy*, 262–80.

Norton, Richard J. "Feral Cities." *Naval War College Review* 56, no. 4 (Autumn 2003): 97–106.

O'Neill, Bard E. *Insurgency and Terrorism: Inside Modern Revolutionary Warfare*. Dulles, VA: Brassey's, 1990.

Orlov, Dmitry. *Reinventing Collapse: The Soviet Example and American Prospects*. Gabriola Island, BC: New Society Publishers.

Ornstein, Norman J., and Shirley Elder. *Interest Groups, Lobbying and Policymaking*. Washington, DC: Congressional Quarterly Press, 1978.

Osterholm, Michael T., and John Schwartz. *Living Terrors: What America Needs to Know to Survive the Coming Bioterrorist Catastrophe*. New York: Random House, 2000.

Parenti, Michael. *The Terrorism Trap: September 11 and Beyond*. San Francisco: City Lights Books, 2002.

Paret, Peter, ed. *Makers of Modern Strategy: From Machiavelli to the Nuclear Age*. Princeton, NJ: Princeton University Press, 1986.

Parfrey, Adam. *Extreme Islam: Anti-American Propaganda of Muslim Fundamentalism*. Los Angeles: Feral House, 2001.

Pedazhur, Ami, ed. *Root Causes of Suicide Terrorism: The Globalization of Martyrdom*. London: Routledge, 2006.

Phares, Walid. *The Confrontation: Winning the War against Future Jihad*. New York: Palgrave Macmillan, 2008.

———. *Future Jihad: Terrorist Strategies against America*. New York: Palgrave Macmillan, 2005.

Pillar, Paul R. *Terrorism and U.S. Foreign Policy*. Washington, DC: Brookings Institution Press, 2001.

Pipes, Daniel. *Militant Islam Reaches America*. New York: Norton, 2002.

Podhoretz, Norman. *World War IV: The Long Struggle against Islamofascism*. New York: Doubleday, 2007.

Pressman, Jeremy. "Leaderless Resistance: The Next Threat?" *Current History*, December 2003, 422–25.

Qiao Liang and Wang Xiangsui. *Unrestricted Warfare: China's Master Plan to Destroy America*. Panama City: Pan American, 2002.

Qutb, Sayid. *Milestones*. Cedar Rapids, IA: Mother Mosque Foundation, n.d.

Raynor, Thomas P. *Terrorism: Past, Present, Future*. New York: Franklin Watts, 1982.

Record, Jeffrey. *Beating Goliath: Why Insurgencies Win*. Washington, DC: Potomac Books, 2007.

Redden, Jim. *Snitch Culture*. Venice, CA: Feral House, 2000.

Reeve, Simon. *The New Jackals: Ramzi Yousef, Osama bin Laden, and the Future of Terrorism*. Boston: Northeastern University Press, 1999.

Reich, Walter, ed. *Origins of Terrorism: Psychologies, Ideologies, Theologies, States of Mind*. Washington, DC: Woodrow Wilson Center Press, 1998.

Reynolds, Michael. "Homegrown Terror." In Badey, *Annual Editions Violence and Terrorism 07/08*, 86–91.

Rheingold, Howard. *Smart Mobs: The Next Social Revolution*. Cambridge, MA: Basic Books, 2002.

Rich, Paul R. "Al Qaeda and the Radical Islamic Challenge to Western Strategy." *Small Wars and Insurgencies* 14, no. 1 (Spring 2003): 39–56.

Richards, Chet. *Neither Shall the Sword: Conflict in the Years Ahead*. Washington, DC: Center for Defense Information, 2005.

Ricks, Thomas E. *The Gamble: General David Petraeus and the American Military Adventure in Iraq, 2006–2008*. New York: Penguin Press, 2009.

Rid, Thomas, and Marc Hecker. *War 2.0: Irregular Warfare in the Information Age*. Westport, CT: Praeger Security International, 2009.

Robb, John. *Brave New War: The Next Stage of Terrorism and the End of Globalization*. Hoboken, NJ: Wiley, 2007.

Robinson, Adam. *Bin Laden: Behind the Mask of the Terrorist*. New York: Arcade, 2001.

Rogan, Hanna. "Abu Reuter and the E-jihad: Virtual Battlefronts from Iraq to the Horn of Africa." *Georgetown Journal of International Affairs*, Summer/Fall 2007, 89–96.

Rosebraugh, Craig. *The Logic of Political Violence: Lessons in Reform and Revolution*. Portland, OR: Arissa, 2004.

Ross, John. *Unintended Consequences*. St. Louis: Accurate Press, 1996.

Rothenberg, Gunther E. "Moltke, Schlieffen, and the Doctrine of Strategic Envelopment." In Paret, *Makers of Modern Strategy*, 296–325.

———. *The Napoleonic Wars*. New York: Collins, 2006.

Rothstein, Hy S. *Afghanistan and the Troubled Future of Unconventional Warfare*. Annapolis, MD: Naval Institute Press, 2006.

Roy, Olivier. *Globalized Islam: The Search for a New Ummah*. New York: Columbia University Press, 2004.

Rubin, Barry, and Judith Colp Rubin, eds. *Anti-American Terrorism and the Middle East: A Documentary Reader*. Oxford: Oxford University Press, 2002.

Sageman, Marc. "Islam and Al Qaeda." In Pedazhur, *Root Causes of Suicide Terrorism*, 122–31.

———. *Leaderless Jihad: Terror Networks in the Twenty-First Century*. Philadelphia: University of Pennsylvania Press, 2008.

———. *Understanding Terror Networks*. Philadelphia: University of Pennsylvania Press, 2004.

Savage, Timothy M. "Europe and Islam: Crescent Waxing, Cultures Clashing." *Washington Quarterly* 27, no. 3 (Summer 2004): 25–50.

Schachner, Nathan. *The Price of Liberty: A History of the American Jewish Committee*. New York: American Jewish Committee, 1948.

Scheurer, Michael. *Imperial Hubris: Why the West Is Losing the War on Terror*. Washington, DC: Brassey's, 2004.

Schneider, Barry R. "Al Qaeda's Modus Operandi: Anticipating Their Target Selection." In Kindt, Post, and Schneider, *The World's Most Threatening Terrorist Networks and Criminal Gangs*, 29–48.

Schweitzer, Glen E., and Carole C. Dorsch, *Superterrorism: Assassins, Mobsters, and Weapons of Mass Destruction*. New York: Plenum Trade, 1998.

Shirky, Clay. *Here Comes Everybody: The Power of Organizing without Organizations*. New York: Penguin Press, 2008.

Shultz, Richard H., Jr., and Andrea J. Dew. *Insurgents, Terrorists, and Militias: The Warriors of Contemporary Combat*. New York: Columbia University Press, 2006.

Shy, John. "Jomini." In Paret, *Makers of Modern Strategy*, 143–85.

Shy, John, and Thomas W. Collier. "Revolutionary War." In Paret, *Makers of Modern Strategy*, 815–62.

Smith, Brent L. *Terrorism in America: Pipe Bombs and Pipe Dreams*. Albany: State University of New York Press, 1994.

Smith, Brent L., and Kelly R. Damphousse. *American Terrorism Study: Patterns of Behavior, Investigation, and Prosecution of American Terrorists*. Rockville, MD: National Institute of Justice, 2002.

———. "Two Decades of Terror." In *The Future of Terrorism: Violence in the New Millennium*, edited by Harvey W. Kushner, 132–56. Thousand Oaks, CA: Sage Publications, 1998.

Smith, Rupert. *The Utility of Force: The Art of War in the Modern World*. New York: Alfred A. Knopf, 2007.

Stanton, Bill. *Klanwatch: Bringing the Ku Klux Klan to Justice*. New York: Mentor, 1991.

Sterling, Claire. *The Terror Network*. New York: Berkley Books, 1984.

Stern, Jessica. "Larry Wayne Harris." In Tucker, *Toxic Terror*, 227–46.

———. *Terror in the Name of God: Why Religious Militants Kill*. New York: HarperCollins, 2003.

———. *The Ultimate Terrorists*. Cambridge, MA: Harvard University Press, 1999.

Stern, Kenneth S. *A Force upon the Plain: The American Militia Movement and the Politics of Hate*. New York: Simon and Schuster, 1996.

Stickney, Brandon M. *All-American Monster: The Unauthorized Biography of Timothy McVeigh*. Amherst, NY: Prometheus Books, 1996.

Stoner, Kelly, and Gary Perlstein. "Implementing 'Justice' through Terror and Destruction: Ecoterror's Violent Agenda to 'Save' Nature." In *Terrorism: Research, Readings, and Realities*, edited by Lynne L. Snowden and Bradley Whitsel, 90–134. Upper Saddle River, NJ: Pearson Prentice Hall, 2005.

Sullivan, John P. "Gangs, Hooligans, and Anarchists—the Vanguard of Netwar in the Streets." In Arquilla and Ronfeldt, *Networks and Netwars*, 99–126.

Sumida, Jon Tetsuro. *Decoding Clausewitz: A New Approach to 'On War.'* Lawrence: University Press of Kansas, 2008.

Sun Tzu. *The Art of War*. New York: Barnes and Noble Classics, 2003.

Swain, Carol M. *The New White Nationalism in America: Its Challenge to Integration*. New York: Cambridge University Press, 2002.

Taber, Robert. *War of the Flea*. Washington, DC: Brassey's, 2002.

Taheri, Amir. *Holy Terror: Inside the World of Islamic Terrorism*. Bethesda, MD: Adler and Adler, 1987.

Takeyh, Ray, and Nikolas Gvosdev. "Do Terrorist Networks Need a Home?" *Washington Quarterly* 25 (Summer 2002): 97–108.

Talbott, Strobe, and Nayan Chanda. *The Age of Terror: America and the World after September 11*. New York: Basic Books, 2001.

Tapscott, Don, and Anthony D. Williams. *Wikinomics: How Mass Collaboration Changes Everything*. New York: Portfolio, 2008.

Taylor, Bron. "Religion, Violence and Radical Environmentalism: From Earth First! to the Unabomber to the Earth Liberation Front." *Terrorism and Political Violence* 10, no. 4 (Winter 1998): 6.

Taylor, Max, and John Horgan. *The Future of Terrorism*. London: Frank Cass, 1999.

Teague, Michael. "New Media and the Arab Spring." *Al Jadid*, n.d., *www.aljadid.com/content/new-media-and-arab-spring*.

Timmerman, Kenneth R. *Preachers of Hate: Islam and the War on America*. New York: Crown Forum, 2003.

Tomajczyk, S. F. *US Elite Counter-Terrorist Forces*. Osceola, WI: MBI, 1997.

Tucker, Jonathan B., ed. *Toxic Terror: Assessing Terrorist Use of Chemical and Biological Weapons*. Cambridge, MA: MIT Press, 2000.

Tucker, Jonathan B., and Jason Pate. "The Minnesota Patriots Council." In Tucker, *Toxic Terror*, 159–83.

Turchin, Peter. *War and Peace and War: The Rise and Fall of Empires*. New York: Plume, 2006.

Van Creveld, Martin. *The Art of War: War and Military Thought*. London: Collins, 2000.

———. *The Changing Face of War: Lessons of Combat, from the Marne to Iraq*. New York: Ballantine Books, 2006.

———. *The Transformation of War*. New York: Free Press, 1991.

Vidino, Lorenzo. *Al Qaeda in Europe: The New Battleground of International Jihad*. Amherst, NY: Prometheus Books, 2006.

Weimann, Gabriel. *Terror on the Internet: The New Arena, the New Challenges*. Washington, DC: United States Institute of Peace, 2006.

Wheaton, Elizabeth. *Codename Greenkil: The 1979 Greensboro Killings*. Athens: University of Georgia Press, 1987.

Whine, Michael. "The Use of the Internet by Far Right Extremists." International Institute for Counter-Terrorism, August 30, 1999, *www.ict.org.il/Articles/tabid/66/Articlsid/720/currentpage/28/Default.aspx*.

White, Jonathan R. *Terrorism: An Introduction*. 3rd ed. Belmont, CA: Wadsworth Thomson Learning, 2002.

———. *Terrorism and Homeland Security*. 5th ed. Belmont, CA: Wadsworth Thomson Learning, 2006.

Whitelaw, Kevin. "The Eye of the Storm." In Badey, *Annual Editions Violence and Terrorism 08/09*, 192–95.

Whitsel, Brad. "'The Turner Diaries' and Cosmotheism: William Pierce's Theology of Revolution." *Nova Religio* 1, no. 2 (April 1998): 183–97.

Wilcox, Laird. *The Watchdogs: A Close Look at Anti-racist "Watchdog" Groups*. Olathe, KS: Laird Wilcox Editorial Research Center, 1999.

Wilcox, Philip C., Jr. "United States." In Alexander, *Combating Terrorism*, 23–61.

Wilkenfeld, Jonathan. "Unstable States and International Crises." In Hewitt, Wilkenfeld, and Gurr, *Peace and Conflict 2008*, 67–78.

Williams, Paul L. *Al Qaeda: Brotherhood of Terror*. Indianapolis: Alpha, 2002.

Woodward, Bob. *Bush at War*. New York: Simon and Schuster, 2002.

Woolsey, R. James. Foreword to Alexander, *Combating Terrorism*, v–vii.

Wright, Robin. *Sacred Rage: The Wrath of Militant Islam*. New York: Touchstone, 2001.

Zakaria, Fareed. "The Return of History." In Hoge and Rose, *How Did This Happen?*, 307–17.

———. "Terrorists Don't Need States." In Badey, *Annual Editions Violence and Terrorism 07/08*, 53.

Zakaria, Fareed. *The Post-American World*. New York: Norton, 2008.

Zayyat, Montasser al-. *The Road to Al-Qaeda: The Story of Bin Laden's Right-Hand Man*. London: Pluto Press, 2004.

Zimmerman, John C. "Sayyid Qutb's Influence of the 11 September Attacks." *Terrorism and Political Violence* 16, no. 2 (Summer 2004): 222–52.

Interviews

Thomas P. M. Barnett, May 20, 2008
Harold Covington, June 4, 2008
Alan Dershowitz, July 1, 2008
Francis Fukuyama, June 30, 2008
Daveed Gartenstein-Ross, December 2, 2008
Rohan Gunaratna, May 28, 2008
Michael V. Hayden, October 21, 2009
Christopher Hewitt, July 7, 2008
Frederick Iklé, June 2, 2008
Anthony Joes, June 25, 2008
Edward Luttwak, June 17, 2009
Darren Mulloy, June 13, 2008
William Pierce, July 12, 2000
Paul Pillar, June 8, 2008
Daniel Pipes, June 9, 2008
John Robb, June 3, 2008
Martin van Creveld, May 28, 2008
Laird Wilcox, July 27, 2009

Index